THE MORAL TEACHING OF
THE NEW TESTAMENT

THE MORAL TEACHING
OF THE
NEW TESTAMENT

RUDOLF SCHNACKENBURG

BURNS & OATES

Original editon "Die sittliche Botschaft des Neuen Testamentes"
Max Hueber Verlag, Munich
Translated by J. Holland-Smith and W. J. O'Hara
from the second revised German edition (1962)

First published in Federal Germany.
This translation © Herder KG and
Search Press 1965, 1975

This edition published by
Burns & Oates 1965
Reprinted 1975, 1982

Nihil Obstat: Joannes M. T. Barton, S.T.D., L.S.S.
Censor deputatus
Imprimatur: † Georgius L. Craven, Epus. Sebastopolis, Vic. Gen.
Westmonasterii, die 17ª Martii, 1964

Printed and bound in Great Britain by
Biddles Ltd, Guildford and King's Lynn
for Search Press Ltd
Wellwood, North Farm Road, Tunbridge Wells, Kent TN2 3DR

ISBN 0 86012 011 2

CONTENTS

I
JESUS' MORAL DEMANDS

Chapter 1: JESUS' PROCLAMATION OF THE REIGN OF GOD AND HIS FUNDAMENTAL RELIGIOUS AND MORAL DEMANDS

Chapter 2: JEWISH MORAL TEACHING AND JESUS' MORAL DEMANDS. THE SERMON ON THE MOUNT

Chapter 3: JESUS' DECISIVE ACTION: THE CONCENTRATION OF ALL RELIGIOUS MORAL PRECEPTS IN THE GREAT COMMANDMENT OF LOVE OF GOD AND NEIGHBOUR

5

CONTENTS

II

THE MORAL TEACHING OF THE EARLY CHURCH IN GENERAL

III

THE MORAL TEACHING OF THE EARLY CHURCH ACCORDING TO PROMINENT INDIVIDUAL PREACHERS

ABBREVIATIONS

Dam.   =   *Damascus Document*
1 QH   =   *Hymns*
1 QM   =   *War Rule*
4 QpPs =   *Commentary on Psalm 37*
1 QS(a)=   *Community Rule, Manual of Discipline*

LThK   =   *Lexikon für Theologie und Kirche*, 2nd ed. 1957 ff.
RAC   =   *Reallexikon für Antike und Christentum*, ed. by T. Klauser, 1950 ff.
RGG   =   *Die Religion in Geschichte und Gegenwart*, Tübingen 1909–13; 2nd ed. 1927–32, 3rd ed. 1956 ff.
ThWB =   *Theologisches Wörterbuch zum Neuen Testament*, ed. by G. Kittel (cont. by G. Friedrich) 6 vols. to date, 1933 ff.
TU   =   *Texte und Untersuchungen zur Geschichte der altchristlichen Literatur*. Leipzig–Berlin 1882 ff.

ATR   =   *Anglican Theological Review*, Evanston 1918 ff.
BZ   =   *Biblische Zeitschrift*, Freiburg i. Br. 1903–29; Paderborn 1931–39, 1957 ff.
EvTh   =   *Evangelische Theologie*, Munich 1934 ff.
ETL   =   *Ephemerides Theologicae Lovanienses*, Bruges 1924 ff.
IKZ   =   *Internationale Kirchliche Zeitschrift*, Berne 1911 ff.
JBL   =   *Journal of Biblical Literature*, Boston 1881 ff.
JR   =   *The Journal of Religion*, Chicago 1921 ff.
JTS   =   *The Journal of Theological Studies*, London 1899 ff.
MSR   =   *Mélanges de science religieuse*, Lille 1944 ff.
MTZ   =   *Münchener Theologische Zeitschrift*, Munich 1950 ff.
NKZ   =   *Neue Kirchliche Zeitschrift*, Leipzig 1890 ff.
NovT   =   *Novum Testamentum*, Leiden 1956 ff.
NRT   =   *Nouvelle Revue Théologique*, Tournai - Louvain - Paris 1879 ff.

OTS = *Oudtestamentische Studiën*, Leiden 1942 ff.

RB = *Revue biblique*, Paris 1892 ff; new series from 1904.

RevSR = *Revue des Sciences Religieuses*, Strasbourg 1921 ff.

RHPR = *Revue d'histoire et de philosophie religieuses*, Strasbourg 1921 ff.

RSPT = *Revue des sciences philosophiques et théologiques*, Paris 1907 ff.

RSR = *Recherches de science religieuse*, Paris 1910 ff.

RTP = *Revue de Théologie et Philosophie;* first series, Lausanne 1888 to 1911; second series, Lausanne 1913–1950; third series, Lausanne 1950 ff.

ST = *Studia Theologica, cura ordinum theologicorum Scandinavicorum edita*, Lund 1948 ff.

TB = *Theologische Blätter*, Leipzig 1922 ff.

TG = *Theologie und Glaube*, Paderborn 1909 ff.

TLZ = *Theologische Literaturzeitung*, Leipzig 1878 ff.

TQ = *Theologische Quartalschrift*, Tübingen 1819 ff; Stuttgart 1960 ff.

TrTZ = *Trierer Theologische Zeitschrift* (till 1944 *Pastor Bonus*) Trier 1888 ff.

TSK = *Theologische Studien und Kritiken* (Hamburg) Gotha 1828 ff.

TZ = *Theologische Zeitschrift*, Basle 1945 ff.

VC = *Vigiliae christianae*, Amsterdam 1947 ff.

VD = *Verbum Domini*, Rome 1921 ff.

ZAW = *Zeitschrift für die alttestamentliche Wissenschaft*, Giessen (Berlin) 1881 ff.

ZKT = *Zeitschrift für Katholische Theologie* (Innsbruck) [Vienna 1877 ff.

ZNW = *Zeitschrift für die neutestamentliche Wissenschaft und die Kunde der älteren Kirche*, Giessen 1960 ff; Berlin 1934 ff.

ZST = *Zeitschrift für systematische Theologie* (Gütersloh) Berlin 1923 ff.

ZThK = *Zeitschrift für Theologie und Kirche*, Tübingen 1891 ff.

GENERAL BIBLIOGRAPHY

A. Works on the Moral Teaching of the New Testament

Alexander, A., *The Ethics of St. Paul*, 1910.

Althaus, P., *Grundriss der Ethik*, 1953.

Andrews, M. E., *The Ethical Teaching of Paul*, 1934.

Benz, K. (Catholic), *Die Ethik des Apostels Paulus*, 1912.

Braun, F.-M. among others (Catholic), *Morale chrétienne et requêtes contemporaines*, 1954.

Dewar, L., *An Outline of New Testament Ethics*, 1949.

Enslin, M. S., *The Ethics of Paul*, 1930.

Herkenrath, J. (Catholic), *Die Ethik Jesu*, 1962.

Hermann, W., *Die sittlichen Weisungen Jesu*, 2nd ed. 1907 (3rd ed. 1922).

Jacoby, H., *Neutestamentliche Ethik*, 1899.

Juncker, A., *Die Ethik des Apostels Paulus*, 2 vols., 1904–1919.

Lagrange, M.-J. (Catholic), *La morale de l'Évangile*, 1931.

Manson, T. W., *Ethics and the Gospel*, 1960.

Marshall, L. H., *The Challenge of New Testament Ethics*, 1950.

Preisker, H., *Das Ethos des Urchristentums*, 1949.

Prunet, O., *La morale chrétienne d'après les écrits johanniques*, 1957.

Scott, C. A., *New Testament Ethics*, 2nd ed. 1936.

Sevenster, G., *Ethiek en Eschatologie in de Synoptische Evangelien*, 1929.

Stelzenberger, J. (Catholic), *Lehrbuch der Moraltheologie*, 1953.

Tillmann, F. (Catholic), *Die Idee der Nachfolge Christi* (*Handbuch der katholischen Sittenlehre*, vol. III), 3rd ed. 1949.

Tillmann, F., *Die Verwirklichung der Nachfolge Christi*, 2 vols. (*Handbuch* vol. IV, 1 and 2), 3rd ed. 1947.

Wagner, F. (Catholic), *Geschichte des Sittlichkeitsbegriffs*, vol. II: *Der Sittlichkeitsbegriff in der Heiligen Schrift und in der altchristlichen Ethik*, 1931.

Wilder, A. N., *Eschatology and Ethics in the Teaching of Jesus*, 2nd ed. 1950.

B. Works Frequently Quoted

Bauer, W., *Griechisch-deutsches Wörterbuch zu den Schriften des Neuen Testaments und der übrigen urchristlichen Literatur*, 5th ed. 1957.

Billerbeck = Billerbeck, P., *Kommentar zum Neuen Testament aus Talmud und Midrasch*, 4 vols., 1922–28.

Bonsirven, J., *Le judaïsme palestinien au temps de Jésus-Christ*, 2 vols., 1934–35.

Bousset, W. and Gressmann, H., *Die Religion des Judentums im späthellenistischen Zeitalter*, 3rd ed. 1926.

Büchsel, F., *Theologie des Neuen Testaments*, 2nd ed. 1937.

Bultmann, R., *Theologie des Neuen Testaments*, 3rd ed. 1953, Eng. tr. *Theology of the New Testament*, vol. I, 3rd imp. 1959, vol. I, 2nd imp. 1958.

Buzy, D., *Les Paraboles*, 16th ed. 1948.

Dalman, G., *Die Worte Jesu*, vol. I, 2nd. ed. 1930, Eng. tr. *The Words of Jesus*, 1902.

Feine, P. and Aland, K., *Theologie des Neuen Testaments*, 8th ed. 1951.

Gewiess, J., *Die urapostolische Heilsverkündigung nach der Apostelgeschichte*, 1939.

Goguel, M., Eng. tr. *The Birth of Christianity*, 1953.

Goguel, M., Eng. tr. *The Primitive Church*, 1964.

Jeremias, J., Eng. tr. *The Parables of Jesus*, rev. ed. 1963.

Kittel, G., *Die Probleme des palästinischen Spätjudentums und das Urchristentum*, 1926.

Liddell, H. G. and Scott, R., *A Greek-English Lexicon*, 9th ed. 1940.

Manson, T. W., *The Sayings of Jesus*, 1949.

Meinertz, M., *Theologie des Neuen Testaments*, 2 vols., 1950.

Moore, G. F., *Judaism in the first Centuries of the Christian Era, the Age of the Tannaim*, 3 vols., 1927–30.

Percy, E., *Die Botschaft Jesu*, 1953.

Schmid, J., *Das Evangelium nach Matthäus*, 3rd ed. 1956.

Schmid, J., *Das Evangelium nach Markus*, 3rd ed. 1954.

Schmid, J., *Das Evangelium nach Lukas*, 3rd ed. 1955.

Schnackenburg, R., Eng. tr. *God's Rule and Kingdom*, 1963.

Spicq, C., *Agapè dans le Nouveau Testament*, 3 vols., 1958–1959.

Stauffer, E., Eng. tr. *New Testament Theology*, 1963.

Völkl, R., *Christ und Welt nach dem Neuen Testament*, 1961.

Volz, P., *Die Eschatologie der jüdischen Gemeinde im neutestamentlichen Zeitalter*, 2nd ed. 1934.

Wikenhauser, A., Eng. tr. *New Testament Introduction*, 4th imp. 1963.

INTRODUCTION

JESUS brought a religious message and it was from that message that his moral demands originated. Any attempt to interpret his preaching in any other way (as a criticism, perhaps, of the civilization of the age, or as a programme of social revolution) is wrong from the outset. Nowhere in the New Testament is it possible to break the unity between religion and morality.

The Old Testament provided Jesus with a wide field of already existing moral views and doctrines, but he also sowed his own seed. It is difficult to distinguish between old and new in the ethical teaching of Jesus; it is almost impossible satisfactorily to describe his attitude to the Old Testament law and the traditions of the Scribes. Yet we must, nevertheless, wrestle with this question if we are to understand the originality and special features of his, and the early Church's, message. Provisionally we may say that Jesus' ethical teaching was religiously conservative, yet startlingly new.

In order to view Jesus' moral message in the right perspective it makes a difference what we regard as the leading idea from his preaching as a whole: the gospel of the goodness and mercy of God our Father, the salvation of souls, the call to discipleship, or the proclamation of the reign of God. In what follows we shall fit Jesus' moral demands principally (though not exclusively) within the framework of his gospel of the reign of God.

Jesus did not elaborate a system of moral theology. His teaching often started from questions put to him by this person or that, and his answers called for immediate decisions. Yet Jesus was not a casuist, nor was he a teacher of "situation ethics". He uncovered the fundamental principles involved in each special case put to him. His moral teaching is concrete, yet gives authoritative precepts.

Essentially, early Christianity built on the moral teaching of Jesus. Yet after Jesus' resurrection the theological emphasis was somewhat differently placed within the Church (consider the development of Christology and soteriology); the events of Pentecost and the experience of the Spirit stirred the minds of the disciples, influences from the surrounding world made themselves felt, and new problems arose. All this was bound to express itself in the moral teaching of the early Church. It is therefore necessary to consider the steps in this development one by one. We shall also have to take into account the broader composition of the early Church (Jewish and gentile Christians; Palestinians and Hellenists, etc.). Then again, as well as the main body of the Church's common preaching, individually strong personalities put their mark on early Christian thought and life. Consequently it is relevant and desirable to study the thought of these moral preachers individually.

The sequence: Jesus – original Jerusalem community – gentile Christianity does not match the chronology of the sources available to us. St. Paul's epistles to the churches are older than the synoptic gospels; the latter contain a collected wealth of tradition very varied in kind. As a result of the relatively late date of their final redaction, the synoptic gospels were not uninfluenced by the theological concepts of the early Church. And although wholly loyal to the Lord's words, the early Church, nevertheless, permitted its own viewpoint and interpretation to show through what it handed on. The date of the composition of many New Testament books (e.g. the epistle of James) is much controverted. But we only refer to the difficult problems involved in this matter to demonstrate the need for discernment in our use of the sources.

I
Jesus' Moral Demands

Chapter One

JESUS' PROCLAMATION OF THE REIGN OF GOD AND HIS FUNDAMENTAL RELIGIOUS AND MORAL DEMANDS

§ 1. THE PROCLAMATION BY JESUS OF THE REIGN OF GOD AND ITS SUMMONS TO MEN

W. Michaelis, *Täufer, Jesus, Urgemeinde,* 1928; G. Gloege, *Reich Gottes und Kirche im NT,* 1929; H. D. Wendland, *Die Eschatalogie des Reiches Gottes bei Jesus,* 1931; K. L. Schmidt, art. "βασιλεία" in *ThWB* vol. I, 1933, 579–92; R. Otto, *Reich Gottes und Menschensohn,* 2nd ed. 1940; J. Héring, *Le Royaume de Dieu et sa venue selon Jésus et l'apôtre Paul,* 1938, 2nd ed. 1959; H. Ridderbos, *De komst van het Koninkrijk,* 1950; R. Morgenthaler, *Kommendes Reich,* 1952; A. N. Wilder, *Eschatology and Ethics in the Teaching of Jesus,* 2nd ed. 1950; W. G. Kümmel, *Verheißung und Erfüllung,* 2nd ed. 1953, Eng. tr. *Promise and Fulfilment,* 2nd ed. 1961; Feine and Aland, *Theologie,* pp. 68–88; Meinertz, *Theologie,* vol. I, pp. 27–69; J. Schmid, *Evangelium nach Markus,* pp. 31–39; H. Roberts, *Jesus and the Kingdom of God,* 1955; J. Bonsirven, *Le Règne de Dieu,* 1957; R. Schnackenburg, *Gottes Herrschaft und Reich* (with further bibliography), Eng. tr. *God's Rule and Kingdom,* 1963.

AT THE beginning of his account of the public ministry of Jesus, the evangelist Mark summarizes Jesus' preaching in the striking words: "The time is accomplished and the kingdom (reign) of God is at hand. Repent and believe the gospel" (Mark 1:15). Thus his preaching was both a proclamation and a warning, an announcement of a divine act and a demand for a response to it from mankind. Everywhere in the New Testament we find that the acts of God are a call to men; the summons arises from the

15

message. The sequence is invariable too, God acts first, and his act lays responsibility on men. Nowhere in the New Testament do we find mere morality, a mere ethical system, but neither do we find a piety that imposes no obligations and is divorced from moral behaviour.

When Jesus appeared, he announced to men that an hour of great significance had come. In the tremendous, millenia-long relationship between God and the human race, which in accordance with God's hidden design had been effected in the centuries before Christ only between God and his chosen people of the covenant, Israel, the moment of fulfilment had come. What did this mean? A promise preceded the fulfilment, the prophetic promise of a future time of salvation, in which God would come to redeem his people[1] and establish definitively his reign.[2] But this new thing, through God's gracious intervention, was not only to be a renewal of the covenant with the people of Israel; it was, at least in comparison with many of the characteristics of the Old Testament hope, to be even more comprehensive, embracing the whole world. The "nations" too will stream to Mount Sion;[3] the peace of Eden will be restored,[4] and a new heaven and a new earth will appear.[5]

[1] Isa. 10:22 (LXX); 33:22; 35:4; 43:3 and 11; 45:17 and 22; 60:16; 62:11f.; Ezech. 34:22; Osee 1:7; Joel 3:5; Wis. 3:17 and 19; Zach. 8:7; 9:9; 10:6. For Later Judaism see Volz, *Eschatologie*, pp. 368f.

[2] Isa. 24:23; 33:22; 52:7f. (with this text, cf. Mark 1:15); Mich. 4:6f.; Wis. 3:14f.; Abd. 21; Zach. 14:9 and 16f. For Later Judaism see *Psalms of Solomon* 5:18f.; 17; the *Prayer of the Eighteen Benedictions* 11; and the beginning of the *Kaddish*. Cf. Dalman, *Worte Jesu*, pp. 310ff.; Volz, *Eschatologie*, pp. 165ff.

[3] Isa. 2:1ff.; 11:10–12; 25:6f.; 60:1ff.; Jer. 12:14ff.; 16:19; Ezech. 17:22ff.; Amos 9:12; Mich. 4:1ff.; Agg. 2:6ff.; Zach. 2:15; Tob. 13:11ff.; 14:8f.; Later Judaism: *Psalms of Solomon* 17, 34f.; *Sibylline Oracles* III, 710ff.; cf. Volz, *Eschatologie*, pp. 171f., 338.

[4] Isa. 11:6ff.; 35; 65:25; Osee 2:20. Later Judaism: Philo, *De Praem.* 88ff.; *Syriac Baruch* 73–4; *Sib.* III, 785–95.

[5] Isa. 65:17; 66:22; cf. 2 Pet. 3:13; Apoc. 21:1; Later Judaism: 1 *Enoch* 45, 4f.; 72, 1; 4 *Esdras* 6:16; 7:75; *Syriac Baruch* 32, 6; 44, 12; 57, 2;

The Jewish nation's hope of salvation had already undergone several changes, and even in the time of Jesus had not yet settled into a single tradition.[6] But all the expressions of this yearning, all the apocalyptic sayings of the prophets and visions of the seers, had one thing in common: the expectation of a final time of salvation. According to the words of Jesus, this "eschatological" time is now accomplished – fulfilled, that is, by his coming and acts. This point is endorsed by a second saying of Jesus. According to Luke 4:16-21, Jesus went one Sabbath day into the synagogue at Nazareth and read from the roll of the prophet Isaias the words, "The spirit of the Lord is upon me. Wherefore he hath anointed me to preach the gospel to the poor; he hath sent me to heal the contrite of heart, to preach deliverance to the captives and sight to the blind, to set at liberty them that are bruised, to preach the acceptable year of the Lord and the day of reward" (Isa. 61. 1ff.). And then he said, "This day is fulfilled this scripture in your ears." In so doing he was claiming to be the bearer of the Spirit in an absolute sense, the anointed of God, that is, the Messias. But to the Jews the Messias was the expected king of salvation of the last days.[7]

Sib. V, 273; *Jubilees* 1:29; 4:26; 2 *Enoch* 33, 1f.; and also *1 QS* IV.:25; *1 QH* XIII:11f. Cf. Volz, *Eschatologie*, pp. 338ff.; E. Sjöberg, "Wiedergeburt und Neuschöpfung im palästinischen Judentum" in *ST* 4 (1950) pp. 44-85 especially pp. 70-74; *id.*, "Neuschöpfung in den Toten-Meer-Rollen" in *ST* 9 (1955) pp. 131-6.

[6] Cf. the suggestions made by Bousset and Gressmann, *Religion des Spätjudentums*, pp. 242-301; Moore, *Judaism*, vol. II, pp. 279-395; Volz, *Eschatologie, passim;* Bonsirven, *Judaïsme*, vol. I, pp. 418-467; S. Mowinckel, *He That Cometh*, Oxford 1956, esp. pp. 261-79.

[7] The expectation of the Messias is not equally strong everywhere in the Old Testament and Later Judaism. It is totally absent from many prophets and also from the Mishnah, although it was very active among the people, as the New Testament itself confirms. Valuable evidence for it is provided by *Psalms of Solomon* 17f. In certain sections of the Apocalypses the Messias does play a bigger rôle, esp. in the *Testament of the Twelve Patriarchs* and the *Sib. Oracles.* Cf. H. Gressmann, *Der Messias*, 1929, esp. pp. 230ff.; Volz, *Eschatologie*, 173-86; Moore, *Judaism*, vol. II, pp.

That Jesus claimed to be the Messias is constantly being disputed; but it provides the only possible explanation of other indisputably genuine utterances of Jesus, such as his reply to the messengers from John the Baptist (Luke 10:24 par.), the claim that he is greater than Jonas or Solomon (Matt. 12:41 par.), the blessing on the eyes that see the acts of Jesus (Matt. 13:16 par.) and his testimony to himself before the Sanhedrin (Mark 14:61 par.). It must, however, be emphasized that Jesus knew himself to be a different kind of Messias from the one his contemporaries had expected. He was a bringer of salvation in a unique and purely religious sense, the eschatological revealer and saviour. Jesus' "Messianic awareness" cannot adequately be expressed in any ready-made category, nor with any existing designation.[8]

Our conclusion must, therefore, be that for Jesus his claim to be the Messias was closely connected with his declaration that the reign of God is at hand. In his person, in his words and deeds, the time of fulfilment had come. And yet it had not come exactly as the Old Testament has expected. The time of fulfilment was not yet the time of completion. In Jesus' preaching the kingdom of God "in power and glory" is still a thing of the future.[9] Does this not mean that the situation in the history of salvation was still the same as it had been in the time of the prophets? No, because in Jesus the Messias had come; because with the mandate and by the power of God he healed the sick, called sinners (Mark 2:15-17 par.), remitted sins (Mark

347ff.; Bonsirven, *Judaïsme*, vol. I, pp. 307–21, 341ff.; J. Klausner, *The Messianic Idea in Israel*, London 1956; Mowinckel, *He That Cometh*, passim.

[8] Cf. Feine and Aland, *Theologie*, pp. 32ff.; Meinertz, *Theologie*, vol. I, pp. 165ff.; W. Manson, *Bist Du, der da kommen soll?* 1952; T. W. Manson, *The Servant Messiah*, 1953; G. Bornkamm, *Jesus of Nazareth*, 1960; A. Vögtle in *LThK* vol. V, 928–31.

[9] The concept of the future rule of God is evidenced by all the synoptic material, even where there is no addition of "with power" or some similar phrase, cf. Schnackenburg, *God's Rule*, pp. 160ff.

2:5-10 par.; Luke 7:36-50), because with divine authority he announced the truths of salvation and the will of God (Mark 1:22 par.), so that the "acceptable year of the Lord", the great and final time of salvation had dawned . . . and the coming of the kingdom of glory become certain – as certain as the coming of harvest after sowing, or as the mighty tree follows from the grain of mustard seed buried in the ground (cf. the parables of growth in Mark 4 and Matthew 13). Indeed, for those who can see, the reign of God (that is, the triumph of God over Satan and his hosts) is already discernible in the acts of Jesus (Luke 11:20). "If I by the finger of God (by the Spirit of God) cast out devils, doubtless the kingdom of God is come upon you" (Luke 11:20 and Matt. 12:28). It is both present and not yet present; it is present in the person of the Messias, his words and saving acts, but not yet present as the cosmic kingdom of peace and glory. There is, however, an intrinsic connection, an irresistible dynamism, linking this beginning and the end, between this "penultimate time" (as Cullmann called it) and the ultimate accomplishment. The last act in the drama of salvation has begun: God himself is bringing his work to an end, despite all the resistance of the Evil One. "Thus in Jesus, promise and fulfilment are linked and mutually dependent, for the promise receives its certainty of fulfilment from the fulfilment already made in Jesus, and because the fulfilment as a provisional one loses its character of being a σκάνδαλον (a stumbling-block or scandal) only because it is known that the promise is still to be fulfilled."[10]

This tension between partial fulfilment and expectancy of the end, between present salvation and future salvation, provides a fertile source of moral obligation. The reign of God having been preached since John the Baptist, everyone has now been invited to share in God's feast (Matt. 22:2–10; Luke 14:16–24). But as this is still a future blessing of salvation, one must prepare

[10] Kümmel, *Promise*, p. 155.

oneself for it, making oneself worthy to share in it. In his metaphorical language, Jesus lays down conditions for "entering the kingdom of God", not thereby implying that we can earn it [it is given us only by the decision of God, and we can only pray for it (Matt. 6:10)], but rather in the sense that only those who now accept and follow the words of Jesus will one day hear him pronounce those other words, "Come, ye blessed of my Father, possess you the kingdom prepared for you from the foundation of the world" (Matt. 25:34).

Underlying these "entering" sayings[11] is a figurative concept with roots in the Old Testament. In Deuteronomy there is set before the Israelites the prospect, providing they keep the divine law, of entry into the promised land of Canaan, of entering into possession of the "inheritance" assigned to them by God. The Septuagint Greek version uses the same words as the Greek New Testament ("entering" and "inheritance"). So, for example, at Deuteronomy 4:1 we read, "And now, O Israel, hear the commandments and judgements which I teach thee that doing them thou mayest live, and entering in may possess the land which the Lord the God of your fathers will give you." (Compare also 6:18 and 16:20.) Furthermore in later times ritual and moral demands were made on anyone who wanted to enter the temple, a custom reflected in the piety of the psalms (see especially Ps. 14:23; 117:19f., in the Septuagint). As the third beatitude shows, there was no difficulty in applying these ideas to "entering into the kingdom of God" (Matt. 5:5).

It was Jesus' keen desire to make men alert, prepared and resolved to total devotion to God, so he showed himself as a prophetic and forcible preacher, rousing bemused human beings who, though able to interpret the signs of coming

[11] Direct verbal references are to be found at Matt. 5:20; 7:21; 18:3 and par.; 21:31; 22:12; 23:13 par.; Mark 9:47; John 3:5; but the idea can also be found underlying a considerably larger volume of material. Cf. H. Windisch, "Die Sprüche vom Eingehen in das Reich Gottes" in *ZNW* 27 (1928) pp. 163-92.

storms on land and in the skies, do not recognize the hour of salvation (Luke 12:56). When he described for them what would happen in the "days of the Son of man" (that is, before and during the parousia – Luke 17:26f.), his intention was to tell them plainly that all these things could already apply to them, his own contemporaries. As people in the days of Noah ate and drank, married and gave themselves in marriage, until suddenly the deluge came and annihilated them, so it shall be at the end. As those dwelling at Sodom went unconcernedly about their business until one day fire and brimstone rained down from heaven and annihilated them all, so it shall be in the final catastrophe before the coming of the Son of man. It also seems to have been Jesus' purpose in many of the parables to point out to his hearers the seriousness of the situation, the crisis of the times, which made it imperative for them to come to a decision.[12] Only a person who is converted and believes can participate in God's reign.

This does not mean that, in order to instruct, Jesus exaggerated. With his coming, the approach of God's reign is really certain. But at the same time it is still uncertain to men how close in time its advent is, how soon God (who is not tied to an earthly measure of time) will bring about the consummation. So Jesus had good grounds for vividly presenting to the minds of his contemporaries both the tribulations of the last days and the coming of the Son of man, the reign of God "in power", so that it became a matter of concern to them.

Some of the sayings of Jesus do indeed present a difficult problem, for they include announcements of the coming of the end at a near point in time.[13] But in contrast to this, Jesus expressly

[12] Cf. C. H. Dodd, *The Parables of the Kingdom,* 2nd ed. 1936, pp. 154ff.; Jeremias, *Parables,* pp. 160–69.
[13] Mark 9:1 par.; 13:30 par.; Matt. 10:23; 23:39 (=Luke 13:35); cf. also "hereafter" (Matt. 26:64); "Quickly" (Luke 18:8); on these texts, see W. Michaelis, *Der Herr verzieht nicht die Verheißung,* 1942; Morgenthaler, *Kommendes Reich,* pp. 52f., 74ff.; Kümmel, *Promise,* pp. 36ff.,

denied both all knowledge of the day and the hour (Mark 13:32), and the possibility of calculating them in advance (Luke 17:20). It is still not possible to give a satisfactory explanation of these logia: they cannot be definitely related to particular situations and hence their original meaning is difficult to ascertain. It is, therefore, not possible to start directly from them to interpret the whole of Jesus' teaching concerning the coming of God's reign. But on the other hand it is important not to lose sight of the fact that Jesus did proclaim that the reign of God is "at hand" (Mark 1:15).[14]

With these prophetic sayings it was his purpose to encourage and strengthen the disciples, and above all to exhort them to a full exertion of their powers. For the time before the end would bring them many difficulties, temptations and trials of faith. This is a main purpose in Jesus' great eschatological discourse (Mark 13 par.); several times over he bids them to "Be ready" (vv. 5, 9, 23, 33). The climax of the whole discourse lies in the thrice repeated cry, "Watch!" (vv. 33, 35, 37). Luke introduces this same exhortation to watchfulness and preparedness at another point in his narrative (12:35–40), and making oneself ready for what is to come, that is, God's great banquet, is urged by Matthew through the parable of the wise and foolish virgins. This parable, like all the others describing the reign of God under the image of a banquet or marriage-feast,[15] is an important addition to the number of texts where reference is

64ff.; Meinertz, *Theologie*, vol. I. pp. 58ff.; Schnackenburg, *God's Rule*, pp. 195–214.

[14] The perfect tense is is often taken to mean "is here, is present"; but cf. Bauer, *Wörterbuch*, 422f.; H. Preisker in *ThWB* vol. II, 329–32, Morgenthaler, *Kommendes Reich*, pp. 45f.; Kümmel, *Promise*, pp. 25–36. Also instructive for the light they throw on the early Christian interpretation are Romans 13:12; James 5:8; Peter 4:7.

[15] Matt. 22:1–10; cf. Luke 14:16–24; Matt. 22:11–14; 25:1–12. See also the ending of the parable of the talents (where joy = the banquet of joy) Matt. 25:21, 23; Luke 12:37; and perhaps also Luke 14:7–11, though this was originally eschatological. Cf. also the sayings about being

made to "entering the kingdom of God". They all contain the warning, "Prepare yourselves and show yourselves worthy to be counted among those who share in it."

Jesus also gave expression to the religious and moral summons implied by the preaching of the reign of God, in other ways. "Seek ye first the kingdom of God and his justice; and all these things shall be added unto you" (Luke 12:31 par.). Like a man who finds a hidden treasure in a field, or a merchant who finds an extremely precious pearl, everyone must be prepared to forgo everything else so as to possess this treasure (Matt. 13:44-46). Even where (as for instance in the beatitudes Matt. 5:3-8) the kingdom of God is shown as a gift of God and a blessing of salvation, it is promised only to men with a certain outlook and an approved way of life. One can inherit it only on the grounds of active love of one's neighbour (Matt. 5:34ff.); one must accept it (or the message concerning it) as a child (Matt. 10:15 par.). Perhaps in that obscure saying (which it is rather difficult to interpret with certainty) regarding the "violent" who carry off the kingdom (Matt. 11:12; Luke 16:16), there is praise for those who since the days of John the Baptist had been making every effort to get into the kingdom of God,[16] just as Jesus assured the Scribe who grasped the meaning of the chief of the commandments, "Thou art not far from the kingdom of God" (Mark 12:34). In this connection we may notice the special demands Jesus made on individuals

---

"accepted" into heaven, Luke 16:9, 22f. (Lazarus) and the contrary saying about being "cast out", Matt. 7:22f. par.; 8:12 par.; 13:41f., 50; 22:13; 25:30; cf. 5:26; 18:34; 24:51; 25:11.

[16] This logion is often interpreted in a hostile sense (as though it meant obstructing or opposing the advent of the kingdom of God); cf. the attempts at exegesis in Bauer, *Wörterbuch*, 255f. and the discussion in Morgenthaler, pp. 48-50; Kümmel, *Promise*, pp. 121f.; Percy, *Botschaft Jesu*, pp. 198-202; D. Daube, *The New Testament and Rabbinic Judaism*, 1956, pp. 285-300; Schnackenburg, *God's Rule*, pp. 129ff.; J. Schmid, *Evangelium nach Matthäus*, pp. 192ff.

who wanted to associate themselves in closer discipleship with him and with the preaching of the message of salvation (Luke 9:57–62; Matt. 19:12; Mark 10:1 par.; see also section 4 below). All these things show the prophetically powerful, messianically unique, immediate summons here and now made by Jesus to men, which no one could evade.

This eschatological summons is as valid today as it was then; but it must not be misinterpreted as an extreme demand made under the pressure of the imminent end, as an "interim ethics".[17] If it were, it would in fact lose its force and validity with the "delay in the parousia", and would have to be left to the enthusiastic apocalyptic sects. The early Church as a whole, however, never viewed its close expectation[18] in that way (cf. section 20), but only as a continual insistent admonition to vigilance and preparedness, sobriety and steadfastness in trial in the world, love of God and the brethren, and so in actual fact as a "perpetual expectation" (H. Schürmann). Jesus' preaching is not motivated by imminent expectation regarding an ascertainable moment of time, but by the situation in the history of salvation created by the advent of God's royal reign in Jesus' activity, and by the last end which is always approaching men and confronts them here and now with a decision. New Testament eschatology holds at least as strongly to the already present fulfilment of salvation in Jesus Christ as it does to expectation for the future, and in fact derives from the former its distinctive character, even if emphasis may be variously placed (cf. Paul, section 29; John, section 32; Apocalypse, section 42).[19] In Jesus' proclamation, too, as well as the prophetical preaching which brings

---

[17] Cf. Schnackenburg, "Interimsethik" in *LThK* vol. V, 727f. See further, section 8.
[18] Cf. F. J. Schierse, "Eschatologismus" in *LThK* vol. III, 1098f.; J. Gnilka, "Parusieverzögerung und Naherwartung..." in *Catholica* 13 (1959) pp. 277–90.
[19] Cf. Schnackenburg, "Eschatologie im NT" in *LThK* vol. III, 1808–93 (Bibliog.).

the "end" close, and compels instant decision, there is the message of the salvific work of God here and now bestowing love and demanding love. "For Jesus then God is encountered not only by being expected in the future but even beforehand in the present by obedience and love."[20] The real ground of moral obligation is the perceptible saving action of God in Jesus' coming and activity, his revelation of redemption, which is both historical and eschatological, and which guarantees the accomplishment which is to come.

§ 2. The Demand for Repentance

A. H. Dirksen, *The NT Concept of Metanoia*, 1932; E. K. Dietrich, *Die Umkehr (Bekehrung und Buße) im AT und Judentum*, 1936; E. Sjöberg, *Gott und die Sünder im palästinischen Judentum*, 1939; O. Michel, "Die Umkehr nach der Verkündigung Jesus" in *EvTh* 5 (1938) pp. 403–13; H. Pohlmann, *Die Metanoia als Zentralbegriff der christlichen Frömmigkeit*, 1938; J. Behm, art. "μετάνοια" in *ThWB* vol. IV, 1942, 972ff.; J. Schniewind, *Das biblische Wort von der Bekehrung*, 1947; F. Tillmann, *Idee der Nachfolge Christi*, pp. 165–70; J. Gewiess, *Metanoia im NT: Die Kirche in der Welt*, vol. II, 1948, pp. 149–52; R. Schnackenburg, "Typen der Metanoia-Predigt im NT" in *MTZ* 1 (1950) No. 4; J. Schmid, *Evangelium nach Lukas*, pp. 125–28; H. Braun, "Umkehr in spätjüdisch-häretischer und in frühchristlicher Sicht" in *ZThK* 50 (1953) pp. 243–58; id., *Spätjüdisch-häretischer und frühchristlicher Radikalismus*, 2 vols., 1957; W. L. Holladay, *The Root šûbh in the Old Testament*, 1958; "La conversion" in *Lumière et Vie* 47 (1960).

THE FUNDAMENTAL though not the ultimate demand made by Jesus on those who wished to participate in the reign of God was that they should repent. The Greek word μετάνοια conveys a Hebrew and Aramaic concept that goes beyond the scope of the Greek meaning "change of mind" and "regret". To the Semitic mind it suggested a man turning away from his former

[20] H. Schürmann, "Eschatologie und Liebesdienst in der Verkündigung Jesu" in *Kaufet die Zeit aus!* (Festschrift für T. Kampmann), 1959, p. 64.

path, now recognized as wrong, and striking out in a completely different direction. Conversion or repentance, therefore, is (a) the total attitude of a man, involving all his powers; (b) a religious action, a resolute total turning to God; (c) not merely a turning away from, and atonement for, sins committed (repentance and penance) but also a new orientation for the future; (d) quite often a conversion in belief, or at least a new and deeper understanding of God and his holy will; (e) finally, an answer to the call of God's grace, a grasping of the opportunity of salvation offered by him.

The goal of religious moral conversion is God. But even in this endeavour to cut oneself off from all one's sins and find one's way back to God it is easy to go astray, for example if the penitent loses his way among externals. To counter this danger, the prophets laid special emphasis on inward turning away from sin and innermost turning towards the holy God, rather than on such penitential practices as fasting, wearing penitential dress and making lamentations. "Rend your heart and not your garments!" (Joel 2:13). Outward proofs of penance must follow the attitude of mind: the "fasting" which is pleasing to God involves freeing captives, breaking bread for the hungry, taking in the homeless and clothing the naked (Isa. 58:6f.). Repentance must, therefore, be expressed in the whole conduct and especially in works of loving assistance.[21]

The preaching of John the Baptist was directly related to the prophetic call to repentance. It was aimed at the moral reformation of the Jewish nation: the nation was not to invoke its descent from Abraham, but only by repentance could escape the threatening judgement of God's wrath and become the eschatological community of salvation (cf. Luke 3:7-9 par.). The baptism of John was a baptism of repentance (Mark 1:4

---

[21] Isa. 31:6; 44:22; 55:6f.; Jer. 3:12ff.; 5:1ff.; 24:7; Lam. 3:40; 5:21; Ezech. 14:6; 18:21ff.; Osee 3:5; 6:1; 14:2f.; Amos 4:6ff.; Zach. 1, 3; Mal. 3:7.

par.) in which the convert acknowledged his sins, (1:5) but was also obliged to bring forth "fruits of repentance" (Luke 3:8 par.). In John's instruction, given to those of various professions (Luke 3:10–14), these fruits of repentance are identified as faithful observance of the moral commandments of God and works of neighbourly love.[22]

In spite of its outward similarity, the call to repentance on the lips of Jesus, the Messias looked for by John, had a deeper significance. With it, Jesus combined the command to believe in the gospel, that is, in the fact that in his acts God's saving will was already in operation and his royal rule already perceptible. Jesus had been sent and empowered to proclaim the boundless mercy of God to men, to forgive their sins, and to redeem the "lost" (Mark 2:10 par.; 2:17 par.). God's readiness to forgive, never preached on such a wide scale in Judaism, and in fact only promised for the last days, is limited by only one condition, repentance.

Radical conversion and repentance was also required in the Qumran community. Anyone who entered it had to be willing to be converted to God's Covenant (1 QS V, 22); the community itself was the "covenant" in which men were "converted to the truth" (1 QS VI, 14), the "Covenant of repentance" (Dam. XIX, 16). Such conversion was understood to be a decisive religious and moral turning to God, "with all the heart and soul" (1 QS XVI, 17). Rites of atonement and ritual ablutions alone do not achieve this; "they shall not be cleansed unless they turn from their wickedness" (1 QS V, 13f.). Nevertheless there are essential differences between this requirement of conversion in Qumran, even though it was eschatological in motive, and Jesus' preaching of penance. (a) Among the Essenes a "return to the law of Moses" was required (Dam. XVI, 1f.; 1 QS V, 8; 4 QpPs 37: I, 2), and this was to be observed in its

---

[22] On this point, cf. H. Sahlin, "Die Früchte der Umkehr" in ST 1 (1947) pp. 54–68.

original purity (according to the sect's knowledge of the Torah), and in its strict form (prescriptions regarding ritual purity and the Sabbath), "in order to atone for the land" (*1 QS* VIII, 6; *1 QSa* I, 3). Jesus' attitude to the law, on the other hand, was quite different (cf. section 5). (b) This conversion was only possible in the "Covenant of God", separated from the rest of the nation, that is to say, in the Qumran community with its strict constitution. Jesus envisaged neither such a separation nor a restriction to the "men of holiness"; he addressed himself to all and particularly to sinners and those who were despised as "without the law". (c) Conversion in Qumran, despite the disposition of soul that was required, consisted nevertheless in concrete obligations of purity, community of possessions, subordination in rank, etc. Jesus gave no such external prescriptions but required radical obedience to the will of God, which ultimately makes deeper, more individual and inescapable demands on men than the law and legal ordinances (cf. section 7 for the commandment of love). (d) Viewed eschatologically, conversion in Qumran was an attempt to induce God to bring about the time of salvation, the "end", but with Jesus, the thankful response to the salvation, already offered by God. With Jesus, metanoia includes belief in the message of salvation and becomes an expression of joy and confidence in salvation.

The ineffable love of God, all-forgiving and prodigal of gifts, drawing the repentant sinner joyfully to his paternal heart, is described by Jesus in three parables in Luke 15, and particularly movingly in the parable of the prodigal son. At the same time, however, Jesus discloses the nature of genuine repentance. The person who repents recognizes and regrets the fact that he is "lost",[23] realizes his hopeless position in relation to the all-holy God and hence his profound wretchedness, and

---

[23] The constant repetition of the word "lose" in this parable should be noticed (vv. 4, 6, 8, 9, 13, 24, 32). "To be lost" and "to perish" (v. 17) were common Greek expressions; cf. also Matt. 18:11 and Luke 19:10. It is therefore used here of eternal damnation.

confesses his sin and guilt. He gives himself over wholly to the judgement of God, without making either excuses or claims on his own behalf, but with profound confidence in the mercy of God. In the parable at Luke 18:9 ff., the publican does not reckon up before God the tally of his good deeds, but only prays that God may be merciful to him, a sinner. In the woman who had greatly sinned, and who washed his feet with her penitent tears at the supper, Jesus recognized a great love for God by which the notorious woman had been completely transformed, and he immediately told her that her sins were forgiven (Luke 7:36 ff.). Because true repentance often stimulates precisely the great sinner to ardent love, and because it is Jesus' vocation as Saviour to bring back to God those who are cast down, he made himself the "friend of publicans and sinners" (Matt. 11:19 par.) and did not avoid their company (Mark 2:16 par.). When they were converted he rejoiced with that joy which God knows when the lost are saved (Luke 15:7–10; Matt. 18:13).

Hence the attitude of mind that most frequently militates against repentance is self-righteousness and presumption. Jesus himself superlatively illustrated this conflict by the parable of the Pharisee and the publican (Luke 18:10–14). The Pharisee, proudly extolling his pious acts before God, is blind[24] to his own human weakness and poverty; he does not need God or his mercy and finds none (Luke 18:14). Such an attitude is usually associated with contempt for others, so Jesus had doubtless such people in mind when he spoke of the elder son who stayed away from the feast given for his brother's homecoming (Luke 15:25 f.) and the discontented labourers in the vineyard (Matt. 20:1–15). Minds as firmly closed as these are no longer capable of thinking generously about God, and in their harsh judgements of their neighbour have lost every spark of love,

---

[24] This was Jesus' frequent reproach to those with this attitude: Matt. 15:14 (= Luke 6:39); 23:16, 17, 19, 24, 26.

and they aroused the wrath of Jesus (cf. Matt. 23). To such Pharisees and Scribes (and there were certainly others like them), he thundered, "Publicans and harlots shall go into the kingdom of God before you" (Matt. 21:31f.; cf. Luke 7:29f.). "You shut the kingdom of heaven against men; for you yourselves do not enter in and those that are going in you suffer not to enter" (Matt. 23:13). Genuine repentance, the repentance that opens to itself the kingdom of God, is only possible when a man knows he is small and slight as a child before God (Matt. 18:3).[25] In his sight we are always unprofitable servants (Luke 17:10); we are always his debtors (Matt. 6:12). But if we ourselves realize this, then the saying that "God exalts the humble" will be proved in us (cf. Luke 14:11 par.; 18:14; see also Jas. 4:10 and 1 Pet. 5:6).

Behind this teaching there lies Jesus' conviction that every man is a sinner in the sight of God. When it was reported to him that Pilate had made a blood-bath among the Galileans attending the sacrifices in the temple, he said to those about him: "Think you that these Galileans were sinners above all the men of Galilee, because they suffered these things? No, I say to you: but, unless you do penance, you shall all likewise perish." And as another example of this he cited the men of Jerusalem who were crushed by the fall of the tower of Siloe (Luke 13:1–5).[26] Jesus' call for repentance, which arose from the actual particular situation, is only intelligible if Jesus considered that all those who heard him were in need of repentance.

[25] The comparison with a child originally refers (Mark 10:15: cf. Luke 18:17), not to the child's humble attitude of mind (Matt. 18:4), but objectively to its smallness in contrast to adults. It may also be meant to recall the child's simplicity and the trust with which it speaks to its father (J. Jeremias, *Parables,* pp. 190f.). Perhaps at Matt. 18:3, if στραφῆτε καί (instead of the normal Septuagint ἐπιστρέφεσθαι for "repentance") is a Hebraism, we should translate, "unless you become again as little children . . ."

[26] Cf. J. Blinzler, "Die Niedermetzelung von Galiläern durch Pilatus" in *NovT* 2 (1957) pp. 24–49.

The saying about the ninety-nine just men who have no need of repentance (Luke 15:7) is not evidence to the contrary. We cannot, however, understand it as intended ironically or add the phrase "in their own opinion", for in the parallel at Matthew 18:11 the saying about the ninety-nine sheep reads only "who have not strayed". In fact, the phrase about the just must be interpreted in relation to that about the sinner. In it, Jesus was accommodating himself to the general opinion about "the just". Jesus taught all his disciples without exception to pray "forgive us our trespasses". To the accusers of the woman taken in adultery he said, "He that is without sin among you, let him first cast a stone at her" (John 8:7).[27]

By his call to repentance, Jesus compelled people to make an immediate decision. Those who heard it from his lips were there and then receiving the call of God's grace: a blessing for one who heard the voice of God and obeyed it, like the chief publican Zacchaeus who, in the gratitude of a heart filled with love for God and his envoy, allowed himself to be inspired by the coming of Jesus to a noble action (Luke 19:1–10). But woe to those who let the hour of God's gracious visitation pass unused! Especially harsh was the reproach Jesus addressed to the Galilean towns which had seen many of his mighty deeds (Luke 10:13–15 par.). Jesus' words here are a typical prophetic warning. His mention of the pagan cities Tyre and Sidon (which, if they had seen such wonders, would long before have "repented in sackcloth and ashes"[28]) is merely a figurative

[27] This pericope did not form part of the original content of St. John's Gospel, but it enshrines an ancient, incontestably historical tradition; see A. Wikenhauser, *Das Evangelium nach Johannes,* 2nd. ed. 1957, pp. 165ff.; for its exegesis see also J. Jeremias in *ZNW* 43 (1950–51) pp. 148f.; F. A. Schilling, "The Story of Jesus and the Adulteress" in *ATR* 37 (1955) pp. 91–106.

[28] The metaphor here, originating from the Old Testament, relates to the customs followed at times of fasting; "sackcloth" is a rough cloth and the word suggests penitential garments. in "Ashes" were usually sprinkled on the head; cf. the example quoted in Billerbeck vol. IV,

expression for the urgency of repentance. What Jesus in fact wanted was not to revive penitential practices wherever he went, but to spread joy. In these sayings about Chorazin, Bethsaida and Capharnaum, the primary concern is not so much with moral repentance as with believing acceptance of God's envoy, which, of course, must be accompanied by perfect submission to God and his will. Whether Jesus' intention was to cry "Too late!" to any of these cities favoured by his activity in them (as he did to Jerusalem, the blind city of God, Luke 14:31) or whether he is addressing a final call to repentance to them, cannot be determined with certainty from these texts, which are not set in the context of a definite situation.

The parable of the barren fig-tree (Luke 13:6–9), connected by St. Luke with Jesus' serious call to repentance, symbolizes the period of grace which the nation (Israel?) has been granted for repentance. The warning voiced in it is sharpened by the mysterious cursing of the fig-tree (Mark 11:13ff., 20f.), a unique prophetic and symbolic action of Jesus, in which condemnation (incurred by guilt) is already definitively expressed.[29]

Jesus' call to repentance, like all his preaching, has, therefore, two sides. His primary message is God's message of joy and salvation. But when he meets with rejection and obduracy, the threat of judgement follows ineluctably from it for the impenitent.

The "hardening", as the attitude diametrically opposed to conversion, and excluding it (cf. following Isaias 6:9ff.; Mark

---

pp. 84f., n. 4. Sometimes, however, one sat among the ashes – as did the King of Nineveh according to Jonas 3:6.

[29] In *RHPR* 33 (1953) pp. 57–60, J. Isaac opposes the hitherto generally accepted interpretation of this text as referring to the whole nation of Israel: but are we not bound on the Old Testament pattern to interpret the symbolic language in this sense? Cf. C. H. Bird in *JTS*, New Series 4 (1953) pp. 177–9; J. W. Doeve, "Purification du Temple et desséchement du figuier" in *NTS* 1 (1954–5) pp. 297–308 (commentary on Jer. 7:20, "My wrath and my indignation is enkindled against this place.").

4:12 par.; John 12:40; Acts 28:26 ff.), raises difficult theological questions. For these texts it must be remembered that (a) the point of view is that of redemptive history, namely in regard to God's chosen people of the Old Covenant and its decision concerning faith in regard to God's eschatological envoy; (b) the individual's opportunity for repentance is not directly affected by the divine decree of hardening (cf. John 12:39 ff. with 42); (c) nothing is said about the duration of the hardening (cf. however Rom. 11:25–32); (d) in the varying forms of the tradition in the gospels, it is possible to recognize certain theological judgements of the evangelists or of the tradition which is their basis.[30]

Jesus' direct summons calls for prompt, radical and lasting repentance. Partial conversion is no conversion; that goes without saying, if Jesus' preaching is properly understood. In the parable of the returning unclean spirit (Luke 11:24–26 par.),[31] Jesus' purpose was clearly to issue an explicit warning against backsliding. "And the last state of that man becomes worse than the first." Men must serve God with undivided heart (Matt. 6:24) and so retain the spirit of repentance. In this way repentance remains the sustaining foundation (though not the centre) of the moral attitude of a Christian. The disciples too took up Jesus' call to repentance (Mark 6:12). In their dealings with one another, disciples are to show readiness to repent and to forgive (Luke 17:3f.). By the command of the risen Lord, "Repent and be baptized" (Acts 2:38) became the fundamental sermon of the early Church after Pentecost.

[30] Cf. W. Trilling, *Das wahre Israel. Studien zur Theologie des Matthäus-Evangeliums*, 1959, pp. 57–77; J. Gnilka, *Die Verstockung Israels. Isaias 6:9–10 in der Theologie der Synoptiker*, 1961.
[31] For more detailed explanation see especially Jeremias, *Parables*, pp. 197f.

§ 3. THE DEMAND FOR FAITH

A. Schlatter, *Der Glaube im NT*, 4th ed. 1927; E. Walter, *Glaube, Hoffnung und Liebe im NT*, 1940; F. Tillmann, *Idee der Nachfolge Christi*, pp. 170ff.; J. Schmid, *Evangelium nach Markus*, pp. 117f.; P. Antoine, "Foi" in *Dictionnaire de la Bible*, suppl. vol. III, 276–310; M. Meinertz, *Theologie*, vol. I, pp. 91ff.; J. Huby, "De la connaissance de foi dans Saint Jean" in *RSR* 31 (1931) pp. 385–421; P. H. Menoud, *La foi dans l'évangile de Jean*, 1936; R. Schnackenburg, *Der Glaube im vierten Evangelium*, 1937; M. Bonningues, *La foi dans l'évangile de Saint Jean*, 1955; A. Weiser and R. Bultmann, art. "πιστεύειν" in *ThWB* vol. VI, 174 to 230 (Eng. tr. *Bible Keywords*, No. 10: "Faith", 1961); A. Decourtray, "La conception johannique de la foi" in *NRT* 91 (1959) pp. 561–76; F.-M. Willocx, *La notion de foi dans le quatrième évangile* (typed dissertation, Louvain, 1962).

THE DEMAND for faith is very closely connected with the call to repentance. Just as repentance is expressed outwardly by accepting Jesus and his messengers (Luke 10:13 par.), so too faith is impossible without the adoption of an attitude of mind which itself is, in the widest sense, a "conversion", a complete turning towards God, a listening to his will, and obedience. The obduracy of the Pharisees and Scribes who did not follow John the Baptist, was both unreadiness to repent and lack of faith (Luke 7:29ff.; Matt. 21:32). Faith is, as it were, the positive side of conversion. "Believe in the gospel" (Mark 1:15) means, believe in the message about the kingdom of God that Jesus brings, not in a cold, uncommitted way, but by accepting in a positive fashion everything it involves for each human being personally. The man who is convinced that God is actively establishing his royal rule is bound above all to strive for his part to fulfil God's royal will. And if God announces his will through Jesus of Nazareth and guarantees his identity by healings and miracles, then one must accept and obey Jesus' words. Consequently faith, like repentance, is a "total" attitude, claiming all man's faculties.

This conception of faith comes from the Old Testament, in

which faith is a total bond with God, a "saying Amen to God" (A. Weiser). To it there certainly belongs recognition of the unicity of Yahweh, but even more, trust in the God of the Covenant, the expectation and hope of his help, the taking refuge in his love, and an absolute holding fast to him and his words. It was faith when after their rescue from the Red Sea, the Israelites held fast to Yahweh and his servant Moses (Exod. 14:31; Ps. 105:12), and it was lack of faith when they murmured against him in the desert (Num. 14:11; 20:12; Deut. 9:23; Ps. 77:22, 32; 105:24). Abraham became a great example of faith by maintaining faith as submission to the almighty God (Gen. 15:6). Isaias, however, the "prophet of faith", affirms in great tribulation, "If you will not believe, you shall not continue" (Isa. 7:9). Faith is the answer of man to God's redemptive action in history, in the life of the people as in that of the individual (cf. the Psalms). If God now announces his eschatological salvation through Jesus and in Jesus, the most important requirement is to believe in this message of salvation, to affirm it with all one's powers, and to accept its consequences. For the same reason the faith demanded by Jesus is always at the same time faith in himself.

It has been questioned whether Jesus really required faith in himself. Leaving St. John's gospel aside for the moment and speaking only of the synoptics, no such explicit demand can be found in anything he said (as regards Matt. 18:6, see the better reading of the Greek at the parallel passage Mark 9:42). Yet in fact, it is everywhere present. Just as Jesus did not openly declare that he was the Messias (hence the so-called "Messianic secret"), so according to the synoptic gospels he did not expressly require faith in himself as the Messias. But just as he wanted people to recognize him as the promised Messias by all he did (Matt. 11:3f. par.; Mark 8:27–30 par.), so too he wanted this Messianic faith to grow among the people and then find expression in a profession of belief in himself. It is clear from his discussion with his disciples at Caesarea Philippi that no other response of faith would satisfy him.

35

At first Jesus was satisfied with faith in the powers of healing invested in him, in the presence of God perceptible in his person. He was able to use such belief as a starting-point for Messianic faith, because healings, the driving out of evil spirits and other miracles forced the question of Messiasship to be raised.[32] After he had taught in the synagogue at Capharnaum, and had exorcized an unclean spirit there, those present were thrown into great excitement: "What thing is this? What is this new doctrine? For with power he commandeth even the unclean spirits; and they obey him" (Mark 1:27). After the stilling of the storm, great fear fell upon them all, and they said to one another, "Who is this (thinkest thou) that both wind and sea obey him?" (Mark 4:40 par.). He skilfully repulsed the malicious accusation of his opponents that when he cast out devils he was himself possessed by Beelzebub, making it clear to everyone that here was "one yet stronger" who had "come from God" (Mark 3:22–27 par.). This is why Jesus accepted the simple faith in miracles, the "faith in the saviour", of the common people, when trust in God's envoy is awakened by it. The woman with an issue of blood had ideas that were still quite primitive regarding the power that flowed from Jesus, but she believed whole-heartedly that in Jesus the helping power of God had come to her, and Jesus assured her, "Daughter, thy faith hath made thee whole" (Mark 5:34 par.).[33] The president of the synagogue who called Jesus to his daughter's death-bed and then received the news of her death, was encouraged by

[32] Cf. A. Richardson, *The Miracle Stories of the Gospels,* 1941 (new imp. 1952), pp. 38ff.; P. H. Menoud, "La signification du miracle dans le NT" in *RHPR* 28 (1948) pp. 173–92; P. A. Liégé, "Réflexions pour une apologétique du miracle" in *RSPT* 35 (1951) pp. 249–54; A. Vögtle, "Jesu Wunder einst und heute" in *Bibel und Leben* 2 (1961) pp. 234–54.
[33] This same formula occurs again, Mark 10:52 and par.; Luke 7:50; 17:19. The Greek word σώζειν has the double meaning "heal" and "save", and so Jesus could also use it in connection with the forgiveness of sins (Luke 7:50), so providing a starting-point for the soteriological faith of the early Church (being saved for eternal life).

Jesus with the words, "Fear not, only believe" (Mark 5:36 par.). In the case of the lame man it was the faith of his helpful friends which called forth from Jesus the absolution of his sins and physical healing (Mark 2:5). The question of faith is central to the narrative of the cured boy (Mark 9:14–29 par.): Jesus sighed over this disbelieving generation (v. 19) and reminded the boy's father that all things are possible to him who believes (v. 23), whereupon the man cried out, "I do believe, Lord; help my unbelief" (v. 23). Jesus let himself be moved by the great faith of the Syro-Phoenician woman to heal her daughter (Mark 7:29; cf. Matt. 15:28). He drew attention with especial praise to the faith of the pagan centurion of Capharnaum, who believed that by a mere word of command from afar Jesus could heal his sick servant (Matt. 8:10 = Luke 7:9).

It is clear that in these cases in which someone else prayed for the sick person, there is no question of magical belief in prodigies nor of the operation of the power of suggestion on the part of the sick person himself. Mark 6:5, therefore, where Jesus is said to have been able to do no miracles in his home town of Nazareth must be understood to mean that a limit was set to his works by the will and wisdom of God. Where he met with obstinate disbelief, he was not permitted to manifest the great signs of salvation.

Jesus instantly rejected the belief that demands signs and marvels.[34] Only an evil and adulterous generation (that is, one unfaithful to God) would demand a sign from heaven (Matt. 12:39). Such people as these, who stand challenging God, would not be moved to acknowledge God's ambassador even by a demonstration miracle in the heavens, for that needs humility and penitence. They will be given only the sign of Jonas (Luke 11:29 par.), that is, probably, the divine attestation of Jesus after his death, at the parousia, when it will be too late for them to repent

[34] Mark 8:11f. = Matt. 16:1f. and 4; Matt. 12:38f. = Luke 11:29; John 6:30; cf. also Luke 23:8f.; Mark 15:32; John 2:18; 4:48.

and the sign they ask for will mean judgement for them.[35] So also at the end of the warning story about the rich glutton and poor Lazarus, Jesus said plainly, "If they hear not Moses and the prophets, neither will they believe if one rise again from the dead" (Luke 16:31).

We must now briefly consider the internal structure of this faith that is described by the synoptic gospels. Above all it is trust in Jesus and in God who is offering salvation through Jesus. The great prophets like Isaias had tended, in a time of darkness and need, a hope of salvation which was to be fulfilled in the last times.[36] This confident hope quite naturally received renewed life from the contact with Jesus, gained strength from his person and confirmation by his acts (cf. Matt. 11:2ff. par.). When the sick and the oppressed have a sincere and religious basis for their faith and confidence in Jesus (see above), it is more than a case of turning to Jesus as a worker of miracles and relief; it is a question of believing in a salvation-giving God who reveals himself in Christ. Those who were impressed by the works of Jesus had already received by their religious education a preparation through which, in contrast to the people of Hellenistic paganism, they were enabled to make definite judgements about the person of the great teacher and wonder-worker. Most commonly, we hear the opinion that he is a "prophet",[37] but on many occasions, too, the people also linked him with Messianic figures, especially with Elias and "the" prophet (expected probably because of Deut. 18:15, see Matt. 6:15; 8:28 par.; John 6:14; 7:40), or else they thought of him as a resurrected John the

---

[35] On this point, cf. Jeremias in *ThWB* vol. III, 412f.; A. Vögtle, "Der Spruch vom Jonaszeichen" in *Synoptische Studien,* Festschrift in honour of A. Wikenhauser, 1954, pp. 230–77.

[36] Cf. Isa. 8:17; 25:9; 28:16; 30:15, 18; similarly Deutero-Isaias 40:31; 43:10–13; 52:6; 57:13; and Jer. 17:5–8. Similar expressions of the same hope may be found in the eschatological cult-psalms 95–98.

[37] Mark 6:15 par.; 8:28 par.; Luke 7:16; Matt. 21:11, 26; cf. also Luke 7:39; 24:19; John 4:19; 9:17.

Baptist (Mark 6:14; cf. 8:28). Clearly faith, in these instances, did not indicate blind trust, an irrational urge; but entailed recognition even if as yet uninformed and immature of the religious significance of Jesus' person and work. It was just this recognition that Jesus wanted to develop further, as he had in the disciples, but the "statement of accounts" rendered at Caesarea Philippi showed that the people had not yet gone beyond a certain stage and it is clear that Jesus saw this as a shortcoming. Both extremes are, therefore to be avoided, excessive emphasis on emotional factors, mistakenly supported by reference to examples in the synoptic gospels; or the onesided over-estimate of that rational conviction which mistrusts all those psychological and frequently imponderable forces that alone make faith capable of living warmth and bring it to full growth.

A purely psychological assessment does not, however, do justice to faith. Jesus makes it clear often enough that, ultimately, faith is a grace. In a cry of exultation, he praises the Father because he has hidden "these things"[38] from the wise and prudent but revealed them to "little ones" (Matt. 11:25 = Luke 10:21). The "mystery of the kingdom of God" has been entrusted to the disciples (Mark 4:11 par.).[39] After Simon Peter, the chief of the circle of twelve, had acknowledged Jesus' Messiasship, Jesus

[38] The fact that the true place of this saying is not known with certainty (cf. the different order in Matthew and Mark), makes it impossible to determine to what "these things" refer. But it could refer to the principal element in the preaching, that is, the fact that God's kingship is perceptible in the acts of Jesus and that the kingdom of God is at hand. Cf. Schnackenburg, God's Rule, pp. 189f.

[39] Probably this means recognition of the presence of the reign of God (see previous note), which remained hidden from most. Cf., among others, G. Bornkamm in ThWB vol. IV, 824f.; M. Hermaniuk, La Parabole évangélique, 1947, p. 282; H. Ridderbos, De komst van het Koninkrijk, p. 120; Jeremias, Parables, p. 15; J. Schniewind, J. Schmid, V. Taylor (The Gospel according to St. Mark, 1952) in loc.; J. Gnilka, op. cit., p. 44. Others again maintain that this saying is secondary, having originated in the Church.

assured him that this truth had been revealed to him not by flesh and blood, but by the Father of Jesus in heaven (Matt. 16:17). Hence it is a sin to scandalize "the little ones" who believe, that is, by acts of malice to tear the faith from the hearts of the simple and unsuspecting followers of Jesus (Mark 9:42 par.). Faith is subject to its own requirements of growth. Even the close disciples of Jesus who were so frequently reproved by their Lord for their "little faith" (that is, for their faint-heartedness, fearfulness, their lack of spontaneous response in faith to some particular situation),[40] sensed the brittleness and inadequacy of their own faith and once begged their master to "increase our faith" (Luke 17:5). The words of Jesus' reply as given by Luke at this point relate to a special kind of faith, which is an extraordinary gift of God's grace yet which is not beyond men's scope. Such charismatic faith, though it be only as "large as a grain of mustard seed" can effect miracles.

The tradition here is not wholly uniform and clear. According to Mark 11:22ff. anyone who does not doubt in his heart can move an obstructive mountain and put it in the sea. According to Luke 17:6, those who have even as little faith as a grain of mustard seed can order a mulberry-tree to uproot itself and plant itself in the sea. Matthew combines the Mark-saying with the cursing of the fig-tree (21:21) and also brings in the saying about faith as big as a grain of mustard seed at another place (17:20), though he too connects it with the example of moving a mountain. The variation in the wording is, however, insignificant in comparison with the fact that the early Church kept a lively memory of the charismatic faith that moves mountains, as 1 Corinthians 13:2 shows.

This strength of faith should be proved in prayer and guaran-

---

[40] This is a favourite expression in Matthew: Matt. 6:30; 8:26; 14:31; 16:8; 17:20. What it meant is shown partly by the context, partly by the synoptic parallels. The scene in which Peter doubts and sinks (14:28–31), a most significant one as far as faith is concerned, belongs to the material peculiar to Matthew.

tees a favourable hearing (Mark 11:24). But from this it follows that the faith that moves mountains brings about what seems impossible not by its own power but by setting in motion God's gracious omnipotence.

That faith, together with baptism, is indispensable if a man is to be "saved", was first explicitly stated by the risen Lord according to the longer (secondary) ending to Mark (Mark 16:16), but is firmly founded on Jesus' fundamental demand for faith and on his preaching as a whole. Luke gives it adequate expression as early as the interpretation of the parable of the sower (8:12). Moreover, the necessity and saving power of faith is also clear from the original saying at Luke 18:8, "But yet, the Son of man, when he cometh, shall he find, think you, faith on earth?" and above all from the saying "For he that shall be ashamed of me and of my words, in this adulterous and sinful generation; the Son of man also will be ashamed of him when he shall come in the glory of his Father with the holy angels" (Mark 8:38 = Luke 9:26; cf. Matt. 10:32f. = Luke 12:8f.). From this it follows that faith is necessary for salvation.

Anyone who agrees that these are the outlines of faith in the synoptic gospels will also see that the constant demand for faith in St. John's gospel is only an organic development. Here faith is the great single expression covering everything that Jesus requires of men.[41] It is Christological faith, that is, the confession that Jesus is the Messias and Son of God (20:31; cf. 11:27). And even now this faith brings possession of eternal, divine life. "He who believes in me, hath eternal life."[42] For the early Church the power of faith to save was the consequence of Jesus' claim to be the Messias. But Johannine faith is not merely recognition and assent. As Jesus' vivid encounters with people whom he leads

[41] See especially John 3:15f.; 6:29; 10:37f.; 12:36, 44ff.; 17:8, 20f.; 20:31.
[42] 3:15, 16, 18, 36; 5:24; 6:35, 40, 47; 7:38; 8:51; 11:25f.; 20:31. Cf. F. Mussner, ZΩH. *Die Anschauung vom "Leben" im vierten Evangelium,* 1952, esp. pp. 144ff.

to faith show, it is both trust and submission. The numerous professions of faith[43] not only praise Jesus with many titles of majesty and dignity, but also reveal personal emotion. The decisive thing, however, remains acceptance of Jesus' claims, and in principle, faith can dispense with Jesus' presence (20:29; cf. 17:20). The moral importance of faith lies in the fact that it has accepted the demand for repentance[44] and requires obedience to the Son of God (3:36), the following of his teaching (8:31f., 51; 12:47f.). Real faith is closely connected with love for Jesus (16:27), which again binds a man to the keeping of his commandments (14:15, 21; 15:10). Jesus repeatedly explained the puzzling disbelief of "the Jews" by references to their moral guilt: they perform works of darkness and shrink from the light (3:19ff.; 5:40ff.; 8:41ff.; 15:24f.). Consequently, if malicious unbelief, which has connections with hate, is seen to arise from the dark depths of the human soul, faith once again is a grace and must be given to a man by God (6:55). No one can come to Jesus unless the Father "draws" him (6:44). Certain persons, entrusted to Jesus by the Father, belong to the flock of the faithful (6:37ff.; 10:26ff.; 17:2, 6, 9), but Jesus gives no information about the mystery of this election. No one is relieved of personal responsibility (9:41; 15:22), the way of faith lies open to all (12:42), and until the end Jesus summons all men with the words, "Whilst you have the light, believe in the light, that you may be the children of light" (12:36).

§ 4. THE CALL TO DISCIPLESHIP

G. Kittel, art. "ἀκολουθέω" in ThWB vol. I, 210–16; F. Tillmann, Idee der Nachfolge Christi, pp. 48–57; A. Oepke, "Nachfolge und Nachahmung Christi im NT" in Allgemeine evangelisch-lutheranische Kirchenzeitung 71

[43] 1:49; 4:42; 6:68f.; (9:38); 11:27; 20:28.
[44] The group of words "repentance" and "repent" has entirely disappeared from St. John's Gospel (and Epistles).

(1938) pp. 850–57, pp. 866–72; J. M. Nielen, "Die Kultsprache der Nachfolge und Nachahmung Gottes und verwandter Bezeichnungen im neutestamentlichen Schrifttum" in *Heilige Überlieferung*, 1938, pp. 59–85; K. H. Rengstorf, art. "μαθητής" in *ThWB* vol. IV, 417–65; W. Michaelis, art. "μιμέομαι" *ibid.* 661–78; H. J. Schoeps, "Von der Imitatio Dei zur Nachfolge Christi" in *Aus frühchristlicher Zeit*, 1950, pp. 286–301; T. Süss, "Nachfolge Jesu" in *TLZ* 78 (1953) pp. 129–40; J. Schmid, *Evangelium nach Lukas*, pp. 178–82; E. Schweizer, *Erniedrigung und Erhöhung bei Jesus und seinen Nachfolgern*, 1955; D. M. Stanley, " 'Become Imitators of Me!' " *Biblica* 40 (1959) pp. 859–77; J. J. Vincent, "Discipleship and Synoptic Studies" in *TZ* 16 (1960) pp. 456–69; R. Schnackenburg, "Nachfolge Christi" in *Der Christ und die Weltwirklichkeit*, 1960, pp. 9–20; K. H. Schelkle, *Jüngerschaft und Apostelamt*, 2nd ed. 1961; A. Schulz, *Nachfolge und Nachahmung im NT* (dissertation, Munich 1959).

IN CONNECTION with the sentences in which he outlines the teaching of Jesus, Mark relates the call of the first disciples, the two pairs of brothers, Simon and Andrew, and James and John (Mark 1:16–20). In this characteristic account of the calling of disciples, Jesus' cry "Follow me!" is paralleled by the remark, "And immediately, leaving their nets, they followed him." So first of all "following" means quite literally "going after" someone, but the mention of the special purpose of this following ("And I will make you to become fishers of men") immediately afterwards gives the expression another, figurative meaning: Jesus was calling them to be his disciples. Such discipleship was immediately comprehensible to Jesus' contemporaries, for the teachers of the law, mostly Pharisees, also collected disciples around them. Such disciples looked upon their rabbi not only as a learned man, passing on the oral teaching to them and expounding it for them, but also a master giving them training in the law.[45] Their discipleship laid the foundations of a living community, a personal relationship between the disciples and the older teacher of the law who, because of his strict observance of the law and his piety, was generally held in the highest respect.

[45] Cf. Billerbeck, vol. I, pp. 527–9; Rengstorf, art. in *ThWB* vol. IV, 437 (Eng. tr. *Biblical Keywords*, No. 6: "Apostleship", 1952).

As Jesus was held to be a rabbi, even if not an academically trained rabbi (John 7:15), and as he also publicly acted like one in his discourses and in his lessons and controversial discussions, his disciples were compared with "the disciples of the Pharisees" and those of John the Baptist (Mark 2:18 par.). But, of course, discipleship under Jesus meant something very different, higher, unique and in keeping with the dignity of the person calling and the work to which he called.

The goal was not the completion of a vocational training followed by "ordination" as a rabbi, but rather lasting communion with God's ambassador (see Mark 3:14). In the circle of his disciples Jesus demanded and received a far higher degree of personal authority than a rabbi: all that counted was his word alone. No one else's opinion, and no objection raised had any validity. There was no disputation of the kind that is usual in the activity of a school. The disciples seldom questioned him and never when it concerned his own behaviour (cf. John 4:27). Moreover, Jesus seems to have seen them more in the rôle of "servants" than would generally appear to have been expected in the relationship between a rabbi and his disciples.[46] This, of course, stemmed only from his claim to sovereign authority and the status this gave his disciples, and was not so markedly expressed in actual service (Mark 10:45 par.). In the Upper Room Jesus deliberately raised this relationship between master and servant to one of friendship (John 15:15). Finally, the mission Jesus laid on his disciples was different from that given to pupils of the rabbis: their task was to be, not the passing on of tenets, but the preaching of his message and the exercising of his powers in his name.

In every text where "follow" has the particular ring given it at Mark 1:18 and does not mean merely "walk behind" in the

---

[46] Cf. Rengstorf, *loc. cit.*, 451f.; there are valuable observations on the unique character of Christian discipleship in A. Schlatter, *Die Geschichte des Christus,* 2nd. ed. 1923, pp. 316ff.

usual sense, what was originally meant was this kind of discipleship. The call to "follow" in this sense was made by Jesus[47] and he made the strongest demands on those he called: they had to leave everything (Luke 5:11; Mark 10:28f. par.), family, house and farm (see also Luke 14:26 par.; Matt. 10:37), money and wealth (Mark 10:21 par.), their former occupations (Matthew-Levi, Mark 2:14 par.) and all economic security (Luke 9:58 par. Matt. 8:20). Hatred, suffering, persecution and death awaited the disciples of Jesus in following their Lord (Matt. 10:10–25 par.; John 15:19f.; 16:1–4). Jesus must have spoken repeatedly of these things.

Luke describes the hardships of discipleship, and at the same time its urgent necessity, in three records of sayings (9:57–62). Matthew collected together the instructions to the disciples on this subject in a missionary discourse (chapter 10). Even the section in Luke 14:25–35 in spite of its introductory remark with its mention of "great multitudes" (v. 25) embodies various elements of tradition originally belonging to the training of the disciples. Note verse 33: complete renunciation of personal property. Within this tradition belong certain extremely radical sayings, as when Jesus declared that the filial duty of burying one's own father must take second place to the preaching of the reign of God (Luke 9:60); or again, that his disciples must love him more than father, mother, children, sisters, brothers, or even their own lives (Luke 14:26).[48] All this is intelligible only on the assumption that Jesus himself knew he was bound to perform the task laid on him by his Father and wanted to engage his disciples to the same lofty mission.

[47] Cf. Mark 2:14 par.; 3:13; 10:21 par.; Luke 9:59f. par.; John 1:43; 6:70; 13:18; 15:16.

[48] The expression here has been given a Semitic colouring: "hate" only means to "love less". The negative phrase appended ("and hate not") signifies logical subordination ("because he does not love me more"). Matthew has expressed the same sense in a form more intelligible to Greek ears (Matt. 10:37).

To the disciples of Jesus the call to follow him was, then, in truth their "vocation". This shows that their "following" was not primarily imitation of him, but consisted in accepting the conditions of Jesus' life, of sharing in his destiny. "The disciple is not above the master, nor the servant above his lord. It is enough for the disciple that he be as his master, and the servant as his Lord" (Matt. 10:24f.).[49] That is the fundamental rule of life for a disciple. But from the disciple's close unity with his Lord (and through him with God), profound consolation is given him, and the well-springs of divine power are opened to him. The Holy Spirit helps the disciple before the seat of judgement (Matt. 10:19ff. par.), and he is promised a most noble reward (Matt. 19:28f. par.).[50] "Fear not, little flock, for it hath pleased your Father to give you a kingdom" (Luke 12:32). It is the disciples who have endured with Jesus in his temptations;[51] he, therefore, also gives them a share in his dominion (Luke 22:28f.).

Within the framework of this concept of community of destiny with Jesus, there also belongs the saying about following the cross, which has been handed down in several forms.[52] To the people of that time the cross was not a symbol of greater or lesser "sacrifice" or even of the burden of the misery and sorrow

---

[49] Matt. 10:25 "It is enough for the disciple if he be as his master", (meaning, if he shares the same fate), occurs often, almost like a proverb, in Jewish writings; cf. Billerbeck, vol. I, pp. 577f.; cf. also John 15:20.
[50] In v. 28 the prospect of a special reward is set before the twelve (cf. Luke 22:30), but in v. 29 (cf. Mark 10:29f.; Luke 18:29f.) all the disciples are promised a rich reward. Cf. the commentaries, and J. Theissing, *Die Lehre Jesu von der ewigen Seligkeit,* 1940, pp. 54–59.
[51] The concept of temptation, which presupposes a situation of eschatological warfare, is now well illustrated by the manuscripts discovered near the Dead Sea; cf. K. G. Kuhn, "Πειρασμός - ἁμαρτία - σάρξ im NT und die damit zusammenhängenden Vorstellungen" in *ZTK* 49 (1952) pp. 200–22.
[52] Mark 8:34 = Matt. 16:24 = Luke 9:23; Matt. 10:38 = Luke 14:27; cf. also John 12:25f.

laid on life in this world, but was the terrifying sign of a shameful death. However the original symbol was meant,[53] its meaning becomes clear in the phrase added in the longer version of the logion "Let him renounce himself" (Mark 8:34 par.). This renunciation of self means a radical abandonment of one's own Ego with all its self-seeking, even to the point of giving one's life. Closely related to this saying is that other, paradoxically worded saying about "saving one's life and losing it". Even if the logion about taking up the cross should be thought of as already having a metaphorical meaning (at least in Luke, cf. "daily"), the image must not be robbed of its strength. From those who follow him, Jesus requires the bitterest suffering and, if profession of faith in him requires it, even the surrender of life itself.

The saying about following in the way of the cross raises an important problem. Is it addressed primarily only to the disciples who have joined Jesus in personal association and "vocational" collaboration, or is it addressed to all? According to Matthew 16:24, Jesus was speaking to the disciples; according to Mark 8:34, to the crowd together with the disciples, and according to Luke 9:23, expressly to everyone. Clearly these remarks about the setting are the work of the evangelists, who thereby also provided an opening for the paranesis of the early Church.

In view of the tradition of Jesus' sayings as it has come down to us, therefore, the distinctions between the teaching of the disciples and the instruction of the people become blurred or are

[53] E. Dinkler "Jesu Wort vom Kreuztragen" in *Neutestamentliche Studien für R. Bultmann,* 1954, pp. 111–29, wants to establish the original meaning as "Let him take His sign (Hebr. 'oth) upon him", that is the sign of belonging to God (in the form of a Hebrew *taw*) which is mentioned in 1 Esdras 9:4 ff., a sign of repentance but also of divine protection. In the community the *taw* was understood as a cross and then applied concretely to Christ's cross. On the meaning of the word, cf. also R. Koolmeister, "Selbstverleugnung, Kreuzaufnahme und Nachfolge" in *Charisteria J. Köpp,* 1954, pp. 64–94.

obscured by the accompanying observations of the evangelists and by the way they assemble collections of sayings. There is an intrinsic reason for this. The demands which Jesus addressed during earthly life to his followers in the narrower sense, that is to say, the disciples who were called by him into personal association with him and to collaborate in his preaching, were transferred in the community after the Resurrection to all Christ's faithful, when there was no longer any discipleship in the former special sense. In fact "disciples" is a standard expression in Acts 6–21 for members of the Church.[54] This linguistic usage, however, also made its way into the gospels, so that Jesus' followers in the wider sense are called disciples (cf. Luke 6:17; 10:1; 19:37; 24:18; John 4:1; 6:60ff. 66; 7:3; 8:31; 9:27ff.; 19:38). In the sight of the early Church the distinction was then no longer strictly drawn between the special demands made by Jesus on the disciples summoned by him to closer collaboration and his demands on all the faithful. This was an understandable and legitimate proceeding when it was desired to retain "discipleship", which now became faith, obedience and service in regard to the invisible Lord who from heaven guides his Church.

From the choosing of the special group of twelve it can be seen how Jesus proceeded in appointing a disciple, "He called unto him whom he would" (Mark 3:13): he chose for himself certain men out of the crowd that thronged to him. It was the same at the time of the mission of the seventy-two disciples: Jesus himself named them (Luke 10:1). As well as this way of selecting "from above", there was another, inner one that separated his followers "from below": Jesus laid special and often individual demands on those who wanted to follow him constantly (see Mark 10:17–22 par.; Luke 9:57–62). From among the radical demands that Jesus made on all who wanted to gain entry into the kingdom of God (see section 1 below, on the Sermon on the Mount), some stand out as only applicable

[54] See Rengstorf in *ThWB* vol. IV, 462f.; Eng. tr. see note 45.

to those who join in a full community of life with him. First among these is the command to renounce all personal possessions and follow him in poverty and abnegation. This is necessary for the preacher of the kingdom of God (Mark 6:7–9 par.). From the rich man "who had many possessions", Jesus explicitly demanded as a condition of discipleship that he should sell everything and give to the poor (Mark 10:21 par.). At Luke 14:33, this condition is formulated quite generally as a requisite in a disciple of Jesus, and from Mark 10:28 it is clear that the twelve followed Jesus on this condition. But Jesus did not address this demand to all who accepted him as God's legate: he called Matthew Levi away from the seat of custom, but not the chief publican, Zacchaeus. As regards the celibate life, Jesus said, "There are eunuchs who have made themselves eunuchs for the kingdom of heaven. He that can take, let him take it" (Matt. 19:12). Here too, the motive is unimpeded dedication to the kingdom of God, so Jesus is thinking here of those who were to preach. Probably the phrase belongs originally to a particular situation in which Jesus seeks to protect those who have renounced married life "for the sake of the kingdom of God"; they were scorned as "eunuchs", but Jesus defended their decision to be quite free for God and the apostolate.[55] He did not advocate celibacy as a precept binding on all. "All men take not this word, but they to whom it is given" (by God). It is on this individual vocation and grace from God that the difference between commandments and counsels is based.

It is rather different in regard to the demand for perfect obedience, which from ancient times has been counted among the three "evangelical counsels". The warning "whosoever shall be greater among you shall be your minister" (Mark 10:43 par.) is a universal law in the community of those who want to give

[55] Cf. J. Blinzler, "Εἰσὶν εὐνοῦχοι. Zur Auslegung von Mt 19:12" in ZNW 48 (1957) pp. 254–70; J. Dupont, Mariage et divorce dans l'Évangile, 1959, pp. 161–222.

expression to love as Jesus understood it (cf. also John 13:34f., with 13:14). But "perfect obedience", which the example of Jesus, the motive of self-renunciation (Mark 8;34) and other motives may have inspired, was an idea of the ancient Church, developed on this foundation, and worthy to be placed beside the other two counsels.

The distinction between commandment and counsel is, therefore, not formally recognizable as such in the gospels, but was only made clear later in the Church; but it has a biblical foundation.[56] It should not be misunderstood in the sense of a morality on two levels. In principle, every human being who repents and believes may receive a special call from God, as can be seen from the example of the rich young man (Mark 10:17–21 par.). This account must not be understood either as though Jesus offered two ways to a man honestly seeking and striving for the kingdom of God, an ordinary one of the ten commandments and an extraordinary one of renunciation of his earthly possessions. Jesus' intention regarding that rich man was a single one from the start. He wished to make of him his disciple, and so lead him to the kingdom of God. He left the man no choice, "One thing is lacking to thee. Go, sell whatever thou hast . . . and come, follow me!" He had recognized that for this rich man, his wealth was the great obstacle to his giving himself completely to God, and asked of him (quite in accord with Matthew 6:24), precisely what he was attached to by the secret fetters of his heart. Jesus did not demand of everyone the complete abandonment of possessions (cf. section 13). The case is typical to the extent that it shows how God can ask something special of a man.

On the other hand there are radical requirements incumbent on everyone who wants to enter the kingdom of God. To these belongs what is contained in the Sermon on the Mount, not in the sense that this is an exhaustive list, but rather as an illustration of the radical obedience that every hearer of Jesus' message owes

---

[56] Cf. *LThK* vol. III, 1245–50.

to the holy God who is now proferring his salvation. It would be wrong to restrict what is demanded in the Sermon on the Mount to a narrower circle of disciples, or to view it only as a "counsel" (cf. section 8). There is one and the same decision regarding acceptance of the message of salvation and adherence to Jesus, whatever particular form the actual concrete call to an individual may take. The commandment of love of God and the neighbour is simply a short formula summarizing God's summons, which involves the whole human being individually, interiorly and ineluctably. But the same pattern emerges in the matter of discipleship too. The duty of confessing Christ (Mark 8:38 par.) is assumed by everyone who follows Jesus. The struggle to belong to Jesus or not penetrates deep into families in the time of disturbance before the end (Luke 12:52ff. par.). Hatred, persecution and death all threaten (Mark 13:12f.), and all the "elect" must reckon with dangerous temptation in the great tribulation (Mark 13:19ff. par.).

If the idea of discipleship in the gospels is to be correctly understood, the coalescing of two planes, that of Jesus' historical life, and that of the preaching of the faith by the early Church after the Resurrection, must not be forgotten. What had once taken place in a unique way, the formation of the circle of disciples around Jesus "that they should be with him and that he might send them" (Mark 3:14), was continued in a new way in the early Church which lived in spiritual association with its Lord, in submission to his word which had once rung out and now remained valid. And in this, not a few special precepts addressed to the disciples were now taken as guiding requirements for all believers. The summons to follow Christ as a disciple now became a call to all the baptized; but nor was it forgotten that this call can work out for the individual Christian in different ways in its actual accomplishment. That is evident, for example, in the way Paul treats the question of marriage and virginity (1 Cor. 7). He limits his wish that all might live as he himself did, unmarried, by the remark "but everyone hath his proper

51

gift from God; one after this manner, and another after that" (1 Cor. 7:7). The gifts which are thus distributed are to be understood in general as an expression of God's varying call to service (1 Cor. 12:4–11; Rom. 12:3–8; Eph. 4:11–16). To follow Christ is demanded of all, but in different ways, according to individual vocation. In St. John's Gospel the call to follow Christ is equivalent in one passage to the summons to belief addressed to all: "He that followeth me walketh not in darkness but shall have the light of life" (8:12; cf. 12:35f.). This following, however, is still a repetition of Christ's path, by way of the Cross, into glory: "If any man minister to me, let him follow me; and where I am, there also shall my minister be" (John 12:26). And in this each person's own lot is also decided (cf. for Simon Peter, John 13:36ff.; 21:18f.; for the "disciple whom Jesus loved", John 21:20ff.).

But here too there is a change in the inner meaning of the word "follow". Following is to be understood here as more than a moral attitude, as an actual imitation.[57] This change is fully marked at 1 Peter 2:31 ff. By his sufferings, Christ has given us an example so that we too may follow in his footsteps. There is nothing strange about this development, for even in the relationship of Jesus' disciples to their master the idea of imitation was not wholly excluded. At least in one respect Jesus set himself as an example for them, in service and utter devotedness: "And whosoever shall be first among you shall be the servant of all. For the Son of man also is not come to be ministered unto; but to minister and to give his life a redemption for many" (Mark 10:44f. par.). This is expressed more clearly still in Luke, which locates in the upper room the dispute between the disciples over precedence (Luke 22:27); and with perfect clarity in St. John's gospel, which records the symbolic act of the washing of the feet. "For I have given you an example, that as I have done

[57] To allow this impulse to occupy a central place from the first (as does T. Süss, "Nachfolge Jesu") might give a wrong slant to one's investigations into the meaning of Christian discipleship.

to you, so you do also" (John 13:15).[58] The idea of the imitation of Christ can scarcely be denied by Paul (see 1 Thess. 1:6; 1 Cor. 11:1 and also Rom. 15:1ff.; Phil. 2:5ff.; although here there is question of more than an exemplar).[59] It is also operative at 1 John 2:6; 3:16 and 4:17; – and was to become still stronger in the Apostolic Fathers, especially Ignatius of Antioch.[60] The chief reason for this is to be found in the growth of the worship of Christ: people not only wanted to live in communion with the glorified Lord, but also wanted to make themselves like him in love and devotion, suffering and death. The idea of a complete community of death and life with Christ is clearly marked in Pauline theology. For Paul the life of faith is a life in, with and for Christ (cf. Gal. 2:19ff.; Rom. 14:17f.; Phil. 1:21ff.), a sharing in and imitation of his death and Resurrection (2 Cor. 4:11; 13:4; Phil. 3:10f.), a real and mystical following of his path.[61] Later Hellenistic (Platonic) ideas of becoming like God and Christ, also bore fruit.[62] In any case the valuable idea of following Jesus as his disciple did not die away after the Lord's departure. In later days it underwent many other changes and to some extent was weakened and lost its distinctive features. Reflection on its original meaning and content is particularly recommendable again today.[63]

[58] As against this, the cry of the Saviour at Matt. 11:29, "Learn of me, because I am meek and humble of heart", must probably not belong here.
[59] W. Michaelis tries to exclude moral imitation from μιμέομαι (in ThWB vol. IV, 670ff.), leaving only the impulse to obedience, to bow to the authority of the Lord (or of Paul).
[60] Cf. T. Preiss, "La mystique de l'imitation du Christ et de l'unité chez Ignace d'Antioche" in RHPR 18 (1938) pp. 197–242.
[61] Cf. A. Wikenhauser, Pauline Mysticism, 1960, pp. 146–62; R. Schnackenburg, Das Heilsgeschehen bei der Taufe nach dem Apostel Paulus, 1950; id., Nachfolge Christi, pp. 16f.
[62] Cf. on this M. Merki, Ὁμοίωσις Θεῷ. Von den Platonischen Angleichen an Gott zur Gottähnlichkeit bei Gregor von Nyssa, 1952.
[63] Reflections intended particularly for priests are given by K. H. Schelkle, Jüngerschaft und Apostelamt, 2nd. ed. 1961.

Chapter Two

JEWISH MORAL TEACHING AND JESUS'
MORAL DEMANDS.
THE SERMON ON THE MOUNT

"IF THOU wilt enter into life, keep the commandments" (Matt. 19:17). From this reply of Jesus to the rich young man (a reply admittedly expressed with less emphasis at Mark 10:19 and Luke 18:20 in the words, "Thou knowest the commandments"), it might be concluded that Jesus in the first place made exactly the same demands as the Jewish teachers of the law at that time. In fact he is deeply rooted in the moral teaching of his people; he too appealed to the will of God as enshrined in the "law". Yet there was something disturbing about Jesus' message. He taught like a man having full divine authority, and not like the Scribes (Mark 1:22 par.). In the name of God he made demands terrifying to men. How far, then, did he follow the Jewish moral doctrine of his own times, and in what respects did he go his own way? If one surveys the synoptic material as a whole, Jesus' attitude to the law of the Old Testament and to the accepted practices of his times, even granting our limited knowledge of those times, remains very puzzling to us, for Jesus' own statements take very diverse and apparently conflicting forms. According to the latest research, the current picture of Jesus engaging in one vehement polemic against the Jewish view of the law at that time is just as much in need of correction as the contrary opinion, originating particularly on the Jewish side, according to which Jesus was one teacher of the law among many and introduced almost nothing new and original. The question is one of more than merely historical significance, and can lead us to a deeper understanding of the religious and moral message of Jesus. The ethos of the Sermon on the Mount, with its sharply-drawn definitions and radical demands, is particularly exciting and disturbing (cf. Matt. ch. 5–7; Luke 6:20–49). Yet this important collection of sayings only condenses what can also be found in other utterances of our Lord.

Selected General Bibliography for the Sermon on the Mount

K. Bornhäuser, *Die Bergpredigt*, 1923.

P. Fiebig, *Jesu Bergpredigt, Rabbinische Texte zum Verständnis der Bergpredigt*, 1924.

G. Kittel, *Die Probleme des palästinischen Spätjudentums und das Urchristentum*, 1926, pp. 84–140.

A. Steinmann, *Die Bergpredigt*, 1926.

H. H. Huber, *Die Bergpredigt*, 1932.

B. Lanwer, *Die Grundgedanken der Bergpredigt auf dem Hintergrund des Alten Testaments und Spätjudentums*, 1934.

J. Schneider, *Der Sinn der Bergpredigt von der Grundordnung christlichen Lebens*, 1936.

F. Traub, "Das Problem der Bergpredigt" in *ZThK* 17 (1936) pp. 193 to 218.

R. Gyllenberg, "Religion und Ethik in der Bergpredigt" in *ZST* 13 (1936) pp. 628–705.

H. Windisch, *Der Sinn der Bergpredigt*, 2nd. ed. 1937.

S. Dimitroff, *Der Sinn der Forderungen Jesu in der Bergpredigt*, 1938.

H. Asmussen, *Die Bergpredigt*, 1939.

T. Soiron, *Die Bergpredigt*, 1941.

M. Dibelius, "Die Bergpredigt" (original English, 1940) in *Botschaft und Geschichte*, vol. I, 1953, pp. 79–174.

E. Percy, *Die Botschaft Jesu*, 1953, pp. 40–108, 123–64.

A. M. Hunter, *Design for Life. An Exposition of the Sermon on the Mount*, 1953.

J. Dupont, *Les Béatitudes*, 2nd ed. vol. I, 1958 (detailed bibliography on pp. 347–54).

W. D. Davies, *The Setting of the Sermon on the Mount*, 1964.

§ 5. JESUS' ATTITUDE TO THE JEWISH LAW

K. Benz, *Jesu Stellung zum alttestamentlichen Gesetz*, 1914; J. Hänel, *Der Schriftbegriff Jesu*, 1919; B. H. Branscomb, *Jesus and the Law of Moses*, 1930; W. G. Kümmel, "Jesus und der jüdische Traditionsgedanke" in *ZNW* 33 (1934) pp. 105–30; A. Oepke, *Jesus und das Alte Testament*, 1938; R. Liechtenhan, *Gottes Gebot im Neuen Testament*, 1942; W. Gutbrod, art. "νόμος" in *ThWB* vol. IV, 1051–57 (Eng. tr. *Biblical Keywords*, No. 11: "Law", 1962); H. J. Schoeps, "Jesus und das jüdische Gesetz" in *Aus frühchristlicher Zeit*, 1950, pp. 212–20; P. Althaus, *Gebot und Gesetz*, 1952; E. Schweizer, "Matthäus 5:17–20" in *TLZ* 77 (1952) pp. 479–84; J. Schmid, *Evangelium nach Matthäus*, pp. 89–94; V. E. Hasler, *Gesetz und Evangelium in der alten Kirche bis Origenes*, 1953; E. Percy, *Die Botschaft Jesu*, pp. 116–23; H. Ljungmann, *Das Gesetz erfüllen*, 1954; W. D. Davies, "Matthew 5:17–18" in *Mélanges bibliques A. Robert*, 1957, pp. 428–56; J. Dupont, *Les Béatitudes*, pp. 130–45; W. Trilling, *Das wahre Israel*, 1959, pp. 138–88; G. Barth, "Das Gesetzverständnis des Evangelisten Matthäus" in *Überlieferung und Auslegung im Matthäusevangelium*, 1960, pp. 54–154; P. G. Verweijs, *Evangelium und neues Gesetz in der ältesten Christenheit bis auf Marcion*, 1960.

THAT IT was not Jesus' purpose simply to set aside the Jewish law is clear from his personal behaviour quite apart from any disputed sayings of his. He shared in the richly developed religious life of his people, which was ruled by the law.

On the Sabbath we find him in the synagogue (Mark 1:21 par.; 6:2; cf. Luke 4:16; 13:10), and on the great pilgrimage festivals among the pilgrims in Jerusalem (Luke 2:41 ff.; John 2:13; 5:1; 7:14; 10:22; 12:12; Mark 11:1 ff. par.), and as a teacher in the synagogues and in the Temple (Mark 1:29 par.; 14:49 par.; John 6:59; 7:14; 8:20 etc.). He celebrated the paschal feast in the traditional way with his disciples (cf. Mark 14:12 ff. par.; Luke 22:15 f.), spoke without disapproval of the temple sacrifices (Matt. 5:23 f.) and of other pious practices (Matt. 6:1–18) in themselves valuable, and paid the temple half-shekel (Matt. 17:24 ff.). He wore the prescribed tassels on his cloak (Mark 6:56; Luke 8:44). And he sent the lepers he healed to show themselves to the priests in accordance with the law (for the cure to be verified) and so that they might take them the purification offering (Mark 1:44 par.; Luke 17:14).

Jesus, then, was really "subject to the law" (Gal. 4:44) and even submitted to its external, ceremonial precepts. Furthermore, among the things he said, there are statements which cannot be interpreted except as acknowledging in principle that the will of God is laid down in the Mosaic law.

"Do not think that I am come to destroy the law or the prophets. I am not come to destroy, but to fulfil" (Matt. 5:17). This much-discussed logion reveals the basic reason why Jesus held to the law. It is the chief constituent of the Old Testament revelation of God ("the law and the prophets"), the expression of the divine will.

There is some dispute over the meaning of the Greek word for "to fulfil" (πληρῶσαι) here. Does it mean "fill up", that is, "complete", or "perfect" (if so, how?) or "fulfil by performance", or "fulfil in accordance with the plan of redemption" (that is, fulfil the promises and types of the Old Testament).[1] It is true that πληροῦν can also signify fulfilment by performance (Cf. Matt. 3:15), but in Matthew it has predominantly the sense of bringing to fulfilment what has been previously announced (by Scripture), and the expression "the law or the prophets" refers here to Scripture too, even though the "law" takes precedence (notice the "or"). In contrast to the quotations which concern the fulfilment of prophetic predictions, what is meant here, therefore, are the requirements contained in Scripture which Jesus will likewise "fulfil", that is to say, bring to their full validity. How that will happen is, of course, not stated in this logion. It remains an open question whether Jesus wished to make God's original will fully clear, whether he

---

[1] On the possible meanings of πληροῦν see Bauer, *Wörterbuch*, 1330/33; H. Ljungman, *Das Gesetz erfüllen*, pp. 19–36; W. Trilling, *Das wahre Israel*, pp. 147 ff.; G. Delling in *ThWB* vol. VI, 289–96, esp. 292f.

intended to reduce the many commandments to the one fundamental precept of the love of God and the neighbour, which comprises and transcends all the others (as E. Schweizer holds), or whether he intended to insist on the true claim of the law to its ultimate pitch of obligation. Probably all these factors are to be understood simultaneously in the programmatic saying. The decisive point of view is that of the history of redemption which is indicated at the very beginning by the words "I am come", which express Jesus' consciousness of his mission.[2]

The two adjoining logia regarding the law (verses 18 and 19), scarcely belong to the same original context as verse 17, and also have a different emphasis to that verse,[3] but probably form a traditional unity themselves.[4] They bear witness to a view of the law which set a high value on surpassing the Torah, though hardly of course in the sense that its slightest prescriptions were to be maintained absolutely literally and carried into effect.[5]

---

[2] The same view is taken by V. E. Hasler, *Gesetz und Evangelium in der alten Kirche bis Origenes,* 1953, pp. 9 ff., though he distinguishes two levels in 5:17–20; but he recognizes precisely in verses 17 and 18c the point of view of redemptive history. J. Dupont, *Les Béatitudes,* pp. 140 f. regards verses 18 and 19 as a supplement due to the evangelist.

[3] Cf. the penetrating investigation of W. Trilling, *Das wahre Israel,* 1959, pp. 138–59.

[4] Cf. H. Schürmann, "Wer daher eines dieser geringsten Gebote auflöst..." in *BZ* 4 (1960) pp. 238–50.

[5] Modern criticism, taking as its basis a literal interpretation, frequently postulates a Jewish Christian tendency of the evangelist who in his own time wished to re-establish the old Jewish law more strongly, and it then expounds verses 18 and 19 as a secondary and tendentious formulation; cf. among others Klostermann's commentary on this passage; Bultmann, *Die Geschichte der synoptischen Tradition,* 2nd ed. 1931, p. 147, Eng. tr. *The History of the Synoptic Tradition,* Oxford 1963; Kümmel, "Jesus und der jüdische Traditionsgedanke", pp. 127 f.; Percy, *Die Botschaft Jesu,* pp. 120 f. — That, however, is open to doubt merely on the ground of the history of tradition, for Luke also transmits verse 18, and in fact in a shorter and clearer form and in a context which points to the source

These two verses were intended rather to express that the whole law (or the will of God which it embodies), was to be taught and practised in a new and perfect way. Then a connection can be seen extending between verse 17 and verse 20, which introduces the section of the antitheses (verses 21–48), which is intended to illustrate that conception of the law. At all events Matthew seems, in 5:17–20 (despite the separation of the individual logia) to have intended such a unity of meaning. But even when the logia are viewed in themselves, the point of view of redemptive history is the dominant one. Jesus knows himself to be sent by God to expound the Old Testament law, in which God's will is inalienably contained, in its true sense, its ever valid claims and the obligation it imposes to act upon it, and in this way to "fulfil" it.

In this way a perspective opens out which is important for the whole problem of Jesus and the Old Testament law. The antithesis "destroy-fulfil" requires the comprehensive meaning "give power and effect to". The Scribes saw the divine will as embodied not only in the law of Sinai, but also, and equally in the "tradition of the ancients" which they interpreted as equally binding.[6] But Jesus was aware of having been sent to reveal the will of God in its original sense and clarify it on doubtful points with divine authority, and where necessary to state and promulgate it afresh and definitively. This task belonged to him together with that of preaching the reign of God. He had to tell people the conditions on which they could enter the kingdom, and enjoin these on them (cf. Matt. 5:20). His person was on the one hand a boundary and a turning-point for the Old Testament (cf. Luke 16:16), and on the other its fulfilment (Luke 10:23f. par.). For him the Old Testament law was from one point of view not an absolute rule, for he

---

common to Matthew and Luke (Luke 16:17). Cf. for further details Schürmann's article referred to in the preceding note.

[6] Cf. Kümmel, "Jesus und der jüdische Traditionsgedanke", pp. 107–18.

had divine authority on his own account to make decisions, whilst from another point of view it was still binding because it enshrined the will of God and awaited interpretation of its true and original sense. "While he proclaimed the absolute will of God, Jesus did not speak as a law-giver, but as God's envoy of the last hour."[7]

We must now examine briefly a few occasions on which Jesus came into conflict with Jewish teachers of the law and which may throw clearer light on his attitude to the law. In discussing the question of the Sabbath, he argued for the dignity of man and for God's original intention against a captious interpretation of the commandment to rest, "The sabbath was made for man, and not man for the sabbath" (Mark 2:27). Though a similar Jewish view existed long before, it was only applied in order to save a human life.[8] For Jesus, however, doing good was a sufficient excuse, especially saving someone from a dangerous illness (Mark 3:4 par.). In controversy with the rabbis Jesus sometimes used their own weapons (cf. Luke 14:1ff.); but he is not accountable to his opponents for the ultimate grounds of his actions. "The Son of man is the Lord of the sabbath also" (Mark 2:28 par.).

It has often been claimed that in this saying "Son of man" means no more than "man" and that the verse therefore only draws a conclusion from Mark 2:27. It would, however, be difficult to believe that Jesus granted everyone the right to dispose freely for himself of an institution which he too recognized as God-given. Verse 27 may imply no more than Mark 3:4 or Matthew 12:12. It is also noteworthy that v. 27 is not to be found in either Matthew or Luke, although they have v. 28. The first three sections of this collection of controversies in Galilee all reach their climax in sayings regarding Jesus' majesty

---

[7] Dibelius, "Die Bergpredigt" in *Botschaft und Geschichte,* vol. I, 1953, p. 130.
[8] Cf. Billerbeck, vol. I, p. 623; vol. II, p. 5.

and mission (cf. Mark 2:10, 17, 19). Would it not therefore seem likely that 2:28 should contain some statement about Jesus' person and dignity? There would therefore seem to be no essential connection between vv. 27 and 28. The conclusion drawn by verse 28 (*Therefore* the Son of man is Lord of the Sabbath also) is the last word on the Sabbath controversy, spoken perhaps by Jesus, perhaps by the early Church. It may be something Jesus once said, in the circle of the disciples, perhaps, as the title Son of man suggests, and which the early Church found useful as a key to the understanding of his actions, so that in Matthew and Luke it crowded out the other logion on this controversy (v. 27). There can, in any case, be no doubt that on his own authority Jesus used great freedom in interpreting the Sabbath prescriptions.[9] This feature cannot be effaced from the picture of the Jesus of history; it is also an index of his difference from the Essenes who in the observance of the Sabbath in some respects went even beyond the prescriptions of the Pharisees.[10]

The controversy over the regulations about ritual cleanliness (Mark 7:1–23; Matt. 15:1–20) gives us a further insight into Jesus' attitude to the law. Jesus defended the disciples when they had neglected to perform the ritual hand-washing, and attacked the "traditions of the ancients" which were regarded as an indispensable extension of the Mosaic law, and indeed as part of the law of Moses from Sinai itself.[11] He retorted to his opponents "For leaving the commandment of God, you hold the tradition

---

[9] Cf. E. Lohse, "Jesu Worte über den Sabbat" in *Judentum, Urchristentum, Kirche* (Festschrift for J. Jeremias), 1960, pp. 79–87.

[10] Cf. *Damascus Rule* X, 14 — XI, 18. Precept XI, 14 is significant: "If a (new-born) beast falls into a cistern or pit, he may not lift it out on the Sabbath." Cf. as opposed to this, Luke 14:5; Matt. 12:11. On the rabbis' discussion of a case of this kind, cf. Billerbeck, vol. I, pp. 629f.

[11] Cf. R. Akiba's words (d. about A.D. 135), "As the whole Torah is the law to Moses from Sinai, so too the least precept is a law to Moses from Sinai" (*Nidda* 45a Bar., quoted by Kümmel, *Jesus*, p. 113).

of men" (Mark 7:8). This description of tradition as a merely human institution, undermined the whole Jewish theory of the law. But Jesus demonstrated the justice of his attack with a concrete example (7:9–13): they neglected the duty of supporting parents, that is, the fourth commandment of the decalogue, because, caught in the net of their own exposition, they permitted corban oaths, even to the detriment of their parents' rights.

The so-called corban oath or vow ("May the usufruct you could have of my property be a gift to God") deprived parents of the usufruct of the property of their son without his being bound afterwards to pay it into the Temple. It has been proved that such things did happen.[12] The rabbis later tried to put an end to the worst evils resulting from these vows.

The second part of this passage (7:14–23), which is built up from several parts, is concerned directly with the clean and the unclean. In his treatment of this question Jesus again deviated considerably from current Jewish views. "There is nothing from without a man that entering into him can defile him; but the things which come from a man, those are things that defile a man" (7:15). He afterwards explained to the disciples that he was thinking here of the evil desires and actions arising from the heart (vv. 18–23). He can scarcely, of course, have been dissecting the law of God into moral and ritual precepts by that, nevertheless he was bringing it back to its central purpose and that meant in fact eliminating everything merely external. And by doing that was he not, in fact, touching upon the very substance of the Torah of the Old Testament? At any rate, he did dethrone the Jewish view that every precept, great or small, whether it concerned the heart or external matters, was equally binding on obedience, because it was "a prescription of the King of all kings".[13] Without further argument or justification,

---

[12] Cf. Billerbeck, vol. I, pp. 71 ff.
[13] Cf. the words of R. Johanan b. Zakkai (d. about A.D. 80) quoted in Billerbeck, vol. I, p. 719, n. 2.

he lays the foundations of a new morality, in fact, re-lays anew the foundations of ethics as such, by making the moral value of an act depend only on inner disposition of heart.

So both as regards form and content Jesus set up discriminating criteria in face of the Jewish "law" viewed as a unitary whole. Just as he repudiated the "tradition of the ancients" in Mark 7, so too he once even played off an earlier text of the Torah against a later (in his judgement on the indissolubility of marriage, Mark 10:1-9 par.), a proceeding unusual, or unheard of among the rabbis. There are other indications too that Jesus placed moral precepts above liturgical and ritual ones. He gave high praise to the Scribe who assented to the principal commandment of love, and who himself observed that it was more important than all "the holocausts and sacrifices" (Mark 12:33f.). Matthew 23:23ff. leads to a similar conclusion, although the qualification made here ("these things you ought to have done, and not to leave those undone") also testifies to a conception of the law which intends to hold fast to all the particular precepts and is only insisting on the importance of the moral commandments and emphasizing the pre-eminence of inner disposition over external legality (verses 25-28). If this latter conception fully corresponds to Jesus' mind, the qualification mentioned may be taking into account the practice of Jewish Christians who remained faithful to the customs of Jewish life. That was not illegitimate, for Jesus was no revolutionary in this matter, either; he was solely concerned with genuine morality on a religious foundation, whatever the form of life.

Although, like the Scribes, Jesus often in controversy appealed to the Scriptures (though in his own individual way) as can be seen in Mark 10 and 12, he did not do so always and as a matter of principle, any more than he justified his actions by reference to them (cf. Mark 11:27-33 par.). His attitude on this was certainly a very great scandal to the Scribes for whom the divine will was enshrined in the law and could be learned only from it. Jesus did in fact claim to teach the will of God authoritatively and not by deduction from the Torah. This is shown most clearly in the antitheses in the Sermon on the Mount (Matt. 5:21–48). For the time being, we can leave on one side the question how far he was saying anything intrinsically new here (see below, section 7). All that is necessary now is to notice the form, style and manner in which he proclaimed the divine will. In spite of their outward form, these six antitheses, with their characteristic, "You have heard that it was said to them of old . . . . But I say to you . . .", are not a unity. In the third antithesis (on adultery), the introduction is different (Matt. 5:31). In the Lucan Sermon on the Mount (Luke 6:20–49), there are real parallels only to the last two Matthean antitheses (on retaliation and love of one's enemies) – though at Luke 16:18 there is also a parallel to the third. In none of these cases, however, does Luke use the antithetical form. Hence many scholars would like to regard as original only the three that are identical in form and which in content are proper to Matthew (those on anger, adultery and swearing); others, only the first two; and still others, all except the third, which is different in form. However that may be, it cannot be doubted that Jesus commonly spoke in this antithetical way.

Even if the formula "But I say to you" was no more than a rabbinic flourish common in disputation[14], it is still quite clear from the antitheses of the Sermon on the Mount, that Jesus was not putting forward his own opinion against the views of others (and having to prove it from the law) as a Scribe would have done, but was authoritatively opposing to the whole of the earlier tradition as it had been taught to previous generations (even including and above all the generation that had lived in the desert), a wholly new understanding of

[14] Cf. M. Smith, *Tannaitic Parallels to the Gospels,* 1951, pp. 27 ff. Kümmel "Jesus und der jüdische Traditionsgedanke" n. 77, had already rejected the view that Jesus was using a special, rabbinic Midrash formula.

God's will, and a radically incisive one, a new teaching with authority (Mark 1:27). The regal style of his judgements, which were dependent neither on the tradition itself nor its principles of interpretation, can be explained only by his Messianic consciousness and mission.

Accordingly, if Jesus' attitude to the Jewish law, which is frequently difficult to understand where individual questions are concerned, and which is uncertain through both the form and the content of particular utterances, is at all susceptible of explanation on a consistent basis, this can only be his claim purely and absolutely to announce God's will. This will he can only recognize in the Jewish conception of the law in a fragmentary way, partly true, partly distorted and diminished by men.

§ 6. The Overcoming of the Legalism of Works and of any Disposition that is not Morally Genuine

J. Jeremias, *Jerusalem zur Zeit Jesu,* 2nd ed. 1958; I. Abrahams, *Studies in Pharisaism and the Gospels,* 2 vols., 1917–24; G. Dalman, *Jesus – Jeschua,* 1922, pp. 62ff.; Billerbeck, vol. IV, pp. 334–52; D. W. Riddle, *Jesus and the Pharisees,* 1928; L. Baeck, *Die Pharisäer,* 1934; G. Schrenk, "Rabbinische Charakterköpfe im urchristlichen Zeitalter" in *Studien zu Paulus,* 1954, pp. 9–45; W. Beilner, *Christus und die Pharisäer,* 1959 (Bibliog.).
G. Schrenk, art. "δικαιοσύνη" in *ThWB* vol. II, 200f. (Eng. tr. *Biblical Keywords* No. 4: "Righteousness", 1951): A. Descamps, *Les Justes et la Justice dans les évangiles et le christianisme primitif hormis la doctrine proprement paulinienne,* 1950; E. Haenchen, "Matthäus 23" in *ZThK* 48 (1951) pp. 38–63; H. H. Schrey and H. N. Walz, *Gerechtigkeit in biblischer Sicht,* 1955; R. Mach, *Der Zaddik in Talmud und Midrasch,* 1957.

In the Sermon on the Mount there is a saying which may be used as a further key to the interpretation of this compendium of Jesus' moral teaching, or at least of Matthew's version of it: "Unless your justice abound more than that of the Scribes and Pharisees, you shall not enter into the kingdom of heaven"

(5:20). It is clear from this that it was not Jesus' intention to start a merely theoretical controversy about the validity and interpretation of the Jewish law, but that what was at stake for him was the fulfilment of the divine will, which, of course, for the Jews principally consisted in the observance of the law, the keeping of the commandments. The goal is "justice", the right disposition towards God, the epitome of good religious and moral behaviour in the sight of God; not merely as in our narrower modern usage, the attitude and virtue grounded in the will to give everyone his due.

Justice in this sense is a leading Old Testament concept, only to be understood by the linking of morality and religion: Man is wholly under the judgement of God. Jesus took over this concept, although the abstract noun is only to be found on his lips in Matthew where it occurs seven times. But he did speak constantly of "the just", and never in such a way as to suggest that he rejected this designation.[15] He denounced only one kind and manifestation of "justice", namely self-righteousness and sham (see especially Luke 18:10–14; Matt. 23:28). He did not deny the justice of those the Old Testament calls just (Matt. 13:17; 23:35) and he sometimes called the citizens of the kingdom of God "the just" (Matt. 25:37; 25:46; Luke 14:14; cf. Matt. 13:43). On his lips it was, however, no longer a leading concept, although for Matthew the expression "justice" was valuable as a summing-up of the complete religious and moral attitude, and useful in view of his Jewish Christian readers.

For pious Jews the decisive question was: How can one attain "justification" in the sight of God? The rabbinic answer was, by accumulating so many merits by fulfilling the commandments and doing "good works" (almsgiving, fasting, acts of philanthropy, study of the law), that they outweigh one's sins in the sight of God; so that one can endure the judgement

---

[15] Cf. Schrenk in *ThWB* vol. II, 190–2 (Eng. tr. *Biblical Keywords,* No. 4: "Righteousness", 1951); Descamps, *Les justes,* pp. 31 ff.; 207 ff.

of God.[16] In practice this led, particularly among the Pharisees, who were zealous for the law, to those traits which so profoundly angered Jesus, and occasioned his most severe criticisms.

The groups he attacked, the Pharisees and the Scribes, were not identical. The Pharisees were a religious party, or rather, according to their own definition, a "brotherhood". Any Jew could join them as long as he was ready to accept their teaching and way of life, the most marked characteristic of which was strict observance of the law according to the traditions of the ancients and the exegesis of Pharisee scholars. Because the centre of the Pharisee's life was the Torah, the number of rabbis from this party was naturally large, although there were also Sadducees among the teachers of the law, who formed a group in the Sanhedrin. The teachers of the law, the Scribes, were more a professional body, for their duties were not restricted to teaching, they also performed juridical functions. They were held in high esteem and their influence in the Sanhedrin was continually increasing.

In requiring from those who wanted to enter the kingdom of heaven a justice greater than that of the Pharisees and Scribes, Jesus had in mind the way in which these models of Jewish piety strove, often, no doubt, with noble aspirations and ardent endeavour (see Paul: Gal. 1:14; Phil. 3:6), to obtain God's approbation. But "pharisaism" was inherent in their views, there is no other possible explanation of the widening gulf between Jesus and his religious opponents and of the fact that Jesus' mission resulted in a new doctrine, although Jesus started from what lay before his eyes, before his gaze which pierced to the heart.

To the Pharisees the most important thing was literal fulfilment of the law. But if this is not accompanied by a deeply religious frame of mind, that is, motives of love and obedience

---

[16] Cf. Billerbeck, vol. I, p. 251; J. Schmid, *Evangelium nach Matthäus*, p. 289; W. Pesch, *Der Lohngedanke in der Lehre Jesu*, 1955, pp. 100ff.

towards God, it must result in legalism, the purely outward observance of the law. With the Pharisees this danger was all the greater because they were striving to acquire as many merits as possible. They prided themselves on it and considered themselves just. This led them to feel contempt for others, for those who "know not the law" (*Am ha-Aretz,* the "people of the land", John 7:49; Luke 18:9) and the result was the caricature Jesus drew with such startling clarity in the parable of the Pharisee and the publican. In this Pharisee there is no longer any sign of humility and readiness to repent in the presence of God, nor yet of that hunger and thirst after justice that comes from God (Matt. 5:6), nor yet again of genuine devotion to God; but, in their place, worship of self disguised as religion.

It would be unjust to Jewish moral teaching to reproach it with having completely neglected interior dispositions. Outward observance of the law was supposed to be accompanied by fear of God in the soul.[17] There was argument whether fear or love of God should be the chief motive.[18] Sayings have come down to us containing a very high doctrine of moral motivation. Thus Antigonus of Sokho, one of the earliest exponents of the tradition of the law (probably three hundred years before Christ) said "Be not like those servants who serve their Lord thinking to receive a reward; but be like those servants who serve their Lord without thinking of any reward: and then the fear of heaven will be upon you."[19] But in later Judaism the thought of merit became increasingly dominant. Many sayings warn against selfish abuse of the law: one should do good for the sake

[17] Cf. Moore, *Judaism,* vol. II, pp. 97 ff.; E. Sjöberg, *Gott und die Sünder im palästinischen Judentum,* 1938, p. 23, n. 2. Even Billerbeck's judgement (that there was literal fulfilment of the law, pure legalism – vol. IV, pp. 13 ff.) is too rigid and one-sided here.

[18] Cf. Moore, *Judaism,* vol. II, pp. 99 f., 194; R. Sander, *Liebe und Furcht im palästinischen Judentum,* 1935; Bonsirven, *Judaïsme,* vol. II, pp. 43 ff.

[19] *Mishnah Aboth,* I, 3.

of God.[20] But was that still possible when one was seeking to justify oneself and extolling one's own merits before God? Just as the breaking itself of a precept of the law was threatened with punishment, so too its very fulfilment was promised reward.[21] In how many cases, then, must the right intention required by the high-minded teachers have been lacking!

Jesus demanded interior disposition as the decisive factor in moral action. He made the heart the centre of the moral personality. Only what comes from the heart defiles (Mark 7:18 par.; see below section 5). He borrowed the words of the prophet Isaias (29:13) "This people honoureth me with their lips, but their heart is far from me" (Mark 7:6 par.). He called those who are pure of heart (that is, single-minded and simple) "blessed" (Matt. 5:8). Our hearts are not to be fixed on earthly treasures, but wholly concerned with God in heaven (cf. Matt. 6:21 par.). The good man brings good things out of the treasury of his heart; the evil man brings wicked things out of the evil store of his heart, "for out of the abundance of the heart the mouth speaketh" (cf. Luke 6:45 and also Matt. 12:34f.). By a lustful look at another's wife a man has already committed adultery with her "in his heart" (Matt. 5:28).

There are also many other sayings which designate the heart as the source of good or evil thoughts. For the Semites, the heart was the seat of thoughts, desires and emotions, and also

[20] Or, as the rabbis said, "for the sake of heaven" (for example *Aboth* II, 2; IV, 11). Cf. the beautiful dictum, *Siphre Deut.* II, 13, 41: " 'To love the Lord your God': perhaps you will say: Look, I am learning the Torah, so that I may become rich, or so that I may be called rabbi, or so that I may be rewarded. But we read, 'To love the Lord your God'; everything you do, do only from love." (See Moore, *Judaism*, vol. II, p. 100.)

[21] Even M. Smith *(op. cit.)*, who strongly attacks Billerbeck's account of Jewish teaching on merit (p. 49ff.), says on the reasons for God's rewarding man, that above all there are very many texts in which someone who fulfils a commandment is promised a reward simply because he has fulfilled it (cf. p. 69).

of the moral judgement, taking over the functions we ascribe to the conscience, for which there is no specific word in the gospels. The sayings about the "light within you" (a metaphor very difficult to interpret) often quoted in this connection, certainly do not refer to conscience.[22]

In spite of the emphasis Jesus put on inner dispositions, he did not despise external action; but rather he demanded that action should be the fruit of disposition (cf. Luke 6:43ff. par.). The beautiful final parable of the Sermon on the Mount, the house built on a rock (Matt. 7:24–27 par.), is a call to men not only to listen to Jesus' words but to put them into action. There is no piety without moral authentication through action. "Not everyone that saith to me, Lord, Lord, shall enter the kingdom of heaven; but he that doth the will of my Father who is in heaven, he shall enter into the kingdom of heaven" (7:21, cf. also v. 22: a saying of Jesus relating to the judgement, and hence independent of v. 21). The parable of the two sons (Matt. 21:28–32) is especially instructive: when Jesus told it he may well have had in mind the Scribes and Pharisees who said yes, but neglected to do what was asked (that is, believe and repent), and the publicans and prostitutes who said no, that is, sinned, but afterwards repented and were converted.[23]

Further development of Jesus' reproaches to the Scribes and Pharisees is found in the "woes" uttered against the Jewish leaders, editorially linked by St. Matthew (Matt. 23:1–36; cf. the

---

[22] According to C. Edlund, *Das Auge der Einfalt* (*Acta Sem. Nt. Upsal.*, 19) (1952), a very thorough monograph, the image is intended to refer to an inwardly upright and unequivocal attitude of man. E. Sjöberg, *Das Licht in dir,* art. in *ST* 5 (dated 1951: published 1952), pp. 89–105, explains the metaphor differently, maintaining it refers not to the organ of light, but the receiving of light, and being filled with it; the point of the logion is then the danger of merely apparent communion with God.

[23] Cf. Jeremias, *Parables,* pp. 80f., 125; see further J. Schmid, "Das textgeschichtliche Problem der Parabel von den zwei Söhnen" in *Vom Worte des Lebens* (Festschrift for M. Meinertz) 1952, pp. 68–84.

various parallels in Mark and Luke) into a vehement indictment.

Verse 3 has given rise to critical discussion. "All things, therefore, whatsoever they shall say to you, observe and do; but according to their works do ye not. For they say, and do not." For, of course, Jesus did not entirely share their view of the law and consequently not their teaching either. The point here, within the pattern of these "woes" is rather to denounce the reprehensible practice of the Pharisees; if their teaching is declared binding, it may be that the later practice of Jewish Christians is being taken into account.

What strikes us first in Jesus' pitiless criticism is that he was attacking the hair-splitting methods of exegesis adopted by the rabbis, exemplified here by their ingeniously reasoned distinctions on the forms of oaths (vv. 16–22) and their instructions about the cleansing of vessels (v. 25). Such pettiness, possibly the result of respect for the letter of the law and regard for the least of God's precepts, might even have been tolerable if it had not led to "straining at a gnat" and "swallowing a camel". But they did, in fact, neglect the weightier things of the law, justice, mercy and good faith, fundamental moral attitudes (v. 23). And whilst they cleansed the outside with excessive care, the inside was full of "rapine and uncleanness" (v. 25), and so their actions become symbolic of themselves.

But even this does not completely account for Jesus' wrath. What really angered him in their attitude was its mendacity and hypocrisy. "They bind heavy and insupportable burdens and lay them on men's shoulders; but with a finger of their own they will not move them" (v. 4). "So you also outwardly indeed appear to men just; but inwardly you are full of hypocrisy and iniquity" (v. 28).

In his study of this section, Haenchen maintains that this attack on hypocrisy may be the wording given by Matthew to the whole "woe" discourse so as to make it attack only false exposition and application of the law, not the law itself. He maintains that Jesus attacked the law in a much more radical way, but Matthew did not realize that, and made of it only a new Christian way of understanding the law. But is not Haenchen attributing to Jesus an attitude to the law which is scarcely in accord with an objective estimation of all the texts?

Although the formula "hypocrites" in this discourse (Matt. 23:15, 23, 25, 27, 29) may be stylization by the evangelist, the attack on hypocrisy itself certainly goes back to Jesus, for it occurs in Mark 7:6; Luke 6:42 par.; 12:56 and 13:15.[24] It was false piety and vanity before men that chiefly led to Jesus' tearing the mask from the hypocrites' faces. In the Sermon on the Mount he picked out three especially esteemed works of piety in order vividly to illustrate his warning for his hearers. "Take heed that you do not your justice before men, to be seen by them": these three works were almsgiving, prayer and fasting (Matt. 6:1–18). His striking description of the hypocrites has impressed itself on people of every period: they have trumpets blown before them when they distribute gifts; they stand ostentatiously at busy street-corners to pray; they pull long faces to show that they are fasting. Jesus nowhere repudiates the pious practices themselves, what he was concerned with was rather the need for a genuinely religious and moral attitude towards God. It is incorrect to raise straightaway here the question of the reward motive (see below section 16). All that was important to Jesus was that by doing good and praying, people should once again find the way to God which those hypocrites had lost. The "hypocrisy" which, in Matthew 6 might be interpreted as subjective dissimulation and sanctimoniousness, receives in other passages, however, a different and more objective meaning. When Jesus in Luke 12:56 reproves his

[24] Thus the explanation of the "leaven" of the Pharisees (and Herodians, Mark; and Sadducees, Matthew) as their hypocrisy in Luke 12:1 may be secondary, as the linking of the "leaven" of the Pharisees and the "leaven" of the Herodians at Mark 8:15 shows. The original sense of the logion remains obscure.

hearers as hypocrites because they know how to read the signs of the weather in the sky and on the earth, but not to discern the signs of the hour in the history of redemption, he is reproaching them with blindness and unbelief. By the pejorative term "hypocrite", Jesus ultimately means a transgression of the divine will, deriving from the guilty rejection of his person, and a plain contradiction between outer legality and genuine morality (Matt. 23; Luke 13:15), alienation from God, despite all their religious practices (Mark 7:6).[25] The Hebrew and Aramaic concept (haleph, halepha), which lies at the basis of our "hypocrite" is more comprehensive and can also mean "godless", "impious". This also explains the mistaken translation in Matthew 24:51 ("and appoint his portion with the hypocrites"); in Luke 12:46 this reads more correctly "with unbelievers".[26] Ultimately all these warnings have a common denominator: the service of God with an undivided heart (Matt. 6:24 par.), guileless and upright, or the love of God with all one's heart and soul (Mark 12:30 par.). Seen from this point of view, Jesus' attitude to the law and his struggle with men spring from a single intention, and his theory and his practice can both be measured by a single criterion: that God's holy will be done, and that it be done for love of him, out of a purer disposition of heart.

§ 7. Jesus' Radicalism: God's Will in its Original Totality as the Strictly Binding Standard

Apart from previously mentioned works, see R. Bultmann, *Jesus*, 1951, pp. 52–113, G. Bornkamm, *Jesus von Nazareth*, 1956, pp. 88–100, Eng. tr. *Jesus of Nazareth*, 1960.

[25] Cf. W. Beilner, art. "Heuchler" in *Bibeltheologisches Wörterbuch*, 1959, 410–13; *id., Christus und die Pharisäer*, pp. 227–32.
[26] Cf. Jeremias, *Parables*, p. 57, note 31.

IT WAS Jesus' desire to free mankind from the intolerable burden of the many commandments and precepts that formed the "hedge" around the Jewish law (Matt. 23:4). He called to himself all those who laboured and were heavily burdened and promised them rest, because his yoke was easy and his burden light (Matt. 11:28–30). In this call of comfort for the heavy-laden Jesus was clearly contrasting his "yoke" with that of the "yoke of the law", a familiar rabbinic expression. Even though the Jews were proud to bend to the divine yoke, nevertheless Jesus made himself the advocate of those to whom the law was a heavy burden. The whole passage seems to have been influenced by the Wisdom literature where in a similar way, personified Wisdom promises her disciples "rest" (cf. Ecclus. 6:24–8; 51:23–7); but the admonition in Jeremias 6:16 to walk in the path of salvation in order to find "refreshment for your souls", can also have exercised influence.[27] In the concrete, Jesus is calling men to follow him, which leads to "rest", that is to say, to eternal life. In the newly-found *Gospel of Thomas* (saying 90), the logion is shorter and in a different order, "Come to me for my yoke is light and my rule gentle and you will find rest for yourselves". The "rest" here is probably the eschatological reward; but on account of it even the present "yoke" is already tolerable (cf. Mark 10:28 ff. par.; Luke 22:28 ff.)

Nevertheless, it was not Jesus' intention to turn men loose in lawlessness and licence. On the contrary he demanded more of them, absolute and unlimited obedience to the holy will of

---

[27] On the "yoke of the law" cf. K. H. Rengstorf in *ThWB* vol. II, 202f.; on the "Call of the Saviour", see esp. T. Arvedson, *Das Mysterium Christi*, 1937, pp. 158–228; A. Feuillet, "Jésus et la sagesse d'après les évangiles synoptiques" in *RB* 62 (1955) pp. 161–96; G. Lambert, "Mon joug est aisé et mon fardeau léger" in *NRT* 87 (1955) pp. 963–69; H. Mertens, *L'hymne de jubilation chez les Synoptiques*, 1957; J. B. Bauer, "Das milde Joch und die Ruhe, Matth. 11:28–30" in *TZ* 17 (1961) pp. 99–106.

God: "Seek ye therefore first the kingdom of God and his justice" (Matt. 3:33). That is the law of action for all those who want to enter the kingdom of God. Everything else that does not serve this highest of ends, must recede and be suppressed if it becomes a hindrance. "And if thy hand scandalize thee (that is, is a stumbling-block), cut it off; it is better for thee to enter into life, maimed, than having two hands to go into unquenchable fire . . ." (Mark 9:43–47 par.). Matthew also records this saying, though in a shorter form and different setting, within the framework of the Sermon on the Mount, to show with what determination we must fight against sexual lust (5:29f.).

This saying alone is sufficient to show how radical moral obligation has become in the teaching of Jesus. But in content all the antitheses of the Sermon on the Mount have the same point. In relation to the Jewish law there are degrees of contrast; it is possible to differentiate between two classes of antitheses. In one, the requirement of the law is accepted and the antithesis intensifies it: in this group, for example, belong the sayings about murder and anger (Matt. 5:21–26), and about adultery (5:27–30). In the second group, "the law is negatived on account of its mitigation through concessions to human weakness, and in the antithesis the divine command is set out",[28] – as in the saying about oaths (Matt. 5:33–37), but more clearly and significantly in regard to divorce (5:31–32), and especially boldly in the sayings on revenge (5:38–42) and loving one's enemies (5:43–48). Basically, however, all the antitheses are not perfectly similar in their inner structure. "The impression" of a self-contained block of essentially the same structure is deceptive. It is clearly a question of a loose collection of examples,

---

[28] Thus E. Dinkler in an essay "Zum Problem der Ethik bei Paulus" in *ZThK* 49 (1952) p. 178. On the commandment against swearing see H. Müller, *Zum Eidesverbot der Bergpredigt,* 1913; J. Schneider in *ThWB* vol. V, 178–81; W. Trilling, *Das wahre Israel,* pp. 183f.

the common basis of which seems to be of a relatively general nature."[29]

A great deal of trouble has been taken to investigate Jewish ethical teaching to see whether Jesus' attacks on strict retaliation, for instance, were justified and also to test the novelty of Jesus' "new" commandments. The result has been not unfavourable to Judaism. It is possible to find in the utterances of the rabbis parallels to all these moral commandments formulated so provocatively by Jesus, some of them saying more or less the same thing and in many points attaining the same heights of morality, others at least coming close to them.[30] To acknowledge this is no more than just. But such comparisons miss the point. It was part of the tradition of the Jewish schools to collect the most diverse utterances of the rabbis so that alongside opinions of the highest merit we can find others confirming how right Jesus was to be scandalized. Then too we must recognize that the New Testament itself is a source of information about the current, customary conceptions dominant in the popular mind at that time. Finally and above all, Jesus' concern was with a unified religious and moral message whose novelty resulted from the significance of the moment reached in the history of salvation.

In spite of their differing degrees of severity, the antitheses taken together do form a unity. "In all these sentences one decisive demand shines out. The good that it is a question of doing must be done totally. Anyone who does it a little laxly, with reservations, just so that at a pinch the outward precept is fulfilled, has not really done it at all."[31]

To enable men clearly to recognize this demand from God, a demand that pierces to the very marrow of the soul, Jesus

[29] W. Trilling, *ibid.* p. 184.
[30] Cf. esp. G. Kittel, *Die Probleme*, pp. 96 ff.; the material on the Sermon on the Mount in Billerbeck, vol. I; and also Percy, *Botschaft Jesu*, pp. 123–64, though he makes certain fundamental reservations.
[31] Bultmann, *Jesus*, p. 79.

made use of a deliberately exaggerated form of speech, hyperbole. The saying about being scandalized, with the obviously unreasonable requirement of cutting off limbs of the body, is a particularly clear example. But Jesus' condemnation of anger and abuse must also be interpreted in the same way. The reason why the three statements hand over the guilty to the lower court, to the Sanhedrin and to eternal judgement, is due to a progression which, however, does not so much concern the punishment to be expected but is intended vividly to depict the aggravation of the guilt in Jesus' eyes. "Jesus mentions judicial institutions here in order to express in a tangible way his purely religious idea" (J. Schmid in loc.). According to recent research,[32] however, it would also be possible that the judgement first mentioned refers to the judgement of God (in hell, cf. Matthew 23:33), the symbolism of the Sanhedrin in that case would signify the council of the community (as in Qumran) which likewise hands over the sinner to the punishment of God, and the third saying finally names the place of eschatological punishment. If that were so, the triple expression would not present a progression but only a variation on the one theme, with the same fundamental idea that it is not the external deed and liability to punishment in the juridical sense which makes a man guilty, but his moral state of mind and the sin against his brother, which God will most strictly requite.

One must not, however, make use of this popular style of teaching, a favourite throughout the Orient, in order to detract from the actual demands it contains. Jesus really was demanding that even the occasion of sin should be radically removed, that brotherly love should not be preserved in any merely external manner, but should extend even to the very impulses of the

---

[32] M. Weise, Matthew 5:21f. — The interpretation of συνέδριον on the basis of the Qumran texts remains doubtful, for that meaning is not found elsewhere in the New Testament. (Cf. on the contrary Matthew 10:17.)

heart and the most secret thoughts, and should lead to renunciation of a real right to retaliation (Matt. 5:38–42).

This last case in particular raises weighty problems. For does Jesus' doctrine not destroy the order of exterior justice essential to social life? And does not this order derive from God? And can these demands, finally culminating in love for one's enemies, be realized at all? We cannot answer these questions until later. It is sufficient at this point to observe that the demands formulated within the framework of the Sermon of the Mount are intended to throw light on the divine will, which is more important than the letter of the law, external action and "natural" human feelings.

From this point of view, the Lucan Sermon on the Mount, which is so frequently overlooked, assumes a new significance. The antitheses of Matthew 5 are not to be found in it, for with their Jewish legal outlook they would be less intelligible and suitable for Christian converts from paganism. Yet the much shorter discourse at Luke 6:20–49 has the same purpose.

"Love for one's enemies and brotherly love" is sometimes taken to be the principle guiding its construction.[33] Apart from the fact that this sequence would be remarkable in itself, (why not the reverse order?) it does not even fit the contents. The sayings about judgements and giving (6:37f.) need not relate especially to the relationships of Christians with one another. The example of the good and bad trees (6:43f.) serves to indicate a criterion by which to recognize a person with a good inner disposition (v. 45), a person, that is, who measures up to Jesus' demands. When, after the sayings on salvation and damnation (which are formulated as a message and not as a warning),[34] Luke starts straight off with love of one's enemies,

[33] Soiron, *Bergpredigt,* pp. 122–7.
[34] Cf. Dibelius, *Die Bergpredigt,* pp. 119f.; Percy, *Botschaft Jesu,* pp. 40–108, esp. pp. 85–89; J. Dupont, *Les Béatitudes,* 2nd ed., vol. I, pp. 265–345.

he clearly does so in order to reveal immediately the completely radical nature of Jesus' moral preaching, just as Matthew demonstrates it by contrasting it with the law of Moses. Jesus requires more than men usually perform, more than what even "sinners" do. This extra thing consists of unlimited, unselfish love, extending even to one's enemies after the example of the merciful Father as Jesus reveals him. God is infinite in kindness, but he also demands a degree of love surpassing all ordinary measures and necessitating severe self-testing and self-conquest. The sayings in the second section (including even those about loveless condemnation of one's brethren, the splinter in a brother's eye, and the plank in one's own, v. 41 f.) are therefore to be seen only as further examples of those divine demands that are exacting for the natural man. Self-testing has therefore to penetrate to the depth of the heart, and men must strive for intention and action to correspond.

If we search for the deeper motives for this radical attitude of Jesus (whose intention was, we recall, to lay an easy yoke on men), we find them primarily in his zeal to win acknowledgement for God's will in its original totality. Moses permitted divorce, wholly with divine permission, "because of the hardness of your heart"; but "from the beginning of the creation" God's will had been something different (Mark 10:1–9 par.). In this case, therefore, we know the grounds for Jesus' prohibition of divorce (also recorded among the antitheses of Matt. 5:31 f.), from a more detailed instructional discourse. It is therefore unthinkable that Jesus would have provided for a new mitigation of the divine will by the so-called "fornication-clause" (Matt. 5:32; 19:9). That would have been nonsensical, not only in the domain of the antitheses, but also in that of the instructional and controversial discourses (see also section 14 below).

Jesus himself did not attack the Mosaic law itself, although he did in part suspend it. It can, however, only be superseded in the name of God, in order to proclaim laws of God never previously promulgated.

One explanation, in keeping with the spirit of modern times, but finding no foundation in any saying of Jesus, is Bultmann's suggestion that men are considered able, and are expected, to see for themselves what is required of them. "Thus God's requirements are intelligible. And consequently the idea of obedience is viewed really radically".[35] But this cannot be right, for Jesus countered the letter of the old law with, "But *I* say to you . . . ."

And yet the will of God, viewed in itself, is not yet the ultimate basis of Jesus' disturbing and revolutionary new demands. Why should the will of God be fulfilled at this time without compromise, in its absolute form and with the most single-minded disposition? Because the reign of God is at hand. Those who have already seen the love of God in the work of his Messias and are convinced by his promises (cf. the beatitudes) will follow God alone and for love of him will rid themselves of all selfishness. Because the eschatological hour of salvation has struck, Jesus has returned to the primordial will of God, unrestrained by the conditions and difficult circumstances of this world, regardless of human weakness and hardness of heart, and has set out the commandments of God wholly free from any of the compromises of daily life, set them forth in their full integrity as what God demands.[36]

Only from this point of view is it possible to understand many of the "objectionable" sayings of Jesus. At Matthew 5:39 he is not setting up a moral system based on cowardice and making a virtue of weakness; at Matthew 5:40f. he is not abolishing all justice, but is commanding individuals in concrete situations to waive their just claims for the sake of love. The candidate for the kingdom of God must do himself violence for God's sake. The passage about loving one's enemies (Matt. 5:43–48)

---

[35] Bultmann, *Jesus,* p. 68; cf. also the section *Die Einsichtigkeit der Forderung,* pp. 76–86; and the criticism by Percy, *Botschaft Jesu,* pp. 164.
[36] Kittel, *Die Probleme,* p. 127.

enshrines this same motive (see v. 46f.), though here another is linked with it, namely that God himself acts differently from what we would expect of his justice, and so we too ought to judge after his pattern (see below, section 17).

It would be ridiculous if such radical demands formed part of an ethical system built on the nature of man. If they were addressed to men in a time of great humiliation and power-lessness they would finally lead to despair. But Jesus proclaimed them at the moment in the history of salvation when God was inaugurating his reign and so they were necessary in order that human beings might respond to God's mighty acts with generosity of heart. And such a response makes the burden light.

However, at this point there arises the great objection, the real problem of the Sermon on the Mount. Can such a morality be realized in this world? Is it not fanaticism or unhealthy rigorism? Should not these sentences be given a different inter-pretation, or mitigated, if morality and life are not to drift apart?

§ 8. The Problem of Practicability

See the bibliography on the Sermon on the Mount; also F. C. Grant, "The Impracticability of the Gospel Ethics" in *Aux sources de la tradition chrétienne* (Essays presented to M. Goguel), 1950, pp. 86–94; T. W. Manson, *Ethics and the Gospel,* 1950, pp. 58–68.

JEWISH authors see the chief difference between the moral teachings of Judaism and the moral demands of Jesus as being that Judaism looks for what is possible and attainable in this world, whilst Jesus requires the impracticable. To the Jew the whole point is that moral instruction should imbue and give form to life, but should not destroy it through its rigorism.[37] Our own

[37] Thus, J. Klausner, *Jesus of Nazareth, His Life, Times, and Teachings* (1925, new imp. 1947) pp. 390 ff.; for further views see Kittel, *Die Pro-bleme,* p. 128.

age, sober and inclined to pragmatism, gives such opinions a sympathetic hearing. Is not Jesus a fanatic in comparison, or at best, an idealist who has lost touch with reality?

Very diverse answers have been given to this problem from the Christian side.

Catholic moral theology firmly maintains both the possibility and duty of carrying out the moral commands of Jesus, but has felt bound to draw certain distinctions between them. Most of Jesus' commandments are binding in their literal meaning; the principal commandment, of love, however, lays down an end which can only be attained by approximation, for love can and should perpetually increase. Many of the demands made by the Sermon on the Mount need interpreting and delimiting; among them, for example, renunciation of one's own rights, and love of enemies; for everything Jesus said "is included among the holy and inviolable ordinances of his Father, given to him and all his disciples as an obligation to be religiously observed."[38] Finally, some of the precepts, the "evangelical counsels" (see above section 4) do not concern everyone, but only those "who can take" them and are called to do so. (It is important, however, to notice that this distinction between commandments and counsels is not applied to the Sermon on the Mount.) In short, in Catholic moral theology the demands of Jesus are interpreted in such a way that they can be fulfilled by men with the help of the grace of God.

In Protestant interpretation of the Sermon on the Mount some fundamentally divergent conceptions are met with. Some resolutely reject the idea that Jesus' demands are to be taken as commandments, because this would involve a relapse into Jewish legalism; with Jesus, they say, all that matters is the inner disposition. Others see it as Jesus' intention to make man aware of his inadequacy in the face of the holy will of God and to direct sinners towards the cross of Christ. Others again, the

[38] F. Tillmann, *Handbuch der kath. Sittenlehre,* vol. IV, 2, p. 258.

"eschatologists", ascribe to Jesus a severer ethic in expectation of the parousia, which they claim he expected in the immediate future. On the other hand others want to defend the supra-historical significance of Jesus' moral message, interpreting it as an ethics of utter obedience to God's summons at any given time.[39]

The attempt by Leo Tolstoy to translate the rigorist demands of the Sermon on the Mount directly into the basis for a new general economic and social order is well known. It is an attempt that must end in anarchy.[40]

The exegete must follow the methodological principle that the utterances of Jesus are to be explained according to their literal meaning and context, by comparison with other sayings and the general pattern of his teaching as a whole. It is a difficult and sometimes almost impossible task, for the logia have not been handed down in their complete form, nor in one unitary context, and this makes it difficult to give a systematic account of them. Individual utterances continue to stick out like craggy boulders. The Sermon on the Mount itself is not a unitary collection. Nevertheless, one must seek its basic conception.[41]

First of all it is plainly to be seen that Jesus was not concerned only with interior dispositions, but wanted his demands to be interpreted as real commandments that are to be converted into action. His purpose was not merely to awaken his hearers out of their moral lethargy, out of habit and self-satisfaction, by the use of a hyperbolic style, nor yet only to create a new "attitude"; he also wanted to give, if not actually a new code

[39] Cf. the summaries, in Windisch, *Der Sinn der Bergpredigt*, pp. 25–42; Soiron, *Bergpredigt*, pp. 1–96.

[40] Cf. J. Ackermann, *Tolstoi und das N. T.* (dissertation, 1928).

[41] The exploitation of preconceived opinions, a warning against false systemification and exegetical infallibility are the strong points of Windisch's inquiry; his work, however, lacks a clear line in positive, theological interpretation (pp. 143 ff.). Dibelius saw more clearly that Jesus' teaching was a new, self-sufficient gospel.

of law, at least new guiding principles, and also to impose a certain pattern of behaviour as obligatory. This emerges from the commanding tone of the antitheses, which have the same ring as the voice of the ancient law-giver. It is confirmed by the concluding parable of the houses built upon sand and rock, in which Jesus contrasts the wise man who hears and does what he says, with the foolish man who rests satisfied merely with hearing it. And the fact that on the day of judgement he will reject the "doers of unlawfulness", although they have prophesied in his name, cast out demons and performed many miracles (Matt. 7:22ff.), can only be interpreted as meaning that it is moral acts which will tip the scale (cf. also Matt. 25:31ff.). As this same saying is also preserved by Luke although in a different form and in a different connection (against Jesus' Jewish opponents), but with the same meaning (Luke 13:26f.), it is not valid to seek in it a new "legalistic" tendency on the part of Matthew.[42]

A logion noteworthy in this connection is that preserved only by Matthew (5:19) to the effect that anyone who abolishes the least of "these" (which?) commandments and teaches men so, shall be called least in the kingdom of heaven (but not excluded, however); whilst he who fulfils them and teaches men to keep them shall be called great. The antithesis here is not between "teach" and "fulfil", but between following and not following "the least of these commandments".

Jesus, then, required an obedience which accepted his authoritative sayings as such. Thus, he certainly meant the prohibition of divorce literally, and not merely as an example of God's uncompromising demands[43] – just as at Matthew 19:12 he really

---

[42] Cf. on this point in addition to the commentaries Windisch, *Der Sinn der Bergpredigt*, pp. 52–54; Percy, *Botschaft*, p. 121f.; H. Schürmann in *BZ* 4 (1960) pp. 238–50.

[43] 1 Cor. 7:10, and even more the absolute form found in Mark and Luke, are proof that the Lord's words were interpreted in this way in the primitive Church. According to Bultmann (*Jesus*, p. 81), anyone reading

acknowledges virginity as a law of life for certain of his followers individually. These radical demands are not least the principles that guided his own activity; they are the mirror of his personality.[44] They are also to be concretely realized in following him (cf. Luke 9:57f. = Matt. 8:19f.); Jesus asks nothing of which he does not himself set the example (cf. Mark 8:34–48 par.; 10:43ff.).

As we have recognized as the very kernel of Jesus' preaching his message regarding the advent of God's reign, we are compelled to ask what was the relationship between the moral life he was demanding and the kingdom of God he announced. Is this perhaps the solution of the problem of practicability?

It has been suggested that Jesus' reference back to the absolute will of God is an "ethics of the kingdom of God" in the sense that Jesus' radical demands will only be realized in the consummated kingdom. For then "man will stand as a new being before God, will have a new heart and will be able properly to do the pure will of God as it is interpreted by Jesus in the Sermon on the Mount . . . . When the kingdom comes, this aeon will cease, and with it the Jewish law will cease being transgressed."[45] According to this interpretation, therefore, Jesus was not making demands on his hearers (or rather only one, to repent and believe), but was merely describing the holy and blessed state of affairs in the future kingdom of God. But

this text as "formal, legal definition by an external authority", has completely misunderstood it. The other view is taken by Windisch, *op. cit.*, pp. 55f., who thinks that the concept of an invalid marriage may have not been familiar to Jesus.

[44] Windisch too says that many of the demands awaken the impression that Jesus brought them forth from his own mind and that the demand and the man must have been inseparable as far as his hearers were concerned (*op. cit.*, pp. 75f.).

[45] H. J. Schoeps, *Jesus und das jüdische Gesetz*, p. 214. Cognate with this is Percy's view that "from the point of view of content, Jesus' demands correspond to that kind of reality Jesus called the kingdom of God and in fact themselves represent part of that reality" (*Botschaft Jesu*, p. 164).

this interpretation is impossible. In the world to come, where they neither marry nor are given in marriage, but are like the angels in heaven (Mark 12:25), the indissolubility of marriage would be meaningless as a commandment. Strict precepts generally will no longer be necessary there, for those who are admitted into it will know the will of God and fulfil it without difficulty.[46]

Jesus' clear and stringent commandments can only be interpreted as conditions of entry. Even if it is true that eschatological motivation is lacking in many of the sayings of the Sermon on the Mount, the whole discourse is, nevertheless, firmly rooted in Jesus' proclamation of the reign of God. Right at the beginning, the beatitudes set the eschatological scene, and in St. Matthew's gospel they are already imperatives by implication. At Matthew 5:20, definitely in a specially prominent place, there is an explicit entry-saying, and others follow it towards the end (7:13, 21, 22f.; cf. also 7:19). The whole passage 6:19–34 which (especially towards the end: have confidence in the merciful Father) has the appearance of a timeless wisdom discourse, is brought back to this perspective by v. 33. Finally the concluding parable (about building houses 7:24–27), must certainly be read eschatologically: with the cloud-burst of storm and rain testing the foundations, Jesus is reminding us of the catastrophes of the last times.[47] It may be, too, that the eschatological situation is the ultimate basis of many other individual sayings, though in their present form this is less distinct because of the paraenetic aim of the evangelist (compare Matt. 5:25f. with Luke 12:57ff.; 5:29 with Mark 9:43ff.; and also 6:10, 19f. and the parable Luke 12:16–21; 7:7ff. and Luke 18:7f.). In fact, "The supposition that the whole of the Lord's message has an eschatological background is a justifiable one."[48]

---

[46] Cf. Goguel, *The Life of Jesus,* Oxford 1954.
[47] Cf. Jeremias, *Parables,* pp. 167, 194.
[48] Dibelius, *Die Bergpredigt,* p. 119.

But how urgent is this pressure of the last times? Is Jesus constraining his followers to heroic efforts because the terrible last age with its bitter trials is imminent? Is Jesus calling the candidate for the kingdom of God to free himself from "this" world, marked out for destruction, so that he shall not be drawn into the catastrophe with it, but may arise from it cleansed as though from a crucible? Are his extreme demands an "interim ethic"?[49] Anyone who reads the Sermon on the Mount dispassionately will not receive that impression, and anyone trying to account for that by the situation of the Church in the evangelist's time and by reference to the fading of expectation of an imminent parousia (but did it in fact fade?) would still have to answer the question how the Church at that time interpreted the urgent precepts.

The austere demands of Jesus are not to be explained by reference to "eschatologism" (that is, as though all perspectives were shortened), nevertheless they are to be interpreted eschatologically. They are valid for the period between Jesus' preaching and the end of the world. He is asking not for final preparations, but for preparation for the end. Jesus' warning on the dangers of riches is instructive in connection with this problem of practicability. The well-known saying, "It is easier for a camel to pass through the eye of a needle than for a rich man to enter into the kingdom of God" expresses by a hyperbole how difficult it is for many to comply with Jesus' demands. But when the disciples were very alarmed and said among themselves, "Who then can be saved?" Jesus looked at them and said to them, "With men it is impossible, but not with God. For all things are possible with God" (Mark 10:25-27). Sharp as Jesus'

---

[49] A. Schweitzer, *Geschichte der Leben-Jesu-Forschung,* 6th ed. 1951, pp. 594ff., Eng. tr. *The Quest for the Historical Jesus,* Oxford 1964; J. Weiss, *Das Matthäus-Evangelium (Die Schriften des N. T.,* vol. I, 4th ed. 1929) pp. 250ff.; E. Peterson, "Bergpredigt" in *RGG,* 2nd ed., vol. I, pp. 907–10. For a criticism see Schnackenburg, "Interimsethik" in *LThK* vol. V, 727f.

warnings are, he matches them with his gentleness towards those who are discouraged. He does not take back what he has said, but refers the disciples to the power of God. Jesus also described how hard it is to enter the kingdom of God by the image of a narrow gate (Matt. 7:14 and Luke 13:24). Here again it was far from his intention to frighten anyone away or to teach that some people are debarred from salvation.[50] Jesus certainly believed his commandments were practicable, because he was certain that God not only asks extremely difficult things, but also helps with his grace (cf. also the many admonitions to pray). It is not possible from any of the sayings to support the view that Jesus wanted only to humble men by the difficulty of his demands and to bring them to awareness of their weakness and sinfulness. Jesus' ethics is an "ethics of the time of salvation" (A. N. Wilder) which prefaces the radical demands by God's message of redemption and follows them with the promises of the kingdom of God.

So then we must let the words of Jesus stand in all their severity and ruggedness. Any mitigation, however well intended, is an attack on his moral mission. But how Jesus judges those who fall short of his demands is quite another matter. His behaviour towards his disciples gives us an object-lesson on this point. He took back even Simon Peter, who denied him three times and yet was the leader in the circle of the twelve, after Peter had bitterly repented his action, and he confirmed him in his position as chief of the disciples and shepherd of his sheep (cf. Luke 22:32; John 21:15–17). Admonition and mercy are found together. It is the mercy of God which always comes first. It comes definitively into history with the person and works of Jesus. But Jesus also longs to awaken the ultimate powers for good in those laid hold of by the love of God and saved from eternal ruin. They should now thankfully

---

[50] Cf. J. Theissing, *Die Lehre Jesu von der ewigen Seligkeit,* 1940, pp. 91, 114.

do the holy will of God in its totality, unalloyed. If in spite of everything they again succumb to human weakness and wretchedness, God's mercy will not fail if they turn back in penitence. To be sure that is not stated explicitly in Jesus' sayings (he calls men to a first repentance and warns them against backsliding), but it is in line with his teaching as a whole (cf. the plenary power to forgive sins, John 20:23). The man who has a genuinely penitent outlook will not misunderstand the two facets of Jesus' mission, the proclamation of salvation to sinners, and the call to complete submission to God. He will neither abuse the mercy of God and despise the commandments of Jesus, nor collapse under the severity of his demands and despair of the grace of God. With the idea of the following of Christ, there is an even closer coincidence of God's guidance and his demands. "The living Christ is there to show the way to all who are ready to follow him. What is more, the strength to follow him is also there. The living Christ has two hands, one to point out the way, and the other to stretch out to help us onward."[51]

[51] T. W. Manson, *Ethics*, p. 68.

Chapter Three

JESUS' DECISIVE ACTION:
THE CONCENTRATION OF ALL
RELIGIOUS MORAL PRECEPTS IN THE
GREAT COMMANDMENT OF LOVE
OF GOD AND THE NEIGHBOUR

§ 9. JESUS' FUNDAMENTAL PRONOUNCEMENT.
COMPARISON WITH JUDAISM

W. Lütgert, *Die Liebe im Neuen Testament*, 1905; J. Moffatt, *Love in the NT,* 1929; H. Preisker, *Die urchristliche Botschaft von der Liebe Gottes im Lichte der vergleichenden Religionsgeschichte,* 1930; E. Stauffer, art. "ἀγαπάω" in *ThWB* vol. I, 44 ff.; G. Schrenk, art. "ἐντολή" in *ThWB* vol. II, 545 ff.; A. Nygren, *Eros und Agape,* 2 vols., 1930–37; F. Weinrich, *Die Liebe im Buddhismus und im Christentum,* 1935; V. Warnach, *Agape. Die Liebe als Grundmotiv der neutestamentlichen Theologie,* 1951; W. Harrelson, "The Idea of Agape in the New Testament" in *JR* 31 (1951) pp. 169–82; C. Spicq, "Le verbe 'ἀγαπάω' et ses dérivés dans le grec classique" in *RB* 60 (1953) pp. 372–97; G. Bornkamm, "Das Doppelgebot der Liebe" in *Neutestamentliche Studien für R. Bultmann,* 1954, pp. 85–93; V. Warnach, art. "Liebe" in *Bibeltheologisches Wörterbuch,* 1959, 502–42 (with detailed bibliog.); C. Spicq, *Agapè dans le Nouveau Testament. Analyse des textes,* 3 vols., 1958–59.

THE early Church, and with it, Christianity throughout the centuries, was profoundly convinced that the greatest of Jesus' achievements in the moral sphere was the promulgation of the chief commandment of love of God and one's neighbour. The message of Christian *agape,* the model and highest expression of which is the mission of the Son of God to redeem the sinful human race, brought something new into the world, an idea and a reality so vast and incomprehensible as to be the highest revelation of God, and quite inconceivable apart from revelation. Yet realization of these facts was only possible after the death of Jesus and could only first be confirmed by the theology of early Christianity (see below sections 23 and 33). The foundation of this revelation was laid by Jesus himself, and furthermore he declared love to be the chief commandment of Christian morality. Our task here must be to examine this both within the framework of his moral teaching and in comparison with Jewish moral doctrine.

All three synoptic gospels record this great act of Jesus in an important pericope which, however, receives different formulation in the three evangelists. In Mark 12:28-34, it is a learned discussion with a well-disposed Scribe who is seeking God, approves Jesus' words, emphasizes the pre-eminence of love over external acts of worship, and is praised by Jesus for doing so. According to Matthew 22:34-40, a Pharisee lawyer tries to trap Jesus; the pericope – clearly the event was the same as that described by St. Mark – is given the form of a controversy. At Luke 10:25ff. the saying about the twofold commandment merely forms the introduction to the story of the good Samaritan, and, surprisingly, is uttered by the questioner himself. The whole passage has a practical aim. The teacher of the law wanted Jesus to tell him what he ought to do to inherit eternal life, and Jesus brought his parable of a merciful act of true neighbourly love to a climax with the words "Go and do likewise" (v. 37). Is it a different encounter of Jesus with a lawyer that is in question in Luke to the one in Mark and Matthew? In neither case are the indications of the situation, the setting, of decisive importance. In Mark and Matthew this is because the passage belongs to a section in which the early Church had brought together four fundamental questions on theological grounds and by reason of their content (Mark 12:13-37).[1] In Luke it is also the case because probably only

---

[1] Cf. D. Daube, *The New Testament and Rabbinic Judaism*, pp. 158-69.

the mention of the Samaritan in the parable led to the insertion of the passage in the Lucan "travel narrative". Of course two occurrences of a similar sort are not inconceivable. Jesus may several times have returned to this doctrine which he considered important. As regards the lawyer in Luke who enunciates of his own accord the summary of the two commandments of love, it would be possible to consider that he had already heard of this from Jesus' own discourses.[2] It is preferable on grounds of the history of the tradition and for reasons of literary criticism, however, to regard one event as having provided the basis for the two differently narrated cases. Stylistically,[3] and in the narrative, the Lucan pericope reveals the shaping hand of the evangelist. His chief concern was with the parable; he wanted to use the "great commandment" as an introduction to it, and constructed the pericope as a whole accordingly. That is also the simplest explanation why here the lawyer himself states the double commandment. "If in the Lucan text the lawyer himself designates the double commandment of love as the way of life indicated by the law, Jesus has only to insist on the actual accomplishment of this commandment, and to say how this must take place."[4] In no event does the Lucan pericope oblige us to take the view that the summarizing of the two commandments is not to be attributed to Jesus but had already been taken over by him.

The repercussions of Jesus' chief commandment may be

[2] Cf. M. J. Lagrange, *Évangile selon s. Luc*, 7th ed. 1948, p. 311; T. W. Manson, *The Sayings of Jesus*, pp. 259–61.

[3] Verse 25 καὶ ἰδού is frequent in Luke; τί ποιήσας corresponds verbally to Luke 18:18 (as opposed to Mark 10:17). In verse 26, πῶς is not used in a Semitic way (How is it possible?), but Hellenistically (What?). In verse 27 the fourfold phrasing is a secondary formulation (cf. J. Jeremias in *ZNW* 50, 1959, p. 272); in verse 28, ὀρθῶς is genuinely Lucan, as opposed to only once in Mark 7:35, and that in a different sense; in verse 29 δικαιῶσαι is only found here and at 16:15 in the whole of the New Testament.

[4] J. Schmid, *Das Evangelium nach Lukas*, p. 190.

traced throughout the New Testament writings and especially in the life of the early Church. Was Christendom right in concluding that Jesus by it had done something of fundamental and unique importance for moral doctrine? This question has to be faced, because in recent times the originality of his pronouncement has frequently been challenged, and because in making it, Jesus did in fact do no more than link together two texts from the Old Testament.

Even in ancient Judaism attempts to reduce the many individual precepts of the Jewish law to a few basic principles had not been unknown. This is not difficult to understand when one recalls that in later times (in the second century A.D.) the commandments totalled 613, including 248 positive precepts and 365 prohibitions. Hillel (c. 20 B.C.) put forward the famous Golden Rule, but in the negative form, as the principle uniting the law (cf. Matt. 7:12 par.); Rabbi Akiba (d.c. A.D. 135) gave the commandment to love one's neighbour (Luke 19:8), and Rabbi Simlai (c. 250) named faith.[5] The distinction between "small" (or light) and "great" (or heavy) commandments is also very old; but it was not uniformly made and did not correspond to what Jesus called the "first" (Mark) or "great" (Matt.) commandment.[6] To Jesus, this was a twofold commandment; he put love of God and love of one's neighbour on an equal footing. On them all the law and the prophets "depend": that is, from them all other commandments can be derived (Matt. 22:40). In a similar way Bar Quappara (c. 220) said that all the chief things in the Torah could be hung from Proverbs 3:6, as from a hook.[7]

Each of these two commandments which were to be found in different passages in the Old Testament enjoyed specially

---

[5] Billerbeck, vol. I, p. 907; cf. also Bonsirven, *Judaïsme,* vol. II, pp. 78 ff.
[6] A "heavy" commandment was primarily one difficult to fulfil, and so also an important or strictly binding commandment; cf. Billerbeck, vol. I, pp. 901 ff.
[7] Billerbeck, vol. I, pp. 907 f.

high esteem in Judaism. The commandment to love God (Deut. 6:5) belongs to the *Shema,* the old confession of monotheistic faith recited every morning and evening by the devout Jew and already customary in Jesus' time.[8] There are striking examples of the seriousness with which Jews regarded this service of God.

In one ancient passage the Talmud (Baraitha) reports, "When Rabbi Akiba was being led away to death, it was the time for the recitation of the *Shema.* They raked off his flesh with iron combs and he took the yoke of the kingdom (reign) of heaven upon himself (that is, he recited the *Shema*). His disciples said to him, 'Master, enough?' He answered them, 'My whole life long I have been concerned regarding this verse 'with thy whole soul'; even if he takes away the soul (that is, life). I said, 'When will it be possible for me to fulfil it? And now, when it is possible for me, ought I not fulfil it?'" (*Berakh.* 61, b).[9]

Neighbourly love was also accounted a primary duty. Rabbi Akiba summed up the whole of the Torah in this one commandment. For him it was just as much the great and universal foundation of the whole Torah, as the twofold commandment was for Jesus. This, moreover, was beyond all doubt the significance of the Golden Rule to Hillel. And so also in the Aristeas letter a Jewish sage puts the Golden Rule before the king of Egypt as a guiding principle for his government, and does so in both positive and negative form. It would, therefore, be wrong to claim superiority for Jesus on the basis of the occurrence of the positive form of the Golden Rule at Matt. 7:12 par.[10] Both gifts made from love (almsdeeds) and services performed from love (personal acts of practical assistance) were held to be paramount "good works", through which one could ensure one's participation in the world to come.

---

[8] Billerbeck's excursus, vol. IV, pp. 189 ff.
[9] Quoted in Billerbeck, vol. I, p. 906.
[10] Cf. Kittel, *Die Probleme,* pp. 109 f.

What was it, then, that Jesus did? His action was threefold: he revealed the indissoluble interior bond between these two commandments; he showed clearly that the whole law could be reduced to this and only this chief and double commandment, and he reinterpreted "neighbourly love" as "love of the nearest person", that is he interpreted it in an absolutely universal sense.

If we are to understand Jesus' purpose in laying down the double commandment of love, we must realize that in it Jesus linked the two commandments and put them into mutual relation. According to Jesus' mind, love of God is to find expression and give practical proof of itself in the equally important brotherly love (Matt. 22:39) and, conversely, brotherly love receives as its foundation and support, the love of God. Detailed examination of the profound interrelation between religion and morality that this involves will be undertaken below (section 11); here it must suffice to point out that no Jewish teacher of the law ever attained such clarity. For ancient Judaism, indeed, there could be no worship without the fulfilment of moral obligations; but the very esteem in which the liturgical and ritual precepts were held and their equation with the purely moral commandments exerted a restrictive effect. Hence the teacher of the law was praised by Jesus (Mark 12:34) because he drew from Jesus' reply to his question the inference that the commandment to love is more important than any sacrifice. Judaism, then, was open to such ideas, but needed positive direction. And although the Jewish religion was certainly a moral monotheism to a degree that raised it above all other forms of religion then known, "justification by works" exposed it to the danger of seeing religious acts as moral "performances" and hence of emptying moral action of its intrinsic value by defective motivation. The work of clarification and purification undertaken by Jesus in regard to the Jewish law and legal practice must not be overlooked in his laying down the double commandment of love. With that Jesus simply set the seal on his work of promulgating the true will of God. With this reciprocal linking of the two commandments, he made a perfect unity of religion and morality and by doing so gave religious as well as moral values their full dignity.

Jesus' contemporary, the Jewish scholar of Alexandria, Philo, writes in one passage of his abundant writings that man's duty towards God is piety and holy service; and towards men, philanthropy and justice, describing these as the highest elements in the uncountable multitude of sayings and precepts.[11] No similar summary resembling Jesus' twofold commandment is known from any Palestinian teacher of the law. But even if it were, Jesus' dictum would still not lose its importance, for any such saying would only be one among others; it would indeed show a better understanding of the law than was usual, but hardly a comprehension as fundamentally profound as that of Jesus, concerned entirely with the primordial will of God. His work is a unity in this respect. The new justice he demands expresses itself in love for God and the neighbour as he envisages it, boundless and issuing from the depth of the soul. His radical demands, going far beyond even the written Mosaic law, are also contained and implied in the commandment of love.

In the *Testament of the Twelve Patriarchs,* a work of exhortation dating apparently from the second century before Christ, love of God and of one's neighbour are linked together several times (*Test. Iss.* 5, 7; 7, 6; *Test. Dan* 5, 3). But here these two commandments are put together in a series with others and not set forward as the principle unifying the whole of moral activity. Furthermore, it is debatable how far this document, which we possess only in an edited form, has been subject to Christian influences.

At Leviticus 19:18 the commandment to love one's neighbour is made to relate only to the "children of thy people", and thus to those who belonged to the religious and national union

---

[11] *De Spec. Leg.,* II, 63.

of Israel. But a stranger, living among the Israelites, was to be thought of as a native: "You shall love him as yourselves" (Lev. 19:34). In later Judaism this commandment was interpreted as relating to the full proselyte, who had accepted circumcision and baptism. To extend it to all men whatsoever was very far from the thoughts of Jews in general. It was Ben Azzai (c. A.D. 110) who first recalled that all men are made in God's image and made this thought a motive for love.[12] Acts of charity towards pagan fellow-citizens are demanded more than once in the Mishnah, but only "for the sake of peace" (and thus from social good sense).[13] Hellenistic Judaism was more strongly imbued with the idea of universal philanthropy, for it was acquainted with the Stoic ideal of humanity. In a chapter "Concerning Philanthropy" (de Virt. 51 ff.), Philo seeks to show that this ideal is to be found in a perfect form in the Old Testament. According to him love should extend from one's fellow-citizens to one's enemies, and even to slaves, animals and plants. In the Testament of the Twelve Patriarchs, especially in the admonitions of Zabulon, on sympathy and mercy, and those of Gad, on love and hate, hatred is described as a satanic and destructive force, and love as the only attitude conformable to God. "Let every one of you love his neighbour and drive hatred out of your hearts; love one another in deed and word and sentiment!" (Test. Gad 6, 1). These are warm and generous words. But Jesus' demand that no limit be set on love of one's neighbour and that one stand by the sufferer with immediate practical help even when he is a national enemy (parable of the Good Samaritan) must still have been one that those listening to him realized they did not hear every day. It presupposes a universality of love that does not derive from noble humanity alone (as in Hellenism), nor venture hesitantly

---

[12] Cf. Billerbeck, vol. I, pp. 358f.; Kittel, Die Probleme, pp. 113–17, maintains that in practice the harsh contrast between Israelite and non-Israelite was to some extent mitigated.
[13] Cf. Billerbeck, vol. I, p. 359 and Kittel, Die Probleme, p. 115.

and reluctantly outside the circle of the chosen people (as in Judaism). The universality of love preached by Jesus was fired by God's all-embracing and all-merciful love. Thus his preaching of love was ultimately based on his preaching concerning God the Father and the advent of the hour of salvation.

§ 10. Closer Understanding of the Great Commandment from Jesus' Words and Deeds

J. Beeking, *Die Nächstenliebe nach der Lehre der Heiligen Schrift*, 1930; F. Tillmann, *Handbuch der katholischen Sittenlehre*, vol. IV, 2, pp. 232–65; R. Bultmann, "Das christliche Gebot der Nächstenliebe" in *Glauben und Verstehen*, vol. I, 1933, pp. 229–44; *id.*, *Jesus*, pp. 95–103; E. Bach, *Die Feindesliebe nach dem natürlichen und übernatürlichen Sittengesetz*, 1914; W. Foerster, art. "ἐχθρός" in *ThWB* vol. II, 813f.; F. X. Durrwell, *La charité selon les synoptiques et les épîtres de s. Paul*, 1955; R. Völkl, *Die Selbstliebe in der Heiligen Schrift und bei Thomas von Aquin*, 1956; "Amour de Dieu, Amour des hommes" in *Lumière et Vie* 44 (1959).

Apart from the great commandment Jesus nowhere spoke explicitly about loving God. But with the parallel commandment concerning brotherly love he indicated a broad field of action for that love. The close connection between the two commandments in the mind of Jesus is clear from Matt. 5:23f. Someone bringing his gift for sacrifice to God to the altar must first go and be reconciled with his brother. Love of God likewise obliges one to forgive. One can ask the heavenly Father for forgiveness of one's sins, if one has oneself forgiven one's debtors, so Jesus taught both in the Lord's Prayer (Matt. 6:12) and in a special admonition (Mark 11:25 par.). From this it is clear what Jesus meant by love of God: not a feeling, an emotional rapture, nor yet mystical bliss, but obedience and service. "Thus there can be no obedience towards God in a vacuum, as it were, no obedience apart from the concrete situation in which I stand as a human being among others."[14]

[14] Bultmann, *Jesus*, p. 99.

It would, however, be wrong to equate love for God narrowly with the manifestation of love for one's neighbour. It is as all-embracing as the meaning of the saying about serving two masters (Matt. 6:24 par.). This practically requires one to leave oneself free for God by overcoming one's leaning towards Mammon. The following passage (6:25–34) requires us to free ourselves from the cares that bind us to the world. As it ends with the exhortation to seek first the kingdom of God and his justice (6:33), we can say that love for God, as Jesus understood it, above all means fulfilling in faith and obedience all the requirements that God has made known through Jesus as conditions for entering the kingdom of God. Thus we can say that everything we have already seen to be part of the content of the moral mission of Jesus is an expression of the love we owe to God, and that this love implies quite concrete guiding principles.

Religious acts properly so called also belong to this love of God. Matthew devotes two sections of the Sermon on the Mount to prayer (6:1–16; 7:7–11) and Luke a significant part of his report of Jesus' journeyings (11:1–13). The Lord's Prayer (Matt. 6:9–13, and in a shorter form with a different rhythm, Luke 11:2–4) is unquestionably a prayer concerned with the kingdom of God; the petition for its coming is the central one.[15] But it also shows clearly how Jesus' gospel of the Father and his proclamation of God's reign belong together. The most important intention is that God should exalt his name[16] and, in his goodness and omnipotence, establish his kingdom. But Jesus' disciples who are still in this world, are permitted to

---

[15] On the Lord's Prayer see I. Abrahams, *Studies in Pharisaism and the Gospels*, vol. II, 1924, pp. 94–108; P. Fiebig, *Das Vaterunser*, 1927; G. Dalman, *Die Worte Jesu*, pp. 283–365; E. Lohmeyer, *Das Vaterunser*, 3rd ed. 1952; M. Meinertz, *Das Vaterunser und der Reim*, 1950; H. Schürmann, *Das Gebet des Herrn*, 1957, Eng. tr. *Praying with Christ*, 1964; H. van den Bussche, *Le Notre Père*, 1960.

[16] The use of the passive shows that it is presupposed that it is God who is acting here; cf. O. Procksch in *ThWB* vol. I, p. 113; J. Schmid, *in loc.*

entrust the anxieties of their earthly life to the Father, and they are also to implore him for protection against the powerful attacks and temptations of the Evil One. In prayer too, what is decisive is the interior disposition. So Jesus endeavours through a constant flow of new sayings, images and parables (Luke 11:5–8; 18:1–5, 7; cf. also Mark 11:24 par.), to awaken in his disciples a solid and unshakeable confidence in the heavenly Father. Prayer is especially important in the eschatological situation of struggle and temptation (Mark 14:38 par.).[17] Confidence is essential to overcome not only anxiety but also terror in the storms of persecution (Matt. 10:26–33 par.). Love for God is very far, therefore, from being a weakly attitude; it engenders courage that even extends to fearless confession of faith and martyrdom. Jesus embodied this love which is obedience and readiness for death itself, in his own person, as his words in St. John's gospel make plain, "But that the world may know that I love the Father; and as the Father hath given me commandment, so do I" (14:31).

It is on the foundation of this utterly resolute love for God that love of the neighbour is built up. Hence unbounded and genuine, heart-felt forgiveness of our brethren is a primary duty. The parable of the merciless servant (Matt. 18:23–35) demonstrates that God's infinite mercy is given us in the expectation that we deal mercifully with our fellow men.

The metaphor of the remittance of debts applied here to forgiveness of spiritual guilt, is also used in the Lord's Prayer. The parable is part of the material found only in the gospel according to St. Matthew. Its connection with the exhortation to forgive repeatedly (v. 21f.) is secondary, for this feature is not prominent in the story and Luke has a parallel saying (17:14) not linked with the parable. In this parable the application in-

---

[17] Cf. K. G. Kuhn, "Πειρασμός—ἁμαρτία—σάρξ im NT und die damit zusammenhängenden Vorstellungen" in *ZThK* 49 (1952) pp. 200–22; *id.*, "Jesus in Gethsemane" in *EvTh* 12 (1952–3) pp. 260–85.

tervenes several times in the narrative itself, for the total of the first servant's debt is unimaginably large, even if he is to be thought of as a steward, and he is incapable of ever paying it by his punishment at the end. Thus behind the king, God is to be seen, and behind the punishment, eternal damnation. This parable itself shows that our love for our human brethren is in fact only an answer to the love of God, a passing on of his mercy. It has learnt from the infinite love for sinners of God and Jesus.

Together with this "spiritual work of mercy", Jesus lays equal weight on the corporal works. The list of them is taken from the great picture of the judgement sketched by Jesus at Matthew 25:31–46 (more material peculiar to Matthew).[18] This indicates a way in which the heathen, who do not know Jesus and yet must stand before the judgement seat of God, can win possession of the kingdom of God. If they have performed works of love towards those in need, the Son of man will reckon their actions as though they treated him in that way; for he looks upon the poor and needy as his "brethren".[19] The duty of helpful love is absolutely binding on those who believe in him. Jesus holds in especially high esteem any act of charity done to those persecuted for his name's sake (cf. Matt. 10:42 = Mark 9:41). At Mark 9:37f. par. there is recorded another saying regarding "receiving" a "little one" ("these" little ones): in receiving a helpless child, one receives Jesus himself.[20]

[18] A. Wikenhauser, "Die Liebeswerke im Gerichtsgemälde Mt. 25: 31–46" in *BZ* 20 (1932) pp. 366–77; J. A. T. Robinson, "The Parable of the Sheep and the Goats" in *NTS* 2 (1955–6) pp. 225–37.
[19] The point here is not the mystical union of Jesus and sufferers. It is a judgement-saying in which acts of charity are identified with acts done for "the least" of Jesus' brethren, that is, those who are suffering.
[20] The basis of this is the old idea that the ambassador is to be honoured in exactly the same degree as the one who sent him. Cf. Billerbeck, vol. I, p. 590. The application of the thought here to a child is striking, as it is elsewhere used of men of God and missionaries; cf. Matt. 10:40f.

Although the interpretation is commonly made, it is debatable whether the guilt of the rich glutton (Luke 16:19ff.) rested on the fact that he paid no attention to poor Lazarus at his gate and did not help him. The introduction to this story simply describes the contrast between the two men, and Abraham answers Dives in torment in the underworld not with a reference to his lack of love, but merely by recalling the property he owned whilst he was alive (v. 25). Important with regard to the question of poverty as this parable undoubtedly is, (see below, section 13), it is also difficult to interpret, perhaps because it assumes familiarity on the part of its audience with a story in which the rich man was a sinner and the poor man just. Judaism frequently regarded the good fortune of the godless as a reward given for occasional good works, yet for their lawlessness, they were excluded from the future aeon. If Jesus had intended to indicate that the glutton was being punished for his lack of love, he would surely have said so more clearly.

Renunciation of worldly wealth and its distribution to the poor were required by Jesus not only of the disciples who wanted to follow him personally (Mark 10:21 par.), but also, to a lesser degree, of all (cf. Luke 12:33 – a Lucan supplement). If God is to give us his superabundant gifts of salvation, we too must give to those who ask (Luke 6:30 par.), and must lend without expecting anything in return (Luke 6:35 par.). And here too, as with forgiveness, the motive is "For with the same measure that you shall mete withal it shall be measured to you again".

It would, however, be wrong to interpret Jesus' exhortation to generous helpful love as though one saw in those in need only an opportunity for religious activity or to gain a heavenly reward. The good Samaritan (Luke 10:30–37) did not ask whether the injured man was a Jew, he had not got one eye on a reward, nor did he hesitate or say much. He simply helped, there and then, setting about it himself, sacrificing something that belonged to him, and was ready to do more than was absolutely necessary. Certainly brotherly love grows from the love of God, but just as certainly it aims at helping anyone in need, simply because he is a fellow human being. The more selfless the service to someone else, the purer the love. We should invite not friends, brethren, relations and neighbours, but the poor, the crippled, the lame and the blind (Luke 14:12–14). We should not give in order to receive *(do ut des)*! As in Judaism too, personal service is valued more highly than financial support. Anyone who loves is ready to give himself. Jesus himself provided the best example of this, by giving his life "for many" (Mark 10:45 par.). "I am in the midst of you as he that serveth" (Luke 22:27). According to John 13:4–15, Jesus humbled himself to perform the slave's duty of washing feet, and by so doing symbolized his love "unto the end" (13:1), that is, his sacrificial and atoning death. But he said to the disciples, "A new commandment I give unto you: That you love one another, as I have loved you" (13:34). John interpreted this as referring to Jesus' sublime love for his friends (John 15:13) and as a summons to brotherly love (1 John 2:10; 3:14ff. etc). He saw this extreme example of laying down one's life for the brethren, not as a single pinnacle attained by the love of Jesus alone, but as an act binding us to do likewise (1 John 3:16).

This early Christian interpretation of the commandment to love makes it clear that the addition of the words "as thyself" to the commandment of neighbourly love is not intended to be taken as a limitation of its scope. Rather, the self-love that is spontaneously and essentially present in everyone should be an unforgettable reminder to us of how far our love for others ought to go. "This 'as thyself' cannot be twisted and explained away; judging with the severity of eternity, it pierces to the inmost hiding places of the love a man has for himself."[21] That is what Jesus had in mind in the Golden Rule: "All things,

[21] Kierkegaard, quoted by Bultmann, *Jesus,* p. 100.

therefore, whatsoever you would that men should do to you, do you also to them" (Matt. 7:12 par.).

Love of friends and love of enemies are only "two different forms of the Christian sentiment of love" (F. Tillmann). Love of the kind Jesus requires often demands painful self-conquest; in loving one's enemies, that is only too obvious. The step from loving one's friends in the right way to loving one's enemies, is not a big one. Not for nothing did Jesus make the symbol of the helpful man a Samaritan, a member of that half-pagan, half-breed nation with whom the Jews were at that time at particular enmity.[22] But in the gospels, enemy primarily means personal opponent, as is also shown by the example at Matthew 5:39. Luke puts in one phrase, "Give to everyone that asketh of thee; and of him that taketh away thy goods, ask them not again" (6:30). The next step is to renounce revenge (Luke 6:29 par.), but loving one's enemies also involves positive action, "Love your enemies. Do good to them that hate you. Bless them that curse and pray for them that calumniate you" (6:27f.). Jesus was not concerned with the psychological difficulties that loving one's enemies might entail. It is enough that this is what God himself does, "who maketh his sun to rise upon the good and bad and raineth upon the just and the unjust" (Matt. 5:45), and imitation of God will make those who love God capable of a similar attitude.

The comparable utterances of the noble Stoics are well-known and are often quoted. Seneca, for example, said, "If you want to imitate the gods, do favours even to the ungrateful; for the sun rises even over the wicked, and the sea is open even to pirates" (*De benef.* VI, 26, 1, cf. also Marcus Aurelius, *In sem.*, IX, 11). But in this pantheistic system there could be no question of a genuine imitation of God. Ultimately the philosophers were moved to make their statements, truly admirable as they are,

---

[22] Cf. Billerbeck, vol. I, 56–60; Jeremias, *Jerusalem zur Zeit Jesu,* vol. II B, pp. 227–31.

by reason alone. Jesus demanded love of one's enemies as the highest expression yet necessary consequence of personal love for God and one's neighbour. Self-conquest was for him not a philosophical exercise, but profound love based on religion.

A practical application of love of this kind, operative both towards friend and foe, is avoidance of loveless condemnation. Here again the religious motive is evident, "Judge not, and you shall not be judged (by God). Condemn not, and you shall not be condemned. Forgive, and you shall be forgiven" (Luke 6:37 par.), and the wonderful saying about the mote or splinter in a brother's eye and the beam in one's own (Luke 6:41f. par.) makes the admonition unforgettable. It is astonishing how Jesus links bold and as it might seem superhuman demands with a very clear-sighted and realistic assessment of the limitations of human nature. He, however, has the right to call men in the name of God out of their narrowness up on to the heights of divine sanctity (cf. Matt. 5:48), for he not only preached this love, but lived it, not least in prayer for his enemies (Luke 23:34): a prayer which, at that moment on the cross and in its moving and incomparable form, is the worthiest testimony to his spirit.[23]

§ 11. The Significance of the Great Commandment for Religion and Morality

See bibliography to sections 9 and 10; also J. Herkenrath, *Ethik Jesu,* pp. 83ff.; F. Tillmann, *Die Idee der Nachfolge Christi,* pp. 136ff., pp. 147ff., pp. 179ff., cf. also J. Fuchs, "Die Liebe als Aufbauprinzip der Moraltheologie. Ein Bericht" in *Scholastik* 29 (1954) pp. 79–87; C.

---

[23] Jesus' petition for his enemies is recorded only in Luke, and is, moreover, not to be found in many important Mss.; nevertheless, it must have originated from a good and ancient tradition, for St. Stephen was clearly moved to offer a similar prayer by his Lord's example. Cf. Acts 7:60. Cf. J. Schmid, *in loc.*

Spicq, "Die Liebe als Gestaltungsprinzip der Moral in den synoptischen Evangelien" in *Freiburger Zeitschrift für Theologie und Philosophie* 1 (1954) pp. 394–410.

THE LINKING together intrinsically of love of God and of one's neighbour, and the interpretation of this double commandment as the core and climax of the whole of moral doctrine, is a great gain for religion as well as morality, and this might perhaps be summarized more or less as follows.

Religion, the relationship of man with God, and its whole wealth of ideas, doctrines, emotions, endeavours and actions can no longer lead to a self-contained ceremonial piety. The Scribe of Mark 12:32f. had already drawn from the words of Jesus the conclusion that the love of God surpasses everything and that brotherly love is more than all the temple sacrifices. Early Christians understood this: "Religion clean and undefiled before God and the Father is this: to visit the fatherless and widows in their tribulation ..." (Jas. 1:27). It can be a strong impetus to the life of the liturgy, worship itself (cf. the Agape, the fraternal feast), but especially to the influence of that life on the activities of the parish community and of individual Christians in the world. For believers in Christ the goal could not be the visionary mysticism which at that time exerted an immense power of attraction over not a few human beings (Hermeticism, the Mystery Religions, Gnosticism). It is not ecstatic visions that lead to communion with God, but love proved in action (cf. 1 John 4:12). At the same time, brotherly love affords genuine and powerful love for God a field of action. Love urges us to act; but God is invisible and afar off to human beings with their bodies and senses. Now, however, human beings can demonstrate their love for God through goodwill and acts of benevolence towards their brethren. The whole problem that people in modern times claim to find in loving God and in the commandment to love, consequently evaporates. Direct acts of worship of God are not thereby suppressed; but rather love makes possible true praise and thanksgiving, confidence and hope. Perfect love overcomes fear (1 John 4:18), but brotherly love can also help, for it assures us of our love for God, soothes our hearts when they condemn us and trouble us (1 John 3:19f.). Jesus also spoke sometimes about fear of God (Matt. 10:28), and his serious warnings about judgement could increase this; but in the great commandment he unmistakably proclaimed love as the decisive attitude. But anyone who asks how it is possible to express such love above all things for the all-holy God, is directed towards the simple path of brotherly love which the good Samaritan took.

These ideas are not a later glorification of Jesus' proclamation of the great commandment; at a very early date they had already been developed from his commandment of love. It is no accident that they are already to be found in the First Epistle of St. John. They are in accord with John's meditations on communion with God and were also called forth by the pseudo-mysticism and gnosis that John had to combat. Without setting out the theme as explicitly as has been done here, he, in fact, worked out the rich benefit the commandment of love affords for a healthy and profound piety (see also sections 33 and 34 below).

The value of the great commandment for morality is perhaps even more important. Unification and interiorization, a morality of intention and of action, love for the poorest and love for all have been extolled often enough; but often not enough account is taken of love of God as the basis of religion. This love alone guarantees the unselfishness which is lacking to almost all human love; it alone makes possible the self-conquest from which the most secret and powerful acts of love spring. Only this love grounded in God, becomes *agape,* which surpasses every natural *eros,* and the praise of which is sung at 1 Corinthians 13. It surpasses the love of friendship, for even without natural affinity it meets others with goodwill, readiness to help, understanding and forgiveness for the sake of God and Christ. In this Christian *agape* the urge towards union has quite receded in favour of pure benevolence and mercy. For that reason it can also extend to those who are not naturally worthy of love and even to an enemy. But where does it derive the stimulus to do so? Again only from love of God, by whom the Christian knows himself to be loved in this self-same way. This "completely different" love of God has been revealed to the Christian in the words of Jesus (Matt. 5:45), in Jesus' saving acts and finally in his death. Because Christian love of the neighbour is related to love of God, it impels the Christian, when it is correctly understood and taken to heart, to the utmost effort, to "perfection", as Jesus himself expressed it (Matt. 5:48).

This Christian perfection in love is different in kind from the Greek ideal of perfection. Its aim is not the attainment of a harmonious personality, morally faultless, self-contained, but of "holiness", as God is holy (cf. Lev. 19:2; 1 Pet. 1:16). In this context, that of loving one's enemies, and of the resolving of the antitheses of the Sermon on the Mount, holiness involves a love that completely surrenders the individual ego, and takes as its model God's incomprehensible love for mankind and for sinners. The expression "perfect" probably derives from Matthew, who is the only evangelist to use it again, in 19:21. In Luke 6:36, the words of the Sermon on the Mount read, "Be ye therefore merciful as your Father also is merciful", and that must have been the original wording, because in the Old Testament the predicate "perfect" is never applied to God (though it is to his actions, Deuteronomy 32:4, his law, Psalm 18:8, and to the way in which he guides), but the predicate "merciful" often is. By his expression Matthew has wished, in accordance with the sense, to bring out and condense for his Jewish Christian readers, the morality demanded by Jesus, which exceeds all previous "righteousness" (5:20), and which concerns the whole man and claims him wholly. Consequently, in Matthew, Jesus also says to the rich young man, when he is asking the hardest of him, "If thou wilt be perfect, go sell what thou hast" (19:21). On the basis of Hebrew thought "perfect" *(tamim)* really means "intact", "faultless", "sound" (often used in this sense of sacrificial animals) and the noun *(tom)* also means "innocence", "purity". The idea is not of a perfecting by stages, but of the integrity of the whole person who belongs to God.[24] In Judaism too we meet with the exhortation, "As God is called merciful and gracious, so be thou also merciful and gracious, and give to every man without reward",[25] but here it is closely linked with other attributes of God that are to be imitated. The command to be perfect and to walk before Yahweh, was already given to Abraham (Gen. 17:1). But to Jesus perfection as he demands it at the climax of the Sermon on the Mount is more, it is in fact the highest peak of love, final renunciation of self and utter devotion to God and fellow men.

By this a goal is set for the moral striving of men, which goes far beyond the range of vision of any philosophical system of ethics and every purely human ideal of perfection, a goal beyond the reach of purely human powers, but not unattainable with the help of God's grace. This moral task set before the Christian, although consisting primarily in the attainment of salvation and of all the blessings of salvation promised by Jesus, is also a source of true happiness and lasting peace in the earthly life of men with one another.

[24] R. Schnackenburg, "Die Vollkommenheit des Christen nach den Evangelien" in *Geist und Leben* 32 (1959) pp. 420–33; J. Dupont, "'Soyez parfaits' (Mt. 5:48) — 'Soyez miséricordieux' (Luke 6:36)" in *Sacra Pagina,* vol. II (1959) pp. 150–62; P. J. Du Plessis, *The Idea of Perfection in the NT,* Kampen 1959, pp. 168–73.

[25] *Siphre Deut.* 11, 22 sect. 49, quoted in Billerbeck, vol. I, p. 372.

Chapter Four

JESUS' DEMANDS FOR LIFE IN THE CONDITIONS OF THIS WORLD

§ 12. JESUS' ATTITUDE TO LAW, POWER, AND THE STATE

H. Windisch, *Imperium und Evangelium im Neuen Testament*, 1931; E. Stauffer, *Gott und Kaiser im Neuen Testament*, 1935; K. Pieper, *Urkirche und Staat*, 1935; K. Bornhäuser, *Jesus imperator mundi*, 1938; G. Kittel, *Christus und Imperator*, 1939; O. Eck, *Urgemeinde und Imperium*, 1940; M. Dibelius, "Rom und die Christen im 1. Jahrhundert" in *Botschaft und Geschichte*, vol. II (1956) pp. 177–228; W. G. Kümmel in *Theologische Rundschau* 17 (1948) pp. 133–42; H. v. Campenhausen, "Zum Verständnis von Johannes 19:11" in *TLZ* 73 (1948) pp. 387–92; W. Bienert, *Krieg, Kriegsdienst und Kriegsdienstverweigerung nach der Botschaft des Neuen Testaments*, 1952; R. Leivestad, *Christ the Conqueror*, 1954; J. Lasserre, *Der Krieg und das Evangelium*, 1956; O. Betz, "Jesu heiliger Krieg" in *NovT* 2 (1957) pp. 116–37; O. Cullmann, *Der Staat im Neuen Testament*, 1956, Eng. tr. *The State in the New Testament*, 1957; O. Michel in *TLZ* 83, (1958) pp. 161–6; H. W. Bartsch, "Die neutestamentlichen Aussagen über den Staat" in *EvTh* 19 (1959) pp. 375–90; R. Völkl, *Christ und Welt nach dem Neuen Testament*, 1961, pp. 108–38 (Bibliog.). See also section 25.

WHAT IS striking about Jesus' judgement of conditions in this world is the realism of his attitude. His parables, with their firm basis in life, and his personal conduct in that political storm-centre of the Roman Empire, would quickly correct anyone who, on the evidence of the Sermon on the Mount, was tempted to see him as a religious visionary and moral reformer out of touch with reality. He is not particular in his choice of material for the parables which are mostly intended to throw light on a single main idea. He describes a king debating with himself beforehand whether with the forces available to him he should involve himself in a war, or sue for peace (Luke 14:31f.); or a disloyal steward about to lose his office and acting with cunning and speed in an attempt to win friends for himself by remitting debts (Luke 16:1–7);[1] or again, a judge who helps a widow obtain justice not for love of justice but in order to get peace for himself at last (Luke 18:1–5). These types are certainly not examples to be followed, and it was not Jesus' intention to put them forward as patterns for war and peace, social life and legal practice.

But when Jesus saw the social and political abuses of his time, was he not offended by them and did he not want to put an end to them? Did he not construct, as well as a system of personal ethics, a system of social ethics, as seems so extremely important to us nowadays? In fidelity to the texts of the New Testament, we are bound to answer: No, at least, not directly. It is a grotesque misinterpretation to characterize him as a social revolutionary because of what he said against the rich, or as the planner of a new social order (cf. Tolstoi) on the basis of his precept to renounce revenge, or as a communist on account of his commandment to love one's neighbour, or as a pacifist in the political sense because of his commandment to love one's enemies, or as an opponent of learning and civilization because of his attacks on the Scribes. All these forms of radicalism are orientated towards this world: none of them can appeal to him for support, for they misconstrue his basic purposes in these pronouncements, purposes which are wholly religious and moral. For his own

[1] A. Vögtle, "Das Gleichnis vom ungetreuen Verwalter" in *Oberrheinisches Pastoralblatt* 53 (1952); J. Jeremias, *Parables,* pp. 45–48; M. Kramer, "Ad parabolam de villico iniquo, Luke 16:8, 9" in *VD* 38 (1960) pp. 278–91; J. Duncan, M. Derrett, "Fresh Light on St. Luke 16" in *NTS* 7 (1960–1) pp. 198–219.

part, he did not allow himself to become involved in "worldly affairs".

When a man from the crowd asked him to settle a dispute about an inheritance, a valid request to make of a rabbi, he replied, "Man, who hath appointed me judge or divider over you?" (Luke 12:13f.). We must not try to deduce from this text a recognition by Jesus of a natural right to property, perhaps, by linking it with the warning that follows against covetousness (v. 15), as though Jesus were attacking the longing of the "disinherited" for possessions. Verse 15 is an independent logion, and the whole section was assembled by the evangelist. Jesus nowhere contested the right to own property, but neither did he anywhere explicitly confirm it.

It is important for us to consider the reason for Jesus' attitude. Did it spring from indifference to the conditions of this world? Did he consider this world so corrupt that no improvement is worthwhile? Did he imagine that the kingdom of God was so near that these questions were pointless in the light of the approaching end? An affirmative answer to these questions cannot be supported from what Jesus said, nor would it be in keeping with the spirit that animated him. His reply to the man who was a party to the dispute over an inheritance also answers our questions: he did not feel that his personal vocation called on him to deal with such matters. Still more fundamental was the attitude he revealed under temptation (Matt. 4:3-10; Luke 4:3-12). Satan strove to turn Jesus aside at the last moment from the path of Messiasship the Father had marked out for him, that is, from work in obscurity, from suffering and death as the "Servant of God", and to persuade him into a political, power-seeking Messiasship. By doing so, the devil hoped to outwit him and subject him to himself. Jesus, however, repulsed him and remained loyal to his vocation.[2]

[2] Cf. Schnackenburg, "Der Sinn der Versuchung Jesu bei den Synoptikern" in *TQ* 132 (1952) pp. 297-326; M. Sabbe, "De tentatione Jesu"

When according to Luke 4:6f. the devil said, "For to me they are delivered; and to whom I will, I give them", this did not mean that all power in this world is diabolical. The devil's claim to dispose of it at will was an empty one (cf. John 19:11). That forces hostile to God stand behind the kingdoms of this world was a view put forward both occasionally in the Old Testament and more strongly by later Judaism, particularly in the apocalypses.[3] Yet the ultimate sovereignty is God's, which in the end overthrows all those in authority and all kingdoms that revolted against him. The idea expressed at Luke 4:6 is fully worked out at Apocalypse 13:2.

Jesus refused to intervene directly and regulate the disordered affairs of this world. His often-repeated "I am come" reveals his consciousness of his vocation: he had been sent to call sinners (Mark 2:17 par.), save the lost (Luke 19:10), give his life as a redemption for many (Mark 10:45 par.). His purpose is to bring the divine life back to the world (John 3:16ff.; 10:10; 12:46f.). Before Pilate he declared, "My kingdom is not of this world" (John 18:36). He fled from the desire of his Galilean supporters to make him a political messianic king and national liberator (cf. John 6:14f.) and rejected Simon Peter's plea to relinquish the path of suffering and death, just as energetically as he repulsed the temptations of Satan in the wilderness (Matt. 16:22f.). The demonstration by the people at the time

in *Collationes Brugenses* 50 (1954) pp. 200–22; J. Dupont, "L'arrière-fond biblique du récit des tentations de Jésus" in *NTS* 3 (1956–7) pp. 287, 304; H. Seesemann in *ThWB*, vol VI, 33ff.

[3] Cf. Isa. 24:21–23; 27:1; *Dan* 7:2ff.; 1 *Enoch*. 89f.; the figure of Beliar in the *Testament of the Twelve Patriarchs* and the *Sybilline Oracles*, and of Mastema in the *Book of Jubilees,* etc. on these see Bousset and Gressmann, *Religion des Judentums,* pp. 331ff.; Volz, *Eschatologie,* pp. 86ff.; H. W. Huppenbauer, "Belial in den Qumrantexten" in *TZ* 15 (1959) pp. 81–89.

But on the other hand, the view has also recently become current that the political might of the powers appointed by God are bound to the fight against evil, cf. E. Stauffer, *Theology,* pp. 64ff.

of the entry into Jerusalem was so peaceful in character that it did not even feature as an item in the indictment against him at his trial. Jesus never suggested that his precept of love is to lead to a "peaceful revolution", to reform and renewal of this world.

Clearly Jesus kept himself apart from the religio-political movement of the Zealots. This party, founded by Judas the Galilean in A.D. 6,[4] under the old theocratic ideal that only Yahweh is to be king of Israel strove to throw off by force the Roman yoke, refused to pay the poll-tax and prepared for a holy war until the Jewish revolt actually did break out in A.D. 66. Probably the Galileans who according to Luke 13:1f. were put to the sword while at sacrifice in the Temple, were Zealots, and possibly also the men who according to John 6:14ff. wanted to take Jesus by force and make him king. Jesus maintained no contacts with the Zealots even if he received Simon the Zealot as one of the twelve. If other disciples from this circle had, as many scholars suppose, possessed Zealot leanings (Judas Iscariot, and the "sons of thunder"), Jesus gave them a clear refusal.[5]

Does this mean, then, that Jesus' moral teaching has no bearing on social life, social ethics, the conditions of this world? To think so would be just as serious a mistake, with equally grave consequences. It was by no means Jesus' wish to shut his disciples and followers out of the "world", perhaps making them, like the Essenes, leave the nation and found closed communities with a special, strict code of morality,[6] or even, whilst remaining within the community of the nation, to form

[4] On the Zealots, see: M. R. Farmer, *Maccabees, Zealots, and Josephus*, 1956; M. Hengel, *Die Zeloten*, 1961.
[5] O. Cullmann, *Der Staat im Neuen Testament*, pp. 5–15; S. G. Brandon, *The Fall of Jerusalem and the Christian Church*, 1951, probably over-estimate the importance of the Zealots for Jesus and for the early Church.
[6] See on this difficult passage (esp. vv. 32–3) J. Schmid, *Das Evangelium nach Lukas*; J. Blinzler, *Herodes Antipas und Jesus Christus*, 1947, pp. 16–20; *id.*, in *Synoptische Studien* (Festschrift for A. Wikenhauser) 1954,

self-absorbed groups, preparing with profound devotion, brotherly love and moral purity for the coming of the reign of God. Jesus sent his disciples out into the midst of the world (Matt. 10:16), and gave them the task of preaching the gospel first to Israel (Matt. 10:5) and then to all the nations (Matt. 24:14 par.; 28:19). They were to carry on his mission (John 17:18; 20:21), and he expressly asked the Father not to take them out of the world, but to preserve them from evil within the world (John 17:15).

The institutions wielding power within paganism and Judaism are not shown in a very good light in the mission discourse (Matt. 10). The disciples, Jesus said, will be dragged before the courts, and these will condemn them. That will be evidence in God's court against those in power (Matt. 10:17). Such bitter persecution has its true place in the terrible period before the end (Mark 13:9-13). By saying these things, Jesus was not giving an explanation of what justifies and gives value to these circumstances; he was merely instructing the disciples in what they must expect in following him. The same is true of John 15:19ff.; 16:1-4.

But Jesus did not wholly avoid the questions everyone has to face regarding the powers of this world. It was impossible for him to do so from the mere fact that his disciples had not forgotten the dream of an earthly, national Jewish messianic kingdom (cf. Luke 19:11; 24:31; Acts 1:6), and could not subdue the striving for power so deeply rooted in every human being. Two clearly independent scenes illustrating this have been handed down to us: the dispute over precedence and the request made by the sons of Zebedee, James and John.

According to Mark 9:33-35, the dispute over precedence occurred on a journey and after it Jesus gave his disciples his stern lesson. Matthew 18:1-5 links it closely with the scene in

pp. 42-46; a contrary view is shown by M. Black, *An Aramaic Approach to the Gospel and Acts,* 2nd ed. 1954, pp. 151-3.

which Jesus led a child among them as a model of humility. St. Luke puts it in a similar position but is even more dependent on the Marcan report (9:46–48). He then repeats it in the room of the last supper (22:24–27), though with the sayings that Matthew and Mark connect with the question put by the Zebedee brothers (Mark 10:41–45 = Matt. 20:24–28). The uncertainty of the tradition should not disturb us if we remember that what is important is not the setting but the words of Jesus.[7]

The saying, "You know that they who claim to rule (Douay: seem to rule) over the gentiles lord it over them; and their princes oppress them (Douay: have power over them)" (Mark 10:42 par.),[8] confirms the realism of Jesus' outlook. It is not a fundamental repudiation of political institutions, but a statement based on observation. But Jesus sees what is dangerous and seductive in power, just as he did in riches.

The saying about being "first and last" is recorded in five forms. The full form (a couplet exhibiting *parallelismus membrorum*) is to be found at Mark 10:43f. and (with slight modifications) Matthew 20:26f.: "Whosoever will be greater shall be your minister. And whosoever will be first among you shall be the servant of all." In a paradoxical form this saying illustrates the quite different order ruling within the circle of Jesus' disciples, who wish to gain entrance to the kingdom of God, from the struggles for power found in the world. This saying is one of Jesus' sharp admonitions and may be compared with the renunciation of legal justice. It does not deny all value to power which like law and justice may have a relative value and be necessary in the conditions of life in this world, but the disciple of Christ must be prepared to renounce it with a view to the kingdom of God. The saying at Matthew 18:4 suggests another saying also recorded several times (Matt. 23:12; Luke

[7] Cf. Schnackenburg, "Markus 9:33–50" in *Synoptische Studien* (Festschrift for A. Wikenhauser) 1954, pp. 184–206.
[8] On the translation, see T. W. Manson, *The Teaching of Jesus,* 2nd ed. 1935 (new imp. 1951) pp. 313–15.

14:11; 18:14): "And whosoever shall exalt himself shall be humbled; and he that shall humble himself shall be exalted." This is a guarantee for the future, in which the use of the passive form conceals God: the humble servant will be exalted by God in the coming kingdom. The two sayings, the warning for the present and the promise for the future, are related. That these and other logia occur more often and in various forms, is due to the fact that they are applicable to various situations and texts and can be fitted in accordingly. They are "unattached" logia.[9]

When he was asked about the poll tax, the tribute money (Mark 12:13–17), Jesus did not shrink from a political pronouncement, yet he avoided anything sensational in it. At the same time he contrived, even with this ticklish question, to guide it back to the religious domain and bring out what he had most at heart. The poll-tax was also a burning problem for the Jews of that time. It had to be paid in Roman currency in the form of a silver denarius, bearing the Emperor's portrait and name, so that by paying it one was acknowledging the sovereignty of a pagan ruler. This involved the Jews in conflicts among themselves, for they acknowledged God, or his representative, as the only king of their nation. As a result, the Zealots refused to pay the poll-tax and the Pharisees could only with difficulty bring themselves to do so, justifying themselves with the thought that it was God who raised (pagan) kings to power and abased them again (Dan. 2: 21).

Jesus' unequivocal decision was that the tax should be paid and he countered his cunning questioner with the argument that by using coins bearing the portrait of the Emperor (and profiting by the Roman economic order) they were recognizing the Emperor's right to strike coinage and consequently, in accordance with the view current in the ancient world, his sovereignty too. They therefore owed[10] him the tax and, as the

[9] Cf. G. Lindeskog, "Logia-Studien" in *ST* 4 (1950) pp. 129–89.
[10] Notice the word "render" (not "give"). Yet it would be wrong to try

universal form of the reply shows, obedience generally in the duties required of citizens. But of his own accord Jesus also added a second clause, which, by its position, must receive all possible emphasis, "and render (give) to God the things that are God's". Just as great, and even greater, is man's duty to God. "The State can demand what is necessary to its existence, but God claims the whole man, and man has to 'give himself back' to him."[11]

How is the sequence of the two precepts to be understood? Is the first perhaps intended to be taken merely ironically? "You may as well give the Emperor what is his, in comparison with God he is nothing but a puppet." This cannot be derived from the literal tenor of the text, and it would have given Jesus' ever-watchful enemies another ground for attacking him. Was it Jesus' intention to suggest that man's duties towards God alone are important, so that his tasks as a citizen are of no account? Or was he, on the contrary, juxtaposing the two spheres as equally well-founded? Did Jesus acknowledge the emperor and state unreservedly, even perhaps as divine institutions? Every possible shade of interpretation has its adherents.[12] Taking into account both the co-ordination between the two clauses and at the same time the crescendo in the second, one is justified in saying that obedience to the emperor does not appear merely as a concession or prudent rule of conduct in practical life; but obedience to God stands on a higher plane and is more imperative. Emperor and God, State and divine rule are for Jesus two realities, belonging to two different orders, though not juxtaposed unrelatedly, and there is no question which of the two for him is the higher, incomparably higher. He leaves the secular and at that time the pagan State,

to argue that the doctrine here is one of "restoration". "Render" is used to emphasize the idea of indebtedness.

[11] R. Völkl, *Christ und Welt*, p. 113.

[12] See the discussion of recent literature in Kümmel, article in *Theologische Rundschau*.

its rights in its own sphere, but only to the extent that the all-embracing rights of God over man are not thereby violated. That implies a reservation in regard to the State, but there is no reservation in regard to God.

However, by taking into account the whole tenor of Christ's preaching, the ideas then current in Judaism, and the way in which Jesus' word of guidance was applied in the early Church, we can perhaps draw the following more concrete conclusions: 1. Jesus did not give the Roman Emperor the halo of rule by divine right, otherwise he could not have contrasted God and the Emperor in the way he did. But he did recognize the Emperor's rights and demanded obedience from his subjects. 2. The state, even the pagan state, has its importance in its own sphere and its provisions (for example, coinage) serve the common good. 3. By emphasizing man's duty to God as the higher, Jesus expresses reservations about the power of the state; it must not encroach on God's dignity, forbid worship of him, or contradict his commandments. 4. Jesus neither draws attention to, nor makes mock of, the limited and ephemeral nature of the state, but he is conscious of its dependence on God's will and power.

The last of these conclusions is confirmed by Jesus' openness in his personal relationship with those in civil power and authority. He administered an unconcealed rebuff to Herod Antipas, his ruler in Galilee, when Herod wanted to remove him from his realm by cunning (Luke 13:31ff.). By God's command he "must" do his messianic works in a definite space of time and could not allow himself to be disconcerted by anybody.[13] Still

---

[13] This is an essential difference between the Qumran community and Jesus or his disciples. See esp. K. Schubert, *Die Gemeinde vom Toten Meer,* 1958, p. 126; A. Vögtle, *Das öffentliche Wirken Jesu auf dem Hintergrund der Qumranbewegung,* 1958; F. M. Cross Jr., *The Ancient Library of Qumran,* 1958, pp. 54ff.; J. van der Ploeg, Eng. tr. *The Excavations at Qumran,* 1958, pp. 229ff.; R. Mayer and J. Reuss, *Die Qumranfunde und die Bibel,* 1959, pp. 148f.

more informative is Jesus' reply to Pilate at John 19:11: "Thou shouldest not have any power against me, unless it were given thee from above (that is, from God)".

This saying is generally interpreted as meaning that Jesus was here tracing the power of the state (in this instance, the Roman state) ultimately back to God. But exegesis of this kind, in the sense of Romans 13:1ff., is hardly acceptable. All Jesus wanted to explain to Pilate in the concrete situation was: I find myself in your power because it is my Father's will. Your threat cannot frighten me because I have consented to my Father's decision (cf. 14:30f.; 18:11). This emerges not only from the perspective of St. John's gospel as a whole, but also from the actual text, for "given thee from above" refers not to "power" (ἐξουσία, a feminine word), but is indefinite and neuter. According to the gospel of St. John, Jesus was aware that everything, including the very "hour" of his death (and glorification) was appointed for him by the Father (cf. 7:30; 8:20; 9:4; 13:1; 17:1); unless the Father so willed, no one could touch him (cf. also 8:59; 10:39). According to Luke 22:53 too, "the hour" of Jesus' enemies and "the power of darkness" began with his arrest. In this Pilate's rôle was not as active as that played by Jesus' Jewish enemies; their sin was therefore also greater, as Jesus goes on to say at John 19:11.[14]

It is instructive here to compare Jesus with Socrates, who although well aware of his innocence, did not flee, but drank the cup of poison. The Greek sage submitted so that the good order of the state might remain undisturbed; Jesus obeyed because he saw his Father's will in what was happening to him (cf. also Matt. 26:52–54; John 18:11). For him, God is higher than the state in two ways: God can demand absolutely more obedience than the state, and he can also take away from the state the power granted to it at any given time.

---

[14] See on the whole section H. von Campenhausen, "Zum Verständnis"; J. Blinzler, Der Prozess Jesu, 3rd ed. 1960, pp. 245ff.

There are many specific questions to which Jesus has given us no direct answers, for example, whether there is a permissible war and whether one may refuse military service. Both those opposed to all war on principle and those maintaining that national emergencies can arise in which the state must have recourse to arms and can demand obedience from its subjects, have appealed for support to the words of Jesus. Decisive texts are lacking on both sides, for Jesus spoke realistically about wars, but did not enunciate a principle. He called for pacific dispositions and love of enemies, but did not deal directly with the emergencies that may face a nation.[15] In this question as in others, it is left to the Church to make the relevant decision in accordance with the mind and guiding principles of Jesus. Instructive examples of such application of moral standards as well as of the attitude to the state and the powers of this world are to be found in the life of the early Church. (On the tension between Romans 13 and Acts 13, see section 26 below.)

§ 13. Jesus' Attitude to Work and Property

A. Steinmann, *Jesus und die soziale Frage,* 2nd ed. 1925; Herkenrath, *Ethik Jesu,* pp. 160–88; F. Hauck, *Die Stellung des Urchristentums zu Arbeit und Geld,* 1921; H. Greeven, *Das Hauptproblem der Sozialethik in der neueren Stoa und im Urchristentum,* 1935; K. Bornhäuser, *Der Christ und seine Habe nach dem Neuen Testament,* 1936; H. Holzapfel, *Die sittliche Wertung der körperlichen Arbeit im christlichen Altertum,* 1941; M. Dibelius, "Das soziale Motiv im Neuen Testament" in *Botschaft und Geschichte,* vol. I, 1953, pp. 178–203; F. Hauck, art. "Arbeit" in *RAC* vol. I, 585–90; H. Bolkestein and A. Kalsbach, art. "Armut" *ibid.,* 698–705; J. Schmid, *Evangelium nach Markus,* pp. 194–6; J. Leipoldt, *Der soziale Gedanke in*

---

[15] Apart from the monographs by W. Bienert (with many problematical points about Jesus) and J. Lasserve (who maintains that the idea of war is incompatible with the gospel), cf. also H. von Campenhausen "Der Kriegsdienst der Christen in der Kirche des Altertums" in *Offener Horizont* (Festschrift for Karl Jaspers) 1953, pp. 255–64; O. Bauernfeind in *ThWB* vol. VI, 512–15; R. Völkl, *Christ und Welt,* pp. 115f.

der altchristlichen Kirche, 1952; A. Richardson, *The Biblical Doctrine of Work,* 1953; E. Percy, *Die Botschaft Jesu,* pp. 89–106; A. Gelin, *Les Pauvres de Yahvé,* 1953; H. J. Kandler, "Die Bedeutung der Armut im Schrifttum vom Chirbet Qumran" in *Judaica* 13 (1957) pp. 193–209; E. Bammel, art. "πτωχός" in *ThWB* vol. VI, 885–915; R. Völkl, *Christ und Welt,* pp. 22–26, pp. 102–5.

JESUS no more intended to change the social system than he did the political order. He never assumed a definite attitude on economic and social problems. Only one thing is clear. In the period of his public ministry, he who had grown up himself in the circumscribed and poor circumstances of the small artisan (cf. Luke 2:24, where the sacrifice offered is that of the poor) and who, like Joseph, had worked as a carpenter (cf. Mark 6:3) kept a great love for simple people who earned their living by the labour of their hands. His parables show how closely he had observed them going about their various occupations: the peasant at his laborious task of farming (Mark 4:3f. par.; Luke 9:62), the labourer in the vineyard (Matt. 20:1–15), the fishermen at work hauling in the nets and sorting the fish (Matt. 13:47–50), as well as housewives at their daily tasks (Matt. 13:33 par.; Luke 15:8f. etc.), servants and household slaves (Luke 12:37f.; 17:7–10, etc.). Jesus shows us almost all the avocations found in his world, merchants and traders, builders, craftsmen, tax-gatherers, soldiers, kings and ministers, judges and physicians, farmers and stewards, peasants and herdsmen. He passes value judgements on none of them; he does not preach on their special duties of state, and does not construct a system of vocational morality. He found already existing among his people a high esteem, based on religion, for work, even physical labour, much stronger than was usually the case in the ancient world.[16] His eschatological mission did not lead him to think little of avocation and work. When he

---

[16] The opinion frequently heard in the past, that physical work was held in universally low esteem in antiquity, has been greatly modified partly through the results of recent research, and partly because we

called his disciples out of the circle of their former lives, he gave them the new avocation of being preachers of the gospel and "fishers of men" (Mark 1:17 par.) or "labourers in the harvest" of God (Luke 10:2 par.; John 4:38).

It was with this in view, not, as with the Cynics, for the sake of human and moral independence, that he required frugality of them (Mark 10:9f. par.). In order to be able to fulfil their apostolic tasks freely and without hindrance, they are to be magnanimous in giving and receiving. "For the workman is worthy of his meat" (Matt. 10:10 par.; cf. 1 Cor. 9:14) is a saying that confirms that Jesus saw the work of discipleship as a new avocation.

Jesus did not in any way attack the system of property. He made no attempt at all to share out the goods of this world more fairly. "The poor you have always with you" (Mark 14:7 par.) is the same realistic, illusion-free view of the world with which he accepted simply as a fact the despotism of the great. It implies neither sanction nor condemnation of economic and class differences; all that Jesus' wholly religious outlook completely excludes, by making love the supreme law, is mutual scorn and enmity, exploitation from above and hatred from below. But he made a unique contribution to what has been called the principal problem of social ethics in the ancient world, the overcoming of social differences, and made it possible for the Church in later times to draw concrete conclusions regarding the economic and social order. Whether they were all of a kind to stand the incorruptible scrutiny of her Lord who encompasses all men alike with divine love, is another question.

Here too there is a striking difference between Jesus and the Qumran community, for in the latter we find a real community

now have a better insight (thanks to the papyri) into the everyday life of ancient times. But it is difficult to draw an ethics of work from the fact of pride in work and attention to work. Cf. the literature on this subject, including Hauck. *Die Stellung des Urchristentums zu Arbeit und Geld,* pp. 38–62; Holzapfel, *Die sittliche Wertung,* pp. 15ff.

of possessions (cf. *1 QS* V, cf. section 1, 2). Full membership was only obtained after two years' novitiate and on the decision of the full congregation. "Then he shall be inscribed among his brethren in the order of his rank for the Torah, for justice, for purity and the sharing of his property . . ." (*1 QS* VI, 22.) The motive for the communal economy in which the differences between rich and poor were abolished was perhaps "an imitation of the form of life . . . which God introduces with the age to come,"[17] as well as a spirit of religious poverty of which traces are also evident in other Qumran writings (*Hymns* and the *War Rule*). There was also the need for a close, strict common life. In Qumran, too, the expression "the poor" meant more than poverty in external possessions. Behind it stands a spiritual and religious attitude, awareness of dependence on God, of guilt and need for redemption, but also of election and divine guidance (cf. the *Hymns*). In the *War Rule* we read, "Thou hast announced . . . to strike down Belial's hordes, the seven nations of vanity by the poor of thy redemption" (*1 QM* XI, 8f.). "The poor" becomes a title of honour and it is perhaps one of the community's own names for itself. In an exposition of Psalm 36, it is said regarding verse 11 ("but the meek shall inherit the land"), "its meaning applies to (all the) 'poor' who have accepted the time of penance", and on verse 22 ("and those whom he blesses will possess the land"), "Its interpretation refers to the community of the poor".[18] The similar application of Psalm 36 in Matthew 5:5 (cf. also verse 3, which is identical in meaning), is striking; but the form of life with work and property in common, the assembly into a "community of the poor", clearly distinguishes Qumran from Jesus' intention.

But did not Jesus direct his sharpest warnings against the rich, hurling his "woes" at them (Luke 6:24) and suggesting

[17] E. Bammel, in *ThWB* vol. VI, 898; cf. F. M. Cross Jr., *op. cit.* pp. 61f.
[18] *4 QpPs 37*:1, 8f.; II, 9f. translated by G. Vermes, *The Dead Sea Scrolls in English*, 1962, pp. 240ff.

that it was almost impossible (that is, only possible with the grace of God) for them to enter the kingdom of God (Mark 10:23 ff. par.)? Certainly these texts cannot be mitigated in any way, but the key to their interpretation is again to be found in Jesus' wholly religious outlook.

As soon as one applies economic standards, one finds oneself in a pathless thicket, for where does wealth begin? Moreover, one attributes inconsistency to Jesus himself, for he permitted himself to be the guest of rich men (Luke 7:36; 14:1), often accepted the hospitality of the well-to-do sisters at Bethania (Luke 10:38–42; John 11:1 ff.; 12:1 ff.) and the support of women of property (Luke 8:3), and drew from the enemies who hated him the cry that he was a glutton and a wine-bibber (Matt. 11:19 par.). He preserved this freedom of action, without any sort of "poor man's resentment", when it seemed helpful in his work. His sharp attacks on the rich receive qualification even from the religious point of view, for he certainly did not intend to exclude from the kingdom of God such people as Nicodemus and Joseph of Arimathea, Zacchaeus the rich publican (Luke 19:1–10) and those friends we have mentioned who supported him. Consequently it cannot be the possession of property as such that is the obstacle, but only wealth that is becoming an idol.

But it is inadmissible to try to make the evangelist Luke alone responsible for Jesus' disowning of the rich on religious grounds, at least in its sharpest form. There is no clearer saying than that recorded by Matthew also, "You cannot serve God and mammon" (Matt. 6:24 = Luke 16:13). This dictum, linked as it is with the image of the household slave who can only serve one lord, presents a dilemma and demands that a choice be made. Mammon, or more correctly *mamon,* means "property", what has monetary value; but in later Judaism it generally also had the pejorative sense of "wealth gained unjustly" (cf. Luke 16:9). Jesus, however, probably did not mean to say that one should reject only dishonest profit but was rather of the opinion, widely current at that time, that injustice is very often involved in the acquisition of wealth, as Luke 16:9 shows.[19]

Jesus' view is well expressed in the text: "And the cares of the world and the deceitfulness of riches and the lusts after other things entering in choke the word; and it is made fruitless" (Mark 4:19). There is an alluring fascination in riches, as there is in power, which a man is too weak to withstand on his own (cf. Mark 10:27 par.). Consequently, the other minimizing interpretation is also excluded, according to which Jesus only demanded that we should free ourselves inwardly from the ensnaring power of wealth. This is not supported by any texts,[20] although there are plenty of others which demand the actual giving away of property, or renunciation of the acquisition of wealth.

In addition to the instructions to the disciples (according to which they, who are going to follow Jesus perfectly, are to leave everything; cf. §4), the warning not to accumulate treasures in this world, but rather with God (Matt. 6:19f. = Luke 12:33), also belongs in this context, as well as the declaration, "For what shall it profit a man if he gain the whole world and suffer the loss of his soul" (Mark 8:36 par.), the parable of the rich fool (Luke 12:16–21) and lastly, at least with the Lucan addition at the end (12:21), the warning against cupidity (Luke 12:15).

Jesus must, therefore, have been closely associated with the idea of poverty and of religious poverty. He regarded poverty as freedom for God and as a condition for the undivided

---

[19] Cf. F. Hauck in *ThWB* vol. IV, 390–2. For the expression "mammon of iniquity" see *Ethiopian Enoch Book* 63:10. Compare "mammon of dishonesty" in the Targumim (Billerbeck, vol. II, p. 220). See also *1 QS* X:19 "My soul shall not desire the riches of violence (hon hamas)"; *Damascus Rule* VI:15 "They shall keep away from the unclean riches of wickedness."

[20] The warning against avarice at Luke 12:15 is directed against the amassing of new wealth. Although avarice is condemned as a sin of the heart and one of the roots of evil in the list of vices at Mark 7:22, that is not to say that nothing counts but intention.

dedication to God, to which in particular the preacher of the gospel is called. But he made of the demand for poverty neither a social programme nor a "law" for all to whom his message was addressed. Voluntary renunciation of earthly possessions remains a special call addressed to the individual and so preserves the character of a "counsel" (see section 4).

The theme of wealth and poverty is undeniably given an especially important place in the gospel according to St. Luke. The question arises whether this evangelist displays a special bias towards "Ebionism", that is, whether he regarded poverty itself as something pleasing to God and was promising the poor, starving in this life, a compensation after death or in the future aeon.[21]

It has been said of Luke that he flagrantly intensified Jesus' sayings against the rich and riches. Careful comparison of the traditional material common to the different evangelists makes it clear, however, that this was the case in only a few places. When treating of the call of the disciples, he generalizes, saying "they left *all things*" (5:11, 28). On the mission of the disciples, according to him, the disciples were not allowed to take anything at all with them (9:3; 10:4), not even a staff or sandals (as against Mark 6:8f.; yet agreeing with Matt. 10:10). In the material which he shares only with Matthew he demands at 12:33, in addition to what Matthew mentions, the sale of property and its distribution as alms – noteworthy for the concept of almsgiving – and in the Sermon on the Mount (6:34f.) he clearly expresses the duty of lending without asking any return and in the parable of the great feast he specifies that the guests invited in the second instance were the poor, the crippled, the blind and the lame (14:21 – the same list as at 14:13). The blessing of the poor, contrasting as it does with the "woes" against the rich, may well be original material (see below).

---

[21] Percy, *Die Botschaft Jesu,* makes great use of this tendency, sometimes even exaggerating it. Thus on p. 105 he says, "Inheritance and possession are irreconcilable with participation in the kingdom of God", and refers the Ebionism said to be traceable in Luke to Jesus himself (p. 106).

But Luke also introduces a great deal of original material on this theme. Thus as early as the infancy narrative there are traits that characterize Jesus' earthly origin as poverty-stricken (1:52f.; 2:7 and 24). Among his discourses and parables we must mention 12:15-21;14:12-14 and 33, (where renunciation of all possessions is declared necessary for every disciple of Jesus), and especially chapter 16, which not only in the main includes special material but is also systematically constructed so as to bear on this theme. Hesitation about the genuineness of this special tradition in Luke, the great compiler, is not justified; at most, the linking of a number of the sayings and parables is his.

That in the Beatitude at Luke 6:20, Jesus meant actually poor people and not "poor" in the metaphorical sense, namely "just", those who, as in many psalms and later Jewish writings acknowledge themselves poor and wretched in the sight of God, cannot be doubted, either, in the light of the Beatitudes that follow, which certainly hold good of those actually afflicted by want and suffering, or in the light of the precisely parallel "woes". In the parable at Luke 18:19ff. the subject is a really poor, bitterly afflicted man who after his death is taken to Abraham's bosom (that is, into blessed company at table with the patriarchs). What gives offence to some in both the "woes" and the parable is the motive of "class warfare" against the rich: they have received their reward (6:24) or as Abraham reminded the rich glutton, "Son, remember that thou didst receive good things in thy lifetime, and likewise Lazarus evil things; but now he is comforted and thou art tormented" (16:25). Yet there is no room here for modern ideas on this question. The form of this story was clearly determined by Jewish concepts of retribution. It is certainly assumed without question that the poor who are addressed also had a moral character fitting them to enter the kingdom of God. A purely economic, materialistic outlook was alien to Judaism: a godless poor man would never have a place in the future aeon merely because of his poverty. Jesus denied it more clearly still when he made fulfilment of the will of God the condition for entering the kingdom of God (Luke 6:46 = Matt. 7:21). The parable of the rich glutton and the poor man Lazarus is also probably dealing with material familiar to Jesus' hearers in a similar form, in which a godless rich man was contrasted with a pious poor man.[22]

The Blessings and Woes in Luke 6:20-6, however, in comparison with the Beatitudes in Matthew 5:3-12, pose the question what the original words and meaning were on Jesus' lips. If the tradition common to Matthew and Luke can only be reconstructed to a certain extent (cf. the work by J. Dupont), it is nevertheless possible to say that Matthew lays all the emphasis on the religious and moral attitude of those who are declared blessed and to whom the kingdom of God and its gifts are promised, while Luke on the other hand stresses the social and earthly position of those addressed. When Matthew has in addition to "poor", the words "in spirit", and to "hungering and thirsting" the words "after justice", his tendency is clear; the further Beatitudes, which are only found in him, concerning the merciful, the clean of heart and the peace-makers emphasize the Matthean interpretation. For the "poor in spirit" there is now another parallel in the *War Rule* of Qumran (*1 QM* XIV, 17). These writings in general, as has been said, are filled with a deep spirit of religious poverty; a single significant passage may be quoted: "With the humble (*'anawim*) [thou art] when their feet sink, with those who are cast down for the sake of righteousness in order to raise up from the turmoil all the poor of grace (*'ebyonei hesed*)" (*1 QH* V, 21f.). Here the "poor" are human beings eager for redemption, who

---

[22] A story similar to that in Luke 16:19ff. is known from Egyptian sources; cf. H. Gressmann, *Vom reichen Mann und armen Lazarus* (Conference-report, Berlin, 1918); for the oldest Jewish version see Billerbeck, vol. II, pp. 231f. Cf. with this T. W. Manson, *Sayings*, pp. 296ff.; J. Jeremias, *Parables*, pp. 182-7; Percy, *Botschaft Jesu*, pp. 93ff.; W. Pesch, *Der Lohngedanke in der Lehre Jesu*, 1955, pp. 6f., 22-4.

are oppressed in this world but who are also inwardly distressed and expect salvation from God alone. This religious poverty has a history that goes back into the Old Testament,[23] and Jesus certainly made reference to this religious conception of "the poor". That is shown above all by his appeal to Isaisas 61:1. He is sent "to preach the gospel to the poor" (Luke 4:18; cf. Matt. 11:5 = Luke 7:22). Consequently, the different version of the Beatitude in Matthew 5:3 and Luke 6:20 must be understood as due to the fact that the two evangelists have interpreted in a special sense in the service of the paraenesis of the early Church, Jesus' originally Messianic call addressed to all men willing for redemption, Matthew more with a view to the religious and moral attitude, Luke socially in regard to the actually poor and needy, but likewise presupposing the corresponding religious disposition.[24] Matthew's expression might perhaps best be rendered "salvation to those who possess the spirit of poverty".[25]

St. Luke, of course, did not falsify in any way the attitude taken by Jesus, but he did strongly underline it in his own manner. A classical example of this is his exegesis of the parable of the unfaithful steward (16:1–7) where he includes a saying which is only extrinsically connected with the material of the parable itself.[26] In the same way the parable of the rich fool (12:16–20)

[23] Cf. A. Causse, *Les pauvres d'Israel*, 1922; W. Satter, "Die Anawim im Zeitalter Jesu Christi" in *Festschrift for A. Jülicher*, 1927, pp. 1–15, H. Birkeland, *'Ani und 'Anaw in den Psalmen*, 1932; A. Kuschke, "Arm und reich im AT mit besonderen Berücksichtigungen der nachexilischen Zeit" in *ZAW* 57 (1939) pp. 31–57; J. van der Ploeg, "Les pauvres d'Israël et leur piété" in *OTS* 7 (1950) pp. 236–70; Percy, *Botschaft Jesu*, pp. 45–81 (who doubts, wrongly, that "poor" also had a metaphysical meaning); A. Gelin, *Les Pauvres de Yahvé* (Bibliog.).

[24] Cf. J. Dupont, *Les Béatitudes*, pp. 217, 293, 297.

[25] J. Schmitt in *RevSR* 30 (1956) p. 269. Yet the addition ἐν πνεύματι "in spirit" is certainly Matthew's, though this is not Schmitt's opinion.

[26] With v. 9, cf. v. 4; in the parable the disloyal steward's aim is that the former debtors should receive him in their homes; but in v. 9, the

was perhaps originally an eschatological crisis parable which he interpreted as referring especially to the egotistical amassing of worldly treasures and thus applied differently, for his hortatory purpose (12:21).[27] So too the accusation made against the Pharisees, that they were greedy for money, must be laid to his account, although a similar reproach made by Jesus, that they devoured the goods of widows, is to be found at Mark 12:40 (Luke 20:47). We should perhaps look for the reason for this attitude of the third evangelist in his own personal piety, and especially in his close contact with certain circles in the original Jerusalem community who were in fact poor and may have called themselves "the poor", meaning it in the religious sense (cf. Rom. 15:26; Gal. 2:10). He does, in fact, describe with warm approval the community of goods practised among the first Christians (Acts 2:44f.; 4:32; 5:1-11; see below, sections 19 and 23). It is scarcely probable that he was moved to extol poverty (and still less to practise it) by certain currents in contemporary pagan hellenistic philosophy.[28]

For the Epistle of St. James, see section 39 below.

The early Christian sect of the Ebionites (the "poor") specially cultivated and developed the ideal of religious poverty. They clearly felt themselves to be the legitimate successors of the

---

plural conceals God, who receives men into everlasting mansions (the same kind of plural may be seen at Luke 6:38; 12:20). Cf. D. Buzy, *Les paraboles*, p. 692, "Verse 9 is not part of the parable; all it has in common with it is a noticeable similarity of situation and style. But, in fact, it belongs to a different group of teachings about wealth. "See also Schmid, *Das Evangelium nach Lukas*. Against this M. Kramer tries to demonstrate a closer connexion between verse 9 and the parable in *VD* 38 (1960) pp. 278-86.

[27] Cf. J. Jeremias, *Parables*, pp. 164f. (Verse 21 is not relevant to the point of the parable, and so is a genuine fragment, but from a conversation that does not belong to the parable, Buzy, *Les paraboles*, p. 667).

[28] So too Hauck, *Die Stellung des Urchristentums zu Arbeit und Geld*, pp. 83-98; Greeven, *Das Hauptproblem*, p. 92. Cf. also H. Zimmermann in *BZ* 5 (1961) pp. 81f.

original Jerusalem community. It is hardly because of their ideas about poverty that they became heretical, but rather because they held fast to the Jewish law. The frequently quoted saying current among them "Wealth is sin" (κτήματα ἁμαρτήματα Ps.-Clement, *Hom.* 15, 9) is shown by the context to mean that what is sinful is not wealth itself, but the avarice bound up with it.[29] Although it became heretical, this group did at any rate take seriously a serious concern of Jesus, which in the official Church was sometimes overlooked or re-interpreted.

§ 14. JESUS' ATTITUDE TO MARRIAGE AND THE FAMILY

Steinmann and Greeven, see section 13. J. Fischer, *Ehe und Jungfräulichkeit im Neuen Testament,* 1919; Herkenrath, *Ethik Jesu,* pp. 188 ff.; H. Preisker, *Christentum und Ehe in den ersten drei Jahrhunderten,* 1927; E. Stauffer, art. "γαμέω" in *ThWB* vol. I, 646–55; A. Oepke, art. "γυνή" *ibid.* 776–90; F. Vogt, *Das Ehegesetz Jesu,* 1936; A. Ott, *Die Ehescheidung im Matthäus,* 1939; K. Staab, "Die Unauflöslichkeit der Ehe und die Ehebruchklauseln" in *Festschrift für E. Eichmann,* 1940, pp. 432–52; F. Büchsel, "Die Ehe im Urchristentum" in *TB* 21 (1942) pp. 113–28; J. Sickenberger, "Die Unzuchtsklausel im Matthäus" in *TQ* 123 (1942) pp. 189–206; U. Holzmeister, "Die Streitfrage über die Ehescheidungstexte bei Matthäus 5:32; 19:9" in *Biblica* 26 (1945) pp. 133–46; J. Bonsirven, *Le divorce dans le Nouveau Testament,* 1948; P. Kletter, *Christus und die Frauen,* 2 vols., 1949–50; F. J. Leenhardt and F. Blanke, *Die Stellung der Frau im Neuen Testament und in der alten Kirche,* 1949; A. Oepke, art. "παῖς" in *ThWB* vol. V, 636–50; J. Leipoldt, *Die Frau in der antiken Welt und im Urchristentum,* 1954; G. Delling, "Das Logion Markus 10:11 (und seine Abwandlungen) im Neuen Testament" in *NovT* 1 (1956) pp. 263–74; F. Hauck and S. Schulz, art. "πόρνη" in *ThWB* vol. VI, 579–95; J. Dupont, *Mariage et divorce dans l'Évangile,* 1959.

THE FOUNDATION of holy and happy marriage and family life is reverence for the dignity of women. What was Jesus' attitude

[29] Cf. H. J. Schoeps, *Theologie und Geschichte des Judenchristentums,* 1949, pp. 196 ff.

to women? He did not undertake to make changes in their legal status, which in the Old Testament and Judaism was far from being one of equality of rights, but his actual behaviour bears witness to high esteem, serious evaluation of their religious aspirations, and delicate tact, rarely encountered in later Judaism.[30] There is also his love, as their saviour, for sinners and prostitutes (Luke 7:36–50; John 7:53–8,11; Matt. 21:31f.), which was totally incomprehensible from the point of view of the Pharisees. But when it seemed necessary to him for his work as Messias, Jesus even overstepped the bounds of Jewish custom and outlook in his dealings with women. He spoke to the Samaritan woman at Jacob's Well, though to do so was considered unseemly for a man and especially for a rabbi (John 4:27).[31] He allowed himself to be touched by the woman with an issue of blood, though that made him ritually unclean (Mark 5:27–34 par.). For the sake of a poor, bent woman "whom Satan hath bound these eighteen years" he broke the Sabbath in order to free this "daughter of Abraham" (a title of honour not often recorded) from the evil besetting her (Luke 13:10–17). He performed a strikingly large number of miracles of healing women (in addition to the above, Simon Peter's mother-in-law, Mark 1:29–31 par.; Jairus' daughter, Mark 5:21 to 43 par.; the daughter of the Syro-Phoenician woman, Mark 7:24–30 par.; Mary of Magdala, Luke 8:2). The sorrow of the widow of Naim moved him to sympathy (Luke 7:13); he did not refuse the request of the Syro-Phoenician woman (Mark 7:28f.). He praised and called attention to the great spirit of sacrifice of the widow who threw her mite into the temple treasury (Mark 12:41–44 par.). He defended the act

[30] Billerbeck (vol. III, pp. 610–13) has compiled a collection of both good and bad judgements on women in Judaism; cf. also the index. The opinion of women held in antiquity generally cannot (even if the final judgement we make is unfavourable) be expressed in a few words; cf. the books on this subject (Preisker, Greeven).

[31] Cf. Billerbeck, vol. II, p. 438; Moore, *Judaism*, vol. II, pp. 269f.

that Mary of Bethania performed for love, anointing his head and his feet (Mark 14:3–8 par.; John 12:1–8). He allowed women among his following and accepted the help they gave (Luke 8:2f.), visited the family at Bethania, and wished both sisters to listen to what he had to say (Luke 10:38). On the way of the Cross he instructed the grieving women (Luke 23:27–31). Even his conversation with the Samaritan woman shows him primarily (at least in the mind of the evangelist), not as a master of spiritual direction but as a preacher of revelation. St. John's account is directly concerned not with the woman's moral conversion but rather with her faith and Jesus gladly allows this woman to help him to make the fields ripe for harvest in Samaria also (vv. 28 ff.). The conversation with Martha (John 11:20–27) is another act of lofty self-revelation on the part of the Johannine Christ. The same evangelist tells of the appearance of the Risen Lord to Mary Magdalene, who becomes his messenger, the first to bring to his brethren the news of his ascent to the Father (20:11–18).[32] The only conclusion to be drawn from all this is that Jesus did not differentiate in his preaching between men and women; women were to hear the word of God, experience messianic salvation and participate in the future kingdom of God in complete equality with men. Then, after the general resurrection, sexual differences will become meaningless, for marriage and giving in marriage will come to an end (Mark 12:25 par.). The religious equality of rights recognized by Jesus for women and given expression by him in practice, this equality of dignity in the sight of God, was bound in the long run to exert a deeper influence and be more conducive to the raising of the dignity of women than

---

[32] On Mary Magdalene, who cannot be identified with the unnamed sinner (Luke 7:36–50) or with Mary from Bethany, cf. P. Ketter, *Die Magdalenenfrage*, 1929; on the report of the appearance of the risen Lord to Mary Magdalene, see P. Benoit "Marie–Madeleine et les disciples au tombeau selon Jean 20:1–18" in *Judentum, Urchristentum, Kirche* (Festschrift for J. Jeremias) 1960, pp. 141–52.

any particular social reforms could have done. Above all, by his attitude, Jesus saved women from being thought of as merely sexual beings, honouring them as human beings, persons, children of God.

Of great significance for the status of women and for marriage and family life was Jesus' decree that according to the will of God originally marriage was indissoluble, and was now obligatorily so again. Already in the Sermon on the Mount there are sharp words against adultery (even that simply committed in the heart by desire), and also against all divorce. But he also took up a definite position on this question in a discussion recorded by Mark 10:2-12 and Matthew 19:3-9.

We need not discuss here all the minute differences between these two accounts: they originate mainly from the different wording of the question put to him by the Pharisees "tempting him", to trap him. According to Mark, "Is it lawful for a man to put away his wife?" and according to Matthew, "Is it lawful for a man to put away his wife for every cause?" (that is, "for any cause?"). Which form of words is the original historical one it is difficult to say. On grounds of the historical background of the age, one would like to follow Matthew, for the problem of grounds for divorce was a well-known point of controversy between the schools of Hillel and Shammai. The gentler and in this instance laxer Hillel expounded the debatable expression "for some uncleanness" at Deut. 24:1 (*'erwath dabhar*) in such a way that anything the husband disapproved of (letting the food burn, for example) could be a ground for divorce; the stricter Shammai would accept only something morally shameful, namely, a sin against chastity.[33] On the other hand it is equally possible to maintain, in favour of the presentation in Mark, that a question concerning grounds for divorce did not represent a trap at all, for Jesus would not have involved himself in any charge, whether he adhered to the views of Hillel

[33] Cf. Billerbeck, vol. I, pp. 312ff.

which were then dominant, or those of Shammai. Clearly the intention was to try to bring Jesus to the point of contradicting Moses, but, in fact, the way the conversation went left Jesus annulling the right to divorce granted by Moses, though, of course without attacking Moses himself; Whatever one's judgement about the starting-point, there can be no doubt about Jesus' decision itself.[34]

Jesus brought two earlier scriptural passages (Gen. 1:27; 2:24) into the field against the Mosaic dispensation allowing a bill of divorce to be made out and the woman sent away (Deut. 24:1). From them he argued that the primordial will of God at the beginning of creation intended the indissolubility of marriage. Moses' "commandment" was given only because of the "hardness of heart" of the Jews, and now the order established at the creation is once again to prevail, so Jesus announces in God's name, "What therefore God hath joined together, let not man put asunder."

By the reference back to the texts in Genesis, woman is assigned equality of dignity with man. "Male and female he created them"; "And they shall be two in one flesh." The husband leaves the community of his family in which he has lived hitherto ("leaves father and mother") and forms with his wife a new community. The two become so completely one that they can never again be separated; such is the conclusion Jesus expressly draws from the Scriptural text, the proof follows precisely from this oneness of husband and wife.

What Jesus said is so unequivocal that it is possible to avoid its binding force only by interpreting his moral mission as a whole as not literally binding or by emptying it of force in some other way. Yet many have claimed to find a basis for making an exception in the text of the New Testament itself,

[34] Cf. on this pericope J. Schmid in *Synoptische Studien* (Festschrift for A. Wikenhauser) 1954, pp. 177–82. (That the report in Mark is of an earlier literary date, but that that in Matthew has probably correctly reproduced the historical questioning.)

in the much-quoted "fornication clause" at Matthew 5:32 and 19:9.

These two texts read, "whosoever shall put away his wife, excepting for the cause of fornication, maketh her to commit adultery; and he that shall marry her that is put away committeth adultery" (Matt. 5:32),[35] and "whosoever shall put away his wife, except it be for fornication, and shall marry another, committeth adultery; and he that shall marry her that is put away committeth adultery" (19:9). The parallel to 19:9 at Mark 10:11 is exactly similar but without the fornication clause; but then Mark does, in fact, continue in v. 12 with the case corresponding more to Roman law, when the wife leaves her husband and marries again. There is a parallel to Matthew 5:32 at Luke 16:18: here too the double case is cited, the husband leaving his wife and the wife her husband, but the form of words is different. And the fornication clause, too, is lacking.

How is this clause to be interpreted? The problem is so difficult and involved that we cannot discuss it fully here. Moreover, none of the explanations hitherto suggested is completely acceptable. However, it is possible to note the following. These additions found only in Matthew, cannot nullify or relax Jesus' fundamental and universal prohibition of divorce. 1. This is clear from the meaning of the context of the two texts. In the Sermon on the Mount (5:32), Jesus' purpose was to go beyond the law as it had been, and replace it with a new commandment from God. If Jesus had actually accepted unchastity (adultery) as an exception, he would have been going scarcely any further than Shammai. But in the discussion, too (Matt. 19:1) we find the sentence "What therefore God has

---

[35] As far as the translation is concerned, the Greek expression used can hardly be said to represent 'erwath dabar (the shame of a thing) at Deut. 24:1, for the governing noun has disappeared (cf. Lagrange on this text). The Greek λόγος can mean both the object and the ground, reason. Bauer, Wörterbuch, 946, tends more towards the second possibility.

joined together, let not men put asunder", in its absolute form, and Jesus simply goes on to draw the conclusion from it. 2. Mark and Luke know nothing of this exception. It is hardly conceivable that they would have omitted so important a pronouncement. 3. 1 Corinthians 7:10f., the earliest interpretation of our Lord's words (which were also known to St. Paul), bears witness to the absolute prohibition of divorce, although v. 11 does acknowledge the possibility of separation without divorce. The conclusion drawn by Protestants and Orthodox from the clause, that in Jesus' mind adultery was a true exception is therefore untenable. (Modern Protestant theologians are coming to concur in this judgement.)

Among attempts at a solution,[36] the following have been influential and may be noted. 1. The suggestion of many Protestant scholars that Matthew inserted the clause to meet a situation arising in the later community (particularly among Jewish Christians) and from the law introduced by the Church. That is, it is interpreted as authentic from the literary point of view but historically unauthentic. Thus any ground is removed for the hypothesis that there is here a real exception of Jesus' forbidding of divorce. We do not know if divorce (and remarriage) was allowed among the Jewish Christians because of the wife's infidelity, and in view of 1 Corinthians 7:10f. it is most improbable. Catholic scholars too understand it as an explanatory insertion by the evangelist for his readers, though one which does not give the possibility of a second marriage but rather deals with a special case. In practice the remark provides for separation without remarriage (see 4. below).[37] 2. The "inclusive"

---

[36] Cf. the surveys and reviews in A. Ott, *Die Auslegung der neutestamentlichen Texte über die Ehescheidung,* 1911; J. Schmid in *Theologische Rundschau* 39 (1940) pp. 56ff.; Holzmeister, "Die Streitfrage"; Bonsirven, *Le divorce,* pp. 38ff.; J. Dupont, *Mariage et divorce, passim.*

[37] F. Neirguck, "Het evangelisch echtscheidingsverbod" in *Collationes Brugenses* 4 (1958) pp. 25–46; A. Descamps in *Studia Evangelica,* 1959, pp. 165f.; J. Dupont, *op. cit,* pp. 81–92, J. Michel in *LThK* vol. III, 679.

interpretation explains the two additional phrases not as exceptions but as special examples of the application of the commandment, as relatively unimportant parentheses. The text then reads "Whosoever shall put away his wife – leaving aside entirely the question of unchastity . . ." (5:32); "I am not speaking now of divorce – in the case of unchastity . . ." (19:9). Thereby Jesus would have clearly indicated his awareness of the controversy, whilst leaving this case firmly on one side and, as it were, setting it apart in parentheses . . . . But if so, he would have been ignoring the most important source of difficulty and his ruling would be valueless. On the other hand, however, some maintain that it was Jesus' intention explicitly to include the question of unchastity ("even for unchastity" could be expressed in Greek in a negative sentence with this particular participle). But it is hardly possible linguistically (for it would have to mean "not even in the case of . . ."). [38] 3. Then there is the view that this clause deals with an exception relating to the times in which it was made and intended for the Jews of those times; that fundamentally Jesus promulgated an absolute prohibition of divorce, but for his Jewish hearers, (some of whom may have contracted second marriages after divorce) he allowed an exception in practice, following Shammai. But given the tenor of Jesus' absolute demands, this is extremely improbable, and, furthermore, it is not indicated in the text. Moreover, the clause looks like a Matthean addition; it is hardly likely to have been left out by Mark and Luke for the benefit of their Gentile readers (as comparison of the synoptic gospels shows, Mark is from the literary point of view here primary as compared with Matthew). 4. Divorce here might mean "separation from bed and board". This has been the "classical" solution since the time of St. Jerome. The most cautious proof of this view, following precisely the tenets of Jewish law and the form of words used by Matthew, runs somewhat as follows. In Jewish law, the husband bore the

---

[38] Cf. Sickenberger, "Die Unzuchtsklausel", pp. 198f.

responsibility for dismissal and was bound to prepare a bill of divorce. But in Jesus' opinion, if he sent his wife away, he drove her into adultery (into breaking the bond of her first, still existing marriage, unless she has already broken the bond of matrimony, in which case she herself bears the responsibility and is already an adulteress (5:32). At 19:9, the position of the insertion after "putting away", but before remarriage, shows that he did allow separation for unchastity, but not a second marriage. Thus what Jesus primarily was doing was to insist on the moral responsibility of the husband, whilst indirectly countenancing mere separation in the case of adultery. This view can find historical support at 1 Corinthians 7:11, where such a practice is presupposed. But the greatest difficulty in accepting it arises from the fact that mere separation with prohibition of remarriage was unknown among the Jews, so that if Jesus was advocating it, he could scarcely have been understood by those listening to him. 5. The interpretation (favoured by Bonsirven) that "fornication" refers to illegal marriages. Bonsirven's theory – linguistically and conceptually unobjectionable (for the word is fornication and not adultery: the Greek word πορνεία can be used of forbidden, invalid marriages, as indeed it is at Acts 15:20 and 29; 21:25; Heb. 12:16) – sees the exception as expressly made by Jesus himself and, following him, by St. Matthew, the Jewish Christian, and as being the marriages forbidden to the Jews (zenuth), in which no valid marriage took place. This explanation, though very attractive in itself, encounters two difficulties. Πορνεία can have this meaning, but usually it has the general meaning "unchastity", on the part of married people, therefore, adultery (although indeed the special expression μοιχεία was used of this). But above all it would make Jesus appear to be saying something self-evident: that a marriage not legally valid can be dissolved. That would seem too obvious to need especial mention.[39]

[39] For a commentary see Dupont, *op. cit*, pp. 107–14.

The "classical solution" is perhaps still the most acceptable, particularly if one may postulate that in some measure Matthew also had in mind the conditions found in the later community; in other words that the unchastity clause was added by him.[40] Jesus may have given indications (cf. 1 Cor. 1:10f.) which the evangelist brought out more clearly. Nevertheless, as we have said, difficulties still remain.

In any case Jesus emphasized most strongly the moral responsibility of married people and, in the conditions then existing, especially that of the husband, and restored marriage to what it should be according to the will of God at the creation, the source and centre of a holy and happy family life in which the married couple and their children serve God with equal dignity and mutual love.

Jesus' high esteem for family life is confirmed by the scene of the children which follows the dispute concerning divorce (Mark 10:13–16 par.). In Jesus' nation children were held in a certain regard (they were not transgressors of the law). There are sayings of rabbis that point out children's moral innocence and pleasingness to God, and people were convinced that children would have a place in the world to come.[41] To the early Church, the scene in which Jesus caressed children, blessed them and said two wonderful things about their sharing in the kingdom of God and about their disposition, was more than a mere episode. It gave children an unchallenged place in the life of the community.

The arrangement of the pericopes here is not a random one. In this section various important pronouncements by Jesus on the problems of social life in the widest sense are assembled: his attitude to marriage (Mark 10:1–12), to children (10:13–16), to earthly possessions (10:17–31), to authority and power

[40] For this view see Dupont, *op. cit.*, pp. 136–57.
[41] Cf. the sayings in Billerbeck, vol. I, pp. 780f. and 786. Further in Oepke, art. "παῖς" in *ThWB* vol. V, 644–49.

141

(10:34–45). In a very large measure the other two synoptics have followed Mark.

All this excludes any depreciation of marriage and family, even in relation to the very essence of the religious life; the early Church did not separate the "natural" and supernatural domain. Furthermore, Jesus also inculcated reverence and care for parents through Mark 10:7–13 par., and also by emphasizing the fourth commandment in his reply to the rich young man (Mark 10:19 par.).[42]

There are admittedly a series of sayings by Jesus which seem to contradict this. Above all, some have been shocked by his own apparently cold attitude towards the members of his own family. When his mother and his "brethren" wanted to speak with him while he was instructing the people crowded round him, he said, "Who is my mother and my brethren?" He looked at those seated round him and said: "Behold my mother and my brethren. For whosoever shall do the will of God, he is my brother and sister and mother" (Mark 3:31–35 par.). He even corrected a woman in the crowd who blessed his mother, saying, "Yea, rather, blessed are they who hear the word of God and keep it" (Luke 11:27). For his own part Jesus had, in fact, cut the bond which had united him for thirty years with Mary and Joseph in family life in Nazareth. Joseph had probably already died; but his mother must have felt rejected to some degree at the marriage at Cana (John 2:4). Yet precisely here it is possible to discern the underlying motive for Jesus' behaviour: his messianic consciousness, his exclusive attachment to his Father's will. That Jesus had not abandoned filial love and care for his mother is proved by his "testament" from the cross (John 19:26). As regards his "brethren", another motive comes into play here; at the time of his public ministry they did not believe in him (John 7:5).

---

[42] The order of the commandments is striking: first the fifth to tenth, and then the fourth. Probably it is intended to present a movement from the negative to the positive commandments.

There is only one interpretation of these sayings: when the Messias gathers his community around him, this is his family and to it all his care and work belongs.

Abandonment of the natural tie of blood-relationship was, however, also demanded by Jesus of his disciples in the narrower sense, those who preach the message of salvation and continue his work. This is the only possible interpretation of the harsh sayings which seem to wound both natural sensibilities and propriety (cf. Luke 9:60; 14:26 par.). For these followers of Jesus the spiritual community of the faithful, the community they serve, replaces the natural community of blood (cf. also Mark 10:29f. par.).

Finally there are sayings of Jesus that even envisage dissensions arising in families on his account (Matt. 10:34f.; Luke 12:51f.; Mark 13:12par.). These are revelations relating to the last terrible epoch, and repeat old apocalyptic prophecies (Mich. 7:6; cf. *Jubilees* 23; 16, 19 etc.). This dissolution of the divinely established order of things is the sign of the disruption of the world before the end. But from the way in which Jesus speaks of them, it is clear that he regarded them as exceptional, in fact, as trials in the eschatological tribulation for disciples and faithful.

Although marriage and family life end with this world, they are nevertheless important for the future kingdom of God. Even in this sphere the Christian must preserve his obedience to the words of Jesus, his single-minded service of God and his self-sacrificing love.

Chapter Five

THE MOTIVES THAT JESUS GAVE FOR HIS DEMANDS

§ 15. THE PRINCIPAL MOTIVE: THE KINGDOM OF GOD AND ITS BLESSINGS

See bibliography to section 1; also Herkenrath, *Ethik Jesu*, pp. 226 ff.; J. Jeremias, *Jesus als Weltvollender*, 1930; G. Dalman, *Die Worte Jesu*, pp. 75–146, Eng. tr. *The Words of Jesus*, 1902; J. Theissing, *Die Lehre Jesu von der ewigen Seligkeit*, 1940; Tillmann, *Idee der Nachfolge Christi*, pp. 241 ff.; Völkl, *Christ und Welt*, pp. 138–53.

SINCE the motive of an act, as well as its object, decisively contributes to determine its moral quality, we must now consider the motives which Jesus gave for his demands. A single unitary principle, something like the categorical imperative of Kant, for example, is as little to be found, of course, as any deliberate reflection on the importance of motive.

This is what we should expect from Jesus' prophetic style of preaching, with its predilection for metaphorical language, sharp, polished aphorisms, the hyperbole and the *mashal* (parable) in its many forms; and we find it confirmed when we take into account the motives which are presented simultaneously with his precepts. Hence the word "motive" here cannot be taken in a strictly delimited sense. Jesus' purpose was to move those who heard him to adopt a particular way of life and form of activity, hence "motive" here must include everything he brought to their attention to move their hearts. Hence too we cannot narrowly restrict our interest to the actual words Jesus used, but must look into his deeper purpose and aim. If we were to measure his utterances by purely formal standards, we should find we were compelled to accord a very large place in his moral teaching to the motive of retribution, to the concepts of reward and punishment; but as will become clear below, to do so would be to miss his real intention.

For the same reason, however, we must reject any attempt to show that Jesus' moral teaching was generally and without exception concerned to serve "the highest of motives", that is, the doing of good for its own sake or rather, for God's sake. In fact it is very difficult to trace this motive among those he mentions, yet the basic attitude of anyone who accepts his message will lead him continually away from selfish motives of every kind and towards loving self-surrender to God. In Jesus' sayings the holy will of God can readily be identified as the highest standard, but scarcely as the highest motive (Herkenrath) for action.

In this respect too Jesus was not so much a theoretical thinker as a practical teacher and educator. Realistically, he accepts man with all his striving and desires, deliberately taking as his starting point the religious and moral ideas current among his contemporaries, seeking to catch the interest of his hearers as they were, with all their narrowness and poverty, and yet all their openheartedness and yearning for God, and so win their support for his mission and demands. Our investigation will, therefore, be able to take account only of the most imperative of the motives he gives, and their significance for moral decision.

Generally speaking, the principle subject of Jesus' preaching, the reign of God and its advent, also provides the most powerful of motives. It is not only an eschatological fact, an act of the saving God, but also the highest blessing of salvation, the essence of all the blessings of salvation, the "central idea of blessedness" (Theissing).

As far as Jewish ideas and the concepts governing them were concerned, this was something in Jesus' message that was new. The expression most frequently used by the rabbis to sum up the blessings of salvation at the end of time was "the world to come" *(ha 'olam ha-ba')*; they often also spoke of "paradise".[1]

That participation in the kingdom of God was to Jesus the chief and most important of the promises, is clear above all from the Beatitudes at Matt. 5:3–10. The first and last Beatitudes both say, "theirs is the kingdom": the kingdom, that is, belongs to the blessed and they will one day enter into it. The intermediate Beatitudes depict the saving promises under various images, all of which, however, are descriptive of salvation at the end of time.

The Beatitudes are metaphors in the prophetic manner. The first three may be compared with Isaias 61:1f., "He hath sent me to preach to the meek, to heal the contrite of heart... to comfort all that mourn" – a text from the prophet that, as we have already seen, Jesus used elsewhere (Luke 4:18) in describing his own mission. Thus there was unity between his self-awareness and his message. It also becomes clear that the words "poor" and "mourning" both refer to the same people and the same circumstances.[2] "Console" is a messianic word (cf. Isa. 40:1; *Apoc. Baruch* 44:7; and Luke 2:25; 16:25) and had become so general an expression that people even took oaths by saying, "May I not see consolation if...".[3] The word did not refer to any special blessing hoped for, but to eschatological salvation as

---

[1] Cf. Dalman, *Die Worte Jesu,* pp. 103f.; Billerbeck, vol. I, p. 181; Volz, *Eschatologie,* pp. 413ff.; Bonsirven, *Judaïsme,* vol. I, pp. 310ff.; 511ff.; J. Jeremias, art. "παράδεισος" in *ThWB* vol. V, 763–71; Schnackenburg, *God's Rule and Kingdom,* pp. 54–63.

[2] The third Beatitude (Blessed are the meek ...) has connections with Ps. 37:11; in some of the MSS. it stands before, and in some after, the blessing of those that mourn and is perhaps not original. In any case, there is little difference between the meek and the mourning.

[3] Cf. Billerbeck, vol. II, pp. 124–6; Schmitz and Stählin in *ThWB* vol. V., 785ff.

such. Consolation in this context usually means not the resurrection, but deliverance in its entirety.[4]

Moreover, the promises in the second group of Beatitudes, which make more definite demands on those looking for the kingdom of God, do not refer to particular blessings of salvation, but only use new images to describe the one all-embracing salvation shared by everyone in the kingdom of God. "Being filled" reminds us of the frequently recurring image of the eschatological banquet or wedding-feast; "mercy" of God's mercy at the last judgement, by which alone we can be saved for the reign of God and the time of salvation. Like "vision of God", "divine sonship" must be interpreted here as an eschatological blessing of salvation, making us worthy of the presence of God.[5]

From this we are forced to draw the important conclusion that the word "reward" in the amplification of the last Beatitude (Matt. 5:11ff.) is also used only as a metaphor, taken like the others from the state of affairs prevailing on earth, but not justifying the transposing of all the ideas (achievement, title, equity) connected with reward on earth to the bliss to come. In a related text, Jesus says to his disciples "Rejoice in this, that your names are written in heaven" (Luke 10:20), written, that is, in the books relating to acts of justice and injustice, kept by God himself on the deeds of men.

The texts treating of entering the kingdom of God, and all the related sayings of Jesus already mentioned above (section 1), all give this as the chief motive for action. We have seen (section 8) that the radical demands made in the Sermon on the Mount are also pre-conditions for entering the kingdom, so that, in fact, these texts enshrine one of the most fundamental of motives in Jesus' preaching of the kingdom and represent his threat and promise, his call to penance as well as his good news.[6]

---

[4] Dalman, *Worte Jesu,* p. 90.
[5] Cf. Billerbeck, vol. I, pp. 207ff.; 219f.; Volz, *Eschatologie,* pp. 395f.
[6] H. Windisch in *ZNW* 27 (1928) pp. 170f.

We can only regret the fact that this motive of eschatological sharing in God's perfect reign has faded nowadays to "getting to heaven", for the result is the mutilation of the great cosmic vision, in favour of the personal bliss of every individual after death, so that the Christian is tempted to think more of the salvation of his own soul than of the consummation of the history of salvation, more of his own blessedness than of the glorification of God – no more than a shift in emphasis, to be sure, but one not unimportant in determining the pattern of our moral endeavours.[7]

Sometimes Jesus does explicitly give "for the sake of the kingdom of God" (or something corresponding to it) as a motive. One example is when talking about the renunciation of matrimony (Matt. 19:12); from the fact that this is not required of everyone, it would seem that he was here concerned with freedom to preach the kingdom of God. Similar expressions are "for Jesus' sake" (or his "name's sake") and " for the sake of the gospel." They appear in two other passages connected with the disciples (Matt. 10:18 par.; 19:29 par.), and as comparison of the synoptic gospels shows, both are making the same point: that following Jesus involves abandoning the good things of this world and enduring persecution when it is necessary to do so to preach the kingdom of God, and that in return the preacher may expect to share in reigning in the kingdom of God (cf. Luke 22, 28 ff.).

Fundamentally, then, the motive is not an ascetic one, that is, it did not originate in the thought of voluntarily taking up some practice in order the more certainly or fully to win God's salvation (or "reward"). Jesus rather was foretelling that these bitter privations and sufferings were unavoidable for those who followed him. It is, however, not at all difficult to see that with the mitigation of persecution, love for Jesus might lead

---

[7] Cf. J. Theissing, "Gottesreich und Vollendung" in *Amt und Sendung* (Beiträge zu seelsorglichen und religiösen Fragen) 1950, pp. 161–90.

men to voluntary acceptance of similar burdens. But then the motive becomes even more important: if we are to keep the spirit of the New Testament, we must also preserve our vision over and beyond the personal sphere outwards towards the coming of God's reign, and the struggle of the Church against the powers of evil and God's final victory.

But Jesus promises the kingdom of God not only to those persecuted "for justice's sake" (Matt. 5:10), but also to everyone who gives to his disciples even as little as a drink of water "in my name"; "he shall not lose his reward" (Mark 9:41 par.). The motive of wanting to do something for Jesus, God's ambassador, should guide the actions of every Christian, right up to the point of surrendering his life for Jesus' sake, and for the sake of the gospel (Mark 8:35 par.). The fact that the promise of a reward is attached, in this case the assurance of gaining eternal life, shows once again that what is ultimately in view is the blessings of salvation in the kingdom of God. Those who give their allegiance to the message of salvation gain for themselves a share in that salvation.

Utilitarian and prudential motives play only an apparent rôle in Jesus' instructions. The "foolishness" against which Jesus warns us in the parable of the rich fool (Luke 12:16–20), is the folly of those people who are unwilling to pay heed to Jesus' warning at this eschatological hour; the prudence recommended by Jesus in the parable of the unfaithful steward (Luke 16:1–7) consists in being concerned about one's own eternal salvation. Thus these two are in fact only metaphors and analogies. By deliberately choosing dramatic cases out of the field of human experience, Jesus addresses himself to human beings as they really are. That the real point behind prudence and folly here, is concern to enter the kingdom of God, is also shown by the parable of the wise and foolish virgins, with the typical image of the wedding feast (Matt. 25:1–12). The exhortation to take the lowest place at a feast is quite misunderstood if it is taken to be a rule of propriety or even merely a straightforward demand for humility, as may easily be proved by trying to follow it out in everyday life. "Feast" ... "shall be exalted" (that is, by God) ... "first" and "last": all these point to the true significance of the parable. "Put away all pride, all self-justification; be converted in humility and repentance, so that God may one day exalt you in his kingdom." It is not inferior motives, but sound and effective didactic principles, then, that caused Jesus to employ this vivid mode of speech, and an argument that went home to the people.

But is this principal motive of the kingdom of God, not itself a reward-motive, and one made even stronger by the threat of exclusion? And does it not, therefore, lack that gold of the love of God which alone can give splendour to any moral action? No, for no one who correctly understands the gospel of the reign of God can make the search for the kingdom of God and his justice into an egotistical struggle for personal reward. In the first place we must remember that it was God who took the first step with the mission of Jesus and his preaching of salvation, and that man can and should only make a humble and grateful response. The coming of the perfect kingdom thus remains wholly and solely the act of God. In the last resort the blessings of the kingdom surpass everything that even the most hardened campaigner could "win" or "earn" for himself. The kingdom of God is a completely different world as compared with all that is earthly, and in Jesus' view it is wholly a gift of the grace and love of God. Jesus' rejection of the piety and morality of the Pharisees was, of course, intended to demonstrate the impossibility of earning oneself entry to the kingdom of God through a justification achieved by works. Here again we can see the profound importance of Jesus' basic demands for repentance and faith (see §§ 2–3); these dispositions prevent us from abusing the motive of the kingdom of God. Furthermore, the centre of Jesus' moral teaching, the great commandment of love, also gives positive support to this motive. That epitome of all Jesus' commandments is indeed given only in the form of a commandment, not as a motive, but as soon as one begins to express in action the commandment to love, love itself proves to be the driving force of all one's endeavours, even of one's seeking the kingdom of God. The "law" of the Sermon on the Mount can only be fulfilled by love. Hence love becomes the deepest impetus of all who are striving purely and simply for the kingdom of God.

§ 16. THE IMPORTANCE OF THE CONCEPTS OF REWARD AND PUNISHMENT

Herkenrath, *Ethik Jesu*, pp. 246–71; F. K. Karner, *Der Vergeltungsgedanke in der Ethik Jesu*, 1927; K. Weiss, *Die Frohbotschaft Jesu über Lohn und Vollkommenheit*, 1927; O. Michel, "Der Lohngedanke in der Verkündigung Jesu" in *ZST* 9 (1931–32) pp. 47–54; M. Wagner, "Der Lohngedanke im Evangelium" in *NKZ* 43 (1932) pp. 106–12; pp. 129 to 39; H. Preisker and E. Würthwein, art. "μισθός" in *ThWB* vol. IV, 699–736; G. Bornkamm, *Der Lohngedanke im Neuen Testament*, 1947; Bo Reicke, "The New Testament Conception of Reward" in *Aux sources de la tradition chrétienne* (Essays presented to M. Goguel) 1950, pp. 195–206; J. Schmid, *Evangelium nach Matthäus*, pp. 287–94; W. Pesch, *Der Lohngedanke in der Lehre Jesu*, 1955.

IT HAS already emerged from our discussion of the motive of the kingdom of God that Jesus spoke unconstrainedly about reward and punishment; but it is debatable whether that was a purely metaphorical or pedagogical manner of expression, or whether the motive of retribution had a genuine settled place in Jesus' moral teaching.

Unfortunately this problem is burdened with the historical, dogmatic and philosophical judgements and viewpoints of earlier generations. Judaism defends itself against the accusation that it advocated a purely selfish ethics of reward. Catholic teaching defends its dogmatic teaching on "merit", which on the basis of the gospel presents an essentially different aspect from the Jewish teaching. Protestantism, however, sees it as one of the offending doctrines against which it makes its protest. But both confessions appeal for support to the teachings of Jesus. German thinkers cling, almost immovably perhaps, to the "idealistic" (in reality, formalist and bloodless) principle of Kant, that good ought to be done for the sake of goodness alone. These approaches to the problem often involve a distorted view of the texts, which are then said to "prove" something that they neither can nor are intended either to prove or to disprove. The exegete is concerned to interpret the texts in accordance with what they actually say, bringing out Jesus' real interests and general viewpoint, and displaying his doctrine against the background of his own times. This might perhaps contribute to eliminate much bias and rigidity of opinion.

It is clear from the idea of judgement, which cannot be excised from Jesus' preaching, that reward and punishment are not used merely metaphorically in his sayings. A terrible judgement awaits anyone who refuses to repent and believe and who despises the salvation proferred by God (cf. Matt. 10:15; 11:22, 24, par.; 12:36; 12:41f. par.). Just requital has its proper place in this divine judgement: "The Son of man . . . will . . . render to every man according to his works" (Matt. 16:27). In making such pronouncements Jesus was not merely repeating the warnings of the prophets or associating himself in a merely external manner with that idea which was so dominant in later Judaism. At Matthew 25:31–46 he draws an original picture of the judgement, showing the decisive factor to be the performance or omission of acts of charity towards Jesus' "brethren", the poorest and least of men. The same standard, this time, forgiveness or non-forgiveness of debtors, seals the fate of the unmerciful servant in the parable at Matthew 18:23–24. And Jesus' words about positive retribution, reward, can and should be taken just as seriously. The one scene in which Jesus' disciples remind their master that they have left everything to follow him, and Jesus sets before them the prospect of a superabundant reward (Mark 10:28–30 par.) is enough by itself to prove that; but Jesus speaks very often of reward and recompense[8] doing so naturally and without restraint, with assurance and emphasis. As the reign of God which he proclaims brings men salvation and bliss, it could not be otherwise. Jesus did not share the illusion that good acts can be done only from one motive and that the highest of all, or that in loving God a man must be forgetful of his own happiness. Genuine morality would be dead, only if striving for one's own happiness claimed pre-eminence or monopoly among motives, or even attempted to abuse the higher values.

If, then, it cannot be denied that the motive of retribution had a place in Jesus' teaching, it becomes more important than ever to define the form and meaning he gave the concepts of reward and punishment. Any misgivings we might have must vanish when we see Jesus himself fighting against a morally base striving after reward, as at Matthew 6:1, "Take heed that you do not your justice before men, to be seen by them; otherwise you shall not have reward of your Father who is in heaven." With these words he blocks the path even of delicate self-seeking, of concealed conceit.

In this passage, Jesus contrasts intention in men's eyes and in God's by three examples taken from the life of devotion as found among the Jews. Anyone giving alms, fasting and praying only "before men", to be seen and praised by them, "has his reward" (has been equitably recompensed as it were, by the approbation of men) (Matt. 6:2, 5, 16). What Jesus meant is quite clear: true piety should look to God. Hence the reward-motive ("and the Father who seeth in secret will repay thee") is not the central thought here. Jesus was not saying that in doing these things one should strive for reward, but that one should do them "before God". Only then do they become

---

[8] Matt. 5:12 par.; 6:1, 4, 6, 18; 10:41; Mark 9:41 par.; Luke 6:35; cf. the metaphors in Matt. 5:26 and par.; 18:34; 25:21, 23, 36 ff. (and with these cf. Luke 19:17, 19, 22 ff.); Luke 12:37, 44, 46, 47–48; 16:19 to 31, etc.

valuable from the religious point of view, and become what, by their nature, they ought to be. The thought of reward is, therefore, only an auxiliary motive, but on the other hand there is no question of interpreting Jesus' manner of expression as a mere accommodation to those listening to him.

The reward promised by Jesus is almost always the future kingdom of God or one of its blessings, such as eternal life (Mark 10:30 par.; Matt. 25:46), or, for the disciples, reigning with Christ (Luke 22:28f.), or again, for the twelve specifically as representatives of the people of God, judgement (and rule?) over the twelve tribes of Israel (Matt. 19:28). The reward promised from the Father, who sees those works of divine love done wholly in secret (Matt. 6:4, 6, 18), is also to be understood eschatologically.

Although Judaism also usually expected the reward to be paid only in the future world, there was an important difference between its attitude to this question and that of Jesus. This was the idea that the "principal" accruing from certain particularly meritorious works (certain charitable acts, peacemaking, study of the *torah*) could remain untouched in heaven whilst "interest" was already being received on earth.[9] Such an idea was completely alien to Jesus, who foretold sufferings and persecutions for his disciples in this world. This seems to be in harmony with another idea, involving a kind of theology of suffering, developed particularly by R. Akiba (d. c. A.D. 135): the idea that the just must suffer a great deal here so as one day to receive a commensurably greater reward.[10] But closer examination reveals essential differences, especially in motivation. According to Akiba, God collects penalties from the just for the few evil deeds done by them in this world, so as to be able to give them a perfect reward in the world to come; and

---

[9] Cf. Billerbeck, vol. IV, p. 491 and texts in support on p. 495.
[10] See W. Wichmann, *Die Leidenstheologie, eine Form der Leidensdeutung im Spätjudentum,* 1930, pp. 56 ff.

similarly he gives the godless an abundance of goods and prosperity in this world, as a reward for the few good works they have done, and in the future world he collects penalties from them.[11] Jesus rejected this whole system of book-keeping. In following him the disciples were to accept persecution "for his name's sake". He nowhere said that the sufferings of the disciples would be retribution for their evil deeds. The Father forgives them sin and guilt, but he also gives them the future glory out of pure goodness and grace. Jesus' conversation with the sons of Zebedee (Mark 10:35-40 par.) is instructive here. From their readiness to accept the cup of suffering and baptism of death so as to win the chief seats in the kingdom of God, it would seem that they may have been influenced by Jewish ideas of this kind. Jesus, however, said to them, "You shall indeed drink of the chalice that I drink of; and with the baptism wherewith I am baptized you shall be baptized. But to sit on my right hand and on my left is not mine to give to you, but (will be given) to them for whom it is prepared (by God)."

The cases in which Jesus did speak of retribution in this world are only apparent exceptions. When he threatened Jerusalem with imminent, external judgement (Luke 19:41-44), this was a sign of its condemnation; the real punishment falling on the obdurate members of the ancient people of God is exclusion from the kingdom of God (cf. Matt. 8:11f. par.). Chastisement in this world is not a substitute for eternal punishment, but only a declaration that it is to come. In certain cases Jesus did in fact recognize sickness or misfortune as consequences of sin (cf. Mark 2:1-12 par.; Luke 13:1-5; John 5:14), but he denied that there was inevitably any such connection (John 9:1-3), and attacked the opinion that the magnitude of the sin could be deduced from the severity of the punishment (Luke 13:2f., 4f.). The reason is clear: for him, every human

[11] *Pesiqtha* 73a and par., quoted by Billerbeck, vol. I, p. 390.

being is a sinner and must repent, and God forgives everyone out of pure goodness and mercy. Only one text speaks of "reward" in this world: Mark 10:30 and parallels, where Jesus promises his disciples a hundredfold indemnity "in this world" (though indeed with "persecutions"), and "in the world to come" everlasting life.

This full style (after "a hundredfold" there comes the detailed list already given in verse 29), is only found in Mark. Matthew and Luke have "a hundredfold", "much more", without repeating "houses, brothers, sisters," etc. and also without the addition of the reference to persecutions. Matthew, indeed, has lost the form "this world . . . the world to come". The Marcan text has often been criticized, and it is not, in fact, smooth-flowing, at least with the enumeration after "hundredfold". As regards content, difficulty has been found in the pattern of the two aeons, which is found elsewhere only at Matthew 12:32, but not in the parallels to this text. Many would like to hold that the first part of the promise is not the primitive form; others, not the second part either. If we accept the straightforward meaning of the texts, as the early Church must have done, the manifold indemnity paid in this world refers to the spiritual family, the Christian community (cf. the Lord's words at Mark 3:33–35 par.). The additional phrase "with persecutions" does, however, indicate that this is not the perfect accomplishment of what Jesus really meant to promise his disciples; it is rather a solace than a reward.

It is very important that the reward promised by Jesus is essentially eschatological, consisting in sharing in the kingdom of God and enjoyment of its blessings, because in the preaching of Jesus the eschatological gifts are strictly supernatural and depend on grace. That in itself indicates that no human being is in a position to make claims on God. But there are even clearer texts available in this central matter of the reward motive. The parable of the servant (Luke 17:7–10) reaches its climax in the sentence, "So you also when you shall have done all these things that are commanded you (by God), say: We are unprofitable servants; we have done that which we ought to do." This rejection of all claims to reward can only be harmonized with Jesus' other references to reward if the recompense coming to us from God is a reward of grace; that is, a reward conceded to us by God of his own accord, and promised us through Jesus. Hence the parable of the labourers in the vineyard (Matt. 20:1–16) is no objection to this, even though the owner of the vineyard did in fact stipulate a certain payment for the day-wage men he recruited. On the contrary, the point of the parable lies in the fact that when the wages were paid in the evening, the master freely out of kindness had the late-comers paid a sum larger than he owed them, and justified his action to the "first" labourers when they complained.

We must agree with Protestant exegetes when they say that the labourers who worked the whole day and received a just wage are included only in order to emphasize more sharply the true nature of the situation and of the reward of the last comers,[12] in other words, that the fixing of the payment is only a part of the setting of the scene and cannot be allegorized. But that is not "the" Catholic interpretation, as many Protestants seem to think.[13] According to Meinertz[14] the only essential idea in the parable is that "God is not bound by earthly concepts of reward, but acts out of goodness and distributes what is really a gratuitous gift". Verse 16a, the saying about the first and the last, has led many into false allegorizing (textual criticism excises v. 16b), but it was probably introduced here by the evangelist,

[12] Preisker, art. "μισθός" in *ThWB* vol. IV, 723, 3 ff.
[13] G. Bornkamm, *Der Lohngedanke,* pp. 17 ff.; also Preisker *loc. cit.* 722, 35 ff. Both appeal particularly to the interpretation given by K. Weiss.
[14] *Theologie,* vol. I, p. 104 and note 1; cf. also D. Buzy, *Les Paraboles,* pp. 219–32 and J. Schmid, *Das Evangelium nach Matthäus,* in loc. This exegesis, which rejects the idea that v. 16a provides the key to interpretation, is found as early as St. John Chrysostom.

as happened not infrequently with the so-called "unattached" or "wandering" logia. This parable may, however, contain an allusion to a real situation. Like the elder brother in the parable of the prodigal son (Luke 15:15–32), the complaining labourers may represent those groups among the Pharisees who took offence at Jesus' love for sinners and at his call to them. As against these advocates of the Jewish systems of justification by works and computation of rewards, Jesus put forward the infinite mercy of God, who acts quite differently from the way human narrowness would like to prescribe for him.

There is a deep gulf here between Jesus' ideas and those of some circles among the Jews of his time. The latter were inclined to reckon up their merits and set them against their debts and then claim a reward (cf. the Pharisee in the parable at Luke 18:10–14). Jesus on the other hand rejected such claims but promised every expectation and more, out of the pure goodness and mercy of God.

It is true that many scholars have rightly been at pains to avoid giving too rigid an account of Jewish doctrines of merit and reward, as though the Jew thought of himself as God's equal contractual partner, and demanded from him the fulfilment of his obligations, as though the relation between them was a purely legal one. Dependence on God was not forgotten, and they were also conscious of having to depend on his mercy; but again, they generally believed that God showed it chiefly "because of the merits of the patriarchs". Many sayings can be found that break the legalistic framework. God may also show his goodness and grant his favour "for his name's sake" alone; he can and will give more than one deserves.[15] But in

15 Cf. A. Marmorstein, *The Doctrine of Merits in Old Rabbinical Literature* 1920, pp. 11 ff.; Moore, *Judaism,* vol. II, pp. 93 ff.; E. Sjöberg, *Gott und die Sünder im palästinischen Judentum,* 1938, *passim,* esp. pp. 184–90; M. Smith, *Tannaitic Parallels to the Gospels* 1951, pp. 49–77 and the collection of texts on pp. 163–84. If Smith really means that there was no significant difference between Jewish and Christian doctrines of reward

the time of Jesus, and even later, the danger that people would think in such legalistic and economic terms must, nevertheless, have been very great. All that is important for us, is to see how strongly Jesus dissociated himself from all such ideas.

The recompense promised by Jesus is a gratuitous gift, not only because we can only gain entry to God's kingdom at all through his kindness, but also because of its superabundance. This is expressed even more clearly than in the parable of the labourers in the vineyard, in the account of the rewarding of the servants who had employed their talents profitably. "Well done, good and faithful servant, because thou hast been faithful over a few things, I will place thee over many things" (Matt. 25:21-23).[16] To the man who gives to his fellow-men out of love, God will one day give a good measure, full, shaken down and running over (Luke 6:38 — the metaphor is that of the corn-measure). Thus God does not requite after the human fashion, but he gives with a liberality unsurpassed and truly divine to those who have proved themselves in the trials of this world.

Just as the "reward" given by God exceeds all measure, so too the punishment he imposes. This is terribly clear from the punishment of the man who buried his talent (Matt. 25:30) and of the overseer who neglected his duty (Luke 12:46). The general principle is "Unto whomsoever much is given, of him much shall be required; and to whom they have committed much, of him they will demand the more" (Luke 12:48). God is great in giving, but also in his demands. And he is equally stern when he sees his goodness abused (see the parable

(p. 71), his erroneous view is the result of his untenable exegesis of Matt. 20:1-16, from which he excludes the feature of a "gratuitous reward". Cf. also Pesch, *Der Lohngedanke*, pp. 81-106.

[16] J. Jeremias, *Parables*, pp. 58ff. sees it as a "crisis" parable, a concrete appeal to the Scribes to recognize their responsibility. From the Lucan parallels it would seem that the reward may originally have remained an affair of this world. But is it quite certain that Jesus did not intend this element in his teaching to be understood eschatologically (even in Luke)?

of the unmerciful servant, Matt. 18:23–35), or in general his commandment to love neglected (Matt. 25:41, 46).

It is instructive to notice how Jesus once again uses the metaphor of expiation by analogy with human affairs. The condemned man cannot be released from his imprisonment for debt until the last farthing is paid (Matt. 5:26); but it is obvious that no human being can ever settle his debt with God (cf. Matt. 18:34). Thus the fire of hell really is an everlasting torment for the damned (Mark 9:48 par.; Matt. 25:41, 46).

Jesus set men before the face of God, whose standards are entirely different from those of human beings. He is both great and incomprehensible in rewarding and punishing, and this is the fundamental reason why human notions of reward and punishment are inadequate to the truths Jesus preached and must be purged of all earthly features.

Does this show, then, that the concepts of reward and punishment were secondary for Jesus? By no means, when the fact of eschatological reward and punishment is concerned. As a motive with which to summon men to seek God alone, to inquire his will and to think about their own eternal salvation, those ideas were even welcome to him. But he did not isolate this motive from his proclamation of God's reign; in striving for their own salvation, human beings are to long for the coming of the kingdom of God. The thought of reward and punishment should not supplant the more important one that we should serve God in straightforward loyalty, without making claims on our own behalf (Luke 17:10), and should love him with all our heart. Thus, any form of religious egotism and eudaemonism is excluded. And in so far as the motive of retribution remains subordinate to the motive of the kingdom of God, it is only a secondary one.

§ 17. GOD AND JESUS AS MODELS

See bibliography to section 4. I. Abrahams, *Studies in Pharisaism and the Gospels* II, 1924, pp. 138–54; F. Tillmann, *Die Idee der Nachfolge Jesu*, pp. 67 ff.; H. J. Schoeps, "Von der Imitatio Dei zur Nachfolge Christi" in *Aus frühchristlicher Zeit*, 1950, pp. 286–301.

F. TILLMANN tried to make use of the idea of following Jesus, in the sense of imitating him, as a guiding principle in expounding the moral doctrine of the New Testament. There can be no doubt that an example embodied in an impressive personality is very important in moral education. So even if the primary meaning of "following" in the gospel was different (see above, section 4), the motive of imitation is by no means absent and we may inquire how it is related to the other motives already discussed.

Behind the idea of God's gracious reward and the hope of gaining a share in the coming kingdom of God there stands, as we have already seen (sec. 15–16), a lofty concept of God, that excludes egotism and eudaemonism. God's primacy is shown in everything: in the commencement of the era of salvation, in the calling of those who were lost, in the strengthening of the morally weak, in the gracious and superabundant future reward. The gaze of the disciple of Jesus is powerfully directed away from his own small self to the great and gracious God, and his vision is given support of the most powerful kind by Jesus' continual references to the heavenly Father. There is, therefore, nothing strange in the thought of God's own nature and ways becoming an incentive, and yet there is a paradox here, for God is transcendent, never attainable by man.

Yet the imitation of God is clearly the motive in the call to love one's enemies (Matt. 5:44f.; Luke 6:35). Because[17] God

---

[17] According to the reading of the Greek manuscripts. In the Latin and Syriac translations, this word is replaced by the relative pronoun, though this scarcely changes the sense.

makes his sun rise over the good and the evil, so we too are to love our enemies, and there is also the sentence "that you may be the children of your Father who is in heaven" that is, there is resemblance between the sons and their Father.

But at this point, of course, the question arises, how exactly this "divine sonship" is to be interpreted. Should it be taken, as at Matthew 5:9, as one of the eschatological gifts, hence as a promised reward? The parallel at Luke 6:35 seems to support this; yet the phrase before it "your reward shall be great" is probably a Lucan supplement (cf. 6:23), attracted by the exhortation to lend without expecting in return. In Luke too the promise "you shall be the sons of the Highest" is based on the example of God in loving one's enemies (in Luke it is even less possible than it is in Matthew to refer this causal clause to the more distant commandment to love one's enemies). And lastly, in Matthew as well as in Luke, the closing phrase "Be you therefore perfect (in mercy), as also your heavenly Father is perfect (in mercy)", once again involves the motive of imitation. Hence there must be an inner link between imitating God and being the children of God.

Is Jesus saying, then, that we ought to prove ourselves to be the children of God by loving our enemies as God does? It is difficult to make this assumption because Jesus nowhere else speaks of being the children of God in the same way (not even when teaching the disciples to pray to the Father), although he does so eschatologically at Matthew 5:9. The Jewish Scribes used "child of God" as a term of distinction for Israel, particularly on account of its possession of the Torah.[18] But clearly Jesus did not mean to base his argument on this; when he spoke of loving one's enemies, that highest expression of his message in contrast to previous views, he was thinking of the whole human race. Jewish theology was, however, also acquainted with the idea of being children of

[18] Cf. the texts in Billerbeck, vol. I, pp. 219f. and 371ff.

God as an eschatological blessing,[19] and Jesus did use this too as an incentive.

There was, however, also to be found in Judaism a middle way, linking present and future together, which employed the concept of "child of God" in moral action. In the *Book of Jubilees* (in an account of the last days) we read: "And their souls follow me and all my commandments and they fulfil my commandments; then I shall be their Father and they my children. And they are all called the children of the living God, and all the angels and spirits shall know, then indeed they shall know, that they are my children and I their Father in truth and justice, and that I love them" (2:24). On the other hand the Rabbis frequently deduced the moral obligations of the Israelites from the thought that they were the children of God here and now – thus, for example, R. Jehuda (c. A.D. 150): "If you behave after the manner of children, you are called children; if not, you are not called children."[20] Jesus' probably eschatological preaching gave the following turn to the idea: Practise love of your enemies, as God practises it; then you will already be imitating your heavenly Father, and he will one day acknowledge you as his children in the fullest sense. It is impossible to decide with certainty whether the wording "shall be sons of your Father" refers to a moral similarity to the Father in the present, or the future eschatological blessing to be bestowed by God by reason of their present efforts. But that is a secondary point, for in either case, Jesus' main purpose remains the same.

There is, therefore, no need to prove that Jesus' exhortation bears no more than a superficial resemblance to certain statements of Stoic philosophers (see above, section 10, towards the end). The vast difference between them becomes obvious when one finds among the pagans motives for loving one's enemies that are simply impossible on the lips of Jesus, for example,

[19] Cf. *Psalms of Solomon* 17, 27, 30; 1 *Enoch* 62, 11; *Assumption of Moses* 10, 3, and the text quoted, *Jubilees* 1, 24.   [20] *Qiddushin 36a*, quoted in Billerbeck, vol. I, p. 220, where there are also further examples.

"I was not born to share in hating, but to share in loving" (Sophocles, *Antigone,* 523), or, "A man who renounces revenge will surely win fame for his gentleness" (Seneca, *De clem.* 1, 7). Jesus' sayings reveal a Semitic feeling for style (parallelism), and are also probably intrinsically linked with the concepts of Jewish theology by the kinds of motives implied.

H. J. Schoeps has recently drawn fresh attention to a twig on the many-branched tree of Jewish theology which it is surprising to find in the otherwise stern and remote concept of God current in later Judaism. Abba Sha'ul (probably second century, though dated by Schoeps in the first), not only deduced Israel's duty to imitate God from the law of holiness (Lev. 19:2), but also interpreted Exodus 15:2 in a mystical sense, by a different way of forming the words, so as to read, "I and HE" *(ani we-hu'),* and interpreted these as meaning: This is my God, I will be like him. These thoughts, which can be followed further in Rabbinic Judaism, indicate the existence of no less than a striving after an *unio mystica.* Imitation of God is to take place in the moral sphere, by striving to attain the same characteristics as God. Ultimate resemblance can only be hoped for in the ultimate consummation. "The imitation of the invisible God is a Jewish paradox."[21]

At the very least these Jewish ideas indicate that some Jews came very close to the thinking of Jesus (although they are first recorded in the era after Christ). And if the Jew of that time strove to imitate God, a God ever further withdrawn from the world and surrounded with ever greater awe, why should this idea not have been used by Jesus, who taught us confidently to approach the Father?

As well as in this fundamental text, the motive of imitating God is also operative in other lessons of Jesus, although perhaps not so obviously. Because the king in the parable at Matthew 18:23ff. had remitted the gigantic debt for his servant, he expect-

21 "Von der Imitatio" p. 288.

ed him also to be prepared to remit the debt of his fellow-servant, "Shouldest not thou then have compassion also on thy fellow-servant, even as I had compassion on thee?" (Matt. 18:33). Perhaps this idea is also implied in the saying "So let your light shine before men that they may see your good works and glorify your Father who is in heaven" (Matt. 5:16), for it may mean that in the actions of Christ's disciples, people should recognize not only the power of God that enables these actions to be done, but also the goodness of God which is reflected in them.

Above all this motive unfolds in a new way that is only possible within Christianity, that is, by the imitation of Jesus. It is noteworthy that Jesus spoke of the imitation of God in connection with his chief concern, love and its highest forms of expression. But he knew that he himself had been sent to preach the love of God to men and actually to bring it to them by declaration of forgiveness and ultimately by his atoning death. In this way, he himself became the visible image of God's love and at the same time a model for those who believe in him. In this context, Jesus did not hesitate to summon his disciples to imitate him (Mark 10:45 par.).

The authenticity of this saying, that the Son of man has come to serve and give his life as a redemption for many, has been constantly attacked by critics. This is a point at which our view of the mystery of Jesus' person and his consciousness of his mission is either open or hopelessly blocked. Was Jesus conscious of standing in the rôle of the suffering Servant of God of Isaias 53, and did he accept his death as a vicarious atonement or not? With the words spoken over the chalice in the Upper Room (Mark 14:24 par.), our present text is the clearest in support of such an awareness in Jesus. According to a recent and very careful study by J. Jeremias, there is a strong historical probability that Jesus did see the key to the necessity and meaning of his passion in Isaias 53.[22]

---

[22] Art. "παῖς θεοῦ" in ThWB vol. V, 653–713, and esp. 711, 21 ff.; see

The gospel of St. John gives formal confirmation that it was Jesus' desire that his humble self-sacrifice should also be an example to his followers. With the profoundly significant act of washing their feet he intended to give them an example, so that they might do what he had done (13:15). Consequently the commandment to love is worded "That you love one another, as I have loved you, that you also love one another" (13:14; cf. 15:12). If one affirms Jesus' awareness that in his person God's power and love has come close to men, the motive to imitate God is transposed to a new plane and is effective in a hitherto unimaginable way. This view gains support when we notice that elsewhere in the gospel, too, statements made about God seem to be transferred to Jesus.

Thus, for example, there is a parallel to the saying about the "mystical" presence of Jesus among those gathered together in his name (Matt. 18:20) in the *Mishnah Aboth*, 3, 2: "When two sit together and words of the law (are spoken) between them, then is the *shekinah* (a name for the presence of God) among them." Jesus' sayings about those who do the works of charity (Matt. 5:35 and 40) parallel something God says in an old *midrash*, "My children, whenever you give a poor man something to eat, I count it as though you had given me something to eat."[23]

As has already been shown, the motive of imitating Christ

also Jeremias' additional note "Das Lösegeld für viele" in *Judaica* 3 (1948) pp. 249–64; cf. also A. Médebielle, "Expiation" in *Dictionnaire de la Bible,* suppl. vol. III, 1938, pp. 122–33; H. W. Wolff, *Iesaja 53 im Urchristentum,* 3rd ed. 1952; C. Maurer, "Knecht Gottes und Sohn Gottes im Passionsbericht des Mk-Ev." in *ZThK* 50 (1953) pp. 1–38; V. Taylor, "The Origin of the Marcan Passion Sayings" in *NTS* 1 (1954–55) pp. 159–67; E. Lohse, *Märtyrer und Gottesknecht,* 1955 (Bibliog.) O. Cullmann, *Die Christologie des Neuen Testaments,* 1957, pp. 59–68, Eng. tr., *The Christology of the New Testament,* 1959; A. Vögtle in *LThK* vol. VI, 1150f.

[23] *Midrash Tannaim,* 15, 9, quoted by M. Smith, *Tannaitic Parallels to the Gospels,* p. 154. On pages 152ff., Smith also gives other examples.

came to its full flowering in the early Church after the death and glorification of Jesus. But with the idea of imitating God and Jesus — and for us here this is the important thing — the motive "for the love of God" acquired an almost immediate validity. God is not only incomprehensibly great and frequently terrifying in his demands, he is also worthy of love above all things and to emulate his love is a joyful task for all those who believe in Christ.

II

The Moral Teaching of the Early Church in General

Chapter One

THE FUNDAMENTALLY ESCHATOLOGICAL OUTLOOK OF THE EARLY CHURCH AND THE RESULTS OF THIS ON ETHICS

§ 18. The Experience of the Workings of the Holy Spirit, and the Influence of This on Moral Conduct

On i and iii: H. Gunkel, *Die Wirkungen des Heiligen Geistes nach der populären Anschauung der apostolischen Zeit und der Lehre des Apostels Paulus*, 3rd ed. 1909; H. v. Baer, *Der Heilige Geist in den Lukasschriften*, 1926; N. Adler, *Das erste christliche Pfingstfest*, 1938; id., *Taufe und Handauflegung*, 1951; J. Gewiess, *Die urapostolische Heilsverkündigung nach der Apg*, 1939; R. Bultmann, *Theologie*, pp. 151–62, Eng. tr. *Theology of the New Testament*, vol. I, pp. 153–64; E. Lohse, "Die Bedeutung des Pfingstberichtes im Rahmen des lukanischen Geschichtswerkes" in *EvTh* 13 (1953) pp. 422–36; E. Schweizer, *Geist und Gemeinde im Neuen Testament und heute*, 1952; P. Bonnard, "L'Esprit Saint et l'Église selon le Nouveau Testament" in *RHPR* 37 (1957) pp. 81–90; B. Willaert, "De Hl. Geest eschatologische gave in Christus" in *Collationes Brugenses* 3 (1957) pp. 145–60; E. Schweizer in *ThWB* vol. VI, 401–13, (Eng. tr. *Bible Keywords* No. 9: "Spirit of God", 1960).

On ii: E. Sokolowski, *Die Begriffe Geist und Leben bei Paulus*, 1903; H. Bertrams, *Das Wesen des Geistes nach der Anschauung des Apostels Paulus*, 1913; W. Reinhard, *Das Wirken des Hl. Geistes im Menschen nach den Briefen des Apostels Paulus*, 1918; E. Sommerlath, *Der Ursprung des neuen Lebens nach Paulus*, 2nd ed. 1927; A. Wikenhauser, Die Christusmystik des hl. Paulus, 2nd ed. 1954, Eng. tr. *Pauline Mysticism*, 1960; id., *Die Kirche als der mystische Leib Christi nach dem Apostel Paulus*, 2nd ed. 1940, pp. 114 ff.; R. Schnackenburg, *Das Heilsgeschehen bei der Taufe nach dem Apostel Paulus*, 1950, esp. pp. 77 ff., pp. 159 ff.; J. Schmidt, "Geist und Leben bei Paulus" in *Geist und Leben* 24 (1951) pp. 419–29; H.D. Wendland, "Das Wirken des Heiligen Geistes in den Gläubigen nach Paulus" in *TLZ* 77 (1952) pp. 457–70; N. Q. Hamilton, *The Holy Spirit and Eschatology in Paul,* 1957; E. Schweizer in *ThWB* vol. VI, 413–36, (Eng. tr. *Bible Keywords* No. 9: "Spirit of God", 1960); O. Kuss, *Der Römerbrief,* 2nd ed. 1959, pp. 540–95; P. Bläser, "Lebendigmachender Geist" in *Sacra Pagina,* vol. II (1959) pp. 404–13; I. Hermann, *Kyrios und Pneuma,* 1961 (Bibliog.).

i. THE basic religious experience of early Christianity was the outpouring of the Spirit. It transformed the disciples from dispirited followers and unenlightened listeners into joyful witnesses to the resurrection and courageous preachers of the message of Christ (Acts 1:8; 2:29–36). Enlightened and impelled by the Holy Spirit, convinced that the risen Lord himself had sent the Spirit from the Father (2:33), they openly proclaimed that Jesus was Messias and Lord before the whole nation and before the leaders of the Jews (2:22–24, 36; 3:20; 5:31 etc.). The Spirit of God found utterance through stammers of amazement and enthusiastic talk about the wonderful works of God (4:31; 8:17f.; 10:46; 19:6), but also made possible a clearer and wiser presentation of the message of salvation. The Spirit of God was not merely an extraordinary (charismatic) gift to the apostles, an equipment of those who preached with wisdom (6:3, 5, 10), but was God's gift to all the baptized (2:38; 8:15, 17; 19:6), or those who were to be baptized (10:44ff.; 11:15; 15:8). The early Church was convinced that here was the fulfilment of Joel's prophecy concerning the eschatological time of salvation, when God would pour out his Spirit upon all flesh (2:16ff.). Therefore, just as Jesus as the Messias had already worked on earth in the fullness of the Spirit (10:38), so too for the early Church the universal outpouring of the Spirit was the great Pentecostal event, the first fulfilment of the work of Jesus, made possible by Jesus' crucifixion and resurrection.

It has long been remarked that little is said in the synoptic gospels about the Spirit, and that what is, is mostly in the gospel according to St. Luke. Especially remarkable is the omission from the words of Jesus of any declaration that the Spirit would be received by all the faithful (but notice the support of the Spirit before the courts, promised at Matthew 10:19f. and its parallel, Luke 12:11f.). C. K. Barrett deals with this question in his recent study.[1] He first rejects certain radical solutions, such as the claim that the concept of the Spirit first arose out of the encounter of the early Church with Hellenism, and then gives several reasons for the silence of the synoptics. Chief among them is that of St. John, "As yet the Spirit was not given (to those who believed in Christ) because Jesus was not yet glorified" (7:39). It is obvious why St. Luke (who also describes the life of the early Church under the guidance of the Holy Spirit) puts greater emphasis on the possession of the Spirit by Jesus and by the faithful (cf. Luke 11:13 with Matt. 7:11). In St. John's gospel (14:16f., 26; 15:26; 16:7, 13f.) it is expressly promised that the disciples of Jesus will receive the Spirit, though for definite functions (teaching, bearing witness, consolation) and under a special title (Paraclete). But all the faithful will become sharers in the Spirit, in a sacramental manner (3:5ff.; 6:63, cf. also 4:14; 7:13ff.). The announcement by John the Baptist of a baptism with the Spirit to be dispensed by the Messias is a bridge between the synoptic and Johannine traditions (Mark 1:8 par.; cf. John 1:33). The early Church understood that during Jesus' ministry he alone as Messias was endowed in the fullest sense with the Spirit, and that only after his glorification would the Spirit of God be poured out on Jesus' community.

But must this exciting experience of the Spirit not also have influenced the moral outlook of the original community? In the Acts of the Apostles it is the extraordinary (charismatic) operations of the Spirit that are most in evidence. The Spirit was seen rather as

---

[1] *The Holy Spirit and the Gospel Tradition*, 1947; cf. also G. W. H. Lampe, "The Holy Spirit in the Writings of St. Luke" in *Studies in the Gospels* (Essays in memory of R. H. Lightfoot), 1957, pp. 159–200.

a religious phenomenon, not as the fundamental moral force in Christian life.[2] In the "summaries", the condensed accounts of the life of the community, there is no mention of the Spirit (2:42–47; 4:32–35; 5:12–16). People were brought under the spell by extraordinary manifestations, including miraculous healings (2:43).

One dramatic example of these was the sudden death of Ananias, and of his wife Saphira (5:1–11). It shows that the guidance of the Spirit of God was also operative, at least indirectly, in the moral sphere. Peter's reproach to this deceitful fellow-member of the community was, "Ananias, why hast Satan tempted thy heart, that thou shouldest lie to the Holy Ghost?" (5:3). And to Saphira he said, "Why have you agreed together to tempt (that is, put to the test) the Spirit of the Lord?" (5:9). The Holy Spirit was recognized as the real guide of the community, watching over its purity, leading it through its trials and supporting it in its temptations. To the young Church, the calm that followed the first persecution was the consolation of the Holy Ghost (9:31), and the disciples won in Pisidian Antioch were "filled with joy and with the Holy Ghost" (9:31). Clearly, then, the Holy Ghost was a strong driving force. But above all he brought into being in the early Church the awareness that a new stage had been reached in the history of salvation, in which God's eschatological salvific acts are taking place. This frame of mind urged men to a revolutionary remodelling of the whole of life. The Spirit gave this band of believers in Christ the conviction that it was God's new divine community of salvation, so compelling the development of a new communal life (cf. section 19). The Spirit strengthened and advanced the Church with "signs and wonders" done at the hands of the

---

[2] Cf. A. Wikenhauser, *Die Apostelgeschichte,* 3rd. ed. 1956, pp. 99–103; H. Gunkel, *Die Wirkungen,* exaggerated the difference between popular early Christian ideas about the Holy Spirit and St. Paul's doctrine. For a criticism, see H. v. Baer, *Der Heilige Geist,* pp. 183–92; Feine and Aland, *Theologie,* p. 138.

apostles and other preachers of the faith,[3] and through the gift of prophecy, which threw light both on present and future.[4]

ii. It was, of course, Paul who first regarded the Spirit of God as the driving force of moral life (Rom. 8:12ff.; Gal. 5:16ff.). The Spirit's activity, constraining all to adopt a new way of life, begins at baptism (Rom. 6:4; 1 Cor. 6:11), in which all Christians receive the same Spirit (1 Cor. 12:13f.; Eph. 4:4f.). Was Paul teaching a new doctrine here? Even in Acts the Spirit is God's normal gift to all the baptized (2:38; 19, 5f.), and despite his more fully developed ideas he still characterizes the Spirit as a "gift" (Rom. 5:5) and, even in the late Epistle to Titus speaks of the abundant "outpouring" of the Spirit (3:6). For the early community as for St. Paul, baptism was the normal place for receiving the Spirit. The exuberance of the *charismatikoi* may have contributed towards giving greater prominence to the moral workings of the Spirit.

Paul clearly saw the danger that the charismatic gifts, particularly ecstatic *glossolalia,* might be overvalued, and behaviour at divine worship unrestrained (1 Cor. 12 and 14). So he guided the faithful towards the incomparably higher way of love (1 Cor. 13). He clearly regarded this too as a manifestation of the Spirit; it has first place among the fruits of the Spirit at Galatians 5:22f. From the account in Acts (which sometimes blurs oppositions), it cannot be clearly determined whether tensions had already arisen in the Palestinian communities as a result of the charismatic gift of the Spirit. Only one thing is certain: everywhere in the early Church the charismatic gift of the Spirit grew gradually weaker and this inevitably resulted in more attention being given to the sacramental operations and ethical impulses of the Spirit. Paul encouraged and made fruitful this theological development, but he found its seeds already present in the theology of the community.

[3] 2:43; 3:6; 4:30; 5:12, 15f.; 6:8; 8:6, 13; 9:34, 40; 14:10, 13; 15:12; 16:18; 19:11f.; 28:8f.   [4] 11:28; 15:32; 19:6; 21:9, 11f.

St. Paul's doctrine of the Spirit cannot indeed be seen as a mere expansion of the ideas already stirring in the primitive Jerusalem community. The *pneuma* as the holy and effective power of God, given to the baptized person and working continually in him, has to overcome the corrupting influence of the *sarx* ("flesh"),[5] human nature inclined to sin. The high moral significance of the Spirit of God is manifested precisely in this struggle. Paul describes it at Galatians 5:16ff. "I say then, Walk in the Spirit; and you shall not fulfil the lusts of the flesh. For the flesh lusteth against the spirit; and the spirit against the flesh. For these are contrary to one another, so that you do not do the things that you would."

The two elements are personified here in a way typical of St. Paul: they fight for the human being, that is, for the Christian who on the one hand is still held captive by "the flesh", his nature as a human being inclined since the fall to evil, and who on the other hand, from baptism onwards, is filled with the Spirit of God and impelled towards good. Each of these forces seeks to prevent the Christian from finally choosing what the opposing force is urging on him, and what in some measure he feels drawn to accept. The Christian's moral task consists in allowing himself to be impelled by the Holy Spirit (cf. also Rom. 8:13f.; Gal. 5:25), so helping him to triumph.[6]

Thus to Paul the spirit of God was the divine power given

---

[5] For this concept cf. W. Schauf, *Sarx. Der Begriff "Fleisch" beim Apostel Paulus unter besonderer Berücksichtigung seiner Erlösungslehre*, 1924; W. Gutbrod, *Die paulinische Anthropologie*, 1934, pp. 145–55, 216–29; E. Käsemann, *Leib und Leib Christi*, 1933, pp. 100–18; Bultmann, *Theology*, 1955, vol. I., pp. 228–41; C. H. Lindijer, *Het begrip Sarx bij Paulus*, 1952; W. D. Stacey, *The Pauline View of Man*, 1956, pp. 154–80; E. Schweizer in *ThWB* vol. VII, 124–38; O. Kuss, *Der Römerbrief*, pp. 506–40.

[6] P. Althaus, "'Damit ihr nicht tut, was ihr wollt'. Zur Auslegung von Gal. 5:17" in *TLZ* 76 (1951) pp. 15–18. Althaus would like to see this as applying not to a double inclination to good and evil, but only to the first: the *Sarx* hindering the Christian's will to good. This is a beautiful and profound idea, but is not apparent from the text itself.

to the Christian and promising him victory in his moral conflict with the world of evil still encircling him and pressing in on him, through his *sarx,* from every side. The Spirit and only the Spirit radically alters for the Christian the situation in the history of salvation, previously hopeless for him, for up till now the powers of destruction clearly had ascendancy (Rom. 7). In the Spirit of God the forces of the world to come have irrupted into this world, the Christian is transferred into community with Christ and has become a "new creature" (2 Cor. 5:17). This, for St. Paul, reveals that eschatological salvation has already been given us, even though what we have received is only the announcement of full salvation, or payment on account, as it were. The Spirit is the "earnest" of our future inheritance (2 Cor. 1:22; 5:5; Eph. 1:14).

Formerly attempts were usually made to interpret the *pneuma-sarx* antithesis from Hellenistic thought. Only a few scholars argued against this for its origin in Judaism. But the latter view has now received strong support from the manuscripts recently discovered near the Dead Sea, for they are characterized by a similar dualism with a corresponding use of the concepts of "flesh" and "spirit" (cf. also Mark 13:48 par.).[7] The only new element in St. Paul is that in place of the spirit already existing in man and inclined to good (called by Paul at Romans 7:23, 25 the *nous*), in place of a human "spirit", that is, there is the Spirit of God himself. This is, at the same time, the Spirit of Christ (Rom. 8:9; 1 Cor. 2:16), given us by the glorified Lord and uniting us with him (cf. Rom. 8:2; 1 Cor.

[7] K.G.Kuhn, "Πειρασμός—ἁμαρτία—σάρξ und die damit zusammenhängenden Vorstellungen" in *ZThK* 49 (1952) pp. 200–22; H. Huppenbauer, "Fleisch in den Texten von Qumran (Höhle I)" in *TZ* 13 (1957) pp. 298–300; W. D. Davies, "Paul and the Dead Sea Scrolls: Flesh and Spirit" in *The Scrolls and the New Testament* ed. by K. Stendhal, 1957, pp. 157–82; R. E. Murphy, "Bśr in the Qumran Literature and Sarks in the Epistle to the Romans" in *Sacra Pagina* II (1959) pp. 60–76; R. Meyer in *ThWB* vol. VII, pp. 109–13.

6:17; 2 Cor. 3:17f.). This fundamental shift in the concept, and change in the pattern of the dualistic struggle, is the result of the Pauline Christology and theology of redemption.

In his moral teaching Paul made much use of this doctrine of the *pneuma,* and especially of its antithesis to the *sarx* (see section 29 below).

iii. The conviction that the Pentecostal outpouring of the Spirit was perpetuated in the act of baptism and that in this way the eschatological acts of God were made manifest persisted side by side with Paul's teaching. The increasing rarity of extraordinary effects of the Spirit did not shake the fundamental attitude of the early Church. That can still be clearly observed within the New Testament. In St. John's gospel the Paraclete references show that the early Church was conscious of the lasting assistance of the Holy Spirit (14:16f.), that they understood him to be the witness to and interpreter of Jesus' message (14:26; 15:26; 16:13), and through him as God's advocate felt strong and victorious in the face of the hostile "world" (16:8-11). The disciples act as witnesses with the Paraclete (15:27) and so become competent to hand on Jesus' teaching and announce it before the world.[8] The picture given in the First Epistle of John agrees with this. As opposed to dangerous pseudo-prophets, the Spirit which is given to the orthodox community shows itself as the true teacher of the faithful by guaranteeing and infusing in them a right confession of Christ (1 John 2:27; 4:1ff.). The Spirit, however, continues and fulfils within the Church Christ's redemptive work. In the sacraments the *Pneuma* is operative and conveys to all who believe in Jesus the divine life from the glorified Christ (cf. John 3:5; 6:63; 7:39; 20:22; 1 John 5:6ff.). The Spirit sent by the Son of man raised on high brings eschatological fulfilment of Jesus' promise of salvation and does this in the Church.[9]

[8] Cf. F. Mussner, "Die johanneischen Parakletsprüche und die apostolische Tradition" in *BZ* 5 (1961) pp. 56–70.
[9] Cf. C. K. Barrett, "The Holy Spirit in the Fourth Gospel" in *JTS* I

The First Epistle of Peter, a work filled with joyful thoughts of baptism, but also with urgent moral exhortations, reflects the sacramental experience of the Spirit. St. Peter was familiar with the "sanctification of the Spirit" (1:2) which the "chosen strangers" have received; as living stones they are being built up into a "spiritual" house, a holy priesthood, to bring forth "spiritual sacrifices" (2:5).[10] The Greek adjective used (πνευματι-κός) expresses more strongly than the English the rôle of the Holy Spirit. It is the Holy Spirit who welds together the new people of God and builds the new temple of God (cf. also Eph. 2:22), and who also gives the new priesthood strength to perform its "spiritual" sacrifices. Moreover, the text is also a witness to the strong sense of forming a community, a sense that was preserved by the thought of the Holy Spirit.

In the First Epistle of John, too, which seems to know nothing of ecstatic experiences of the Spirit among orthodox Christians (and to want to know nothing of them), the reception of the Spirit (3:24; 4:13) is the well-spring of Christian living and also manifests its fruitfulness for sinless conduct. The "seed of God", probably a metaphorical expression for the Holy Ghost,[11] dwells in the man begotten of God and makes him incapable of sinning (3:9); but this divine capacity also demands serious moral effort of the child of God, and particularly love, which is the characteristic mark of the man begotten of God (2:29; 3:10; 4:7).

(1950) pp. 1–15; K. Wennemer, "Geist und Leben bei Johannes" in Geist und Leben 30 (1957) pp. 185–98; D. E. Holwerda, The Holy Spirit and Eschatology in the Gospel of John, 1959; A. Corvell, Consummatum est. Eschatology and Church in the Gospel of St. John, 1959; R. Schnackenburg, "Die Sakramente im Johannesevangelium", in Sacra Pagina II (1959) pp. 235–54.
[10] On this text, see J. Blinzler, "'IEPATEYMA. Zur Exegese von 1 Pet. 2:5, 9" in Episcopus (Festschrift for Card. Faulhaber), 1949, pp. 49–65.
[11] Cf. R. Schnackenburg, Die Johannesbriefe, 1953, in loc. and pp. 190f.; cf. also P. de Ambroggi, Le Epistole Cattoliche, 2nd ed. 1949, and J. Michl, Die katholischen Briefe, 1953, in loc.

The writer of the short Epistle of Jude, whilst denying that heretics possess the Spirit (v. 19), presupposes that the true Christian enjoys it, and links with this thought exhortations to living faith, prayer in the Spirit and perseverance in the love of God (v. 20f.).

Finally the Apocalypse of John bears witness not only to the Spirit of prophecy (1:10; 4:2; 14:13; 19:10) but also to his admonitory influence over the Christian communities (2:7, 11, 17 etc.). Whether the Spirit is considered in his extraordinary or his interior, invisible workings; emphasized in his functions as witness, helper, wonder-worker, prophet, teacher or admonisher; known as the inward force urging man to what is good, or as the source of the building up of the community; he remains the factor determining the thought and life of the early Church, the bond between it and its heavenly Lord, driving its history forward and pointing to the future.

§ 19. THE AWARENESS OF BEING A NEW COMMUNITY, AND THE FORMATIVE POWER OF THIS AWARENESS

E. v. Dobschütz, *Die urchristlichen Gemeinden. Sittengeschichtliche Bilder,* 1902; E. Peterson, *Die Kirche aus Juden und Heiden,* 1933; J. Schneider, *Die Einheit der Kirche nach dem Neuen Testament,* 1936; A. Wikenhauser, *Die Kirche als der mystische Leib Christi nach dem Apostel Paulus,* 2nd ed. 1940; N. A. Dahl, *Das Volk Gottes. Eine Untersuchung zum Kirchenbewußtsein des Urchristentums,* 1941; L. S. Thornton, *The Common Life in the Body of Christ,* 2nd ed. 1944; O. Michel, *Das Zeugnis des Neuen Testaments von der Gemeinde,* 1941; W. G. Kümmel, *Kirchenbegriff und Geschichtsbewußtsein in der Urgemeinde und bei Jesus,* 1943; Stig Hanson, *The Unity of the Church in the New Testament,* 1946; M. Goguel, *La naissance du christianisme,* 1946, Eng. tr. *The Birth of Christianity,* 1953; id., *L'église primitive,* 1947, Eng. tr. *The Primitive Church,* 1964; L. Cerfaux, *La théologie de l'église suivant saint Paul,* 2nd ed. 1948, Eng. tr. *The Church in the Theology of St. Paul,* 1959; W. G. Kümmel, "Das Urchristentum" in *Theologische Rundschau* 17 (1948–49) pp. 3–50, pp. 103–42; 18 (1950) pp. 8–53; A. Oepke, *Das neue Gottesvolk in Schrifttum, bildender Kunst und Weltgestaltung,* 1950; *Ein Buch von der Kirche,* ed. by G. Aulén and others, 1951; P.-H. Menoud, *La vie de l'église naissante,*

1952; Bo Reicke, *Glaube und Leben der Urkirche,* 1957; H. Schlier, *Die Zeit der Kirche,* 2nd ed. 1958; E. Schweizer, *Gemeinde und Gemeinde-ordnung im Neuen Testament,* 1959, Eng. tr. *Church Order in the NT,* 1961; V. Warnach, art. "Kirche" in *Bibeltheologisches Wörterbuch,* 1959, pp. 432–59 (Bibliog.); R. Schnackenburg, *Die Kirche im Neuen Testament,* 1961, Eng. tr. *The Church in the New Testament* (in print).

As WE have already seen, thanks to the outpouring of the Spirit, the original community at Jerusalem understood itself to be the community of salvation of the last times, the true "Israel of God" (cf. Gal. 6:16; Eph. 2:12), God's community, the "Church of God" (Acts 20:28; 1 Cor. 10:32; 11:22; 15:9; Gal. 1:13; 1 Tim. 3:5, 15).

It thus resumed the self-awareness of the old Israel which was formed particularly in the generation living in the desert under the influence of the covenant sealed at Sinai. The Jewish Christians of Jerusalem were probably less conscious of the novelty of their foundation as a community than of the fact that the ancient prophecies had been fulfilled. They saw themselves as the legitimate heirs of the old people of the covenant, as the true Israel, to whom the Messias had been sent. The Jews, they believed, should have recognized in Jesus the promised Messias sent from God, or should at least do so now, when God himself had borne witness to Jesus in his resurrection from the dead (Acts 3:13ff.; 4:10ff.; 5:30ff.; 7:51ff.; 13:29ff.). Seeing themselves in this light, it was probably quite soon that these early Christians began to call themselves "the saints" (Acts 9:13, 32, 41; 26:10; Rom. 15:25ff.; 1 Cor. 16:1; 2 Cor. 8:4; 9:1, 12; Eph. 2:19), a designation which the gentile Christians also later made their own (Rom. 1:7; 12:13; 16:2, 15; 1 Cor. 1:2; 6:1f. etc.).[12] The typology of the "people of God" of the New Testament, which was already implied by the term "com-

---

[12] Cf. R. Asting, *Die Heiligkeit im Urchristentum,* 1930, pp. 133–98; O. Procksch in *ThWB* vol. I, pp. 107–10; Dahl, *Das Volk Gottes,* pp. 185f.; Cerfaux, *The Church,* pp. 118–144; H. Kosmala, *Hebräer — Essener — Christen,* 1959, pp. 50–62 (in connection with Qumran).

munity (of God)" (ἡ ἐκκλησία τοῦ θεοῦ) is particularly developed and used to the full from the ethical point of view at Hebrews 3:7–4:13,[13] but it also is the basis of Paul's considerations at 1 Corinthians 10:1–13 (cf. also 1 Pet. 2:5, 9f.).

Thus although the young community at first maintained close ties with the religious and liturgical life of the Jews, met in the temple (Acts 2:42; cf. 3:1ff.; 5:20f., 42), and — at least the Judaeo-Christian branch headed by James — long preserved the Jewish way of life (cf. Act 21:17–26; Gal. 2:11–14), it in no way felt that it was only a Jewish "sect". Confession of Jesus as Messias, holding fast to the doctrine of the apostles, the breaking of bread (Eucharist and communal meal),[14] special gatherings for worship in private houses and common prayer (Acts 2:42, 46; 5:12) show that it was a separate community in faith and worship. Its way of life was inevitably strongly affected by these practices. Full of the memory of their Lord's commandment to love, they lived together in harmony and fraternity and expressed this by voluntary works of charity, so that a kind of community of goods appeared (cf. section 23). The first onset of persecution drew the community even more closely together (4:23–31; 8:1–3; 12:1–23). Although it was not free from inner tensions, as is clear even from the conciliatory account in Acts, which tends to give little prominence to such differences, its controversies, first the "murmuring of the Greeks" against the Jews over the question of supporting the poor (6:1) and later the question whether converts from paganism ought first to be circumcised and made subject to the Jewish law (15), could be settled without overthrowing the whole edifice.

[13] On this point see E. Käsemann, *Das wandernde Gottesvolk* (1939); F. J. Schierse, *Verheißung und Heilsvollendung. Zur theologischen Grundfrage des Hebräerbriefes*, 1955.
[14] J. Gewiess, *Die urapostolische Heilsverkündigung nach der Apostelgeschichte*, 1939, pp. 146–57; P.-H. Menoud, "Les Actes des Apôtres et l'Eucharistie" in *RHPR* 33 (1953) pp. 21–36.

The "Greeks", from whose ranks the seven men were taken (Acts 6:1–6), seem to have been more strongly aware of the novelty and specific difference of the confession of Christ and the form of religion involved by it. The accusation against Stephen, that he had spoken against the holy place and the law (6:13), seems from what follows in 6:14 not to have been without some foundation, in view of the allusion to Jesus' saying about the destruction of the temple (cf. Mark 14:58 par.; 15:29 par.; John 2:19) and Stephen's own speech, in which he radically attacked the Jewish worship of temple and sacrifice (7:41ff.). If this is so, the demarcation line between Christianity and Judaism was already more strongly drawn in this group of Hellenistic Christians.

In any case, early Christianity was a group movement from the beginning, and the formative power that derived from the life of the community for the individual member, must not be underrated. One can feel the moral earnestness of the early Church everywhere, whether among the Jewish Christians zealous for the law, who compelled the admiration of their compatriots (Acts 21:20; cf. also 15:5, former Pharisees), the Hellenists or the gentile Christians. This must be compared with the multitude of religious groups, ritual societies and conventicles in contemporary paganism. It has often been repeated that Hellenistic Christianity had close links with the mystery cults and it has been accused of important borrowings from their ideas, for example the *kyrios* cult and sacramental piety, but the arguments in support are generally largely untenable,[15] breaking down particularly in regard to moral conduct. Some mystery cults were not, of course, entirely devoid of influence on

---

[15] From the manifold literature cf. esp. G. Kittel, *Religionsgeschichte und Urchristentum,* pp. 19–32; K. Prümm, *Der christliche Glaube und die altheidnische Welt,* 2 vols., 1935; H. Rahner, "Das christliche Mysterium und die heidnischen Mysterien" in *Eranos-Jahrbuch* 11 (1944) pp. 347–449; M. P. Nilsson, *Geschichte der griechischen Religion,* vol. II, 1950, pp. 651–72, Eng. tr. *History of Greek Religion,* 1925.

morality,[16] but they hardly gave a definite moral education. "Measured by the standards of the moral demands they made, Christianity and the mysteries were like separate worlds, between which flowed no stream of living influence of any kind."[17]

The concept of community current in the original community of Jerusalem was also fostered and promoted in Paul's mission communities, composed predominantly of gentile converts, above all by the personal merit of this exceptional man. It was often no easy task. The first Epistle to the Corinthians gives some idea of the explosive force of disunity sometimes threatening to disrupt these young foundations. With a great deal of patience, skill and motives based on faith Paul had to wean from their wholly human and "carnal" way of thinking (3:1f.) the different groups that had formed in this exceedingly lively community, and which gave allegiance to particular individuals among the first generation of Christians (1 Cor. 1:2). Lack of brotherly love, intensified in part by social differences, became noticeable even in their meetings for worship and were preventing worthy celebration of the "Lord's supper" (11:17–34). Finally the extraordinary gifts of the Spirit themselves, the *charismata,* gave rise to unrest and division in the community (*ibid.* ch. 12–14).[18] To St. Paul the painful thing was that he himself had aroused heated feelings, and among the most difficult of his tasks was disposing of his personal opponents and establishing a truly paternal and apostolic bond with the whole community (cf. 2 Cor.). Elsewhere Judaizing intriguers were threatening to destroy his work (Galatians) and false teachers were endangering the integrity of the faith (Colossians). Paul

---

[16] Cf. J. Leipoldt, "Der Sieg des Christentums über die Religionen der alten Welt" in the *Festgabe für L. Ihmels,* 1928, pp. 49 ff.; G. Kittel, *op. cit.,* p. 115; K. Prümm, *Religionsgeschichtliches Handbuch für den Raum der Altchristlichen Umwelt,* 1943, pp. 296 f., 323–6.

[17] H. Rahner, *loc. cit.,* p. 384.

[18] Cf. P. Neuenzeit, *Das Herrenmahl. Studien zur paulinischen Eucharistie-Auffassung,* 1960.

nevertheless contrived, not only to establish and hold together the communities, but also to awaken a common Christian consciousness in all the "churches of Christ" (Rom. 16:16). It was not left to later times and a different stage of development to give rise to the thought that Christians are a new, "third" race;[19] St. Paul himself contrasted the Christian celebration of the Eucharist, with Jewish and pagan worship (1 Cor. 10; 14–22) and warned his Christians to give offence neither to Jews nor Greeks, nor to "the Church of God" either (1 Cor. 10:32). Visits, messengers and letters wove links between his missionary communities and as a sign of their unity with the first community at Jerusalem, St. Paul organized the great collection, as he had pledged himself to do before the leading men of Jerusalem (Gal. 2:10), devoting himself to its success with the full weight of his personality (1 Cor. 16:1ff.; Rom. 15:26) and from deeply religious motives (Rom. 15:27; 2 Cor. 8–9). When it had been made, he delivered it himself, taking no account of the danger involved (cf. Acts 21:10–17; 24:17).

On the other hand, the individual community was not without its significance. It was the embodiment and representative of the "Church of God" in the place where it lived out its life. Thus in the salutation of his letter, St. Paul addressed himself to "the Church of God that is at Corinth" (1 Cor. 1:2; 2 Cor. 1:1).[20] So too within the letters, the transition from individual community to whole Church is sometimes blurred, as at 1 Corinthians 12, where Paul uses the metaphor of the body, first of the Corinthian community with its χαρισματικοί, but then in

---

[19] Cf. A. v. Harnack, *Mission und Ausbreitung des Christentums*, vol. I, 4th ed., 1924, pp. 259–89.

[20] Cf. A. Schweitzer, *Die Mystik des Apostels Paulus*, 1930 (2nd ed. 1954) p. 104f.; K. L. Schmidt, art. "ἐκκλησία" in *ThWB* vol. III, 508, 538f. (Eng. tr. *Biblical Keywords*, No. 2: "The Church", 1950); Wikenhauser, *Die Kirche*, pp. 4ff. Cerfaux, *The Church*, pp. 187ff. (for a different view); U. Wickert, "Einheit und Eintracht der Kirche im Präskript des ersten Korintherbriefes" in *ZNW* 50 (1959) pp. 73–82.

v. 28 suddenly seems to be thinking of the Church as a whole.[21] A striking illustration of the moral purity required of the community is offered us by the expulsion from the church of the man who committed incest (1 Cor. 5). Paul was shocked to find that a man who would be condemned by the heathen themselves was still tolerated among the ranks of the Christians: "Know you not that a little leaven corrupteth the whole lump? Purge out the old leaven . . ." (v. 6 f.). Christians cannot and are not, of course, to withdraw from this world and its many licentious people, usurers, robbers and idolaters, but if other Christians behave in such ways, they must break off connections with them. His last word on the question is "Put away the evil one from among yourselves" (v. 13).

To St. Paul also belongs the merit of having given a theological foundation and development to this idea of the unity of Christian believers. He takes baptism, which gives the Spirit, the same Spirit, to all, as the foundation of his theology of the community; all, whether Jews or Greeks, slaves or free, men or women, become "one in Jesus Christ" (Gal. 3:28). Through the one Spirit baptism builds all into one body, the Body of Christ (1 Cor. 12:13, 27). Paul develops the ethical significance of this at Romans 12:4 ff. and Colossians 3:11 ff. In the epistles of the captivity, Colossians and Ephesians, the metaphor of the Body of Christ is further developed with the help of the concept of Christ as the head of the body.[22] This theology of the Church is developed particularly in Ephesians, and full consequences drawn from it for the practical exhortation of gentile Christians. These former pagans, who have now been taken into the ancient people of God by God's great saving decree, are exhorted here to "walk worthy of the vocation in which you are called, with all humility and mildness, with patience, supporting one

---

[21] Cf. Wikenhauser, *Die Kirche,* pp. 77 f., 88 ff., 143 ff.; in contrast to this view, but hardly correct, Cerfaux, *The Church,* pp. 193 f.
[22] In addition to the literature already mentioned see E. Käsemann,

another in charity; careful to keep the unity of the Spirit in the bond of peace; one body and one Spirit..." (4:1ff.).[23] The representation of the Church under the image of a body receiving life and growth, unity and control (4:16) from Christ its head, is completed by other no less significant metaphors. The Church, made up of Jews and gentiles, is God's city (2:19), a building constructed by God, a holy temple (2:20ff.); the "matrimonial" bond between Christ and the Church is put as a model before Christian married couples (5:22-23). "One Lord, one faith, one baptism" (4:5), these words, ring out like hammer-blows with which early Christian preachers forged unity within each community and between communities.

The moral exhortation addressed in the First Epistle of Peter to the baptized pagans is not purely individualistic either. It uses the image of the building of a holy temple and priesthood (2:1-10). It also reminds readers of their honour as Christians: by their well-doing they should silence the ignorance of foolish people who slander Christians (2:15). A Christian self-awareness is beginning to appear, built not on human institutions and habits, but on the election of God. As the Johannine Epistles show, the struggle against false teachers strengthened

Leib und Leib Christi, 1933; E. Mersch, *Le Corps Mystique du Christ*, 2 vols., 2nd ed. 1936; E. Percy, *Der Leib in den paulinischen Homologumena und Antilegomena*, 1942; L. Malevez, "L'Église, Corps du Christ" in *RSR* 32 (1944) pp. 27-94; J. A. T. Robinson, *The Body*, 1952; H. Schlier, "Corpus Christi" in *RAC* vol. III, 437-53; P. Benoit, "Corps, Tête et Plérôme dans les épîtres de la captivité" in *RB* 63 (1956) pp. 5-44; J. Reuss, "Die Kirche als 'Leib Christi' und die Herkunft dieser Vorstellung bei dem Apostel Paulus" in *BZ* 2 (1958) pp. 103-27; E. Schweizer in *TLZ* 86 (1961) pp. 161-74, 241-56.

[23] Cf. F. Mussner, *Christus, das All und die Kirche*, 1955; H. Schlier, *Der Brief an die Epheser*, 1957, pp. 90-96. P. Pokorny, "Σῶμα Χριστοῦ im Epheserbrief" in *EvTh* 20 (1960) pp. 456-64; C. Colpe, "Zur Leib-Christi-Vorstellung im Epheserbrief" in *Judentum, Urchristentum, Kirche* (Festschrift for J. Jeremias), 1960, pp. 172-86; R. Schnackenburg, "Gestalt und Wesen der Kirche nach dem Epheserbrief" in *Catholica* 15 (1961) pp. 104-20.

this closer inner unity. The "antichrist" who left the ranks of the orthodox Christians had, in fact, never really belonged to them "for if they had been of us, they would no doubt have remained with us" (2:19). And finally the external organization as it grew stronger also promoted the development of the Church: well-instructed, reliable and well-tried ministers had to concern themselves with moral exhortation as well as the preaching of the word (see the Pastoral Epistles). Thus there grew up that attitude to the "Church" which we may call "catholic", "that thou mayest know how thou oughtest to behave thyself in the house of God, which is the church (ἐκκλη-σία, community) of the living God, the pillar and ground of the truth" (1 Tim. 3:15).

Were the ethical influences emanating from early Christianity felt in the contemporary world? The moral seriousness, fraternal love, chastity, peacefulness and ability to suffer, of Christians, contributed not a little to the triumph of Christianity, for in the long run their lesson was stronger than calumny and oppression. In this sphere Christianity was superior to all the forces at work in that age. The strong moral movement that emerged in the pagan world through the new philosophy was surpassed, just as were the weak tendencies present in the mystery religions.[24]

§ 20. THE EXPECTATION OF THE PAROUSIA, AND ITS INFLUENCE

General: F. Holmström, *Das eschatologische Denken der Gegenwart*, 1936; H. D. Wendland, *Geschichtsanschauung und Geschichtsbewußtsein im Neuen Testament*, 1938; G. Delling, *Das Zeitverständnis im Neuen Testament*, 1940; M. Werner, *Die Entstehung des christlichen Dogmas*, 1941 (and on this W. Michaelis, *Der Herr verzieht nicht die Verheißung*, 1942); O.

[24] K. Müller and H. v. Campenhausen, *Kirchengeschichte* vol. I, 1, 3rd. ed. 1941, p. 107; cf. also A. v. Harnack, *op. cit.*, pp. 226ff.; K Bihlmeyer and H. Tüchle, *Kirchengeschichte,* vol. I, 12th ed. 1951, pp. 134ff.

Cullmann, *Christus und die Zeit*, 2nd ed. 1948, Eng. tr. *Christ and Time*, 1951; *id.*, *Le retour du Christ*, 3rd ed. 1948; T. F. Glasson, *The Second Advent*, 2nd ed. 1947; A. Oepke, art. "παρουσία" in *ThWB* vol. V, 856–69; R. Morgenthaler, *Kommendes Reich*, 1952; T. F. Glasson, *His Appearing and His Kingdom*, 1953; W. G. Kümmel, *Verheißung und Erfüllung*, 3rd ed. 1956, Eng. tr. *Promise and Fulfilment*, 2nd ed. 1961; J. A. T. Robinson, *Jesus and His Coming*, 1957; E. Grässer, *Das Problem der Parusieverzögerung in den synoptischen Evangelien und in der Apostelgeschichte*, 1957; (on this see O. Cullmann in *TLZ* 83 [1958] pp. 1–12; J. Gnilka in *Catholica* 13 [1959] pp. 277–90); R. Schnackenburg, *Gottes Herrschaft* pp. 135–48, pp. 189–98, Eng. tr. *God's Rule and Kingdom*, 1961, pp. 195–214, pp. 271–283.

On Paul: F. Tillmann, *Die Wiederkunft Christi nach den paulinischen Briefen*, 1909; F. Guntermann, *Die Eschatologie des heiligen Paulus*, 1932; B. Brinkmann, "Die Lehre von der Parusie beim heiligen Paulus und im Henochbuch" in *Biblica* 13 (1932) pp. 315–34, 418–34; J. Schmid, "Der Antichrist und die hemmende Macht (2 Thess. 2:1–12)" in *TQ* 129 (1949) pp. 323–43; B. Rigaux, *Les Épîtres aux Thessaloniciens*, 1956, pp. 195–280.

On John: R. Bultmann, "Die Eschatologie des Johannes" in *Glauben und Verstehen*, vol. I, 1933, pp. 134–52; K. Kundsin, "Die Wiederkunft Jesu in den Abschiedsreden des Johannes" in *ZNW* 33 (1934) pp. 210–15; G. Stählin, "Zum Problem der joh. Eschatologie", *ibid.*, pp. 225–59; A. Wikenhauser, *Das Evangelium nach Johannes*, 2nd ed. 1957, pp. 275–80; D. E. Holwerda and A. Corell see above, note 9.

FOR the faith of the early Church, Jesus was not only the Messias who had already come, but also the ultimate saviour and judge, whose coming was still awaited. Only when he appears with divine power, coming on the clouds of heaven *(parousia)*[25] will his work be complete. But did the expectation of the parousia give stronger force to the moral teaching of the early

[25] "Parousia" is a technical word for the appearance of a divinity in power or for the coming of the emperor or other ruler in splendour (especially his coming into his province). Hence this expression was used by the early Church of the coming of Christ in power (his first coming in this sense, not his return); cf. Matt. 24:3, 27, the only examples of its use in the gospels. Cf. Bauer, *Wörterbuch*, 1248ff. and Oepke, art. "παρουσία" in *ThWB*.

Church? Did the imminent expectation of Christ's victory over all the still active powers of evil, mark the attitude of the early Christians to this world, and their manner of life, with a special stamp?

M. Werner (see bibliography) maintains that the intensely eschatological mood of the primitive Church was the decisive factor of the early period; it was only with the hellenization of Christianity that a change came about, bringing with it the appearance of dogmatic theology. The hypotheses of the Eschatologists (A. Schweitzer, J. Weiss etc.) are therefore still with us. Werner's work has, however, encountered a great deal of criticism. The thesis of E. Grässer, too, that the "delay in the parousia" progressively created a series of problems to which various answers were given in the early Church and which can still be identified in the synoptic gospels, is disputable (cf. Cullmann, Gnilka). Luke, of course, wanted to minimize the question of the date of the parousia (cf. Luke 17:20f.; 19:11; 21:7, 24 *ad fin.;* Acts 1:7f.), and to give room for the spread and mission of the Church; but in doing so he was only drawing a conclusion from Jesus' teaching, which did not determine the time of the parousia.

There is very little trace in Acts of any direct influence of the concept of the parousia on the moral life of the original community. But it must be remembered that Acts recounts only a little of the "teaching of the Apostles" (2:42) within the first community, being rather a book of the missions. The words spoken by the angel at Jesus' ascension give some indication of how present the thought was within the Jerusalem community. "This Jesus who is taken up from you into heaven shall so come as you have seen him go into heaven" (Acts 1:11).

The account, given only by St. Luke (Luke 24:50f.; Acts 1:4–12), of the bodily ascension of Jesus on the fortieth day after the resurrection, has been said to be a later or special stage in the development of tradition and theology. According to some scholars, the resurrection and parousia may have originally been a single event as far as the disciples of Jesus or one group of them, were concerned. Yet in the account in Acts, we find the Galileans and Jerusalem group united, and according to other texts, the parousia was part of the earliest apostolic kerygma.[26]

Both in St. Peter's mission sermon to the people (2:20f.) and his discourse to Cornelius and his household (10:42), he deals explicitly with Jesus' second coming and office as final judge. In both cases it is not merely an article of doctrine, but also a motive for action, intended to move men to repentance and faith in the Lord glorified by God. With the Jews, St. Peter was able to assume a common fund of eschatological ideas and only needed to emphasize that Jesus was the Messias who was taken up into heaven "until the subjection of all things" when God will send him to usher in the "times of refreshment".[27] This is given as a motive urging the Jews to listen to the prophet-messias foretold by Moses (v. 22f.). For the pagans, too, the warning about the future "judge of the living and the dead" was certainly intended to make them aware of the seriousness of the decisions facing them; the thought of the judgement formed part of early Christian missionary preaching to the heathen (cf. 1 Thess. 1:10; Acts 17:31). Hence we can conclude that the thought of the parousia was used to the full in exhorting the faithful, though, of course, not as a threat but rather as a stimulus. For the rest, this lofty eschatological temper found expression above all in worship. Clear evidence of this is to be found in the petition *Maranatha* (Come, Lord!) which originated in

---

[26] Cf. J. Gewiess, *Die Urapostolische Heilsverkündigung*, pp. 31–38, On Christ's ascension see P. Benoit, "L'Ascension" in *RB* 56 (1949) pp. 161–203; *id.* in *Bibellexikon,* ed. H. Haag, 1956, 714–19.

[27] That is, the Messianic age, bringing the nation "peace" (cf. Hebrews 3:18–4:11) or "quickening", cf. the parallels in *Aboth* IV, 17 (quoted in Billerbeck, II, p. 626). It was expected that this age would be accompanied by a renewal of creation and a restoration of all things: cf. the commentaries and F. Mussner in *LThK* vol. I, 708f.

the Aramaic liturgy of Palestine (1 Cor. 16:22; Acts 22:20; Didache 10:6).[28]

In the Pauline epistles the expectation of the parousia is a strong motive influencing not only the tone and strength, but also in part the kind of admonition for the present world with its troubles. Catholic scholars, too, admit that in the earliest epistles to the Churches, St. Paul seems to count seriously on the imminent coming of the Lord, believing that he himself and some of those he is addressing will see within their own lifetimes this act of God that will save them from all their tribulations.[29] Longing gave expectancy wings, even though the apostle knew that the time was uncertain (1 Thess. 5:1ff.) and he himself subdues exaggerated and over-confident immediate hope (2 Thess. 2:1–12).

In this passage St. Paul teaches that before the appearance of Christ at the parousia there must first be a "falling away" and that the "man of lawlessness" must be revealed. He, however, will be held back by a hindrance, by someone who will impede him. Of whom or what this should be interpreted (the allusion generally favoured is the Roman Empire) it is no longer possible for us to determine.[30]

The idea that the parousia is not far away and that the time of tribulation preceding it will increase terrestrial wretchedness, gave added force to the apostle's counsel of virginity (1 Cor. 7:25–31). He certainly did not want married people to end their

---

[28] Cf. K. G. Kuhn in ThWB vol. IV, pp. 470–5; G. Bornkamm, "Das Anathema in der urchristlichen Abendmahlsliturgie" in TLZ 75 (1950) pp. 227–31; J. A. T. Robinson in JTS 4 (1953) pp. 38–41; for a different view see C. F. D. Moule in NTS 6 (1957–8) pp. 307–10.

[29] Cf. Tillmann, Wiederkunft, pp. 46–93; Guntermann, Eschatologie, pp. 34–85; J. Sickenberger, Die Briefe des hl. Paulus an die Korinther und Römer, 4th ed. 1932, and O. Kuss, Die Briefe an die Römer, Korinther und Galater, 1940 on 1 Cor. 7:25ff.; cf. also M. Meinertz, Theologie, vol. II, pp. 215–17; B. Rigaux, Épîtres, pp. 222–7.

[30] Cf. the essay by J. Schmid listed in the bibliography; also Rigaux, op. cit., pp. 259–80.

marriages (compare his general principle, directed by pastoral prudence: "Let every man abide in the same calling in which he was called" – v. 20; cf. also v. 17); nevertheless, he counsels the unmarried not to enter into matrimony, so as not to have a "tribulation of the flesh", that is, for the outward man.

Exactly how high the "eschatological temperature" was here, will depend on our translation of vv. 26 and 29. Does the adjective with "necessity" mean "present" or "(immediately) pending?" Both philologically and from the point of view of St. Paul's usage either interpretation is possible, and hence up till now the views of exegetes have been divided. In the first case the last terrible trial would already have come; in the second, the time before the end is still to come. Taking into account the use of the word at 2 Thessalonians 2:2 and the tenor of this passage, the latter view may justifiably be defended. With regard to v. 29, too, the question arises as to whether the time till the parousia "is short", "has been shortened" or "is compressed" (that is, is heavy with significance).[31] However this may be, it is not possible to argue away the fact that the hope was for the near future, particularly as the expressions used have eschatological overtones.

In v. 25, St. Paul makes it adequately clear that his advising virginity was his personal opinion; but the point reached in the history of salvation and the prospect of the parousia in the near future, nevertheless altered perspectives and St. Paul infers as a matter of principle regarding the attitude to earthly things, that they lose their importance and the Christian does well to exercise a certain reserve towards them. Those who had wives should be as though they had none; those who wept, as though they did not weep; those who rejoiced, as

---

[31] The expression is used in a few manuscripts at Acts 27:15 of the taking in ("shortening") of the sails: this was its usual application; cf. Liddell and Scott, *Lexicon*, vol. II, 1735. For the last translation, cf. Delling, *Zeitverständnis*, p. 89f.; L. Nieder, *Die Motive der religiös-sittlichen Paränese in den pln Gemeindebriefen*, 1956, pp. 54–58, 133f.

though they did not rejoice; those who buy, as though it were not to keep; "they that use this world as though they used it not, for the fashion of this world passeth away" (vv. 29–31).

But St. Paul energetically opposed erroneous conclusions based on immediate expectancy of the end, such as were made when, in Thessalonica, many of the members of the community were no longer willing to pursue their daily work in an orderly way (2 Thess. 3:6–12).[32] Even apart from special questions the apostle liked to use the parousia as a theme in his preaching on morals. Christians should be "without blame" on the day of the Lord (1 Thess. 3:13; 5:23; 1 Cor. 1:8; Phil. 1:10). Paul is not threatening here; as a warning he rather adduces exclusion from the kingdom of God (1 Cor. 6:9f.). It is more to awaken joyful readiness to receive the Lord at his parousia free from moral offence (1 Thess. 4:17), for "God hath not appointed us unto wrath; but unto the purchasing of salvation by our Lord Jesus Christ" (1 Thess. 5:9).

At 2 Corinthians 5:1–10 and Philippians 1:21–23, the apostle is concerned more closely with "individual eschatology", that is, the thought of one's own death and fate thereafter. This change of attitude, which was probably due to the apostle's personal situation (at 2 Corinthians 1:8f., great danger of death; at Philippians 1:12ff. uncertainty regarding the outcome of his case), was no light matter for St. Paul; he struggled through under the influence of the elevating thought that he himself would soon be "with Christ".[33] But there is no trace that he felt any difficulty over

---

[32] Cf. M. Dibelius, *An die Thessalonicher I und II. An die Philipper,* 3rd. ed., 1937, p. 57: those living disorderly lives were surely not amoral loafers, but Christians driven to do so by eschatological considerations; cf. also K. Staab, *Die Thessalonicherbriefe usw.,* 1950, *in loc.;* Rigaux, *Épîtres,* on this text; C. Spicq, "Les Thessaloniciens inquiets étaient-ils des paresseux?" in *ST* 10 (1956) pp. 1–13.

[33] On the "change of stimulus" and the development of Paul's eschatological ideas, cf. C. H. Dodd, *NT Studies,* 1953, pp. 108–28; on 2 Cor. 5:1–10, see E. B. Allo, *La seconde épître aux Corinthiens,* 1937, pp. 137–55;

the delay in the parousia. The expected imminence of the parousia is therefore not the essential element in the doctrine, although it was clearly important in moral motivation: Continual vigilance and preparedness, sobriety and self-criticism, an honourable way of life without offence are required (1 Thess. 3:13; 5:1–11; Rom. 13:11–14; 1 Cor. 1:8; 11:31; Phil. 1:10). The Christians are "to redeem the time" (Eph. 5:15f.; Col. 4:5). The idea of the parousia was by no means restricted to St. Paul alone; it was common property among the first Christians. According to 1 Peter 1:7, on that joyful day the proof and test of the faith will be revealed, more noble than gold refined in the fire, and this hope should spur Christians on to a sober, temperate way of life (1:13f.). They should even be glad to share the sufferings of Christ, so that they will be able to be happy and rejoice at the revelation of his glory (4:13). The author of the Epistle to the Hebrews also bases his exhortation to new religious zeal and more steadfast readiness to suffer on the nearness of the parousia (10:25, 37), and even James, who weaves so few specifically "Christian" themes into his exhortations to a life of faith active in works, writes, "Be you therefore also patient and strengthen your hearts; for the coming of the Lord is at hand" (5:8).

From none of these teachers, however, does one gain the impression that they were deducing an "interim ethic" from the fact of the nearness of the parousia. Expectancy was alive, but it was neither all-consuming nor oppressive. The fact that their eyes were fixed on the end did indeed make these Christians pilgrims and strangers on this earth, but it did not estrange them from their worldly tasks and did not plunge them into an apocalyptic fever. We can even see indications of composure

155–60; H. Lietzmann, *An die Korinther I–II*, 4th ed. 1949, pp. 147ff., with the additions by Kümmel pp. 202ff.; A. Feuillet, "La demeure céleste et la destinée des chrétiens" in *RSR* 44 (1956) pp. 161–92, 360 to 402; E. E. Ellis, "2 Cor. 5:1–10 in Pauline Eschatology" in *NTS* 6 (1959–60) pp. 211–24.

(as already in the aging Paul) about the actual time of the parousia. Had eschatological tension relaxed? Had perhaps even some theological remoulding taken place? These questions become acute with the writings of St. John. In this independent theology, all the emphasis is put on the present blessings of salvation: to him who believes "everlasting life" (or, more briefly, "life") is already given (John 3:16, 36; 5:24; 6:40 etc).[34] In St. John's gospel the parousia is definitely mentioned only at 21:22 (in the supplementary chapter, 14:3 is controverted). Even the other things expected in the future (resurrection of the dead and final judgement) become noticeably less important.

For these reasons many scholars, especially Bultmann and his followers, would like to eliminate them root and branch; they explain John 5:28f. and the references to the last day at 6:39, 44, 54 and 12:48, as editorial additions to the gospel which, they say, was originally devoid of any "dramatic" eschatology concerning the future. But this interpretation, made possible only by violent exercises in literary criticism, is rightly rejected by the majority of scholars. John held firmly the future hope even though he did also shift its emphasis (Cf. Stählin, Wikenhauser, Oepke, Holwerda, Corell).

Johannine Christianity lives more on its joyful awareness of having found salvation, of having already obtained true, indestructible life, and of being, through Jesus Christ, in the most intimate communion conceivable with God. It is well aware of the fact that this world is nevertheless dark, full of sin and dread of death. But with and in Jesus Christ, it has already overcome this world of death. Completely? No, only provisionally, in an intense awareness of election and victory. When it was drawn into bitter conflict, the prospect of the parousia and consummation again assumed a heightened significance. This is the case in the first Epistle of St. John where false teachers,

[34] Cf. F. Mussner, ZΩH. *Die Anschauung vom 'Leben' im vierten Evangelium unter Berücksichtigung der Johannesbriefe*, 1952, esp. pp. 144 ff.

openly and perilously disturbing the orthodox communities (cf. 4:1, 5), are called "antichrists" (2:18, 22; 4:3), and where it is said that with their appearance it has become manifest that the "last hour" has come (2:18). But the orthodox Christians are not only conscious of being enlightened by the Holy Spirit (cf. 2:20, 27) and inwardly strengthened by God himself (4:4), they also look forward to the parousia when they hope they will not be "confounded" by Christ (2:28).

Those scholars who want to see in John a "demythologized" eschatology explain this return to the old form of eschatological thought either by editorial revision, or by postulating a second writer who kept more firmly to the usual early Christian line than his master. But such critical exertions are unnecessary, unless one's aim is also to press the gospel of St. John into service to repudiate the old eschatology of the early Church.[35]

Finally the Apocalypse of John, which already looks back on a great multitude of martyrs and forward to worse onslaughts of persecution, is written with prophetic gaze fixed on the imminent final catastrophes, and also with the ardent wish that the Lord may come soon (1:3; 3:11; 22:7, 10, 12, 20). Though expectation is so vivid, we find no trace of misgivings or even thought about the fact that the parousia had not yet come (at the end of the first century!).

Only one New Testament document concerns itself explicitly with this question, because in the meantime doubters and mockers have appeared. This is the second Epistle of St. Peter. The theological answer it gives, that with the Lord, a day is as a thousand years and a thousand years as a single day (3:8), leads to a moral exhortation: the Lord is patient and wants everyone to have an opportunity to repent (3:9). Thus we find that even in communities wearied with waiting, something was still felt of the power to rouse, of belief in the parousia.

[35] For a criticism, see R. Schnackenburg, *Die Johannesbriefe,* 1953, pp. 11 ff., 30 f., 126 f., 146.

Then the question is raised what the enduring lesson of this intense eschatological awareness of the early Church is for Christian morality. It cannot be simply set aside as a phenomenon due to temporary conditions or even as a dangerous apocalyptic tendency. The early Church understood, rather, the eschatological situation of the Christian in this world, the existence which characterizes him between redemption that has already taken place and the fulfilment which has still to come, his *status viatoris,* his wayfaring condition, not only in the sense of his transitory earthly life, but also in the sense of his pilgrimage with the Church through the ages towards the end of this aeon and this world. In this way, the historical character of man and the rôle of the Church in redemptive history, as God's pilgrim people, is brought out more strongly than in later scholastic theology. From that there springs an eschatological attitude which does not push aside the final events that are to come, to the fringe of the believer's mind, but on the contrary views them, in prospect and as approaching, as a perpetual summons to vigilance and sobriety, to responsible action in the world, to combat and struggle against the destructive powers of evil and to living hope and joyful confidence. God's future decision, salvation or judgement, determines the present decision of man; the present situation assumes a decisive character for the future. Events of the last days are not only doctrines which are also recited and professed at the end of the Creed, but truths that impose obligations, and their importance for every human being and for the whole of human society becomes manifest and tangible. No Christian can escape responsibility for the course of history, for the future of the Church, for the salvation of the nations. In his age, in his historically conditioned existence, summoned by the events of history, he has to fulfil the tasks which God has set that age, and him as a child of that age. He does not live in a dimension above history or in a private sphere marked off from what happens in the rest of the world, but must work out his salvation in this world and in its history which is actually taking place, and he can only do this as a member of the Church, of that redeemed community which advances through the centuries to meet its Lord, and which both by its message and the blessings which it has power to impart, is to force back and conquer the forces of perdition in the world, gather together in itself men and nations that are willing for redemption, to submit all things to the dominion of Christ, and lead to the perfect kingdom of God. In this sense a renewal and revival of an "eschatological attitude" in the spirit of the early Church, might well be called for.

Chapter Two

THE EARLY CHURCH AS THE
ADMINISTRATOR OF JESUS' LEGACY

§ 21. CRITICISM OF THE JEWISH LAW; THE CONTROVERSY
ABOUT ITS FURTHER VALIDITY AND SIGNIFICANCE

See the bibliography to section 5, especially the two studies by V. E. Hasler and P. G. Verweijs; add P. Benoit, "La loi et la croix d'après saint Paul" in *RB* 47 (1938) pp. 481–509; F. Torm, "Die erste christliche Gemeinde und ihr Verhältnis zum Judentum" in *ZST* 13 (1936) pp. 403–28; P. Bläser, *Das Gesetz bei Paulus*, 1941; C. Maurer, *Die Gesetzeslehre des Paulus nach ihrem Ursprung und ihrer Entfaltung dargestellt*, 1941; J. Klausner, *From Jesus to Paul*, 1944, pp. 496 ff.; M. Goguel, *L'église primitive*, pp. 508 ff., Eng. tr. *The Primitive Church*, 1964; R. Bultmann, "Christus des Gesetzes Ende" in *Glauben und Verstehen*, vol. II, 1952 pp. 32–58; *id., Theologie*, pp. 117 ff., 544 ff., Eng. tr. *Theology of the New Testament*, I, pp. 109 ff., II, 203 ff.; M. Dibelius, "Die Bekehrung des Cornelius" in *Aufsätze zur Apostelgeschichte*, 1951, pp. 96–107, Eng. translation *Studies in the Acts of the Apostles;* P. Gächter, "Petrus in Antiochia (Gal. 2:11–14)" in *ZKT* 72 (1950) pp. 177–212; G. Bornkamm, *Das Ende des Gesetzes. Paulusstudien*, 1952; C. H. Dodd, *Gospel and Law*, 1951; *id.,* "Ἔννομος Χριστοῦ" in *Studia Paulina in honorem J. de Zwaan*, 1953, pp. 96–110; S. Lyonnet, *Liberté chrétienne et loi nouvelle*, 1953. – Cf. also K. Barth, *Evangelium und Gesetz*, 2nd ed. 1956; S. W. Joest, *Gesetz und Freiheit*, 2nd ed. 1956; G. Söhngen, *Gesetz und Evangelium*, 1957.

JESUS had vigorously criticized Jewish legal righteousness and its theory, but he had never rejected the law itself unreservedly,

197

or fundamentally (Cf. section 5). Hence the question was bound to arise for the early Church what attitude should be taken in future to the Jewish law of the Old Testament. Inquiry into this question will be of more than merely historical value to us, for in considering it we shall meet the ethical problem of law and freedom and the theological problem of the Spirit and moral obligation.

At first, the members of the original Jerusalem community continued to live outwardly in the ordinary Jewish way. How else would it have been possible for their people not to look upon them as a disloyal separate community, but to look on them with benevolence (cf. Acts 2:47) and for many, including even priests (6:7) and Pharisees (15:5) to join them? But these Jewish Christians did not preserve the Jewish way of life merely from habit or expediency. According to the account in Acts, St. Peter only overcame his scruples about having dealings with gentiles, as a result of a divine vision (10:10–16), and only dared to give Cornelius and his household baptism after the Spirit had manifestly been poured out upon them (10:44–48) – speaking with tongues! – and then considered it necessary to justify this action before the brethren in Jerusalem (11:1–18). It may be that Luke has given special prominence to this story, which according to him also played a part in the proceedings of the so-called Council of Jerusalem (15:7–9, 14), in order to emphasize God's intervention in the transition to the mission to the gentiles.[1] Philip, the "Hellenist", had no hesitation in giving baptism to the Ethiopian chamberlain, who was probably not a full proselyte, but only a "god-fearer" (8:26–40).

[1] Dibelius' essay (see Bibliography), where it is maintained that the account in Acts of the Apostolic Council is unhistorical; a similar view is found in E. Haenchen, *Die Apostelgeschichte,* 3rd ed. 1959, pp. 404–10. For the opposite view cf. A. Wikenhauser, *Die Apostelgeschichte,* 3rd. ed. 1956, pp. 177–81; P. Benoit, "La deuxième visite de S. Paul à Jérusalem" in *Biblica* 40 (1959) pp. 778–96. See also J. Dupont, *Les sources du Livre des Actes,* 1960, pp. 67–70.

Clear proof that the original community was still closely linked with Judaism is provided by Acts 21:20–26.

When St. Paul returned to Jerusalem after his considerable success in the missions (and with the proceeds of a big collection in his luggage, but also with gentile Christians in his company, Acts 21:16, 29), James and other leading men in the Jerusalem community said to him, "Thou seest, brother, how many thousands there are among the Jews that have believed; and they are all zealous for the law", and then they asked him if, in order to dispel all the rumours against him, he would redeem with money the Nazarite oath taken by four men, (a custom in the Jewish practice of oaths and offerings) and St. Paul humoured them.

Now it may be true that Paul himself when in a Jewish milieu "also walked keeping the law" (cf. Acts 21:24; 1 Cor. 9:20); but as the apostle of the gentiles he had broken with the law on his own account, as he had also done even more markedly for his new gentile Christians. At the Council of Jerusalem he urged a gospel for gentile Christians free of circumcision and the law, against all opposition (Acts 15; Gal. 2:1–10). With regard to the more far-reaching question whether Jewish Christians still living according to the Mosaic law should share a common table with gentile Christians, he withstood St. Peter himself to his face, in the course of an incident at Antioch and informed that leading apostle that the "truth of the gospel" would brook no ambiguous attitude, and that the law, having become unimportant for salvation, could not be allowed to stand as a wall of separation between the two parties (Gal. 2:11–14). St. James' four prohibitions (the "Apostolic Decree") may owe their existence to a compromise reached over this problem of "inter-communion" (Acts 15:20, 29; 16:4; 21:25).[2]

---

[2] Cf. J. Dupont, *Les problèmes du Livre des Actes d'après les travaux récents,* 1950, pp. 67–70; A. Wikenhauser, *Apostelgeschichte,* 3rd ed. pp. 179f.; E. Haenchen, *Die Apostelgeschichte,* 3rd. ed. pp. 410–14.

Paul in no way denied the right of Jewish Christians, themselves to live after the Jewish manner. Probably we should identify the "weak" in Rome (Rom. 14:1–15:3) mainly with former Jews who could still not accustom themselves no longer to observe certain days (14:5) and the distinction between clean and unclean foods (14:14, 20). Paul was even ready to show them consideration.[3] It was only by the Judaizers that he saw "his gospel" of justification by faith alone and not through the works of the law (Gal. 2:16) attacked, emptied of meaning and destroyed, and his missionary work among the gentiles threatened. These Judaizers required that the gentiles also be circumcised before baptism, and so he fought like a lion (Galatians) against these dangerous false teachers and propagandists, who had already been condemned at the Jerusalem assembly by the senior apostles.

Various motives, personal and theological, brought the great apostle of the gentiles to pass his very unfavourable judgements on the Mosaic law. After his own conversion from Pharisee zealous for the law (Phil. 3:5f.) to ardent disciple of Christ, he recognized the powerlessness of the law "to give life" (Gal. 3:21). After that, in trenchant theological terms, he preached the gospel of the saving grace of God as a way of salvation diametrically opposed to the law with its justification through works. In his meditation on the designs of God in human history, he saw the law as a thing that was intended to play a leading rôle only for a certain time, namely, between Moses and Christ. Although the law in itself is divine and good (Rom. 7:12), it was introduced in the period of calamity between Adam and Christ "that sin might abound" (Rom. 5:20), and to give men "the knowledge of sin" (Rom. 3:20). It developed

---

[3] M. Rauer, *Die Schwachen in Korinth und Rom nach den Paulusbriefen* (1929), is clearly of the opinion that there were also many Gentile Christians among the "weak"; but on this see J. Sickenberger, *Die Briefe des hl. Paulus an die Korinther und Römer*, 4th ed., 1932, pp. 283 ff., and the other commentaries.

into a gaoler, imprisoning human beings under the rule of the power of sin and held them fast (Gal. 3:23). This whole pattern of thought arises, of course, out of the experience of salvation in Christ: the power of sin to which man is provoked by a law, which in itself is good, was to show itself as "sinful above measure" (Rom. 7:13), and the grace of God, breaking the rule of sin and death, and making superabundant salvation possible for all mankind, was to be made manifest (Rom. 5:15–21). Consequently the way of justification through the law was closed for St. Paul, and for everyone, Jews and gentiles, only the way of faith in Jesus Christ is available (Rom. 3:20f., 28; Gal. 2:16). And so, for the faithful and the redeemed, Christ really is "the end of the law" (Rom. 10:4; cf. Gal. 3:24f.).

This Pauline teaching, taking the law of Moses as a whole and declaring it obsolete and superseded as far as the history of salvation is concerned, seems to be at odds with the ethical view that in it man is confronted with the eternally valid holy will of God. But Paul did not mean in the least to free Christians, redeemed by the blood of Christ (and therefore justified by grace alone), from moral obligations. On the contrary. Man is now freely and fully to devote himself to the service of God, to whom he belongs through baptism (Rom. 6), and through the Spirit given him, he is to mortify the deeds of the (sinful) flesh (Rom. 8:13), and also to walk in the Spirit in whom he lives (Gal. 5:25). The apostle even speaks of the "law" of the Spirit, which has freed him from the law of sin and death (Rom. 8:2) and makes the concrete demand that people should serve one another in love, "For all the law is fulfilled in one word: Thou shalt love thy neighbour as thyself" (Gal. 5:14).

The apostle requires, therefore, that the law of God should be done; but with the Christian this fulfilment takes place in a different way from that of the old law. He does not receive a multitude of precepts coming to him from without, and with which he cannot adequately comply; he hears within him the voice of the Spirit, simultaneously impelling him towards what is good and enabling him to do it. Thus the "law of the Spirit" is not a new code of laws (condensed into the commandment to love, perhaps), but rather an impulse towards the good coming from the Holy Spirit. At Romans 7:22f. Paul had already spoken in a similar way of a "law", a "good" law in man's mind (νοῦς) and another law in man's members, driving him to sin. Through the Holy Spirit the good "law" wins the upper hand in the redeemed, in so far as they allow themselves to be impelled by him. S. Lyonnet describes the difference between the "old" law and the "new" as follows: "The first law or laws, whatever they are, are spiritual in the sense that they are given to man by God as rules of conduct to which he must conform; only the new law is fulfilled, accomplished in us through the Holy Spirit. It is a principle of action, a new interior dynamism, which the law as such could obviously never be."[4]

For Paul's related concept of freedom see below, section 28. St. Paul also calls this divine summons to Christians, which thanks to the Holy Spirit is fulfilled primarily by love, the "law of Christ" (Gal. 6:2), and those who obey it (again by the power of the Holy Ghost), are "in the law of Christ" (1 Cor. 9:21).

It would be wrong to imagine this Pauline "law of Christ" as a purely inward inspiration of the Holy Spirit, for its fulfilment by love must also have reference to Jesus' promulgation of the great commandment, and moreover, St. Paul elsewhere refers on occasion to Jesus' precepts (cf. 1 Cor. 7:10, 25; 9:14; 14:37). It is, of course, problematic and controverted, how far it is possible to trace in his writings even more indirect allusions to the sayings and instructions of Christ.[5]

---

[4] *Liberté*, p. 8.

[5] C. H. Dodd in Ἔννομος Χριστοῦ ... tries to extend the evidence as far as possible. This may be questionable, but his main principles — that every Christian is offered the guidance and help of the Holy Spirit in accordance with the doctrines and teachings of Jesus — cannot be denied.

So then, even in Paul, the opponent of legalism of every kind (cf. also 2 Cor. 3:6), there is a *nova lex Christi* (a new law of Christ), and it is wrong to characterize the mere mention of it (particularly in the Apostolic Fathers) as a falling away from the gospel of grace, from "pure" Pauline Christianity. What is really important always is man's inner understanding of the law: whether he is once again to fulfil the law by his own strength, according to the letter making claims to achievement and reward, or whether in love and obedience, under the impulse of the Holy Spirit, with no thought of justifying himself thereby. The gospel of St. Matthew, another witness to early Christian thinking in this point, clearly intends to present Jesus as a new law-giver; the preacher of the Sermon on the Mount is a new Moses, announcing the absolute, holy will of God from the mountain of the Beatitudes as Moses did from Sinai. Only this will is not be accomplished in the old "pharisaical" manner, but with unreserved love.

Many scholars ascribe to Matthew a tendency to leniency in his attitude to the law, for instance E. Haenchen on Matthew 23 (see above pp. 71–2), and V. E. Hasler on Matthew 15 in comparison with Mark 7. The principle enunciated by Jesus in Mark concerning what is clean and unclean: that it is inner disposition alone that ultimately determines the nature of a moral action (Mark 7:15), is, they think, expounded by Matthew merely as an explanation of the special case of unwashed hands.[6] Although particular remarks of this kind may in part be valid, Matthew is, on the other hand, our best witness to Jesus' radical position in the Sermon on the Mount.

There is no doubt that Paul by his radical rejection of the Jewish law went far beyond Jesus' attitude to the law. But this is connected with the condition of the history of redemption

---

[6] *Gesetz und Evangelium in der alten Kirche bis Origenes*, 1953, pp. 20f. For an opposite view compare Barth, "Das Gesetzesverständnis des Evangelisten Matthäus" in *Überlieferung und Auslegung im Matthäusevangelium*, 1960, pp. 80ff.

after the crucifixion and resurrection of Jesus; his expiatory death is now the sole basis of salvation, the Spirit now the strength of moral action. Retention of the way of life dictated by the Jewish law would be quite compatible with this, as is shown by Jewish-Christian practice; but it lost all value for achieving salvation, and in relations with the gentiles who lived "without the law" it led to practical difficulties, as is shown by the incident at Antioch. Therefore sooner or later the Jewish rule of life and its ritual instructions had to be given up. Paul more than any other recognized and defended the basic principles resulting from the way of redemption revealed by Christ — through faith and not the works of the law.

The view of the law in the Epistle of James is also instructive. Although he defends the doctrine that faith without works is dead (2:14-26), thereby apparently coming out against the Pauline formulations (though only apparently — see below, section 36), he fundamentally shared the view that the will of God is to be fulfilled in a new way, above all through love (2:8ff.), and speaks of the "perfect law of liberty" (1:25; 2:12, cf. 2:8). He too sees "works" not as a means of justification, but only as the necessary completion and consequence of faith, and so is not far from the Pauline formula "faith that worketh by charity" (Gal. 5:6; cf. also section 35 below). The first Epistle of John also speaks simply and repeatedly about "fulfilment of the commandments" (cf. 2:3, 4; 3:22, 24; 5:2, 3), though still without slipping into a new legalism. The repudiation of the Mosaic law as the way of salvation did not in the least, therefore, lead to the rejection of the divine law as a moral standard. Of course, it long remained obscure in the early Church how far the law of Sinai fulfils this function and how far it was superseded, corrected or remodelled by the teaching of Jesus.

The later "classical" explanation, that the Christian is no longer bound by the Jewish ceremonial or ritual law, but is by the moral law (and especially the decalogue), is already heralded by Mark 7:15-23 and was suggested by the Epistle of James. This, strongly influenced by the Old Testament and Jewish tradition as it is, inculcates the moral instructions of Jesus sternly and austerely, but never ritual precepts.[7] Nowhere, however, in the New Testament is it clearly stated that we must differentiate between the moral and the liturgical and ritual precepts.

The Epistle to the Hebrews has no bearing on this problem. It makes full use of liturgical conceptions of the Old Testament typologically, to express its main idea, that the true high priest of the new covenant, Jesus Christ, is leading the redeemed community of the new covenant to the heavenly sanctuary, to true and perfect salvation. Ritual and observances are, therefore, not its theme, but only the background.

In order to understand the continued absence of clarification of this matter in the Church in the earliest times, we must remember that, unlike the later Church, it found itself not only in a theological, but also in a practical difficulty with regard to the Jewish law. It was, of course, the traditional and in the main established way of life among the Jewish Christians, for whom the law was scarcely susceptible of neat division in this way. The question of the law was still tormenting Jewish Christianity in the second century, and partly led to the heresy of the Ebionites.[8] And at the other end of the scale an exaggerated Paulinism, represented by Marcion and his followers, also became a heresy. The main body of the Church had to pursue its course between these two extremes. The Apostolic Fathers give various solutions. Ignatius of Antioch rejects "life after the manner of the Jews" for Christians, because the prophets had already lived in the manner of Christ Jesus (*Ep. ad Magn.* 8:1f.); we must therefore learn to live in the Christian way (10:1).

---

[7] See further section 37.
[8] Cf. H. J. Schoeps, *Theologie und Geschichte des Judenchristentums,* 1949, pp. 117–218.

Barnabas reinterpreted the liturgical and ritual laws of the Old Testament, seeing in them only a restraining yoke. "Hence he abolished it, so that the new law of our Lord, which is not a yoke of restraint, should contain no offerings prepared by men" (2:6). In essence the position to be adopted in the future has already been won: rejection of the ritual law and preservation of the moral.[9] Life, however, cannot be guided only by the general moral precepts of the Old Testament (the decalogue) and the few positive directions of Jesus supplementing them, so people (especially Irenaeus, and the Alexandrians) turned back to the natural moral law. The Church, too, issued new guiding principles and decisions on the strength of the divine authority given her. In this way there grew up a new canon of law and virtue. This development was surely inevitable. It is, however, impossible here to inquire what justification there is in the objections of those Protestant scholars who see in it the emergence of a new legalism and a general betrayal of the purpose of the preacher of the Sermon on the Mount, of the apostle Paul and of the whole New Testament.

The lasting importance of this struggle for a correct under-standing of the law lies in recognizing what a problem the "law" as such is. It is necessary as an expression and stable form of the divine will, but in its details it is often questionable. It can be a good signpost for the Christian in his moral endeavours, but it can also mislead into the legalism Jesus wanted to overcome. It can give shape to life, but it can also destroy it. Consequently there can never be an end to scrutiny of the detail of its actual form and administration, as well as to the examination of conscience by Christians, to determine whether the *nova lex Christi* is for them a gaoler in the Pauline sense, or the perfect law of liberty.

[9] In addition to the Apostolic Fathers, see Hasler, *op. cit.,* pp. 29 ff. For a rejection of the new "early Catholic" interpretation of the law, cf. esp. the representations made by Goguel and Bultmann (see bibliography).

THE EARLY CHURCH AS ADMINISTRATOR OF JESUS' LEGACY

§ 22. THE DEMANDS OF DISCIPLESHIP. THE EARLY CHURCH
AND ASCETICISM

General: F. Martinez, *L'ascétisme chrétien pendant les trois premiers siècles de l'église*, 1913; H. Strathmann, *Geschichte der frühchristlichen Askese in der Umgebung des werdenden Christentums*, vol. I, 1914; *id.*, art. "Askese" in *RAC* vol. I, 758–63 (and Bibliog. 794); H. Koch, *Quellen zur Geschichte der Askese und des alten Mönchtums*, 1933; J. Stelzenberger, *Die Beziehungen der frühchristlichen Sittenlehre zur Ethik der Stoa*, 1933; M. Hansen, *Het ascetisme en Paulus' verkondiging van het nieuwe leven*, 1938; M. Viller and K. Rahner, *Aszese and Mystik in der Väterzeit*, 1939; H. v. Campenhausen, *Die Askese im Urchristentum*, 1949; H. Preisker, *Das Ethos des Urchristentums*, 1949, pp. 81 ff.; J. Steinmann, *Saint Jean-Baptiste et la spiritualité du désert*, 1955, Eng. tr. *St. John the Baptist and the Desert Tradition*, 1963; H. Braun, *Spätjüdisch-häretischer und frühchristlicher Radikalismus*, 2 vols., 1957.

On i (Poverty): see the bibliography to section 13. Add O. Schilling, *Reichtum und Eigentum in der altkirchlichen Literatur*, 1908; M. v. Dmitrewski, *Die christliche freiwillige Armut vom Ursprung der Kirche bis zum 12. Jahrhundert*, 1913; A. Bigelmair, "Zur Frage des Sozialismus und Kommunismus der ersten drei Jahrhunderte" in *Festgabe für A. Ehrhard*, 1922, pp. 73–93; *id.*, art. "Armut II" in *RAC* vol. I, 705–09; J. Leipoldt, *Der soziale Gedanke in der altchristlichen Kirche*, 1952.

On ii (Virginity): See the bibliography to section 14. Add E. Fehrle, *Die kultische Keuschheit im Altertum*, 1910; H. Koch, *Virgines Christi* (*TU* 31, 2), 1907; P. Tischleder, *Wesen und Stellung der Frau nach der Lehre des heiligen Paulus*, 1923; M. Müller, *Die Forderung der Ehelosigkeit für alle Getauften in der alten Kirche*, 1927; G. Delling, *Paulus' Stellung zu Frau und Ehe*, 1931; *id.*, art. "παρθένος" in *ThWB* vol. V, 824–35; K. Heussi, *Der Ursprung des Mönchtums*, 1936; B. Kötting, *Die Beurteilung der zweiten Ehe im heidnischen und christlichen Altertum* (dissertation, Bonn), 1943; E. Alzas, "L'apôtre Paul et le célibat" in *RTP* 38 (1950) pp. 226–32; J. J. v. Allmen, *Maris et femmes d'après saint Paul*, 1951; K. H. Rengstorf, in *Verbum Domini manet in aeternum* (Festschrift für O. Schmitz), 1953, pp. 131–45; L. Hick, *Die Stellung des heiligen Paulus zur Frau im Rahmen seiner Zeit*, 1957; E. Kähler, *Die Frau in den paulinischen Briefen*, 1960; X. Léon-Dufour, "Mariage et continence selon saint Paul" in *A la rencontre de Dieu* (Mémorial A. Gelin), 1961, pp. 319–29.

On iii (Fasting): J. Schümmer, *Die altchristliche Fastenpraxis*, 1933; J. Haussleiter, *Der Vegetarismus in der Antike*, 1935; J. Behm, art. "νῆστις" in *ThWB* vol. IV, 926–32; A. Guillaume, *Jeûne et charité dans l'Église latine des origines au XIIe siècle*, 1954.

On iv (Attitude to the World): A. Juncker, *Ethik des Apostels Paulus,* vol. II, pp. 127ff.; C. Schneider, "Paulus und die Welt" in *Angelos* 4 (1932) pp. 11–47; R. Löwe, *Kosmos und Aion,* 1935; H. Sasse, art. "αἰών" in *ThWB* vol. I, 202; *id.,* art. "κόσμος" in *ThWB* vol. III, 882–96; A. Siemon, *Die Stellung zur Welt im Ur-Buddhismus und im Ur-Christentum* (dissertation, Bonn), 1941; R. Bultmann, "Das Verständnis von Welt und Mensch im Neuen Testament und im Griechentum" in *Glauben und Verstehen,* vol. II, pp. 59–78; R. Schnackenburg, *Die Johannesbriefe,* pp. 117–20; F. Mussner, *Christus, das All und die Kirche,* 1955; R. Völkl, *Christ und Welt nach dem Neuen Testament,* 1961 (Bibliog.).

JESUS' call to discipleship, which was originally a summons to personal sharing of life and the work of a disciple, soon became in the early Church a symbol of the union of faith with Jesus and moral imitation of him (cf. section 4). The result was that the radical demands of poverty, abnegation, celibacy, and readiness to suffer became the imperative concern of all Christians. On the other hand it was not forgotten that, unlike John the Baptist, Jesus had not renounced on principle the use of wine (Matt. 11: 19; John 2:1–11) or banquets (Mark 2:15 par.; Luke 7:36; 11:37; 14:1), and had generally been lacking in all the ascetic traits people expected to find in a prophet. He had not demanded celibacy of all his disciples, but only of those who were able (Matt. 19:12). As in the question of the law, the early Church possessed various utterances of Jesus on these matters, but which did not make it possible to solve every separate problem unequivocally (cf. the question of fasting, Mark 2:18ff. par.).[10] The gravity of Jesus' preaching of repentance was beyond question, and yet his advent inaugurated the time of salvation. Hence the early Church itself had to become clear how Jesus' instructions were to be understood in the actual detailed shaping of its life. To us, its behaviour is a valuable supplement to what we know

---

[10] On this point cf. K. T. Schäfer, ". . . und dann werden sie fasten an jenem Tage" in *Synoptische Studien* (Festschrift for A. Wikenhauser) 1954, pp. 124–47.

from the gospels and a precious object-lesson, but it certainly does not present us with a stable and uniform picture. Its attitude to many questions varied, and the judgements of its leaders varied to some extent. But that is rather a sign that it had understood Jesus: the best guiding principle in moral action is not a law determined from without, but the will of God, often difficult to recognize and needing to be rediscovered as situations and conditions change.

i. The Question of Poverty

From the account in Acts, there is no doubt that the original Jerusalem community practis d some kind of community of goods, in which everything belonged to the brethren "in common" (4:32). That this should not be interpreted as Christian "communism" is, however, clear from the following points:

Those who owned property contributed voluntarily. St. Peter's reproach to Ananias was, "Whilst it (the piece of land) remained, did it not remain to thee? And after it was sold, was it not in thy power?" Thus there was neither compulsion nor pressure to renounce property nor, on disposing of it, to pay the whole price into the common purse.

The contribution of all one's property, in spite of the verse "Neither did anyone say that aught of the things which he possessed was his own" (4:32), was not general. The action of Joseph Barnabas (4:36f.) is specially praised and emphasized.

The contributions by individuals to the common purse were made not because on principle they had repudiated private property, but for the poor members of the community. As the controversy between "Hebrews" and "Hellenists" over the maintenance of widows makes plain (6:1), the poor were given daily food and maintenance, and this was seen as a service of love (διακονία). This community of goods was hardly conceived as an economic programme, and if it had been it would have foundered lamentably, for the community grew still poorer and needed support from the gentile Christian communities (Gal. 2:10).

Matters were quite different in the "Community of the Covenant of God", very probably a leading group among the Essenes (cf. above section 13).[11] This sect imposed the obligation by its rule, that is, by its very constitution, therefore, of "community with respect to the Torah and possessions".[12] Finds of coins at the principal site at Khirbet Qumran and in the immediate vicinity where Essenes lived, seems to confirm the existence of a real community of goods among this monk-like order.[13] These differences make it unlikely that the first Jerusalem Christians were directly influenced by Essene ideas. They doubtless took Jesus' pronouncements against wealth and in favour of boundless love for the brethren, and tried to translate them into action.

We owe the idealistic account in Acts to St. Luke, who also collected the largest number of Jesus' utterances against the rich in his gospel and, to some degree, intensified them (see above, section 13). Judaism itself was a fertile soil for religious poverty, which may have surrounded Jesus in his youth (cf. the Lucan infancy narratives). But the characteristics and special elements in the practice of the original community unmistakably reveal Jesus' spirit.

Strong warnings against wealth and even vigorous accusations

[11] Opinion on the situation in Qumran and the motives for the community of possessions is not yet unanimous. Cf. S. E. Johnson, "The Dead Sea Manual of Discipline and the Jerusalem Church of Acts" in *ZAW* 66 (1954) pp. 106–20; C. Rabin, *Qumran Studies*, 1957, pp. 22–36 (there was to a certain extent private property in Qumran also); E. Bammel, in *ThWB* vol. VI, pp. 898f.; J. Maier, *Die Texte vom Toten Meer*, vol. 2, 1961, pp. 13 and 86f.

[12] *1 QS* V:2; cf. also Fl. Josephus, *Bell. Jud.* II, 122 with regard to the Essenes.

[13] In Khirbet Qumran about 250 coins were found, but there were none in the nearby caves. "From this we may conclude that the members of the community were not permitted cash and that the treasury was centralized in the Khirbet": R. de Vaux O.P. in *RB* 60 (1953) pp. 560f.

against the rich are again voiced in the Epistle of James. Prosperous members of the community must not despise the poor, for God chose those who were poor in the eyes of the world to be rich in faith and heirs of the kingdom (2:5f.). To the author of this epistle, the fundamental attitude to be adopted to poverty and wealth has been hardened by the unpleasant experience he has had with the rich even within the community (cf. 2:2f., 6f.; 5:4f.). The result is that Jesus' warnings are confirmed and receive a new impetus here. The social problem and its consequences have penetrated even into the life of religion within the Church. St. James (see also section 39 below) was not the only man who spoke out in the ancient Church; and the result was that, above all in its charitable works, it developed in the main satisfactorily.

ii. Virginity

With regard to virginity, too, the early Church imposed no general decisions binding on all its members, or even on the preachers of the gospel alone. For his own part, as an apostle, St. Paul observes, "Have we not power to eat and to drink? Have we not power to carry about a woman, a sister, as well as the rest of the apostles and brethren of the Lord and Cephas?" (1 Cor. 9:4f.). The actual question here is not that of married life or the life of virginity, but rather the right to maintenance from the communities. Hence it cannot be immediately concluded that the apostles and "brethren of the Lord" had continued to live married lives. In order to illustrate his apostolic freedom, Paul is here indicating the aids which he too might allow himself on his journeys and saying that among them is a travelling companion. Yet the form of expression and usage here ("a woman" not "an assistant") suggests that St. Paul was, in fact, thinking of a wife.[14]

[14] Cf. J. B. Bauer, "Uxores circumducere (1 Cor. 9:5)" in *BZ* 3 (1959) pp. 94–102.

Just as the great apostle to the gentiles voluntarily renounced his right to material support from the communities (9:12, 15, 18), so too his celibate life was the result of a personal decision. Questions raised at Corinth over marriage and virginity (1 Cor. 7) confronted Paul with the difficult task of rejecting a wrongly motivated sexual abstinence whilst upholding the ideal of virginity. As against the trend of thought (influenced by Gnosticism?) that "it is good for a man not to touch a woman", he warned with sober commonsense that married people should not shun one another for too long so that they might not, through the weakness of the flesh, fall into sins against chastity (vv. 1–5). He advised the unmarried too, to marry rather than "be burnt" (v. 9). But by praising Christian marriage, in which there is nothing sinful, he did not mean to detract from the ideal of virginity. Ideally he wished as far as possible all to live as he himself did; but he knew that to do so requires a special *charisma* (v. 7). His reasoning is truly Christian, but not ascetic in the sense which maintains that repudiation of the satisfaction of desires in itself means a holier life. Paul was impelled by two closely related considerations: the expectation of the parousia and the interior bond with the Lord. The idea that married people would suffer more physically in the time of tribulation before the end (see above, section 20), clearly gave added point to his counsel of virginity, but the deeper, essentially Pauline reason for it, was that the unmarried person concerns himself with the things of the Lord "to be holy both in body and in spirit" (7:32–34). To belong only to the Lord: that is the idea that led later generations to the concept of the mystical marriage. But Paul's motive was more eschatological: going forward singlemindedly to meet the Lord. It is the same motive that St. Paul put before all the Corinthians, but here given special application to the married: they must be "without crime in the day of the coming of our Lord Jesus Christ" (1 Cor. 1:8).

Right down to the present day it has remained a matter for controversy whether 7:36–38 presupposes the custom, first indisputably recorded in the third century and then quickly suppressed by the Church, by which young men and girls lived under the same roof in a kind of spiritual marriage, after taking vows of virginity.[15] Is this text concerned with a father who is having difficulties of conscience over whether his "virgin" (daughter) should marry, as earlier exegetes (till the end of the nineteenth century) assumed and most Catholics and not a few Protestants still maintain today? Or ought we not rather to see it as referring to a man who was in doubt as to whether it might not be better if he were to marry his spiritual bride? The difficulty in accepting the earlier exegesis has been that the man's inner conflict is described in such strong terms (particularly in v. 37: "steadfast in his heart" . . . "having power of his own will"), that it would be difficult to read this as referring to a father; and even more the brief advice (with no indication of a change of subject) in v. 36: "Let them marry". The more recent view, that this text refers to a young man "over age" comes into conflict with the philological difficulty that γαμίζειν has been found only in the sense "give in marriage" (and not "take in marriage"). However, in later Greek the verb could apparently mean "to marry" and there is also the fact that the expressions "having power over his own will" and "having no necessity", were frequently used for sexual desire.[16] On the other hand, it is pointed out in favour of the traditional view, that according to the legal ideas of antiquity, the father had an almost unlimited right to dispose of his daughter, and so was responsible for her marriage.[17] The interpretation that takes the text to refer to a young man of strong temperamental inclination,

---

[15] Cf. the summary of the controversy in E. B. Allo, *Première épître aux Corinthiens*, 2nd ed. 1934, pp. 189–94; more recent views are to be found in Lietzmann and Kümmel, *An die Korinther I–II*, 4th ed. 1949, pp. 178f.
[16] Lietzmann and Kümmel on this text; Bauer, *Wörterbuch*, 299 s. v.; G. Schrenk in *ThWB* vol. III, 60f. (under θέλημα).
[17] Cf. S. Lösch in *TQ* 127 (1947) p. 224; P. Ketter, "Syneisakten in Korinth? Zu 1 Kor: 7:36–38" in *TrTZ* 56 (1947) pp. 175–92.

however, deserves to be preferred; there only remains the difficulty that there is no other evidence of "spiritual betrothals" at that time. Consequently, the hypothesis of such a custom has been abandoned recently and the text understood simply of a young Christian who is contemplating the question of marriage. This view, which is gaining ground, and which has been carefully elaborated by W. G. Kümmel, and supported by J. Leal through analysis of the structure of the chapter, may very well in fact represent the solution of the problem.[18]

It is especially important that the missionary should be "free for the Lord". Like Paul, other preachers may have remained unmarried "for the sake of the kingdom of God" (cf. Matt. 19:2) in order to dedicate themselves indefatigably to missionary work. But the early Church bound no one to do so. In the "Mirror for Bishops" (1 Tim. 3:2-7) we find only the requirement that this prelate should be the husband of only one wife, which may have been a first step towards the ideal of celibacy.[19] The vision of St. John of the 144,000 virgin men "who were not defiled with women" (Apoc. 14:4), cannot with certainty be

[18] H. Kruse, "Matrimonia Josephina apud Corinthios" in *VD* 26 (1948) pp. 344-50; D. Marinelli, "De Virginibus in 1 Cor. 7:36-38" in *Studii Bib. Franc.* Liber Annuus 4 (1953-4) pp. 184-218; W. G. Kümmel, "Verlobung und Heirat bei Paulus" in *Neutestamentliche Studien für R. Bultmann,* 1954, pp. 275-95; M. Chadwick in *NTS* 1 (1954-5) pp. 267f.; J. Leal, "Super virgine sua (1 Cor. 7:37)" in *VD* 35 (1957) pp. 97-102.

[19] This requirement is often interpreted as meaning that the bishop should not take a second wife in addition to his own — cf. M. Dibelius, *Die Pastoralbriefe,* 2nd ed. 1931, p. 33; von Campenhausen, *Die Askese,* p. 45; for a contrary view, see B. Kötting, *Die Beurteilung;* C. Spicq, *Les Épîtres Pastorales,* 1947; J. Freundorfer, *Die Pastoralbriefe,* 1950, on this text; H. Conzelmann (in the new edition of Dibelius' commentary, 3rd ed. 1955, p. 43) mentions that on funeral inscriptions it was worthy of special note that one had been married once, that is, in contrast to those who had been several times divorced. J. Jeremias too (in *N. T. Deutsch,* vol. 9, 5th ed. 1949, on this text) refers to the commandment not to marry again after separation.

used in the discussion of the ideal of virginity, for this description may be no more than a metaphor either for the martyrs or for the persecuted Christian community in general (cf. 7:2ff.), which has kept itself clean of all pagan worship of idols ("fornication"), and will celebrate the marriage feast with the lamb (19:7f.; 21:2, 9).[20]

iii. Fasting

Early Christianity shows a certain reserve with regard to abstinence from food and drink. In comparison with the Church of the second century, in which the practice of fasting became more and more common, the early Church was filled with the mood of joy in salvation;[21] the first Christians "took their meat with gladness and simplicity of heart" (Acts 2:46). Fasting from penitence and sorrow (cf. Mark 2:18ff.) must be distinguished from fasting for special purposes, to which a special power to strengthen prayer was ascribed.[22] Thus the gentile Christian community of Antioch held a general liturgical fast before sending out its first missionaries (Acts 13:2f.). Paul and Barnabas laid their hands on the presbyters they appoint-

---

[20] Thus von Campenhausen, *Die Askese*, p. 43f.; G. Delling in *ThWB* vol. V, p. 835; A. Wikenhauser, *Die Offenbarung des Johannes*, 3rd ed. 1959, p. 112; M. E. Boismard in *RB* 59 (1952) pp. 161–72. In contrast, E. B. Allo, *S. Jean, L'Apocalypse*, 3rd ed. 1933, on this text together with most of the Fathers and many modern Catholic exegetes stands fast by the literal meaning as do many Protestants also; see for example, J. Behm, *Die Offenbarung des Johannes*, 5th ed. 1949; E. Lohmeyer, Die Offenbarung des Johannes, 2nd ed. 1953, *in loc.*

[21] The characteristic expression for this is ἀγαλλιᾶσθαι, see particularly 1 Pet. 1:6–8; 4:13. R. Bultmann in *ThWB* vol. I, pp. 19f.: "The word is characteristic of the consciousness of the community, which knows that by God's saving act it has been constituted the eschatological community of the last days."

[22] This is probably the meaning, too, of the additions found in some manuscripts at Mark 9:29; Acts 10:30; 1 Cor. 7:5.

ed over the communities in the missions only after fasting and praying (14:23). One of the reasons why ascetical forms of abstinence were rejected, was the appearance of Jewish-gnostic heretics who followed such practices out of contempt for the material world and dread of making themselves unclean (cf. Col. 2:21–23; 1 Tim. 4:1–5). Against them, Paul defended Christian freedom and attachment to God, on the ground that theirs were human precepts which served vain glory (Col. 2:22f.). But he also gives a more profound reason saying that everything God has made is good and, sanctified with a blessing, should be enjoyed with gratitude (1 Tim. 4:3ff.).

iv. Asceticism and the Christian Attitude to the World

Nevertheless, St. Paul did not fail to recognize the necessity of strict self-discipline. With regard to the exigencies of his apostolic office he said, "Everyone that striveth for the mastery refraineth himself from all things. And they indeed that they may receive a corruptible crown; but we an incorruptible one." Then he compares himself with a runner and a boxer: "I chastise my body and bring it into subjection" (1 Cor. 9:25–27). There was a general early Christian attitude to the "world", equally removed from flight and from morbid craving, a mistrust of it as alluring and dangerous. Paul's well-known phrases muting both terrestrial joy and terrestrial sorrow, pleasure in acquisition and enjoyment (1 Cor. 7:29–31), do indeed outwardly resemble Stoic exhortations but their eschatological motive separates them by an abyss from the Stoic ideal of *apatheia*. The Christian's aim is not an interior, imperturbable peace and insensibility, but the eternally indestructible blessings of the coming aeon (cf. also Rom. 8:18; 2 Cor. 4:17f.). His purpose is not to foster the best elements in the personality but to obtain salvation from God. St. John exhorts Christians, "love not the world, nor the things which are in the world ... the world passeth away and the concupiscence thereof; but he that doth the will of God abideth for ever" (1 John 2:15-17). James warns us against friendship with the world, which is enmity towards God (4:4); we should keep ourselves "unspotted from this world" (1:27). And according to 2 Peter 1:4, Christians are to flee from the corruption which is in the world because of concupiscence.

This pessimistic view of the "world" or of the present epoch of human history, is nothing new. It was, in fact, characteristic of later Judaism and of many currents in Hellenism. It was a result of the *euangelion*, the message of salvation and joy that Jesus brought, that no acosmic or gnostic dualist mood developed, and that in spite of what have been called the "irremediable distresses of the creation", and in spite too of all the persecutions and sufferings, the joy in salvation and confidence in victory survived in the early Church. That spirit pervaded the fundamental moral attitude and directed it towards the positive precepts and especially to love. Where ascetic tendencies do appear, through missionary zeal, or the eschatological atmosphere and the situation of strife in a world still dominated by evil, the motives are positive, and drawn from Christian beliefs.

§ 23. The Great Commandment of Love, its Reception and Development in the Early Church

See the bibliographies to sections 9 and 10; add E. Troeltsch, *Die Soziallehren der christlichen Kirchen und Gruppen*, 1912; W. Liese, *Geschichte der Caritas*, vol. I, 1922; A. v. Harnack, *Die Mission und Ausbreitung des Christentums in den ersten drei Jahrhunderten*, 4th ed. 1924, vol. I, pp. 170–220; P. Richter, *Die Liebestätigkeit in der alten Kirche*, 1930; H. Bolkestein, *Wohltätigkeit und Armenpflege im vorchristlichen Altertum*, 1939; K. Prümm, *Christentum als Neuheitserlebnis*, 1939; H. Bolkestein and W. Schwer, art. "Almosen" in *RAC*, vol. I, pp. 301–07; G. Stählin, art. "ξένος" in *ThWB* vol. V, pp. 16–25; C. H. Ratschow, "Agape. Nächstenliebe und Bruderliebe" in *ZST* 21 (1950) pp. 160-82; L. R. Stachowiak, *Chrestotes*, 1957.

JESUS having made the twofold commandment to love God and one's neighbour the foundation of the moral doctrine of the New Testament, we must now ask how this was reflected in the doctrine and exhortation of the early Church.

It is not often possible to discern a direct echo of Jesus' words in the New Testament authors. Paul declared that all commandments (in the second half of the decalogue) are summed up in one: "thou shalt love thy neighbour as thyself" (Rom. 13:9). To the Galatians he wrote, "Bear ye one another's burdens and so you shall fulfil the law of Christ" (6:2). Bearing one another's burdens probably means, above all, accepting and pardoning the weaknesses and failings of the brethren (cf. Col. 3:13f.), a favourite thought of Jesus himself, an application of the great commandment. It is noteworthy, however, that the apostle did not bring out the link between loving God and loving one's neighbour which is so marked a characteristic of Christian morality; indeed, on the whole he seldom speaks of the love of God (Rom. 8:28; 1 Cor. 2:9; 8:3; 2 Thess. 3:5). Yet love was for him the highest of all values, surpassing the *gnosis* (knowledge) that was then so highly esteemed (1 Cor. 8:1); it is the most precious of gifts (Rom. 5:5; Gal. 5:22), more precious than all the extraordinary gifts of the Spirit (1 Cor. 13).

St. Paul's rapturous hymn to love, the "canticle of love", which we clearly owe to the apostle himself (was it perhaps composed earlier and incorporated into the epistle?),[23] would

[23] The rhythmical form and arrangement in strophes, reminiscent of Hebrew poetry, raise ch. 13 above the main stream of statements about the charismata (ch. 12–14). Even if it was an already existing hymn, it was not unsuitably introduced here to extol the "higher way" surpassing all the charismata. "There is, however, no valid reason to doubt its Pauline origin" (J. Héring, *La première épître de s. Paul aux Cor.*, p. 115, Eng. tr. *The First Epistle of Paul to the Corinthians*, London 1961). For bibliography see H. Riesenfeld, *Étude bibliographique sur la notion biblique d'Agape*, 1941; id., "Note bibliographique sur 1 Cor. 13" in *Nuntius* 6 (1952) pp. 47f.; see also G. Harbsmeier, *Das Hohelied der Liebe*, 1952; H. Schlier, "Über die Liebe, 1 Cor. 13" in *Die Zeit der Kirche*, 1956,

not have been possible without Jesus, for the way in which Paul here describes the value, nature and continuing importance of charity is Christian through and through. The Greek-speaking Church deliberately chose the word *agape* to signify Christian love.[24] Its essence is selflessness, pure benevolence, and even more, readiness to bear and to forgive (13:4-7). A great deal has been written about the triad faith, hope and charity (v. 17), but it too would seem to be genuinely Christian.[25]

For St. Paul too Christian love attains its utmost in love for enemies (Rom. 12:14-21). The list of the virtues at Colossians 3:12 specifies them as heartfelt compassion, kindness, humility, gentleness, patience. These demands made on Christians, so often decried as "passive" virtues and "weaknesses", in fact reflect Jesus' heroic moral doctrine of abnegation of self, as the motive propounded in the following verse shows.

In the New Testament generally self-love is seen not as a limitation but rather as a stimulus to love of one's neighbour. The *Letter of Barnabas,* which uses Jesus' commandment of love in many admonitions on following the "Way of Light", shows itself in this respect closer to the mind of Jesus than many more modern moral theologians, when expounding it: "thou shouldst love thy neighbour more than thy life" (19:5).

The Epistle of James does not expressly base its insistence on brotherly love, which it sees the as essence of the "royal law" (2:8), on Jesus' maxim. Only one writer has deeply understood and clearly expressed the inner connection between love of

pp. 186-93; C. Spicq, "L'ἀγάπη de 1 Cor. 13" in *ETL* 31 (1955) pp. 357-70.

[24] The word is found in the Septuagint and in Jewish-Greek literature; in the non-Jewish Hellenistic language it is only found with certainty in Egypt; cf. E. Stauffer in *ThWB* vol. I, pp. 34ff.; A. Ceresa-Gastaldo, "ΑΓΑΠΗ nei documenti anteriori al NT" in *Aegyptus* 31 (1951-2) pp. 269-306; C. Spicq, *Agapè, Prolégomènes* . . ., 1955.

[25] Cf. E. B. Allo, *Prem. ép. aux Cor.* pp. 351-3; Meinertz, *Theologie,* vol. II, p. 196; Lietzmann and Kümmel, *An die Korinther I.,* vol. II, pp. 66-68.

God and love of one's neighbour, St. John, who appears in one passage to appeal directly to Jesus' commandment (1 John 4:21). Subsequent ages have never been able to better this poet and preacher of divine and fraternal love.[26]

The new perspectives opened to the theology of salvation after Easter made Paul and the other teachers of the faith of the New Testament give other grounds for Jesus' esteem for love in addition to those indicated by their Lord. For them now, the chief exemplar was God's loving dealings with fallen man. Paul saw a proof of God's love for his enemies in the fact that, whilst we were still sinners, Christ died for us (Rom. 5:8, 10). God did not spare his own Son, but delivered him up for us all (Rom. 8:32). This is the guarantee of the promise that in the future he will give us everything with Christ, and of the certitude that in the meantime nothing can separate us from the love of God (8:39). The love of Christ, too, shines forth for him, Christ who "loved me and delivered himself for me" (Gal. 2:20). He exhorts all Christians to "walk in love as Christ also hath loved us and hath delivered himself for us" (Eph. 5:2) and in particular puts before husbands as an example Christ's self-sacrificing love for his Church (Eph. 5:25). St. John realized that love of this unique kind only came into this world through God's act (1 John 4:10), but also drew the corollary from this prior love of God for us: the urgent duty of loving the brethren (v. 11).

In yet another way the outpouring of the Spirit deepened the Church's ideas about love. Love is not primarily moral effort but an inner transformation which comes to us from God by grace. It is the highest good, most worthy of our aspirations (1 Cor. 13:1-3, 8-13), a fruit of the Spirit (Gal. 5:22). For

[26] Explicit or implicit quotations of the commandment to love are to be found in *Didache* 1, 2; *Epistle of Barnabas* 19, vv. 2, 5; *Justin's Apology* 16, 6; *Dialogue with Trypho* 93. In the *Didache* and the *Epistle of Barnabas* the commandment to love is fitted into the old doctrine of the two ways, and has a lot of other moral exhortations with it.

John, it determines the nature of the children of God. One does not become a child of God by being made like God morally, but through being begotten of God (in baptism). The moral endeavour follows the supernatural act of grace. In true Christians love is a spiritual force, a kind of divine stamp which should be more and more deeply impressed on them. Christian love is of a special nature. It is "love in the Spirit" (Col. 1:8), a feature which distinguishes Christians from the world (1 John 3:10, 13f.; 4:7f.), but also the inner law of the structure of the Church, the "Body of Christ" (Eph. 4:16). It should continually increase "in knowledge and in all understanding" (Phil. 1:9; cf. 2 Thess. 1:3).

With the growth of the communal life of the early Church, charity also found rich opportunity for expression and development. In fact, it can be shown that the early Church pointed out immediate practical goals for the love which Jesus had viewed as motive of all good. The outstanding example is the care of the poor already mentioned, the voluntary community of goods in Jerusalem, and the great collection made by gentile Christians for the mother Church. When we recall such concrete exhortations as James 2:15f. and 1 John 3:17f., we see the error of the modern view that the commandment of love was by its very nature susceptible of no explicit, positive stipulations.[27] But neither did the early Church succumb to the danger of once again listing the commandment of love as one commandment among many; for John at least, there was only one new commandment, to love the brethren (1 John 2:7–11), this comprises "all justice" in itself (cf. 3:10 and section 33 below).

Christian love of the brethren has sometimes been regarded as a narrowing of universal brotherly love. It cannot be denied that there is a certain gradation, different shades of feeling, but without lessening the universality of love. Paul too writes, "Let

---

[27] Bultmann, *Theology*, vol. II, p. 222; cf. vol. I, pp. 18 f.; *id., Jesus,* pp. 97ff.

us work good to all men, but especially to those who are of the household of the faith" (Gal. 6:10), and at 1 Peter 2:17 we read, "Honour all men. Love the brotherhood" (that is, your Christian brethren — cf. 5:9). In times of self-defence and persecution such preference for the brethren in the faith is natural and justified, as long as those outside in want are not forgotten.

Care for the poor (Acts 6:1ff.; 1 Tim. 5:9f.) was not limited to material support. People were also at pains to train the communities to respect the "least of Christ's brethren" (cf. 1 Cor. 11:22; Jas. 2:1–5). Much was contributed by communal acts of worship with the liturgical banquet and celebration of the Eucharist. Care for the poor was always a matter of honour to the early Church. Hospitality also was specially practised.[28] This, of course, was a custom held in universal high esteem in the ancient world and regarded as sacred. To the young Church, Jesus' saying "I was a stranger and ye took me in" (Matt. 25:35) gave a deeper reason for hospitality which also gained heightened significance from missionary practice. The wandering messengers of the faith were dependent for their support on the communities, if they did not want to beg, like pagan priests. The lofty inspiration of this hospitality is made clear to us at 3 John 5–8: those who support the missionaries become "fellow-helpers of the truth" (v. 8). In 1 Peter the example given of the love which "covereth a multitude of sins" (4:8),[29] is, in fact,

[28] In the New Testament: Romans 12:13; Heb. 13:1f.; 1 Pet. 4:9; 3 John 5–8 (cf. 10); and as a requirement for bishops, 1 Tim. 3:2; Titus 1:8; and for widows, 1 Tim. 5:10. cf. H. Rusche, *Gastfreundschaft in der Verkündigung des NT und ihr Verhältnis zur Mission*, 1958.

[29] The similar saying recorded in James 5:20 is generally seen as a quotation from Proverbs 10:12 – where, in the Septuagint, the wording and meaning are different. The text probably refers to power of love to save man from sin in the sight of God, cf. Jesus' words to the sinner at Luke 7:47. Cf. C. G. Selwyn, *The First Epistle of Peter* (2nd ed. 1947) *in loc.* The same idea is also expressed in 1 *Clem.* 49, 5; 50, 5; 2 *Clem.* 16, 4. It was "perhaps familiar as a proverb" in the early Church (J. Michl, *Die Katholischen Briefe* [1953] on James 5:20).

hospitality "without murmuring" (v. 9). In the ages which followed it remained a matter of deep concern for the Church.[30]

The love that Jesus demanded, however, was not to be fully demonstrated by physical welfare schemes and organized charity. The exhortations concerning inner disposition, and spiritual works of charity remain preponderant. The brotherly forgiveness demanded by Paul in Jesus' spirit (Col. 3:13; Eph. 4:32), was wonderfully illustrated in the life of this passionate man himself. He told the Corinthians to forgive and fraternally welcome one of the members of the community who had repented after doing the apostle a great injustice and causing him great grief. He himself had already forgiven "but for your sakes have I done it in the person of Christ; that we be not overreached by Satan" (2 Cor. 2:7–11; cf. 7:12). But fraternal correction too can be a work of charity (Rom. 5:14; 1 Thess. 5:14; 2 Thess. 3:15). The call to waive one's claims to legal justice for love's sake is redolent of the spirit of the Sermon on the Mount.

Lawsuits which members of the Corinthian community had brought before pagan courts gave him occasion to discuss this question (1 Cor. 6:1–11). There seems to be a certain contradiction here, in that Paul first recognizes the recourse to the court as valid, asking only that reconciliation be made through Christian brethren (vv. 1–6), but then demands total renunciation of the right to justice (vv. 7–8): "Why do you not rather take wrong? Why do you not rather suffer yourselves to be defrauded?" But what we have here, as often in St. Paul, is what E. Dinkler has described as "a rapid forward-movement of thought, an intensification of the idea, a more radical formulation of the demand in the course of writing", the higher ideal, which cannot be a principle of general legislation by the Church,

---

[30] See von Harnack, *Mission und Ausbreitung,* vol. I, pp. 200ff.; J. Marty, "Sur le devoir chrétien de l'hospitalité aux trois premiers siècles" in *RHPR* 19 (1937) pp. 288–95; Stählin in *ThWB,* vol. V, pp. 23f.

is expressed by Paul in questions which are intended to rouse the depths of the Christian conscience.[31]

The exhortations against seeking revenge (1 Thess. 5:15; Rom. 12:17; 1 Pet. 3:9) come even nearer to the words of the preacher of the Sermon on the Mount. 1 Peter 2:21ff. puts before slaves, who were often unjustly treated, the picture of the innocent but tortured Lord who "when he was reviled, did not revile; when he suffered, he threatened not".

Exhortations to kindness, forbearance, patience, moderation and so on are often formulated in lists of virtues, and it cannot be denied that there is much in them that was formal, worn with usage and traditional, taken over from pagan and Jewish-Hellenistic paraenesis, moral exhortation.[32] Every preacher pays his tribute to the taste of his times. But this fact must not blind us to the Christian motives interwoven with them. The same is true of the so-called "domestic codes" containing instruction for married couples, parents, children and slaves and showing the tendency to subordinate daily life to the Lord.[33] It would not, however, be right to draw from generalities, far-reaching inferences about the actual conditions in individual communities. On the other hand, there had already been good cause to repeat the frequent encouragements to concord (see above,

[31] Cf. E. Dinkler, "Zum Problem der Ethik bei Paulus. Rechtsnahme und Rechtsverzicht (1 Cor. 6:1–11)" in *ZThK* 49 (1952) pp. 167–200; L. Vischer, *Rechtsverzicht und Schlichtung. Die Auslegungsgeschichte von 1 Kor. 6:1–11,* 1955.

[32] Cf. A. Vögtle, *Die Tugend- und Lasterkataloge im NT,* 1936; S. Wibbing, *Die Tugend- und Lasterkataloge im NT und ihre Traditionsgeschichte,* 1959. In this latter work it is shown in conjunction with the Qumran texts (esp. *1* QS IV, 3–14) that Paul is influenced also by a tendency in Later Judaism to make up lists of virtues and vices.

[33] Cf. K. Weidinger, *Die Haustafeln. Ein Stück urchristlicher Paränese,* 1928; D. Schroeder, *Die Haustafeln des NT, ihre Herkunft und ihr theologischer Sinn,* 1959. Schroeder has shown, against Weidinger's view, that it is not simply a matter of taking over a popular Hellenistic moral system. Cf. also section 27.

section 19). In an especially eloquent passage Paul exhorts the Philippians to "fulfil (his) joy, that you be of one mind, having the same charity, being of one accord, agreeing in sentiment. Let nothing be done through contention, neither through vain glory; but in humility, let each esteem others better than themselves . . ." (2:1 ff.). Then comes the most sublime example: the self-emptying and humbling of the pre-existent Son of God from equality with God to the form of a servant and to obedience unto death. The formal eloquence of the preceding exhortation is forgotten in the presence of this highest of arguments.

The danger of losing the unity of theme in the midst of so many separate exhortations is obviated by the emphasis put on love. At Colossians 3:14 charity is defined as the "bond of perfection" and in the enumeration at 2 Peter 1:7 it is made the peak and crown. The *First Epistle of Clement* also seeks to preserve the pre-eminence of love, but after extolling the other virtues at great length, it finds itself somewhat short of breath: "You see, beloved, how great and wonderful love is, and its perfection cannot be exhaustively described" (50:1).

Chapter Three

NEW PRINCIPLES AND DECISIONS

§ 24. THE NEW LITURGY AND THE REQUIREMENTS OF PIETY

F. J. Dölger, *Sol salutis. Gebet und Gesang im christlichen Altertum*, 2nd ed. 1925; L. Duchesne, *Origines du culte chrétien*, 5th ed. 1925; A. Duhm, *Der Gottesdienst im ältesten Christentum*, 1928; W. Bauer, *Der Wortgottesdienst der ältesten Christen,* 1930; H. Greeven, *Gebet und Eschatologie im Neuen Testament*, 1931; *id.* in *ThWB* vol. II, pp. 801–8; G. Harder, *Paul und das Gebet*, 1936; J. Leipoldt, *Der Gottesdienst der ältesten Kirche – jüdisch? griechisch? christlich?* 1937; J. M. Nielen, *Gebet und Gottesdienst im Neuen Testament*, 1937; P. Schubert, *Form and Function of the Pauline Thanksgivings*, 1939; P. Vielhauer, *Oikodome. Das Bild vom Bau in der christlichen Literatur vom Neuen Testament bis Clemens Alex.*, 1939; E. Lohmeyer, *Kultus und Evangelium*, 1942; O. Cullmann, *Urchristentum und Gottesdienst*, 2nd ed. 1950, Eng. tr. *Early Christian Worship*, 1953; E. Sjöberg, "Kirche und Kultus im Neuen Testament" in *Ein Buch von der Kirche*, 1950, pp. 85–109; Meinertz, *Theologie*, vol. II, pp. 166ff.; W. Hahn, *Gottesdienst und Opfer Christi*, 1951; B. Reicke, *Diakonie, Festfreude und Zelos in Verbindung mit der altchristlichen Agapenfeier*, 1951; G. Delling, *Der Gottesdienst im Neuen Testament*, 1952; P.-M. Menoud, "Les Actes des Apôtres et l'eucharistie" in *RHPR* 33 (1953) pp. 21–36; H. Schlier, "Die Verkündigung im Gottesdienst der Kirche" in *Die Zeit der Kirche* 1956, pp. 244–64; A. Dietzel, "Beten im Geist" in *TZ* 13 (1957) pp. 12–32 (Comparison with Qumran); E. Schweizer, *Der Gottesdienst im Neuen Testament*, 1958; A. Hamman, *La prière I: Le Nouveau Testament*, 1959; H. Schürmann, art. "Kult im Neuen Testament" in *LThK* vol. VI, 662–65 (Bibliog.).

J. Jeremias gives the fullest bibliography on the Eucharist in his *Die*

Abendmahlsworte Jesu, 3rd ed. 1960, Eng. tr. *The Eucharistic Words of Jesus,* 1955; H. Schürmann, *Der Paschamahlbericht Lukas 22: (7–14) 15–18,* 1953; *id., Der Einsetzungsbericht Lukas 22: 19–20,* 1955; *id., Jesu Abschiedsrede Lukas 22: 21–38,* 1957; see further P. Neuenzeit, *Das Herrenmahl. Studien zur paulinischen Eucharistieauffassung,* 1960; J. Betz, *Die Eucharistie in der Zeit der griechischen Väter* II/1: *Die Realpräsenz des Leibes und Blutes Jesu im Abendmahl nach dem Neuen Testament,* 1961.

PRAYER and worship are forms of religious expression and do not belong directly to the field of morals; yet Christian piety is so closely concerned with morality that we must look briefly at the prayer and liturgical life of the first Christians. In doing so we shall restrict ourselves to what was new and characteristic in early Christian worship and to its influence on moral behaviour.

At first the religious life of the first Christians in Jerusalem was characterized by a strong feeling of close unity. They continued "with one accord" in the temple (Acts 2:46), where they met together in the court of Solomon (5:12). The surveillance of the new group by the Jewish religious authorities and the interrogation of its leading men John and Peter, resulted in their drawing even closer together in their faith in Jesus the Messias. They all met, too, in private houses for their special assemblies, the "breaking of bread" (2:46), perhaps the celebration of the Eucharist,[1] instruction by the apostles (5:42) and prayer (12:12). After the first release of the apostles Peter and John by the Sanhedrin, they raised their voices "with one accord" to God and put themselves under his continuing

---

[1] The question is still undecided. This view is rejected by Steinmann, among others, in *Die Apostelgeschichte,* 4th ed. 1934, pp. 40–42; J. Behm, in *ThWB* vol. III, p. 729; and judgement is reserved by J. M. Nielen, *Gebet,* pp. 226–31; A. Wikenhauser, *Die Apostelgeschichte,* 3rd ed. 1956, pp. 55f.; J. Gewiess, *Die urapostolische Heilsverkündigung,* p. 152 and *LThK* vol. II, col. 706 ff. connect it with the Eucharist; and M. Meinertz, *Theologie,* vol. I, p. 132, and P. H. Menoud, "Les Actes", interprets it of the Eucharist.

protection in a prayer recorded for us in Acts 4:24–30. They recognized his guidance in the destiny of his "holy servant Jesus"; they desired his help in their own open preaching of God's word, and he heard their request by filling all those present with the Holy Spirit (4:31). They ascribed special power to prayer in common (cf. Matt. 18:20), and this could be manifested in spiritual phenomena. When Peter was kept in strong ward by Herod Agrippa I, the prayer of the community ascended to God ceaselessly for him (12:5).

The picture of a Church continually at prayer and enkindled by the Spirit of God is also drawn for us by Paul in 1 Corinthians 14. Here the foreground is indeed filled by manifestations of the *pneuma:* ecstasies, revelations and spirit-filled, edifying utterances; but these too remain a service of prayer … (v. 13 ff.). The only thing of which there is no explicit mention is the reading of the Scriptures which formed a major ingredient of the Sabbath liturgy in the synagogue, an indication that the communities of Christ had not simply taken over the Jewish pattern.[2] In these assemblies the Spirit came upon many members of the community so that they stammered and prayed in that indeed unintelligible but still fascinating way which St. Paul called "speaking with tongues" *(glossolalia).*[3] Others were instructed by the Spirit in the interpretation (vv. 26–28) of these sounds (which may indeed have been special words: cf. the "tongues of men and of angels" in 1 Cor. 13:1). Others, again, possessed the Spirit of prophecy by which they addressed eloquent discourses of edification and encouragement to the community (v. 3), sometimes even expounding mysteries (cf. v. 26), or foretelling the future (cf. Acts 11:28; 21:10f.; and perhaps 21:9).

[2] Cf. W. Bauer, *Wortgottesdienst,* p .19; M. Goguel, *L'église primitive,* pp. 270 ff.
[3] Cf. E. B. Allo, *1 Cor.,* pp. 374–84 (with additional bibliographies); J. Behm, art. "γλῶσσα" in *ThWB* vol. I, 721–26; H. Lietzmann, *An die Kor.,* pp. 68–71; J. J. Martin, "Glossolalia in the Apostolic Church" in *JBL* 63 (1944) pp. 123–30; J. Gewiess in *LThK* vol. IV, 972 f.

These manifestations, which introduced an irrational, ecstatic element into divine service, induced St. Paul to issue certain moral warnings. He wished those endowed with "tongues" to speak only when there was also an interpreter present, so that the whole community could benefit by what they said and be inwardly edified. "Let all things be done to edification" (v. 26). These words were meant in no subjective, pietistic sense, as we might too easily understand them today, but were aimed at securing the real building up[4] of that supernatural community which Paul characterized in the profound metaphors of "the body of Christ" (1 Cor. 12; Rom. 12; Eph. 4:12ff. etc.), "the temple of God" (1 Cor. 3:16f.), and the "habitation of God" (Eph. 2:20–22). They seem also to have sung together "psalms, hymns and spiritual canticles" (Col. 3:16; Eph. 5:19).

Another characteristic of divine service in the early Church was its relation to Christ. One of the oldest formulae of prayer, undoubtedly originating in the Aramean-Palestinian liturgy was *marana – tha* (Our Lord, come!) (1 Cor. 16:22). It bears witness to the lively yearning for the parousia found among the first Christians (cf. section 20), and also to their devotion to Christ. After Easter those who believed in Christ prayed not only according to the instructions their Lord had given them, but also to their Lord himself. The epistles of the New Testament contain more traces of hymns to Christ than might at first appear.

One such hymn to Christ is certainly preserved at 1 Timothy 3:16, and at least a fragment of another at Ephesians 5:14. But the well-known hymn of praise at Philippians 2:6–11, on the Lord humbled to death and exalted to God's right hand, should also be understood as a piece of writing liturgical in form, whether it was composed by Paul himself or only taken over by him, perhaps with a few additions.[5] Furthermore, the text glorifying

[4] Cf. P. C. Trossen, "Erbauen" in *TG* 6 (1914) pp. 804ff.; P. Vielhauer, *Oikodome;* O. Michel in *ThWB* vol. V, pp. 39–47.
[5] Lastly, see Cerfaux, *Christ in the Theology of St. Paul*, pp. 347–97; J. R. Geiselmann, *Jesus der Christus,* 1951, pp. 130–54 (with further bibliog-

Christ at Colossians 1:15–20; 2:9–15 seems to present more material of a similar kind, though the hand of St. Paul is more clearly discernible. Recently it has been suggested that it is possible to recognize still more fragments of old hymns behind many passages in the epistles.[6]

The community of Christ took its cult of the *kyrios* (the Lord), which distinguished it both from Judaism and from paganism, very seriously. St. Paul says sternly, "If any man loves not our Lord Jesus Christ, let him be anathema" (1 Cor. 16:22).[7] It is not certain, although it seems probable, that it was already customary to celebrate Sunday, the day of Jesus' resurrection.[8]

Another element with significance for the moral sphere was the profession of faith, the creed. We have, of course, to distinguish between the liturgical, doctrinal and missionary uses of

raphies); M. Meinertz, "Zum Verständnis des Christushymnus Phil. 2:5–11" in *TrTZ* 61 (1952) pp. 168–92; J. Jeremias in *Studia Paulina in honorem J. de Zwaan*, 1953, pp. 152–54; L. Krinetzki, "Der Einfluß von Is. 52:13–53:12 auf Phil. 2:6–11" in *TQ* 139 (1959) pp. 157–93.

[6] Cf. R. Bultmann, "Bekenntnis- und Liedfragmente im 1 Petr." in *Coniect. Neotest. XI in honorem A. Fridrichsen*, 1947, pp. 1–14; E. Käsemann, "Eine urchristliche Taufliturgie" in *Festschrift for R. Bultmann*, 1949, pp. 133–45 (Col. 1:15–20); W. Nauck, "Eph. 2:19–22 — ein Tauflied?" in *EvTh* 13 (1953) pp. 362–71; G. Schille, *Liturgisches Gut im Epheserbrief* (unprinted dissertation, Göttingen, 1953); F.L. Cross, *1 Peter — a Paschal Liturgy*, 1954; M. E. Boismard, *Quatre hymnes baptismales dans la première épître de Pierre*, 1961.

[7] Cf. G. Bornkamm, "Das Anathema in der urchristlichen Abendmahlsliturgie" in *TLZ* 75 (1950) pp. 227–30; J. A. T. Robinson, "Traces of a Liturgical Sequence in 1 Cor. 16:20–24" in *JTS* 4 (1953) pp. 38–41; C. Spicq in *NovT* 1 (1956) pp. 200–4; C. F. D. Moule in *NTS* 6 (1959 to 60) pp. 307–10.

[8] The oldest traces are in 1 Cor. 16:2; Acts 20:7 and Apoc. 1:10 (at least for the expression "day of the Lord"); then in *Didache* 14:1. Cf. C. Callewaert, "La syntaxe eucharistique à Jérusalem berceau du dimanche" art. in *ETL* 15 (1938) pp. 34–73; Foerster, art. in *ThWB* vol. III, pp. 1095f.; H. Riesenfeld, "Sabbat et Jour du Seigneur" in *NT Essays* (in memory of T. W. Manson), 1959, pp. 210–17.

creeds,[9] but there is always a link too with moral profession of faith. Jesus himself had made the courageous confession of his name a duty binding on all his followers (Mark 8:38 = Luke 9:26; Matt. 10:32f. = Luke 12:8f.). The more clearly the early Church differentiated itself from its surroundings, and the more conscious it became of its individuality, the more prominent profession of faith in Jesus became. St. Paul, no doubt with a liturgical (baptismal) practice in mind said, "For if thou confess with thy mouth the Lord Jesus and believe in thy heart that God hath raised him up from the dead, thou shalt be saved. For with the heart, we believe unto justice; but with the mouth, confession is made to salvation" (Rom. 10:9f.). A clearly formulated profession of faith became still more important when it was necessary to take defensive measures against false teaching, as we can see from the Johannine writings (see below, section 33). This led to the content of the faith (*fides quae creditur*) becoming increasingly important.

In addition, strong moral influences flowed from the deepest mystery of Christian worship, the celebration of the Lord's supper.

At Corinth abuses arose at these meetings, which were clearly restricted to the baptized and which took place in the evening. Jesus' sacred institution was celebrated within the framework of a common meal, the partaking of the Eucharist being linked with a fraternal meal, the *agape*,[10] so organically linked with it, that the whole celebration apparently bore the name "the Lord's

---

[9] Cf. O. Cullmann, *Die ersten christlichen Glaubensbekenntnisse*, 1949: he lists Baptism and the Catechumenate, Liturgy, Exorcisms, Persecution, and polemic against false teachers as the five reasons for the appearance of the confessions of faith (that is, as formal creeds).

[10] Cf. Allo, *1 Cor.*, pp. 285–93, and in a different way L. Thomas in *Dict. de la bible*, suppl. I, 134–53. Nevertheless, the ancient controversy as to whether a communal meal, an agape meal, was formerly linked with the Eucharist may be answered positively; cf. also Bihlmeyer-Tüchle, *Kirchengeschichte*, vol. 1, pp. 125f.

supper" (1 Cor. 11:20).[11] But the wealthy, arriving early, did not wait to eat and drink (v. 21) until the poorer members of the community (who were probably mostly slaves) had arrived. These latter should have been entertained by their better-endowed brethren in the faith, in token of love. But they went hungry. And the result, in the apostle's opinion, was that the character of the Lord's supper had been destroyed. This lack of the sense of Christian community was something "unworthy" which angered Paul (v. 27) and, according to his account, called down divine punishments on the community: there were many among them who had fallen sick, and not a few who had died (v. 30).

The Lord's supper manifested and actualized through the common use of the Eucharistic bread and wine the supernatural society in Christ, the "Body of Christ" (cf. 1 Cor. 10:17). This should also have been demonstrated in a loving attitude of mind and have been expressed in the celebration itself. Therefore Paul requires a serious self-examination (1 Cor. 11:28), particularly (according to the context) with regard to the attitude one has towards the brethren, who also participate. Whoever does not give the body (the eucharistic body of our Lord) especial reverence (and that includes his relation to the community as the "body of Christ" cf. 10:17) eats and drinks judgement unto himself (v. 29).[12] Although the gospel of St. John gives even greater prominence to the mystical effects of the holy Eucharist, being filled with eternal, divine life, and entering into the closest conceivable union with Christ and God (cf. 6:53–58), Jesus clearly also wished that those united with him should bring forth moral fruits of love (cf. 13:14f., 34f.; 15:9f., 12, 17).

Thus it was already recognized that the faithful should share

[11] See further P. Neuenzeit, *Das Herrenmahl,* pp. 69–76; H. Schürmann, "Die Gestalt der urchristlichen Eucharistiefeier" in *MTZ* 6 (1955) pp. 107–31; *id.,* "Eucharistiefeier" in *LThK* vol. III, 1159–62.
[12] For this controverted verse see P. Neuenzeit, *op. cit.,* pp. 37f.

in Jesus' bequest to them with holy reverence and discern the Body of the Lord, that is, distinguish between it and common food (1 Cor. 11:29). Paul had occasion to refer to this in connection with another special problem, whether Christians might be allowed to participate in pagan sacrificial meals (1 Cor. 10:14–22).

St. Paul forbade this in very clear terms. Participation in such pagan acts of worship, even though they were so devoid of meaning, is something different from eating the flesh of sacrifices offered for sale in the public markets (v. 25). But he himself raised an objection which was also brought forward by the "strong" in conscience (cf. 8:4), that there are in fact no false gods and hence the flesh of sacrifices offered to the gods is nothing in itself (10:19). The kernel of his reply does not lie, as has been objected, in a magical and superstitious idea that in a sacrificial meal the devils won influence over those who ate (cf. v. 20), but rather refers to the dignity and sanctity of the Christian liturgical meal and the honour of the Lord. Christians cannot be at one and the same time "partakers with devils" and united with Christ; they cannot drink both the chalice of the Lord and the chalice of devils; they cannot share in the Lord's table and in the table of the devils (vv. 20b–21). That would involve provoking the Lord, impugning his honour and arousing his anger (v. 22). Far from exhibiting less noble ideas, then, this very passage reveals the high moral influence of Christian worship.[13] St. Paul also guards against magical interpretations of the sacrament at the beginning of chapter 10 (vv. 1–13).

The apostles had no need to exhort people to attend the services of the early Church. But the author of the Epistle to the Hebrews found it necessary to call on some members of the Church to do so (10:25); so already in the second generation lassitude had begun to be perceptible. The responsible shepherds of the communities saw this as a deadly danger, and rightly so, for if

---

[13] On this point see H. v. Soden, *Sakrament und Ethik bei Paulus,* 1931.

the faithful cut themselves off from the warm life of the community, shun sermons and loving encouragement (Heb. 10:24) and no longer draw from the wells of salvation, they cannot prosper as Christians and will not be able to stand before the Lord at the parousia (10:25). The sober St. James gives another practical direction for divine service. The rich man "having a golden ring, in fine apparel" is not to be shown to the best seats and a poor man to a poor and uncomfortable seat (2:2f.). Some measure of lukewarmness, probably in the liturgical life too, had appeared in the Laodicean community by the time of the Apocalypse. It earned a very strong rebuke from John the Seer (3:14–18).

On the other hand the many noble songs of the heavenly court and the redeemed that we hear in the Apocalypse,[14] give us some impression of the developing liturgy of the Church of Jesus Christ on earth. God's final victory and the justification of the persecuted are contemplated in bold visions and celebrated in hymns of anticipation. It cannot be doubted that these hymns of praise to the Almighty and the Lamb who was slain and is now worshipped (cf. esp. 5:6–14; 7:10; 15:3f.; 19:6ff.) also rang out in a similar way in the services of the Christian communities and gave fresh heart to the Church of the martyrs.[15] They were surely more effective than many sermons in stimulating the great virtues, unshakeable faith and steadfast readiness to suffer, necessary at that time of conflict (cf. 13:10; 14:12).

[14] Cf. Apoc. 1:8; 4:8 and 11; 5:9f., 12 and 13; 7:12; 11:15 and 17f.; 12:10–15; 15:3f.; 19:1f., 5 and 6–8.
[15] According to E. Peterson, ΕΙΣ ΘΕΟΣ, 1926, p. 313, the doxologies of the Apocalypse are borrowed from the language of Aramaic acclamations. See further L. Mowry, "Revelation 4–5 and Early Christian Liturgical Usage" in *JBL* 71 (1952) pp. 75–84; T. F. Torrance, "Liturgie et Apocalypse" in *VC* 11 (1957) pp. 28–40; G. Delling, "Zum gottesdienstlichen Stil der Johannesapokalypse" in *NovT* 3 (1959) pp. 107–37; S. Läuchli, "Eine Gottesdienststruktur in der Johannesoffenbarung" in *TZ* 16 (1960) pp. 359–78 (who certainly goes too far).

NEW PRINCIPLES AND DECISIONS

§ 25. THE ATTITUDE TO PUBLIC AUTHORITIES

See the bibliography to section 12; add W. Bauer, *Jedermann sei untertan der Obrigkeit!* 1930; F. J. Dölger, "Zur antiken und frühchristlichen Auffassung der Herrschergewalt von Gottes Gnaden" in *Antike und Christentum* 3 (1932) pp. 117–27; S. Lösch, *Deitas Jesu und antike Apotheose*, 1933; L. Gaugusch, "Die Staatslehre des Apostels Paulus nach Röm 13" in *TG* 26 (1934) pp. 529–50; W. Foerster, art. "ἐξουσία" in *ThWB* vol. II, pp. 559–71; J. Straub, *Das Herrscherideal in der Spätantike,* 1939; E. Stauffer, *Christus und die Cäsaren,* 1948, Eng. tr. *Christ and the Caesars*; W. Schweitzer, *Die Herrschaft Christi und der Staat im Neuen Testament,* 1949; F. Keienberg, *Die Geschichte der Auslegung von Röm 13:1–7* (unprinted dissertation, Basle) 1952; K. H. Schelkle, "Staat und Kirche in der patristischen Auslegung von Röm. 13:1–7" in *ZNW* 44 (1952–3) pp. 223–36; J. Héring, *A Good and a Bad Government,* 1954; O. Kuss, "Paulus über die staatliche Gewalt" in *TG* 45 (1955) pp. 321–34; H. Schlier, "Die Beurteilung des Staates im Neuen Testament" in *Die Zeit der Kirche,* 1956, pp. 1–16; L. Goppelt, *Der Staat in der Sicht des Neuen Testaments,* 1956; A. Strobel, "Zum Verständnis von Röm 13" in *ZNW* 47 (1956) pp. 67–93; E. Käsemann, "Röm. 13:1–7 in unserer Generation" in *ZThK* 56 (1959) pp. 316–76 (Bibliog.); P. Meinhold, *Römer 13. Obrigkeit, Widerstand, Revolution, Krieg,* 1960.

JESUS' decision over the question of the poll tax (Mark 12:13–17 par.; see above, section 12) showed the early Church the line it should take in its attitude to the public authorities, but that terse saying did not relieve it of the task of determining its actual relations with those in authority. It was soon involved in some very delicate questions. How ought it to react to the demands of the Jewish authorities — who also claimed religious authority? How should missionaries deal with Roman officials, and how should they act when brought before their tribunals? At that time, too, the cult of the ruler and emperor was casting its shadow over the Christian community, which recognized the glorified Messias Jesus as its only Lord.

The complex events and ever-changing experiences that befell the young Church were not without their influence on the pronouncements of the writers of the New Testament. If we do not succeed in finding in the New Testament a single answer settling all the questions relating to the relationship between the early Church and the state, it must be remembered that these writers were addressing themselves to a certain situation and their purpose was rather to give practical admonition than to deal with this set of problems exhaustively from the point of view of theory and theology. Furthermore the Christian communities hardly represented a political factor with which the powerful Roman state had to reckon, at most a very minor one (cf. Tacitus *Annals* XV, 44). It is mostly a question, therefore, of the relations of individual Christians with the state and its rulers. At the same time, however, a judgement of principle must underlie these practical, concrete pronouncements. We must, therefore, first examine the individual replies and then, if it is possible, discern the general principle which governs these replies.

The interrogation of the apostles before the Sanhedrin at Jerusalem (Acts 4:5–22; 5:17–40) contains, besides St. Peter's discourse, the adoption of a definite attitude towards the orders of the Jewish authorities. Peter acted with the frankness which Jesus had encouraged in his disciples (Acts 4:13f.; and cf. Matt. 10:19f.). When they were forbidden to preach, Peter and John replied "We must obey God rather than men" (4:19; 5:29). The fact that it is possible to find parallels to this dictum both in Judaism and paganism (see the commentaries), is less significant than the fact that the apostles dared to defy the highest, theocratic authority of their nation. St. Stephen even went on to sharp polemics (Acts 7:51–53).

All the more striking, therefore, is the loyalty to the Roman state and its organs, for which there is a great deal of evidence in the New Testament. Even when Roman officials showed themselves unfriendly, we can detect an effort to soften this impression. This is true even of Jesus' trial, in which the gospel accounts from Mark to John show increased intention to absolve

Pilate.[16] It is also true of the accounts of the missionary journeys of St. Paul, his imprisonment and first trial.

At Philippi Paul and Silas were scourged and thrown into prison. When the town magistrates learned that they were Roman citizens they apologized and gave the missionaries an escort to the town boundaries (Acts 16:19–24, 36–40). At Thessalonica the Jews are made responsible for the uproar against St. Paul and the new Christians; they accuse the missionaries of acting contrary to the imperial ordinances, by saying that "there is another king, Jesus" (Acts 17:7). We hear a Jewish slogan here which caused a lot of trouble for the early Church. But we also recognize a tendency constantly exhibited by Luke in his narrative, that of demonstrating the political innocuousness of Christianity. At Corinth the Roman proconsul Gallio appears completely uninterested in the charges brought by the Jews and decides that the case concerned an internal controversy over religion (Acts 18:13–17). In the riot of the silversmiths at Ephesus some of the Asiarchs are shown as well-disposed towards Paul and warn him not to show himself to the crowd (19:31). In general the Roman authorities behave correctly; one does, of course, feel that they were looking at things from a political as well as a juridical point of view: they did not want to arouse the easily excitable Jews and involved themselves as little as possible.[17] However, a Roman tribune actually saves Paul from death during the riot among the crowd in Jerusalem and also permits him to address the people (21:31–22:24). The development of events here is dependent on the fact that Paul identifies himself as a Roman citizen. The trial at Caesarea shows the Jews, through the lawyer Tertullus, making a further attempt to make out Paul and the

---

[16] See R. Bultmann, *Die Geschichte der synoptischen Tradition*, 2nd ed. 1931, p. 305; M. Goguel, *Das Leben Jesu*, 1934, pp. 311ff., Eng. tr. *The Life of Jesus*, 1954; K. H. Schelkle, *Die Passion Jesu in der Verkündigung des NT*, 1949, pp. 24ff.; J. Blinzler, *Der Prozess Jesu*, 3rd ed. 1960, pp. 47ff.

[17] Cf. Acts 18:16f.; 23:16ff. and 23ff.; 25:1ff.

"sect of the Nazarenes" to be seditious (24:5). To counter their endeavours Paul cleverly attempted to shelter beneath the cloak of the tolerated Jewish religion (cf. 24:10–21; 25:8; 26:5–23).[18] The venality of the proconsul Felix is not concealed (24:26f.), but is balanced by the fairness of his successor, Festus (25:12, 17 to 21, 25). The captain who, during the shipwreck, saved his prisoners from death, is mentioned with praise (27:43) and the light imprisonment in Rome is emphasized (26:16, 30f.).

First-hand statements in the epistles make it clear that in this account Luke was not following a personal bias but reveals a general concern of the early Church. Despite St. Paul's not always satisfactory experiences with the Roman authorities, there is not a word in his writings against the empire. On the contrary, there is the much discussed passage at Romans 13:1–7, which binds Christians in conscience to obey the government of the state.

It is certainly perverse to try to cut this section out of St. Paul's chapters 12–15 as an interpolation. The admonitions are usually fairly loosely strung together in the paraenetic sections. If St. Paul wanted to give the Christians of Rome a survey of his preaching as a whole, he could hardly omit to say something about the attitude to the state. At first sight the context in which this happens is certainly surprising, namely between an admonition not to requite evil with evil but with good (12:17–21), and the summing-up of all the commandments in that of love of the neighbour (13:8–10). That should scarcely mislead anyone into far-reaching theological conclusions, however. Where else was the section on the attitude to secular authority to be inserted? The paraenetic part begins with an eschatological outlook and closes with the same point of view (13:11–14). The next chapter deals with the same special concrete question of what action should be taken in regard to the "weak" in

---

[18] Cf. E. Schürer, *Geschichte des jüdischen Volkes im Zeitalter Jesu Christi*, 4th ed. 1909, vol. III, pp. 97ff., and esp. 111.

Rome. After the chief exhortations, the question of "civic duties" is also dealt with. Perhaps the apostle's intention is clearest in verse 8 which immediately follows, "Owe no man anything, but to love one another" (μηδὲν ὀφείλετε cf. ἀπόδοτε τὰς ὀφειλάς in verse 7). The Christian is to meet what he owes the State authorities (obedience, payment of taxes, respect); fundamentally the apostle does not ask more. It is important to observe that this instruction too is still comprised within the eschatological perspective, even though no such motive (in this case restrictive in force) appears in the actual admonition.

Hence the interpretation of "powers" (ἐξουσίαι) as angelic powers is exegetically unacceptable.[19] The singular form (vv. 1b, 2a, 3b) must be given the well-attested meaning "the authorities, magistrates",[20] and besides, these ἐξουσίαι are identical with the "princes", rulers, ἄρχοντες (v. 3). A. Strobel (cf. bibliography) has shown with reference to abundant sources that the terminology is marked by the official style of the time; he considers that the writing of the passage "presupposed some knowledge of Roman administrative and civil law".

---

[19] This interpretation is supported by (among others) G. Dehn, "Engel und Obrigkeit", essay in *Theologische Aufsätze für K. Barth,* 1936, pp. 90ff.; K. L. Schmidt, "Das Gegenüber von Kirche und Staat in der Gemeinde des NT", in *TB* 16 (1937) pp. 1ff.; K. Barth, *Rechtfertigung und Recht,* 2nd ed. 1948, pp. 14ff.; O. Cullmann, *Königsherrschaft Christi und Kirche im NT,* 2nd ed. 1946, pp. 25f., 44f.; O. Cullmann, *Christus und die Zeit,* 2nd ed. 1948, pp. 169–86, Eng. tr. *Christ and Time,* 1951; W. Schweitzer, *Herrschaft.* It is opposed by G. Kittel, *Christus und Imperator,* pp. 48ff., M. Dibelius, *Rom und die Christen,* pp. 6f.; W. Kümmel, art. in *Theologische Rundschau* 17 (1948–49) pp. 136f.; H. v. Kampenhausen, essay in *Festschrift for A. Bertholet,* 1950, pp. 97–113; G. Bornkamm, art. in *ZThK* 47 (1950) p. 224, n. 2; H. H. Schrey, art. in *Theologische Rundschau* 19 (1951) p. 194, pp. 201–203.

[20] Cf. W. Bauer, *Wörterbuch,* 503f. s. v. 4; Liddell and Scott, *Lexicon,* v. I, p. 599, s. v. II; W. Foerster, art. in *ThWB* vol. III, p. 560, 34ff.; pp. 563, 18ff.; A. Strobel, "Zum Verständnis von Röm 13"; E. Käsemann, "Röm 13:1–7 in unserer Generation", pp. 351–61.

The duty of obedience laid on the faithful by the apostle is clear but surprising by the absence of any limitation. The power of the state is given to it by God (v. 1 b); it is God's minister for good (v. 4a) and bears the sword to deter evil-doers (vv. 4b–c). Hence it can demand obedience in conscience (v. 5). The officials who collect taxes and act honestly, are ministers of God (v. 6) and it is the Christian's duty to pay taxes and tolls and give honour where it is due (v. 7). The statement that the powers that be are ordained of God (v. 1c) is especially significant, making it possible to refer the power of the state directly rather than remotely back to God, the primordial source of all power. But this is the precise point from which we must set out if we are to reach that true understanding which has been made more difficult for us by our way of thinking in terms of natural law, of what belongs to an essence and is always valid.

Semitic thought was directed towards the historical and the concrete, the course of history as governed by God. God deals with men and nations according to his pre-ordained plan. The ideas propounded by Paul are already to be found in the Old Testament and later Judaism, but Paul does not repeat everything that can be found there. Even the Jewish nation did not always see the peoples and kingdoms to which it was subjected and delivered up, as the offspring of hell. The prophets succeeded in seeing the great kings as rulers who had received their power from God in order to fulfil the limited and transitory task assigned to them.[21] Even for later Judaism, which usually saw "this aeon" as dark and evil, the kingdoms of this world were still forces of order erecting a dam against chaos, but their rule is only provisional and their time is measured. They, in fact, hold their power from God; but its continuance lies in his hand and they have neither a right nor an assurance of permanence. They

[21] Cf. Jer. 27:5ff.; 28:14 (Nabuchodonosor); Isa. 41:2ff., 25; 45:1ff. (Cyrus); Dan 4:17ff. On this point see O. Procksch, *Der Staatsgedanke in der Prophetie*, 1933; H. Gross, *Weltherrschaft als religiöse Idee im AT*, 1953.

may be destroyed at any time, and insofar as they misuse the power given them by God, they will one day, at the universal judgement, be made to answer for it. The great vision of the seventy shepherds of the nations at 1 *Enoch* 79–90 is especially informative on this point: God has appointed seventy shepherds (that is, angels of the nations) to pasture his sheep (89:59) and each of them completes the period appointed to him (90:1). God even tolerates their unworthy acts and the fact that the sheep are eaten by wild beasts; but he causes an exact account to be kept of the conduct of the shepherds and one day he calls them to account: "Take these seventy shepherds that I appointed over the sheep; they indeed accepted them, but they killed more of them than I commanded them. And then were the shepherds judged, condemned and thrown into the lake of fire" (96, 22 and 25).[22] Similar views are met with in Rabbinic Judaism.[23]

This historical-theological outlook probably also lies behind St. Paul's statements. The state, with its organs of power, is not an absolute authority, but is established only temporarily, for this present aeon (cf. the glance forwards to the parousia at 13:11f.), and has been given by God the task of being his helper towards an order of justice. The question of how the Christian should conduct himself towards an unjust, tyrannical or even atheistic government is not discussed by the apostle. He was envisaging actually existing authorities, and no doubt even idealized them, emphasizing the duty of obedience towards them. There can be no doubt that he saw the Roman empire as it then existed as a state serving good order and justice. It is, however,

[22] On the angels of the nations, see Billerbeck, vol. III, pp. 48ff., and also 1 *Enoch* 46, 5; *Apocalypse of Baruch* 82, 9; Wis. 6:1ff.

[23] Cf. the saying of R. Aibo (c. 320): "In the past the kingdom (that is, rule) was with Israel; but when they sinned, the kingdom was taken away from them and given to the nations of the world" (*Midrash Esther,* 1, 2; quoted in Billerbeck, vol. I, pp. 877. See also vol. III, pp. 303f.

scarcely probable[24] that he considered it also had a positive rôle in the history of salvation, as is frequently claimed by the old interpretation of 2 Thessalonians 2:6f. (which said, for instance, that "the withholder" was the Roman state, or the emperor), and this view cannot be supported by any other texts.

The same exhortations to reverence and obedience to public authorities are found at 1 Peter 2:13-17, and now "honouring the king" (that is, the emperor) is put next to fearing God (because of Proverbs 24:21?). It is very probable that both exhortations stem from a common source.[25] The positive attitude is the more striking because the author had already mentioned persecutions "for justice's sake" and for the sake of the Christian name (3:14-17; 4:12-19); although these were no more than persecutions by fellow citizens and isolated abuses and blunders on the part of the authorities.[26] The letter exhorts Christians, on the other hand, not to allow themselves to be punished as murderers, thieves, evil-doers or informers "but if as a Christian, let him not be ashamed, but let him glorify God in that name" (4:15f.). He also says, however, "be not afraid of their fear, and be not troubled" (3:14) and indicates the eschatological perspective, "for the time is come that judgement should begin at the house of God. And if first among us, what shall be the end of them that

---

[24] The interpretation of this as referring to the Roman State, goes back to Tert., *Apol.* 32, I; *ad Scapul.* 2; *De Carnis Res.* 24, and is again advocated by (among others) O. Eck, *Urgemeinde*, pp. 67ff.; Stauffer, *Theology*, pp. 84 and notes pp. 274; Goguel, *Birth of Christianity*, 1953, pp. 502ff.; and opposed by M. Dibelius, *Rom und die Christen*, pp. 12ff.; J. Schmid, "Der Antichrist und die hemmende Nacht" in *TQ* 129 (1949) pp. 323ff., esp. 338f.

[25] Thus E. G. Selwyn, *The First Epistle of Peter*, 2nd ed. 1947, pp. 426-9. He maintains that the text in 1 Peter is the oldest reproduction of this source.

[26] Cf. Selwyn, *op. cit.*, and pp. 52-56; J. Michl, *Kath. Briefe*, 1953, p. 197, dates 1 Peter back to the eve of the Neronian Persecution, a less outspoken view is given by K. H. Schelkle, *Die Petrusbriefe, der Judasbrief*, 1961, pp. 7-11. See further section 40.

believe not the gospel of God?" (4:17). Finally, similar exhortations are also found in Titus 3:1-3 and 1 Timothy 2:1-3, where in particular prayer for the authorities is recommended, a practice which was also followed in Judaism.[27] We are probably dealing with a common topic in early Christian homilies.

There also occur in the New Testament declarations completely rejecting earthly power, and these are, in fact, directly connected with the apotheosis of rulers. The apocalyptic book of the New Testament was not the first to reveal the horror of early Christianity at this diabolical idolatry of self on the part of a ruler who, by it, ceases to be the servant of God and makes himself his rival and adversary. The frightful end of King Herod Agrippa I was seen by the Jerusalem community not so much as the punishment of God upon his crimes against them, as upon his blasphemous claim to be a god; for that, "an angel of the Lord struck him" (Acts 12:19-23).

The persecution of Christians under Domitian, whose menacing shadow was what chiefly occasioned the composition of the Apocalypse of John, was causally connected with the worship demanded by the emperor (cf. Apoc. 13:4ff. and 15; 14:9 and 11; 16:2; 19:20). The Christian community immediately reacted against this attack on the honour of God. The angel with the "everlasting gospel" announced to all nations "with a loud voice", "fear the Lord and give him honour . . . and adore ye him that made heaven and earth, the sea and the fountains of waters" (14:6f.). For the sake of this confession of faith in the one true God, Christians were ready to accept all sufferings, whether imprisonment or death by the sword

---

[27] Cf. Jer. 29:7; *Mishna Aboth* III, 2a; R. Chananja, the leader of the priests (before A. D. 70), said: "Pray for the well-being of the government; for if there were no fear of it, we would already have devoured one another alive." In later times, this thought was repeated in relation to gentile authorities. Cf. *Aboda Zara,* 3b; 4a; in Billerbeck, vol. III, p. 304. According to Flavius Josephus, it was the usual practice to offer a daily sacrifice for the emperor (*Bell. Jud.* II, pp. 409f.).

(13:10),[28] but they were also certain that by doing so they would triumph and rule with Christ in the end (20:4).

It is significant that the Apocalypse ascribes the power of the state which is blasphemously abused, not to God, but to Satan. The "dragon" (Satan), gave "his own strength and great power", to the "beast", (the embodiment of the blasphemous regime (13:2)), just as Satan had already claimed he could do, in the course of Jesus' temptation, according to Luke 4:6. Here we can see the other line in the early Christian assessment of the state. The state that deifies itself, the ruler who exceeds his competence and treads the honour of God under his feet, is an instrument of Satan.

The early Christian conception of the state consequently remains unharmonized to a certain extent; but Jesus' exhortation to give to Caesar the things that are Caesar's, and to God the things that are God's lies at the point of intersection of the two lines, one leading to God and the other to Satan. Romans 13 and Apocalypse 13 are not two mutually exclusive pictures, but rather the two different sides of one coin, both of which, from the beginning, had their proper value in the New Testament vision of the history of salvation. Or again, to change the metaphor a little, the current coins keep their value as long as God accepts them in payment, but they became deceitful, devilish money, as soon as the portrait of the ruler on them changes into the idol of a power hostile to God, that God himself will one day dethrone.

§ 26. DUTIES OF STATE. CHRISTIAN MARRIAGE AND THE FAMILY.
THE SLAVE QUESTION

See the bibliography to sections 14 and 22; add K. Weidinger, *Die Haustafeln, ein Stück urchristlicher Paränese*, 1928; H. Schuhmacher, *Das Eheideal des heiligen Paulus*, 1932; A. Vögtle, *Die Tugend- und Laster-*

[28] On this text, which is often incorrectly interpreted, see J. Schmid "Zur Textkritik der Apokalypse" in *ZNW* 43 (1950–1) pp. 122ff.

kataloge im Neuen Testament, 1936; K. Wennemer, "Jedoch ist weder die Frau ohne den Mann noch der Mann ohne die Frau im Herrn" in *Geist und Leben* 26 (1953) pp. 288–97; S. Wibbing, *Die Tugend- und Lasterkataloge in Neuen Testament,* 1959; D. Schroeder, *Die Haustafeln im Neuen Testament,* 1959; K. H. Schelkle, *Die Petrusbriefe, der Judasbrief,* 1961 pp. 96–98; F. Hauck and S. Schulz, art. "πόρνη" in *ThWB* vol. VI, pp. 579–95 (Bibliog.).

On v: A. Steinmann, *Sklavenlos und alte Kirche,* 4th ed. 1922; J. J. Koopmans, *De servitute antiqua et religione christiana,* 1920; E. Lohmeyer, *Soziale Fragen im Urchristentum,* 1921; K. H. Rengstorf, art. "δοῦλος" in *ThWB* vol. II, pp. 264–82; M. Dibelius, "Das soziale Motiv im Neuen Testament", in *Botschaft und Geschichte,* vol. I (1953) pp. 178–203; C. Haufe, "Die antike Beurteilung der Sklaven" in *Wissenschaftliche Zeitschrift,* Leipzig 9 (1959–60) pp. 603–16.

i. General

DID the early Church work out an ethics of her own for different states of life? It is difficult to affirm it. Vocational ethics in the modern sense was unknown, unless one can take the awareness of the preacher (that he was the "minister of Christ and dispenser of the mysteries of God" — cf. 1 Cor. 4:1) as being such a thing for one state of life. Nothing of the kind is found for the secular professions. St. Paul advises, "Let every man abide in the same calling in which he was called" (1 Cor. 7:20).

The word "calling" (κλῆσις) here need not have the meaning of status in the secular sense, although the apostle is thinking, in fact, of slaves and free men (v. 21), as well as the circumcised and uncircumcised (v. 18f.), and in the context of the chapter, especially of married and unmarried people. Thus the word is used comprehensively and in its fundamental sense: when he is "called" in the religious sense (to faith and baptism), a man is already in some worldly vocation which in itself is unimportant (cf. v. 19), but which in one way or another can be filled with religious significance.[29] "Under the overwhelming

[29] On this text see A. Juncker, *Ethik des Apostels Paulus,* vol. II, pp. 160–6; K. L. Schmidt, art. in *ThWB* vol. III, pp. 492f., n. 1; G. Harder in *TLZ*

influence of the New Testament's message of salvation, everything falling within the definition of calling and avocation is immediately absorbed more exclusively than ever into the realm of religion and becomes significant from the point of view of theology and the history of salvation."[30]

The admonitions in the New Testament epistles concerning marriage and family life must be handled carefully if they are to be interpreted as an early Christian vocational ethics. They are for the most part to be found in the so-called "household codes";[31] but it has recently been recognized that these codes reflect a type of admonition already to be found in Judeo-hellenistic propaganda and in the popular philosophy of paganism, and which was taken over into early Christian homiletics, although, of course, enlarged and deepened with Christian motives.[32] The catalogues of virtues and vices[33]

79 (1954) pp.367–72; E. Neuhäusler, "Ruf Gottes und Stand des Christen" in *BZ* 3 (1959) pp. 43–60; and on the concept of vocation in general E. Egel, *Die Berufungstheologie des Apostels Pl.* (unpubl. diss., Heidelberg 1939); W. Schwer, "Beruf" in *RAC* vol. II, pp. 141–56; W. Bieder, *Die Berufung im NT,* 1961.

[30] W. Schwer, "Beruf" in *RAC* vol. II, p. 149.

[31] Col. 3:18–4:1; Eph. 5:22–6 and 9; 1 Pet. 2:18–3:7; cf. 1 Tim. 2:8–15; 5:3–8 (widows); 6, 1–2 (slaves); Titus 2:2–10. Such Christian household codes also figure in early Christian literature of the first post-NT period, cf. 1 *Clem.* 1, 3; 21, 6–9; *Epistle of Barnabas* 19, 5 and 7; *Didache* 4, 9–11; Polycarp *ad Phil.* 4.

[32] Cf. R. Knopf, *Die Apost. Väter* I (Handbuch zum NT, Suppl. vol. I) 1920, pp. 18f.; M. Dibelius and H. Greeven, *An die Kol., Eph., Phlm,* 3rd ed. 1953, excursus pp. 48–50; K. Weidinger, *Die Haustafeln;* D. Schröder, *Die Haustafeln.*

[33] Examples of lists of vices are to be found at Rom. 1:29–31; 13:13; 1 Cor. 5:10–11; 6:9–10; 2 Cor. 12:20–21; Gal. 5:19–21; Eph. 4:31; 5:3–5; Col. 3:5–8; 1 Tim. 1:9–10; 2 Tim. 3:2–4; Didache 2, 1ff.; 5, 1ff.; *Hermas,* 8. Catalogues of virtues appear at Gal. 5:22–23; Phil. 4:8; Eph. 4:2–3; Col. 3:12–14; 1 Tim. 4:12; 6:11; 2 Tim. 2:22; 3:10; 1 Pet. 3:8; 2 Pet. 1:5–7. In addition see H. Lietzmann, *An die Römer,* 4th ed. 1933, excursus pp. 35f.; A. Vögtle, *Lasterkataloge;* S. Wibbing, *Lasterkataloge.*

which must be linked in the first place with a tradition of Later Judaism (S. Wibbing), and which only display a stronger admixture of Hellenistic concepts from the Pastoral Epistles onwards, are even less in the service of a vocational ethics, for they are addressed to all men and seek to bring before their eyes the two ways of "light" and "darkness" (cf. the Qumran texts). Differences of class and profession played no part in the early Church; in contrast to Judaism there were no "despised professions".[34] Jesus himself had already ignored such barriers (by associating with "publicans and sinners"), and Paul emphasized the unity of all in Christ (Gal. 3:28; 1 Cor. 12:13; Col. 3:11), and even recognized in the vocation of members of lower classes a disposition of God's saving plan, "that no flesh should glory in his sight" (1 Cor. 1:26-9). It is understandable, therefore, that the early Church did not elaborate a special ethics for any particular class or profession. Nevertheless its adoption and christianization of the "domestic codes" shows sympathetic awareness of the natural states of life. In the Pastoral Epistles there are lists of qualifications for bearers of office (1 Tim. 3:1-7, 8-13; Tit. 1:7-13), and a "rule for widows" (1 Tim. 5:3-16); but these and similar instructions are envisaged from an ecclesiastical and pastoral point of view and at the most represent the rudiments of a "vocational ethics".

ii. Sexual Purity (Chastity)

The early Church was very much concerned about self-control and discipline in sexual life. In the time of the emperors the old Roman strictness had given way to frightful licentiousness which spread throughout society, especially in the cities, and led to an increasing decline in social life. Consorting with courtesans and prostitutes was hardly thought of as vice any

---

[34] See Jeremias, Jerusalem zur Zeit Jesu, 2nd ed. 1958, vol. II B, pp. 174 to 84; id., "Zöllner und Sünder" in ZNW 30 (1931) pp. 293-300.

longer; adultery and divorce were commonplace and the reform laws of Caesar Augustus were evaded by sham marriages.[35] Even if the accounts given by the moral philosophers are over-drawn, even if the picture of unnatural vice sketched by Paul in Romans 1 derives, at least in part, from the missionary preaching of Hellenistic Judaism, the fact of moral weakness cannot be doubted. At 1 Corinthians 5–6 we are given a glimpse of the true state of affairs at Corinth and also of the frame of mind of the Christian community there. The warnings to flee from licentiousness, to follow the Lord and not prostitutes, and to regard the body as the temple of the Holy Spirit, were urgently necessary. It is, therefore, no accident that in the lists of vices, idolatry (which was often combined with debauchery), unchastity and avarice are given a prominent place[36] and that in 1 Thessalonians 4:4ff. St. Paul sees the sanctification required by God first of all as purity in married life and honesty in busi-ness. In the list of vices at 1 Corinthians 6:9f. he warns, and the motive here is specifically Christian, that "neither fornicators, nor idolaters, nor adulterers, nor the effeminate, nor liers with mankind ... shall possess the kingdom of God". All these things should belong to the past, pre-Christian, pagan part of his readers' lives. Similar warnings in other epistles[37] reveal, however, that the power of the heathen vices was not so quickly broken even after baptism.

---

[35] Cf. Preisker, *Christentum und Ehe,* p. 21: "In order to circumvent Augustus' law against celibacy, mock-marriages were arranged with poor men, who made themselves available for this rôle against a money payment." On the promulgation of the law itself, cf. *op. cit.,* pp. 63ff.
[36] On unchastity in particular see Rom. 13:13; 1 Cor. 5:9f.; 6:9; 2 Cor. 12:21; Gal. 5:19; Eph. 5:5; Col. 3:5; 1 Tim. 1:10; Apoc. 9:21; 21:8; 22:15.
[37] Cf. 2 Cor. 12:21; Gal. 5:16f., 19–21; Eph. 2:1–3; 4:17–20; Col. 3:7; Tit. 3:3ff.; Heb. 13:4; 1 Pet. 2:11; 4:3; 2 Pet. 2:10, 14; 1 John 2:15.

iii. The Conception of Marriage

The early Church took its stand, as Jesus had done, on the account of creation, in which it saw the primordial will of God. The text of Gen. 2:24 "they shall be two in one flesh" was the foundation of the early Christian ethics of marriage (cf. 1 Cor. 6:16f. and Eph. 5:31). Jesus' exegesis and precept bound it to maintain strictly the indissolubility of marriage (1 Cor. 7:10), although difficulties quickly arose, especially in mixed marriages between Christians and pagans (1 Cor. 7:11–16). Between Christians St. Paul allowed, at the most, simple separation without remarriage (7:11).

The so-called "Pauline privilege" which has found a place in Canon Law (C.I.C. 1120–1124, 1126), and is there strictly delimited, is based on 1 Corinthians 7:15 ff. When in a purely pagan marriage one partner accepts the Christian faith and the other is not willing to continue the marriage, the Christian party is free to contract a new marriage. According to the context, of course, Paul is only dealing with the question whether separation is permissible in such a case; he does not speak of remarriage. Nor can the right to remarry be inferred from οὐ δεδούλωται. However verses 15c to 16 are interpreted, whether as intended to console the Christian party (taking verse 16, therefore, in the sense of "leave that in the care of God"), or as an exhortation rather to continue the marriage because perhaps the conversion of the pagan partner may still be possible after all (this was the view of John Chrysostom and Thomas Aquinas and one that has found favour again today[38]), there is no mention of remarriage. The general tendency of the passage (cf. verses 10 ff.) would not seem to point in that direction either, especially if the interpretation we have just

---

[38] For the evidence see J. Jeremias, "Die missionarische Aufgabe in der Mischehe (1 Cor. 7:16)" in *Neutestamentliche Studien für R. Bultmann,* 1954, pp. 255–60.

mentioned were accepted. The Pauline privilege, therefore, is an extension of the Pauline concession of separation, developed by the Church's teaching authority in favour of the believing partner. For the Church's decision in this, however, the point is of importance that the Christian partner in such a case is abandoning a natural marriage in order to contract a Christian, sacramental marriage.

The fact of indissolubility alone was enough to elevate the early Christian ethics of marriage far above the level of those of Judaism and paganism. In its sharp condemnation of adultery, early Christianity was scarcely more severe than Jewish morality, and some Stoic philosophers can be mentioned with honour in this matter, especially Musonius Rufus.[39] But their condemnation was incomplete when there was still a way out through the side-door of divorce. In its principle of indissolubility, Christian marriage had a foundation on which a high ideal of marriage inevitably built, even if here and there less noble views had to be overcome.

Less clear is what the New Testament has to say about the status of the sexes and particularly the position of the wife in marriage. No utterance of Jesus on the relationship of married people to one another is known to us, although his fundamental attitude makes it impossible for the Christian to despise women (see above, section 14). Paul several times calls the husband the "head" of the wife (1 Cor. 11:3, 5; Eph. 5:23), and requires obedience of the wife (Eph. 5:22, 24; Col. 3:18; Tit. 2:5; cf. 1 Pet. 3:1ff.). This has sometimes been seen as implying the inferiority of the wife.[40] In 1 Corinthians 11:3ff., however, it is clear that St. Paul was attempting to explain the place of the sexes in the divine plan of creation without making value judgements.

[39] See Preisker, *Christentum und Ehe*, pp. 20ff.

[40] Preisker, *op. cit.*, pp. 137ff.; Delling, *Paulus' Stellung zu Frau und Ehe*, accuses the Apostle of being antipathetic to marriage (pp. 57ff.) and to women (pp. 96ff.). For an opposite view, see esp. E. Kähler, *Die Frau in den paulinischen Briefen*, 1960.

The argument in these verses turns on a question of usage and custom: whether a woman should attend divine service with her head covered or uncovered. The Christian women of Corinth were against covering their heads, probably not, as was long thought, from a yearning for emancipation, but because this Jewish custom was strange to them.[41] Paul had difficulty in suggesting clear reasons of propriety. This passage, which in detail is very difficult, brings together several kinds of ideas, among which the most important for us are those drawn from the account of the creation. According to verse 3, the head of the woman is the man, the head of the man, Christ, the head of Christ, God. In verse 7, St. Paul deduces from Gen. 1:27 that the husband is "the image and glory of God". "But the woman is the glory of the man. For the man is not of the woman; but the woman of the man. For the man was not created for the woman; but the woman for the man" (v. 7b. ff.). This all points to a lower position, and is intended as a reason why woman should cover her head, Paul seeing this as a sign of her dependence and subordination to man. But the following verses, added perhaps by St. Paul to prevent this misunderstanding, exclude any attribution of lower value to woman. "But yet neither is the man without the woman, nor the woman without the man, in the Lord" (v. 11). At this point he has come close to the great vision at Galatians 3:28, according to which, among the baptized, who have "put on Christ", even the difference between man and woman has lost its significance, "for you are all one in Christ Jesus". However, we must not conclude that within the community, brethren and sisters were equal whilst, in the family that is, in marriage, they were not;[42] for communion with Christ

---

[41] Cf. A. Oepke in *ThWB* vol. III, pp. 563f.; S. Losch, "Christliche Frauen in Korinth (1 Cor. 11:2–16)", art. in *TQ* 127 (1947) pp. 216–61 (proving from the point of view of religious history that leaving the head unveiled had a positive religious significance in many cults); Lietzmann and Kümmel, *An die Kor.*, appendix p. 184.

[42] Preisker, *Christentum und Ehe*, p. 138.

embraces the whole of man's life and cannot be split into a religious and a domestic domain. It is more correct to say that the two texts complement one another. Even in communion with Christ natural conditions are not abolished, but only lose their power to separate, and natural subordination (of the "weaker" to the "stronger" sex) is surmounted through this order "in the Lord". The man too has a "head" over him: Christ (11:3). Hence this pattern of relations of subordination should not be thought of from a legalistic point of view at all. Ephesians 5:22 ff. prescribes for the man, the "head" of the woman, love as the law of his conduct, on the model of Christ. "Paul knows (in the light of his knowledge of how Jesus Christ expresses his sovereignty) that the true exercising of authority consists in love."[43] Even the "subordination" of the woman, which at Colossians 3:18 is distinguished from the "obedience" of children (3:20), does not envisage a servant-status for the wife, but only indicates the place she is to fill according to the order of the creation. How far St. Paul's outlook was due to his Jewish past, or how far he adopted the phrases in the household codes (merely "christening" them by the addition of "in the Lord"), need not be discussed here. The meaning and scope of what he said are clear. In Paul's religious perspective it is ultimately not a question at all of the idea he has of the natural characteristics of the sexes but only of their equal worth before God. Consequently, what he has to say retains its significance even if at the present time the natural relation between the sexes is perhaps differently viewed, even in questions concerning their "equality of rights".

In the household code in the Epistle to the Ephesians the relation of Christian married people to one another is immeasurably ennobled by a purely Christian chain of thought,

[43] J. J. von Allmen, *Maris et femmes d'après s. Paul,* 1951, p. 34. He also points out that the subordination of wife to husband is based on the order of the creation, and not on their susceptibility to temptation (p. 35).

in which the bond between Christ and the Church is seen as the model for Christian marriage (5:22–33). Husbands should love their wives as Christ has loved the Church and given himself for it. Baptism is seen as proof of Christ's concern for the purity, holiness and spotlessness of the Church. Then, using the metaphor of the head and the body to describe the relationship between Christ and Church, St. Paul admonishes husbands to love their wives as their own bodies. This excludes any misuse of the position naturally belonging to the man as head. In the same way women are to be subject to their husbands as to the Lord and show them respect (v. 33). From the fact that marriage is seen as a reflection of the union of Christ with his Church its unity derives even greater stability and dignity. In the well-known verse 32 "great sacrament" can hardly be said to refer directly to Christian marriage, for if it did, this latter would be the pattern for the union of Christ and the Church, whereas throughout the passage the reverse is the case. Even verbally this passage would then be difficult. The text must, rather, explain the quotation from Genesis at v. 31 by reference to the union between Christ and the Church. But the comparison running through the whole suggests that Christian marriage is patterned on the prototype of Christ and the Church.[44]

Hence the idea that for Paul marriage was no more than a sexual partnership, is untenable. It cannot be concluded from

[44] For the various attempts that have been made to interpret v. 32, cf. Schumacher, *Das Eheideal*, pp. 78 ff., who himself, on no firm exegetical basis, supports the exegesis rejected above. As against this view, see M. Meinertz, *Die Gefangenschaftsbriefe des hl. Paulus*, 3th ed. 1931, on this text; G. Bornkamm, art. in *ThWB* vol. IV, pp. 829; Ch. Masson, *L'épître aux Éphésiens*, 1952, on this text; H. Schlier, *Der Brief an die Epheser*, 1957, pp. 261 ff., who makes the very relevant point: "In so far as the event referred to in Genesis 2:24, the mystery of the marriage between Christ and the Church, is repeated in the earthly marriage between man and wife, this latter partakes of that mystery and in that sense is itself a mystery" (pp. 262 f.).

1 Corinthians 7 either, with its entirely different perspective, the ideal of virginity, that for St. Paul marriage is only a necessary evil. Even in this chapter Paul speaks of a mutual "sanctification" of the married couple, and even of a "sanctification" of the unbelieving partner by a believer (v. 14). Even though the concept of sanctification in question here may be a broader one (meaning perhaps "consecration"),[45] Paul is, nevertheless, extending the process of sanctification to the bodies and sexuality of Christians (cf. 1 Cor. 6:12–20); hence marriage cannot be something merely profane, but must have its share in the "new creation" (2 Cor. 5:17).

In one text, however, statements do occur which appear strongly to disparage the female sex. This is 1 Timothy 2:9–15. As a reason why women should be silent in church (cf. also 1 Cor. 14:34f.) it suggests, that Eve was created only after Adam, and that she, not Adam, allowed herself to be deceived by the serpent. The task of the wife is maternity, through which she will be saved (v. 15). But for this text it should be remembered that Jewish views are being taken over here and that a definite abuse was being fought, namely the appearance of "prophetesses" at the services, accompanied by an unhealthy aspiring to extraordinary gifts and activity which were diverting women from their proper tasks in home and family.[46]

iv. Parents and Children

The relation of parents to their children is characterized, as in Judaism, by the authority of the parents and strict discipline, which is, however, a sign of real love (cf. Heb. 12:7–11). From children, the apostle requires obedience in all things

[45] For the concept of sanctification presupposed here, cf. R. Asting, *Die Heiligkeit im Urchristentum*, 1930, pp. 208 ff.; Allo and Lietzmann and Kümmel, app. pp. 176 f., on this text; Allmen, *op. cit.*, pp. 28 f.

[46] Cf. N. J. Hommes, "Taceat mulier in ecclesia" in *Arcana revelata* (Festschrift for F. W. Grosheide), 1952, pp. 33–34.

(Col. 3:20; Eph. 6:1). The inclusion of disobedience in lists of vices at Romans 1:30 and 2 Timothy 3:2 reminds us of the similar concern in the popular ethics of paganism to strengthen family ties.[47] Yet fathers should not discourage their children by excessive severity (Col. 3:21; Eph. 6:4).

The metaphorical use of "father" and "children" suggests a deeper Christian attitude to children. Paul felt he was the father of the Corinthian community because, "in Jesus Christ, by the gospel, I have begotten you" (that is, the Christians of that city), and he writes intending to admonish them as "beloved children" (1 Cor. 4:14f.). For the sake of his children, the Galatians, he undergoes the pangs of childbirth afresh (Gal. 4:19). Again, he repeatedly calls Timothy his beloved son (1 Cor. 4:17; cf. 1 Tim. 1:2; 2 Tim. 1:2; 2:1), just as he does Titus (Tit. 1:4) and Philemon (Philem. 10). He praises Timothy to the Philippians, because he has served him "as a son with the father" (Phil. 2:22). In the Third Epistle of John, the "ancient" also writes to his beloved Gaius, "I have no greater grace than this, to hear that my children walk in truth" (3 John 4), and this venerable person who conceals himself behind the Johannine Epistles delights in using the title "little children". The Christian's heightened reverence and love for the heavenly Father, the Father of the Lord Jesus Christ, also ennobled his idea of paternity in general (cf. Eph. 3:14f.; 4:6; 1 Cor. 8:6; 1 Pet. 1:17; 1 John 3:1).

There has been a great deal of discussion more recently about the status of children in the communities and especially about infant baptism.[48] There are hardly any clear and indisputable texts in the New Testament available here. It may be noticed

---

[47] See Vögtle, *Lasterkataloge*, p. 201.
[48] Cf. J. Jeremias, *Die Kindertaufe in den ersten vier Jahrhunderten*, Eng. tr. *Infant Baptism: The First Four Centuries*, and the literature he indicates (pp. 117–20). A criticism of Jeremias' thesis seeking to demonstrate the practice of infant baptism in the early Church (except the earliest period, for which he assumes a divergent practice on the grounds of

that whole households were baptized (cf. 1 Cor. 1:16; 16:15, 19; Rom. 16:5; Col. 4:15; Philem. 2). Whether it is possible to draw upon the analogy with Jewish practice in the conversion of (full) proselytes, depends on how far the links between the baptism of proselytes and Christian baptism are considered to be demonstrated. The pericope Mark 10:13–16 and parallels has also been considered to prove by its functional context in the life of the Church that the early Church did not exclude children from baptism.[49] It is difficult to form a judgement about 1 Corinthians 7:14c. Is it to be inferred from this text that in that very early period the children of a purely Christian marriage were not baptized because they were held to be already "holy" through their parents? Is this conclusion certain, despite the phrase "your children"? J. Jeremias considers that about the middle of the first century throughout Christendom in all probability children born of Christian parents were not baptized, and that the apostolic Church between A.D. 60 and 70 then started to baptize not only the children of converts (as it had from the beginning) but also children born in the Church and to do this even in their infancy.[50] However that may be, the text at all events testifies to the high esteem for children, even when only one of the parents was a Christian.

Examination of the gospels from the point of view of form criticism, too, permits certain inferences regarding the position of children in the Christian community. The pericope "Suffer little children" (Mark 10:13–15 parallels) does not preserve an "idyll" from the life of Jesus but was important to the early

1 Corinthians 14c), is to be found in: K. Aland, *Die Säuglingstaufe im Neuen Testament und in der ältesten Kirche*, 1961.
[49] O. Cullmann, *Die Tauflehre des Neuen Testamentes*, 1948, pp. 65–73 Eng. tr. *Baptism in the New Testament*, had already sought to prove that behind μὴ κωλύετε stands an old formula from the baptismal rite. J. Jeremias, *op. cit.*, pp. 61–68, has developed the thesis with more abundant material.
[50] Jeremias, *Kindertaufe*, pp. 57 and 68.

Church as indicating the importance of children, quite apart from the question of baptism. The child belongs in the Church and enjoys the love and blessing of Jesus. The Lord himself has laid it down that such as these (children) have a share in the kingdom of God. The other logion concerning the child as an example (Mark 10:15), which Matthew transmits in connection with the dispute concerning precedence among the disciples, a saying regarding admittance to the *basileia* (cf. sections 1 and 2), shows at least that Jesus regarded children benevolently and that for him they represented vividly a fundamental requirement for entry into kingdom of God, childlike humbleness and childlike trust in God the Father. The third saying about children that has been preserved regarding "receiving a child in Jesus' name" (Mark 9:36; Luke 9:48; Matt. 18:5), pointed out the community's duty of caring for children. And so the early Church, even more resolutely than Judaism,[51] took children seriously as members of the community and regarded love and care for them as a binding charge laid on her by the Lord.

v. Masters and Slaves

At that time slaves also were members of a household. Their lot was often very difficult for they were subject to their master's whim without rights or protection. There were, of course, Romans with a humane outlook, and manumission was not rare. Stoic philosophy also succeeded in awakening a consciousness of ethical freedom in slaves who outwardly were unfree.[52] But all this makes little difference to the bleak general picture confronting the student of the ancient world. Did Christianity bring a change here? Outwardly only very slowly, for its banners did not bear the slogans of an economic and social revolution. But the early Church could not avoid adopting an

[51] See A. Oepke in *ThWB* vol. V, pp. 644–7.
[52] See esp. the dissertation of Epictetus (who was himself a freedman) on Freedom, IV, 1. See also H. Schlier, in *ThWB* vol. II, pp. 488 ff.

attitude of mind towards slaves or refuse to give moral guidance on their proper treatment, especially as in every gentile Christian community a significant proportion belonged to this class.

In admonishing slaves the early Christian preachers used all possible incentives to reconcile them to their lot. Paul demonstrated to them the Christian concept of freedom: slaves, he said, called "in the Lord" are the Lord's freedmen, just as those who are legally free are the Lord's slaves (1 Cor. 7:22); in this way the external differences lose their significance. Paul clearly did not mean to say merely, "Act as though...", he meant what he said much more definitely. The Christian slave stands in a relation to the Lord Jesus Christ similar to that of those manumitted under the civil law to the master who freed them: he is their patron.[53] It is from this angle that we must understand the disputed precept at v. 21 b, "If thou mayest be made free, use it rather", make all the more use, that is, of your calling as a slave (and not, as some exegetes would have it, the opportunity to become free: that would destroy the sequence of ideas).

Baptism makes all the faithful "whether Jews or gentiles, whether bond or free" into a single body, the Body of Christ (cf. 1 Cor. 12:13; Gal. 3:28; Col. 3:11). In the household codes (Eph. 6:5–8; Col. 3:22–25), slaves are admonished to display special virtues of their state: obedience, avoidance of eye-service, and interior joy in work. They should look on their servitude as though they were serving Christ the Lord, who will one day give them their reward. These are significantly weaker motives: one senses the influence of secular ethics. But at 1 Peter 2:18–25 the exhortation once again rises to truly Christian heights: slaves when treated unjustly should remember their innocent but suffering Lord. Here the religion of the cross shows its superiority to Stoic philosophy. 1 Timothy 6:1–2 distinguishes between Christian and pagan masters. To the latter, slaves should be respectful, honest and loyal

---

[53] Cf. W. Elert, art. in *TLZ* 72 (1947) pp. 265 ff., esp. 266, n. 1.

"lest the name of the Lord and his doctrine be blasphemed". At Titus 2:10 the same thought is expressed even more finely "that they may adorn the doctrine of God our Saviour in all things". For the sake of the good name of the brethren, they should not despise Christian masters; that is, they should not forget the limitations put on them by their social position. Clearly this presupposes kind Christian masters whose kindness could easily be abused.

The admonitions in the household codes to masters who have slaves, seem rather lifeless. They do, of course, bind masters to act justly and remind them of the judgement to come, at which there will be no respect of persons; but in the light of Christ's message, this is much too little. Here again we have existing material with only slight specifically Christian features. We should be compelled to doubt the moral earnestness of the early Church if we did not possess evidence of the most profoundly moving kind that shows how an apostle personally addressed a Christian master, namely the Epistle to Philemon. Here St. Paul appeals with tact and warmth for the runaway slave Onesimus, whom he had himself baptized in prison and was now sending back to the good Christian Philemon. Although, as an apostle, St. Paul might have commanded him, he asks this wealthy man, his friend, to receive Onesimus not as a slave but as a beloved brother. Whether in v. 21 St. Paul was suggesting to his friend that he should manumit Onesimus, or receive him back into personal service, is disputed. But it may be that in asking that, we are asking the wrong question, and what St. Paul really wanted to see was a fraternal relationship established between the Christian master and his slave, joint participation in the Lord's Supper and the exchange of the fraternal kiss after prayer. This would be much better than an act either of law or of favour.[54]

[54] Cf. H. Greeven, *Hauptproblem der Sozialethik*, pp. 52ff.; M. S. Enslin, *The Ethics of Paul*, pp. 208f.

The early Church tried to alleviate the slave's lot in the profoundest way, by love, and by so doing it initiated a process of interior education that inevitably led, in the end, to the abolition of slavery.

III

The Moral Teaching of the Early Church According to Prominent Individual Preachers

Chapter One

PAUL

§ 27. THE PRESUPPOSITIONS OF PAULINE MORAL TEACHING. MAN AND THE POWERS ABOVE HIM

See the textbooks of New Testament theology, esp. F. Prat, *Théologie de saint Paul*, 38th ed. 1949, vol. II, pp. 53–90; Meinertz, vol. II, pp. 12–39; Bultmann, *Theologie*, 4th ed., pp. 193–270, Eng. tr. *Theology*, vol. I, pp. 192–269; see further W. Schauf, *Sarx*, 1924; K. T. Schäfer, "Der Mensch in neutestamentlicher Auffassung" in *Das Bild vom Menschen* (Festschrift für F. Tillmann), 1934, pp. 25–35; W. G. Kümmel, *Röm. 7 und die Bekehrung des Paulus*, 1929; *id., Das Bild des Menschen im Neuen Testament*, 1948, pp. 20–40, Eng. tr. *Man in the New Testament*, 1963; E. Käsemann, *Leib und Leib Christi*, 1933; W. Gutbrod, *Die paulinische Anthropologie*, 1934; P. Bläser, *Das Gesetz bei Paulus*, 1941; A. Kirchgässner, *Erlösung und Sünde im Neuen Testament*, 1950; H. Mehl-Koehnlein, *L'homme selon l'apôtre Paul*, 1951; C. Ryder Smith, *The Biblical Doctrine of Man*, 1951; C. H. Lindijer, *Het begrip Sarx bij Paulus*, 1952; C. H. Dodd, P. I. Bratsiotis, R. Bultmann, H. Clavier, *Der Mensch in Gottes Heilsplan nach dem Neuen Testament*, 1953; *Anthropologie religieuse* ed. C. J. Bleeker, 1955; J. P. Hyatt, "The View of Man in the Qumran 'Hodayot'" in *NTS* 2 (1955–1956) pp. 276–84; W. D. Stacey, *The Pauline View of Man*, 1956; J. Schmid, art. "Anthropologie, biblische" in *LThK* vol. I, 604–15; O. Kuss, *Der Römerbrief*, 2nd imp., 1959, pp. 506–40; H. Braun, "Röm 7:7–25 und das Selbstverständnis des Qumran-Frommen" in *ZThK* 56 (1959) pp. 1–18; E. Schweizer in *ThWB* vol. VII, pp. 124–36.

St. Paul, the great apostle of the gentiles, was not only passionately stirred by the ideas he disseminated; in a large measure the pattern of his thought must be seen as determined by his deepest personal experience. As he himself saw his life, it fell into two sharply distinct periods (cf. especially Phil. 3:7ff.) — the time of his Jewish legalistic self-justification, and that of his justification by God, granted to him on the ground of faith in Jesus Christ. The turning-point is clearly marked, the event outside Damascus, when Christ the risen Lord appeared to him (1 Cor. 15:8), and, as he himself felt, seized him as though he were a fugitive and set him on a new road, along which he afterwards tirelessly pursued the reward of victory promised in heaven (Phil. 3:13f.). Formerly struggling for salvation with all his human powers, but in vain; then saved by the mighty intervention of God: that is how he saw himself from that time on. But this personal experience, this inner knowledge of faith, also gives its direction to the whole pattern of his thought. Corruption and salvation, human powerlessness and divine power not only confront one another for him, but for every human being, indeed for the whole human race. Paul saw the lives of those he addressed as divided, just like his, into a "then" and a "now" (cf. Col. 1:21; 3:7f.; Eph. 2:2ff., 11ff.; 5:8). But he also saw human history as divided into a period of sin and calamity from Adam to Christ, and a time of salvation from Christ onwards (Rom. 5:12–21). Although other factors may also have contributed to this dualistic view of the history of salvation (cf. the late Jewish doctrine of the "two aeons"), Paul lived it, as it were, in his own self. The joyful consciousness of having found salvation in Christ, of possessing a new life in him (2 Cor. 5:17), of living in faith only for him who "loved him and delivered himself for him" (Gal. 2:20), determined his negative view of the past as well as his present confidence. It is only in faith and the situation in the history of redemption that he grasps the state of man before Christ and without Christ (Rom. 1–2), in its shattering perdition and hopelessness.

Moreover, this inwardly vehement man saw as cosmic forces the powers of good and evil that contend for man, powers that we are so ready to transfer to the human heart. Sin and death are the real powers of destruction, which through the disobedience of Adam, the (physical) ancestor of the human race, have entered the world (Rom. 5:12) and exercised their terrible rule there since. Sin ruled in the age of calamity and guilt before Christ, as an absolute monarch (Rom. 5:21). The real horror of it, however, is that it merits the loss of everlasting life, thus setting up the rule of death (5:14, 17). Death, eternal ruin, is the real calamity which human beings fear, but the power of sin drives them ineluctably towards that ruin. The only choice is whether one will obey sin (like a slave-master) "unto death", or will serve "justice", that is, God, in order to attain life (cf. Rom. 6:16–18, 22). At Romans 6:13 sin is also described as a military force, and using this metaphor, Paul coined the theologically significant sentence, "The wages of sin is death; but the grace of God, life everlasting in Christ Jesus our Lord" (6:23). Just as the power of sin of necessity pays its soldiers with death, so, out of grace, but equally certainly, God gives everlasting life as a gift, because of Jesus' act of atonement and the communion with Christ we receive by faith and baptism. At Romans 7:14 there is yet another metaphor: we are sold into the power of sin, we become prisoners of the "law of sin" (7:23) and are freed only by the "law of the Spirit" (8:2). But how does this master, sin, get power over us? From the fact that it finds in human beings themselves footholds from which to master them, until it inhabits them completely (Rom. 7:20).

This introduces us into an interesting but difficult region in the world of Pauline thought, his doctrine of man, his anthropology. It is not possible to go into this more deeply within the framework of this outline. For the detailed anthropological concepts and views he employed, reference should be made to the relevant works, particularly those of Scharf, Gutbrod, Bultmann and Stacey.

The sphere of the *sarx,* the "flesh", in man, is one which sin makes entirely its own. Because unredeemed man is "of the flesh", he is subject to sin (Rom. 7:14). When and because we were "in the flesh", the sinful lust of our members acquired power, so that we brought forth fruit unto death (Rom. 7:5). In unredeemed man (that is, in his *sarx*), so St. Paul explains, there dwells nothing that is good (7:18). The thinking of the *sarx* is orientated towards death and is at enmity with God; hence "in the *sarx*" we cannot please God (8:6–8). Even now that we are Christians, if we live "according to the flesh", we shall die (8:13).

In that way the *sarx* itself appears as a power working for evil and as an associate of sin. It is not a "part" of man, as it were his bodily, sensual side in contrast to the intellectual sphere of the soul, and so cannot be understood on the basis of the dualism of soul and body. Even sins which we would consider sins of the "spirit" such as envy, jealousy and anger are "works" of the *sarx* (cf. Gal. 5:20f.); and even more the false "glorying" before God, the appeal of the Jew to his privileges (2 Cor. 11:18), the striving of the Greek for human wisdom (cf. 1 Cor. 1:26), are in accordance with the *sarx*. The basis, therefore, is the Hebrew and Semitic anthropology which takes man as a whole but can view him from various standpoints. Certainly the concept of *sarx* refers to the corporeal and sense-endowed character of man but nevertheless signifies the whole man in his frailty, liability to temptation, and slavery to sin. Man as *sarx* confronts God and, trusting to himself, is powerless and prone to evil. The power of sin uses the weak *sarx* as a point of attack (cf. Rom.7:5,25), in order in this way to take possession of the whole man. The expressions in the Qumran texts are significant, "ungodly flesh" (*1 QS* XI, 9), "the sin of flesh" (*1 QS* XI, 12—for any sin), and even "the spirit of flesh" (*1 QH* XII, 13). Because man is "flesh", he is transitory and unsubstantial, but also evil and sinful. And so Paul can even say that God has sent his son "in the form of the flesh of sin" (Rom. 8:3). The *sarx* only becomes a really "sinful" power which leads to transgressions, when man submits to its domination, makes it a rule of his action (κατὰ σάρκα), and delivers himself up to its sinful desires and passions. Unredeemed man, however, is in fact, on account of his weakness, hopelessly its slave.

However, Paul also employs another usage, in which "flesh" and "in the flesh" do not have a negative character but merely signify our earthly existence in a neutral way (cf. 2 Cor. 10:3; Gal. 2:20; Phil. 1:22, 24; Eph. 2:11; Philem. 16). But whenever the pattern of human life is determined only by the *sarx* (and not by the *pneuma*), it becomes ungodly and inimical to God, that is, it assumes a negative character. This is clearly the meaning of 2 Corinthians 10:3, "For, though we walk in the flesh, we do not war according to the flesh. For the weapons of our warfare are not carnal, but mighty to God unto the pulling down of fortifications . . .". Hence as Christians we do not owe it to the *sarx* to live according to the *sarx* but in the Spirit, we are to mortify the works of the flesh (Rom. 8:12f.). He who sows in the *sarx* will reap corruption from the *sarx* (Gal. 6:8).

The sphere of the *sarx* manifests itself in the body, σῶμα (another concept with many possible connotations), insofar as this is the seat of the desires and passions (Rom. 6:12). These evil impulses, bound in service to the power of sin, may also receive the added designation: "of the *sarx*" (Gal. 6:16; Eph. 2:3; cf. also Rom. 13:14). "Body" is favoured by Paul when he is speaking of the "members" (Rom. 6:13) which serve the power of sin either as its weapons or as its slaves (6:19). For the sinful passions are, according to Paul, at work in our members (Rom. 7:5); hence we must mortify those "members which are upon the earth" and are the cause of many vices (Col. 3:5).

Finally there is another contributor to the constellation of evil, the law (ὁ νόμος; see above, section 21). Although in itself it is holy (Rom. 7:12) and spiritual (Rom. 7:14), its effects have been catastrophic, because "I am carnal" (7:14). The actual effect of the law is to promote the power of sin, for by its injunction "thou shalt not covet", it awakens the desires sleeping in the flesh (Rom. 7:7f.), and so it enables the power of sin to invade man and subject man to itself.

Paul describes the co-operation between the power of sin, the law and concupiscence in the difficult and very controverted seventh chapter of the Epistle to the Romans. The dark and despairing struggle of man against the violent assault of sin and abandonment to death described by St. Paul in verses 14ff. is not, as Augustine, the Reformers and earlier Protestant exegetes thought, and as modern Protestant exegesis now largely admits,[1] to be interpreted as referring to the redeemed, nor is it to be explained as Pauline autobiography. It refers to unredeemed mankind, here introduced by the stylistic device as "I". It is scarcely a matter, either, of distinguishing different periods of human life before Christ (finding, perhaps, in v. 9a a reference to the time before the giving of the Mosaic law, and in v. 9b–13 to the period that followed). The whole chapter is to be seen as a thematic description, carried through vigorously with objections and vivid metaphor, of the problem of sin and the law. Verses 1–6 are devoted to the basic thesis and plan; verses 7–13 to the justification of the divine law, which has been made use of and abused by the power of sin (which again, for its own part, must serve the divine plan of salvation); and verses 14–25, to the operation of the law and sin in the unredeemed human being.[2]

---

[1] Cf. the two works by Kümmel and the views quoted by him in *Das Bild*, p. 28, note 59. See further G. Bornkamm, "Sünde, Gesetz und Tod" in *Das Ende des Gesetzes, Paulusstudien*, 1952, pp. 51–69; O. Michel, *Der Brief an die Römer* (H. A. W. Meyer, Part 4, 10th ed.) 1955, pp. 140–58. The new views about Christians, advocated by A. Nygren in his *Römerbriefkommentar*, 1955, have been answered by P. Althaus, "Zur Auslegung von Röm. 7:14ff." in *TLZ* 77 (1952) pp. 475–80.

[2] For the train of thought see especially Bornkamm, *op. cit.* He rightly terms the section 7:7–13 as a defence of the Law.

There is one other misunderstanding we must be careful to avoid. In 7:14–23, Paul is certainly not describing a struggle between a higher, nobler part of the natural man and the dark powers within him driving him towards sin, but is making a general statement about the hopelessness of the resistance to this overpowering by the power of sin. Paul's account may give the wrong impression because he was trying to emphasize the fact that the human being in question "was conscious of being lost in sin and hence of doing evil and not fulfilling the law".[3] In reality, for Paul, the whole unredeemed human being is sold under sin: (the "I" is "carnal" v. 14); just as the whole man is called to redemption. This will be completed only when God re-awakens our "mortal bodies" through the Holy Spirit who dwells in us (8:11). The question whether an unredeemed human being can do absolutely nothing good is another matter altogether (see below, section 30, 2). But the conclusions we have reached here through the exegesis of Romans 7 are important, because they make untenable the theory that St. Paul thought of the realm of the body and the senses as corrupt in itself and so depreciated what belongs to the body and matter, in a Platonic or Gnostic manner, and held there is a dualism within man himself. His more Jewish presuppositions make it certain that this was not the case.[4]

The way in which all these powers of evil work together is shown most strikingly at Romans 7:5, "For, when we were

---

[3] Kümmel, *Das Bild des Menschen,* p. 33. It should be noticed that in vv. 15–21, "I" is the subject of both the (good) will and the (evil) action. From this unresolvable contradiction, St. Paul draws the conclusion that another active subject, the indwelling power of sin, stands beside and behind the "I". V. 22 may in reality be a parallel statement under another image. Following Paul, then, we may say that good and evil fight together within man (and in unredeemed man, as experience shows, the good is defeated). But it would be mistaken to think of these two forces as divided between two parts of man, the body and soul.

[4] Cf. W. D. Stacey, *Pauline View,* pp. 154–73; E. Schweizer in *ThWB* vol. VII, pp. 131–4.

in the flesh, the *passions of sins,* which were by the *law,* did work in our *members,* to bring forth fruit unto *death*"; but St. Paul also continues, "But now we are loose from the law of death, wherein we were detained; so that we should serve in newness of Spirit, and not in the oldness of the letter" (v. 6). Here, then, we are given the outline of the new state of affairs. To be filled with the Spirit of God is the beginning of redemption, but it is also a moral call to a new and real service of God. Yet we are still temporarily surrounded by the old evil aeon "this age" (Gal. 1:4; cf. Rom. 12:2; 1 Cor. 3:18), and the children of God, and with them the whole creation, are still waiting for the perfect revelation of the glory of God, when the creation will be truly set free from its slavery to ephemerality, from the curse of sin and the stigma of death (cf. Rom. 1:18ff.) St. Paul's view of the consequences for morality of the position now reached in the history of salvation, this standing "between the ages", a position, rich in tensions, between the beginning and the end of redemption, is examined in greater detail in the following sections.

§ 28. The Firm Anchoring of Moral Precept in the State of Salvation Bestowed upon us by the Grace of God

See the bibliography to section 27. See also E. Tobac, *Le problème de la justification dans saint Paul,* 1908 (New imp. 1941); R. G. Bandas, *The Master-Idea of St. Paul's Epistles or the Redemption,* 1925; R. Bultmann, "Das Problem der Ethik bei Paul" in *ZNW* 23 (1924) pp. 123–41; H. Windisch, "Das Problem des paulinischen Imperativs", *ibid.,* pp. 265–81; W. Mundle, "Religion und Sittlichkeit bei Paulus in ihrem inneren Zusammenhang" in *ZST* 4 (1927) pp. 456–82; H. D.Wendland, "Ethik und Eschatologie in der Theologie des Paulus" in *NKZ* 41 (1930) pp. 757–83, pp. 793–811; A. Wikenhauser, *Die Christusmystik des heiligen Paulus,* 2nd ed. 1956, Eng. tr. *Pauline Mysticism,* 1956; G. Staffelbach, *Die Vereinigung mit Christus als Prinzip der Moral bei Paulus,* 1932; S. Djukanovic, *Heiligkeit und Heiligung bei Paulus,* 1939; E. Mocsy, "Problema imperativi ethici in justificatione paulina" in *VD* 25 (1947) pp. 204–17, pp. 264–69; R. Schnackenburg, *Das Heilsgeschehen bei der Taufe nach dem Apostel Paulus*, 1950; A. Kirchgässner, *Erlösung und Sünde im Neuen Testament*, 1950, pp. 147–57; G. Bornkamm, "Taufe und neues Leben bei Paulus" in *Das Ende des Gesetzes*, 1952, pp. 34–50; L. Nieder, *Die Motive der religiös-sittlichen Paränese in den paulinischen Gemeindebriefen*, 1956; C. Haufe, *Die sittliche Rechtfertigungslehre des Paulus*, 1957. On the concept of freedom in Paul: O. Schmitz, *Der Freiheitsgedanke bei Epiktet und der Freiheitsgedanke des Paulus*, 1923; W. Brandt, *Freiheit im Neuen Testament*, 1932; H. Schlier, art. "ἐλεύθερος" in *ThWB* vol. II, pp. 484–500; E. G. Gulin, "Die Freiheit in der Verkündigung des Paulus" in *ZST* 18 (1941) pp. 458–81; Bultmann, *Theologie*, 4th ed., pp. 331 ff., Eng. tr. *Theology*, vol. I, pp. 330 ff.; G. Bornkamm, "Die christliche Freiheit" in *Das Ende des Gesetzes*, pp. 133–38; S. Lyonnet, *Liberté chrétienne et loi nouvelle*, 1953; H. Ridderbos, "Vrijheid en wet volgens Paulus' brief aan de Galaten" in *Arcana revelata* (Festschrift für W. Grosheide) 1951, pp. 89–103; U. Neuenschwander, "Das Verständnis der christlichen Freiheit bei Paulus" in *Schweizer Theologische Umschau* 24 (1954) pp. 104–12; E. Grässer, "Freiheit und apostolisches Wirken bei Paulus" in *Ev Th* 15 (1955) pp. 333–42.

AT THE beginning of the Christian way of salvation stands, for St. Paul, salvation by grace, the gift from God of justification on the ground of faith in Jesus Christ. But just as God's working in the preaching of Jesus called on men to make a choice and bound them to fulfil the divine will without reserve, so also according to St. Paul, God's saving act binds man to the service of the new Lord, to whom he submits freely and joyfully. This happens in baptism, in which the vocation of the believer is effectually fulfilled.[5] Baptism — which, also according to Paul, every believer undergoes; there can be no doubt about that — is the place where every individual shares in salvation, where he enters into communion with Christ and becomes a member of

---

[5] Unlike eternal "election", "calling" is related directly to the concrete acceptance of faith and baptism, cf. Rom. 8:30; 9:24; 1 Cor. 1:9; 7:15, 17 ff.; Gal. 1:6, 15; 5:8, 13; Eph. 4:1, 4; Col. 3:15; 1 Thess. 2:12; 4:7; 5:24; 2 Thess. 2:14; 1 Tim. 6:12; 2 Tim. 1:9. On this see K. L. Schmidt, in *ThWB* vol. III, pp. 488–90.

the "Body of Christ".[6] But it is precisely this deeply significant sacramental act itself which is for St. Paul the point of insertion of moral obligation. Baptism by immersion gave the apostle the opportunity to destroy the misunderstanding of the libertines, according to which we can and should sin in order to increase grace (Rom. 6:1 ff.). If the person baptized is immersed in the water (St. Paul argues), disappears under the surface and so is "buried", the "old man" of the power of sin dies, by being "crucified with Christ" (Rom. 6:6); he is now dead to sin; how then can he sin any more? But at the same time the neophyte receives a new life, by being united "with Christ", who was raised from death by the power of the Father, and shares in his resurrection life. This divine life will, of course, only be revealed in its plenitude and glory at the resurrection at the last day (Col. 3:3f.), but it is already ours now, and we belong to it. God has already "quickened (us) together with him" (Col. 2:13; Eph. 2:5); and we are also to live for him (Rom. 6:11). It is the tension between what we already possess and what we do not yet possess which demands so imperiously our ethical probation; this alone makes what we have already received our permanent possession, and makes it possible for us to hope to receive the full inheritance in the future from God.

St. Paul varied these basic ideas in his moral teaching by the use of constantly changing new images and points of view. We are transferred from slavery or military service under sin to the service of God (Rom. 6:12–14; 16–23). Through Christ we are reconciled to God, but we must also reconcile ourselves with God (2 Cor. 5:19, cf. 20). The Spirit of God dwells in us and drives us on, but we must allow ourselves to be impelled by him and mortify the (sinful) works of the body (Rom. 8:11; cf. 13). We live in the Spirit, now we must walk in the Spirit (Gal.

[6] The Pauline texts on baptism are collected and discussed in Schnackenburg, *Das Heilsgeschehen*, pp. 1–77; cf. also pp. 115–20. See further J. Schneider, *Die Taufe im NT*, 1952; "Le baptême dans le NT" in *Lumière et Vie* 26–27 (1956); G. Delling, *Die Zueignung des Heils in der Taufe*, 1961.

5:25). We have died with Christ, and now we must mortify our members upon the earth (Col. 3:3; cf. 5). Our "old man" has been crucified with Christ (Rom. 6:6), but we in turn must put off the old man and put on the new (Eph. 4:22–24; Col. 3:9f.).[7] Sometimes the indicative and the imperative are juxtaposed: "Purge out the old leaven, that you may be a new paste, as (indeed of course) you are unleavened" (1 Cor. 5:7). This sudden glance back to what the Corinthians already are, namely, persons purified from the old leaven of malice and wickedness (v. 8), can only refer to baptism, which is here adduced as a strong ground for the obligation of holiness which is incumbent on them. "Be what you already (through grace) are": this is the very point made by the words at Ephesians 4:1: "Walk worthy of the vocation in which you are called."

It has been held that the tension between the sinlessness of the Christian and the call not to sin can only be accounted for, by saying that Paul did not succeed in reconciling his doctrine of justification, especially his "magical" and sacramental ideas about baptism, with his ethics.[8] But it is now widely admitted that this tension is an essential part of his thinking about the history of salvation.[9] Yet the dogmatic explanation, going back to Luther, that the Christian may be at one and the same moment justified and a sinner, still survives in many forms. On the basis of clear Pauline texts, the Catholic doctrine of justification concludes

---

[7] In Col. 3:9f. it would be possible to interpret the participles as referring back to baptism; but the context, and Eph. 4:24 make it more likely that they are to be understood as imperatives; cf. Dibelius and Meinertz, in loc.

[8] Cf. H. J. Holzmann, *Lehrbuch der neutestamentlichen Theologie*, 2nd ed. 1911, vol. II, pp. 222ff.; P. Wernle, *Der Christ und die Sünde bei Paulus*, 1897; H. Windisch, *Taufe und Sünde im ältesten Christentum bis auf Origenes*, 1908; H. Weinel, *Theologie des NT*, 4th ed. 1928, pp. 249ff., and on the history of this problem cf. Kirchgässner, *Erlösung*, pp. 3–20.

[9] Cf. Mundle "Religion"; F. Büchsel, *Theologie*, p. 137; A. Oepke in *ThWB* vol. I, p. 539; G. Schrenk in *ThWB* vol. II, p. 213; G. Bornkamm, *op. cit.;* P. Althaus, *Der Brief an die Römer*, 5th ed. 1946, pp. 53–55.

that Paul saw baptism as conveying a real forgiveness of sins and genuine, objective sanctification (see especially 1 Cor. 6:11).[10] That for the Christian the power of sin has already been overcome, and yet has not yet been completely expelled, is due to the fact that we still live in "the mortal body" (Rom. 6:12) and hence within the sphere of influence of the *sarx* with its lusts and passions (Gal. 5:16f.; cf. 24). Death, the last of the powers of destruction, has indeed been defeated in principle by the resurrection of Christ, but has not yet been finally swept away. This will be done only at the resurrection on the last day (1 Cor. 15:26 and 54f.). Thus the eschatological perspective was essential to St. Paul (see below, section 29), and the moral exhortation follows inevitably from this.

But before we examine more closely the Christian struggle against those powers of destruction which still exist, even though they may not be terrifying any more, let us note the moral value implicit in St. Paul's basic thought: God's freely given saving gifts impose the obligation on man to fulfil what he owes to God. Paul thus traces back to God all power to act morally, yet summons men most imperatively to action. He makes impossible any kind of conceited and dangerous building on our own strength (cf. 1 Cor. 10:12) yet rouses the innermost powers of man. He is not attempting to explain the ultimately impenetrable mystery of co-operation between God and man,[11] but to teach man what his authentic moral attitude before God should be, and demand it from him. The result is, that religion and morality are brought into the closest possible relationship; faith imperatively demands proof in moral action,

[10] Cf. Tobac, *Le problème,* and especially Kirchgässner who gives a detailed discussion in his book of the Protestant opinion on this point; his positive reply is given on pp. 147–57.
[11] On this point, cf. R. Schulz, *Die Frage nach der Selbsttätigkeit des Menschen im sittlichen Leben bei Paulus,* 1939; Kirchgässner, *Erlösung;* p. 147f.; G. Söhngen, *Die Einheit in der Theologie,* 1952, pp. 224ff.; C. Haufe, *Rechtfertigungslehre.*

especially in love (Gal. 5:6) and moral endeavour is nothing unless it is based on God's saving power, that is, on the Holy Spirit. That is more than providing morality with a religious motivation; it is giving it a supernatural foundation. Man's despairing failure on the plane of his purely "natural" existence (cf. Rom. 7), becomes a new, hopeful start on the plane of his new life in Christ. St. Paul affirmed that there could be a natural ethics grounded in the law written in the heart (Rom. 2:14; see below, section 30, 2), but conscious of the realities of history he wrote, "All have sinned and are in need of the glory of God" (Rom. 3:23). The "law" of faith (that is, the new order of salvation based on faith) makes all boasting impossible (Rom. 3:27).

Furthermore we can see in this fundamental concept of St. Paul the chief source of moral motives. The attempt has been made to regard the basis of Pauline morality as union with Christ; but this motive is accompanied by many others springing from faith, divine election and vocation, reconciliation with God, the gift of the Spirit, etc. The most general and important of all the motives in the plenitude of motives flowing from the wealth of the world of Pauline theological ideas, is to be found in the divine work of salvation as it is preached in the message of Christ.[12] Besides, St. Paul is not an avowed system-builder, but rather a man filled with passionate love for Christ, who by preaching and pleading, teaching and exhorting, is trying to bring human beings to Christ. With this missionary and pastoral purpose, he uses all the motives at his disposal, but gives first place to the supernatural arguments based on his doctrine of redemption. The passion of the thinker and the intense drive of the lover of souls show themselves not least in the multitude and close weave of his moral arguments.

As an example of this we may quote Paul's attempt in 1 Corinthians 6:12–20 to keep the Corinthians (whose city was a slough of sexual excesses — according to Strabo VIII, 6, 20

---

[12] Cf. L. Nieder, *Die Motive*, pp. 143–5.

there were over a thousand temple prostitutes at the Temple of Aphrodite) from fornication. Several quite separate motives are urged in this terse extract. First, in verse 12, the apostle meets the slogan of the libertines, "All things are lawful to me", in the same slogan-like style, "But all things are not expedient", and again, with a play on words, "All things are lawful to me — but I will not be brought under the power of any". Next, in vv. 13–14, he counters the dangerous objections, "Meat for the belly, and the belly for the meat; but God shall destroy both it and them." In his reply he deals with both these propositions, saying, (a) "the body is not for fornication, but for the Lord; and the Lord for the body", and (b) "God hath both raised up the Lord and will raise us up by his power". Then he begins again ("Know you not . . ."), making the Christian counter-attack. He contrasts carnal union with harlots with the union, also extremely close, but in the Spirit, between the faithful and Christ. The Christian cannot surely leave the communion of Christ and join the harlots, (vv. 15–17).[13] There follows another new beginning, in which St. Paul exhorts his readers, "Flee fornication". Now he suddenly introduces a motive that seems very much of the natural order and, from the logical point of view, not even very convincing: "Every sin that a man doth is without the body; but he that committeth fornication sinneth against his own body" (v. 18). Probably he is appealing here not to reason, but to the feeling that unchastity encroaches more than other sins (than perhaps theft or robbery) on the inner domain of a human being. But now the key-word "body"

---

[13] Even within this Christ-motive, as we may call it, two partial elements can be discerned. Paul first characterizes the bodies of Christians as "members of Christ" (cf. the metaphor of the body and the members, 12:12ff.). These (so we must probably understand) cannot be taken away from Christ and made the members of a harlot. This recalls to the apostle the close relation between the sinner and the harlot; he regards them as "one flesh" (quoting Genesis 2:24). Just as close is the relation between the believer and Christ, but they are "one spirit".

leads him straight to another motive that is meaningful only to the faithful: "Or know you not that your members are the temple of the Holy Ghost, whom you have from God?" (v. 19a). And finally the thought of God, the giver and lord of all things reaches its climax in the divine act of redemption, through which we became entirely his property: ". . . and you are not your own. For you are bought with a great price,[14] glorify and bear God in your body" (vv. 19b–20).

The basic mood the apostle awakens in this way in Christians is one of joy and gratitude.[15] But above all he speaks of liberty as what is gained from justification by God (that is, the blessing of salvation), and as what characterizes our present state of redemption. The Christian should be aware of this great gift and it should lead him to good moral behaviour in freedom. It is very important to him for the contrast it presents to his former servitude to the law and sense of powerlessness. "By the freedom wherewith Christ has made us free, stand fast and be not held again under the yoke of bondage" (Gal. 5:1): such is the appeal St. Paul makes to those Galatians who were on the point of allowing themselves to be talked into circumcision by the Judaizers. We hear a joyful cry of liberty at the end of Romans, the account of the terrifying struggle against being overcome by the power of sin. Because his fundamental conception showed him liberation from the powers of evil as being at the same time union with God, he guards Christian liberty

---

[14] The Greek expression does not mean "at a high price" but "for a cash payment" — as is proved by the papyri. The thought here is not that of religious redemption of slaves, nor of the ransoming of prisoners of war (see W. Elert in *TLZ*, 1947, pp. 265–70) but simply of purchase (ἀγοράζειν; for ransom Gal. 3:13; 4:5 has ἐξαγοράζειν), through which the purchaser acquires the right of ownership. Cf. Nieder, *Die Motive*, pp. 50 and 69.

[15] Cf. Rom. 7:25; 8:35–9; 15:13; 1 Cor. 1:4–7; 2 Cor. 4:15; 8:7–9; 13:11; Eph. 1:3–14; 3:20f.; Phil. 4:4–7; Col. 1:11–14; 2:7; 3:17; 1 Thess. 1:6; 2:13; 3:9; 5:16–18; 2 Thess. 2:13f. Cf. M. S. Enslin, *The Ethics of Paul*, pp. 295 ff.

against the misunderstandings which constantly have beset, and still do beset, this concept. Freedom is not independence of everything, but only independence from evil; true moral freedom is freedom to do good. Hence Paul says at Galatians 5:13, "You, brethren, have been called unto liberty. Only make not liberty into an occasion for the flesh; but by charity of the Spirit serve one another". The outcome of true liberty is the fulfilment, that is the "doing" (cf. v. 14) of the whole law through love, as Jesus preached it. In the following verses it is made clear that this is possible through the Spirit of God given us. "But if you are led by the Spirit, you are not under the law" (v. 18), and yet you fulfil the good that God willed in the law.

In these words the antinomy we should otherwise be bound to find in Paul is resolved: Christians are freed from the law, and yet fulfil the law; they are free, yet they are serving. What Paul found burdensome in the old law was less its precepts than the threat of punishment connected with them, which for everyone who did not keep the law, could not but turn to malediction (Gal. 3:10–12); less its validity than its coercive rule; less its compulsion itself than the compulsion to sin that was bound up with it. It is from this that believers in Christ have been freed, because they do not find salvation by the way of faultless observance of the law, but by the mercy of God. The new Christian liberty that Paul is referring to, will be clear to us if we remember its orientation (freedom *to* . . .) and its possibility (by the Holy Ghost . . .). We already possess the freedom to do good (that is, moral freedom) through the Holy Spirit, who impels us from within, guiding us and giving us the power of victory over the *sarx* (cf. Gal. 5:16). Hence we attain to the virtues (v. 22f.) not by our own strength, but as a "fruit of the Spirit", and need no longer fear the curse of the law, as "against such there is no law" (v. 23). The nature of freedom as on the one hand a blessing of redemption and on the other a moral duty, is disclosed by this double view of it: that it is both "freedom from" and "freedom to".

At this point we can see the difference between the concept of religious liberty in Paul and the high ethical ideal of liberty of the Stoics. For the Stoic sage, liberty was defined as the power to act of oneself (αὐτοπραγία) and he went forward to moral freedom (freedom to do good). But he saw this as consisting in self-mastery, in freedom from passions (ἀπάθεια), in the steadfastness to remain unshaken by all the blows of fate (ἀταραξία), in short, in full control over oneself.[16] To St. Paul such self-mastery was a deception and a lie, for human beings are never fully capable of it, and either without noticing it or without admitting it, remain imprisoned by the world of the *sarx,* the sinfulness of their fallen nature. It was axiomatic to him that we must be given true liberty by God, for it is the divine *pneuma* that overcomes the *sarx.*

When Paul sees the highest demonstration of Christian liberty as residing in love (Gal. 5:13), another valuable consequence of his fundamental idea appears: the Spirit of God at work in us does not lead us to an ethics of personality in which the moral ego rests in itself and finds happiness therein, but to active participation in the community. Just as the Holy Spirit necessarily makes us members of the Body of Christ at baptism (cf. 1 Cor. 12:13; Gal. 3:28), so also he builds this up through our moral actions, through love. Even his extraordinary gifts are given us only "for the profit of all" (cf. 1 Cor. 12:7; cf. 14:26), and the growth of the Body of Christ is accomplished "in love" (Eph. 4:15f.; cf. Rom. 12:9ff.). Thus, even in "social ethics", if one likes to call it such, there is to be found confirmation of Paul's basic concept, that the Christian's whole moral activity is only the operation, the working out of the divine powers given us, an allowing oneself to be moved by the Holy Spirit.

[16] For a more detailed discussion, cf. the bibliographies.

§ 29. BETWEEN THE AGES. THE CHRISTIAN'S STRUGGLE WITH
THE POWERS OF EVIL STILL EXISTING IN THE WORLD

See the bibliographies to sections 27 and 28; add H. Braun, *Gerichts-gedanke und Rechtfertigungslehre bei Paulus*, 1930; F. V. Filson, *St. Paul's Conception of Recompense*, 1931; G. Didier, *Désinteressement du chrétien. La rétribution dans la morale de saint Paul*, 1955. — A. Pott, *Das Hoffen im Neuen Testament*, 1915; R. Bultmann and K. H. Rengstorf, art. "ἐλπίς" in *ThWB* vol. II, pp. 515–31; W. Grossouw, "L'espérance dans le Nouveau Testament" in *RB* 61 (1954) pp. 508–32; "L'Espérance" in *Lumière et Vie* 41 (1959); M. Goguel, "Le caractère, à la fois actuel et futur, du salut dans la théologie paulinienne" in *The Background of the New Testament and its Eschatology* (in honour of C. H. Dodd), 1956, pp. 322–41; E. Neuhäusler, art. "Hoffnung" (in Scripture) in *LThK* vol. V, 416ff. – M. Dibelius, *Die Geisterwelt im Glauben des Paulus*, 1909; G. Kürze, *Der Engel- und Teufelsglaube des Apostels Paulus*, 1915; E. Langton, *Essentials of Demonology*, 1949; M. T. Unger, *Biblical Demonolgy*, 1952; M. C. H. Macgregor, "Principalities and Powers..." in *NTS* 1 (1954–5) pp. 17–28; G. B. Caird, *Principalities and Powers*, 1956; H. Schlier, *Mächte und Gewalten im Neuen Testament*, 1958; M. Ziegler, *Engel und Dämonen in der Bibel*, 1958.

THE MORAL doctrine of St. Paul has two focal points: the redemption already given us by God impelling us towards the sanctification of our way of living, and the salvation we have not yet attained demanding the exertion of all our powers if we are to achieve it. The Corinthians had no lack of the gifts of grace, and they were awaiting the revelation of the Lord Jesus Christ, who would strengthen them until the end, so that in the day of Jesus Christ (the parousia), they might be without crime (1 Cor. 1:7f.). The eschatological point of view was indispensable to the whole of Paul's thinking.

But this orientation towards the last end raises a problem of which Protestant theology is very conscious. How can justification by faith be reconciled with the threatened judgement on the basis of works?

Lutheran theology ascribes the salvation of man to the grace of God alone and still regards human beings as sinners even if they are pardoned in the judgement of God. It has difficulties in reconciling this with the Pauline doctrine of a judgement according to works. How can the Christian who in spite of his sinfulness can confidently expect to be acquitted by God at the judgement on the grounds of his faith in Jesus Christ, then be asked about his works? For judgement according to works involves the possibility of one of two verdicts, eternal salvation or damnation. In recent times attempts have sometimes been made to soften this "contradiction". The explanation, for example, is suggested that Paul was thinking of the judgement of Christians as a saving judgement, even if he does not usually express this thought in his admonitions. In spite of all his shortcomings and in spite of the sin inhering in him, the Christian will nevertheless be acquitted on the grounds of what God or Christ has done.[17] But if one argues in this way, is not one taking all true seriousness and force from the motive of judgement in Paul? And can it be shown that Paul's threats of exclusion from the kingdom of God for Christians who sin greatly (cf. 1 Cor. 6:9f.) were only intended rhetorically?[18]

There is an overwhelming amount of material in the texts foretelling a strict testing by the final judge and requital according to one's acts. "We must all be manifested before the judgement seat of Christ, that everyone may receive the proper things of the body, according as he hath done, whether it be good or evil" (2 Cor. 5:10; cf. Rom. 14:10). Paul continually warns his Christian communities that vicious people will not inherit

---

[17] P. Feine and K. Aland, *Theologie*, p. 235; H. Preisker, art. in *ThWB* vol. IV, pp. 726 ff.; and on the other side, F. Büchsel, *Theologie*, pp. 122 ff. and art. in *ThWB* vol. III, p. 939, n. 68. Filson, *Récompense*, pp. 83 ff.; 116 ff. According to H. Braun, *Gerichtsgedanke*, Paul intensified the thought of judgement (pp. 48:59); he expected God to bring about the moral perfecting of Christians (p. 66), but is sometimes inconsistent (pp. 96 f.). For a criticism of the various Protestant views cf. C. Haufe, *Rechtfertigungslehre*, pp. 41–68.

[18] It cannot be proved that the Apostle ceased to count great sinners among the Christians; cf. Kirchgässner, *Erlösung*, pp. 136–47.

the kingdom of God (1 Cor. 6:9f.; Gal. 5:21; Eph. 5:5). The wrathful judgement of God still menaces such sinful Christians (Col. 3:5f.). "Be not deceived; God is not mocked. For what things a man shall sow, those also shall he reap" (Gal. 6:7f.). The completely typological pattern of thought in 1 Corinthians 10:1–13 is intended to save Christians from false confidence that they might indulge in through trust in the sacraments. Paul does, indeed, in almost all these texts, proceed to restore the confidence of the recipients of the epistles by a reminder of God's faithfulness and the strength he gives them. It would be difficult, however, to see his warnings as no more than pedagogical threats or metaphorical retention of Jewish ideas.

For St. Paul, not even the Christian can escape the general judgement of God "who will render to every man according to his works" (Rom. 2:6; cf. 2 Cor. 11:15; Gal. 5:10; Eph. 6:8 and 2 Tim. 4:14). This doctrine formed part of Paul's basic missionary preaching (1 Thess. 4:6). But the apostle expected that the Christian, once saved from the wrathful judgement of God and filled with the Holy Spirit, who inclines him towards what is good, would never again fall into the old vices, and that as a result his primary salvation would be permanent. We have been acquitted (Rom. 5:1) and we shall be acquitted (cf. 5:19). This picture of the judgement in which we see deliverance from sin and guilt on the one hand as having already taken place, and on the other as still to come, always refers to God's sentence of mercy granted because of Christ's atonement;[19]

---

[19] The verb "justify" is usually used in the present or preterite tense, cf. Rom. 3:24; 3:28; 5:1 and 9; 8:30; 1 Cor. 6:11; Gal. 2:16, etc. Yet we also meet it in the future: Rom. 3:30; 5:19 (but other futures are either logical futures or used from the point of view of the OT: Rom. 3:20; Gal. 2:16bc; 3:8 and 24). From the point of view of God, justification is a single act: hence the present tense at Rom. 8:33. For this idea, cf. E. Tobac, *Le problème*, pp. 192–209; G. Schrenk in *ThWB* vol. II, pp. 221f.; H. W. Heidland, *Die Anrechnung des Glaubens zur Gerechtig-*

but it presupposes that between his first justification and final acquittal at the last judgement, the Christian has died to the power of sin (Rom. 6:11) or been cleansed by the discipline of the Lord (1 Cor. 11:32), and does not incur the sentence of eternal damnation. St. Paul says with conviction that Christians will not be "condemned with this world" (1 Cor. 11:32), and often distinguishes them as those who are saved from the others who perish.[20]

In the Catholic view, the way out of the difficulty is not to be found by watering down the sayings about the judgement but by understanding justification differently. Salvation does, indeed, come only by the grace of God; but after baptism, the cleansed and sanctified human being must co-operate with the grace of God. And at the last judgement God or Christ will examine him very closely about the "good works" that he has done in that way with the help of God. But does not such a doctrine open the door to the return of Jewish ideas of achievement and reward? No, there is no possibility in this doctrine either for any boasting among men (Rom. 3:27). Such "works" are rather a "fruit of the Spirit" (Gal. 5:22), and the reward is a gratuitous gift. Paul, too, speaks of "work";[21] he avoids the plural quite deliberately in order not to recall the thought of the Jewish works of the law. Hence judgement according to his works of every human being individually is not a disturbing

keit, 1936. Even Bultmann, Theology, vol. I, pp. 276, says that if God justifies the sinner, 'making him righteous' (Rom. 4:5), the sinner is not merely 'regarded as if he were' righteous, but is really justified, that is, acquitted from his sins by God's judgement.

[20] Cf. 1 Cor. 1:18; 2 Cor. 2:15; cf. 4:3: οἱ σῳζόμενοι is probably to be interpreted as a gerundive, the salvation lies in God's plan. See 1 Cor. 1:21; and also 5:5; 10:33; 1 Cor. 11:32 (negative); 1 Thess. 2:16; 2 Thess. 2:10.

[21] Gal. 6:4; Eph. 6:13; Phil. 2:12 (the verb); cf. also the "work" of the preacher of the faith, which will be tried at the judgement, 1 Cor. 3:13ff.; 9:1; Phil. 1:22; for other work in the Church, cf. 1 Thess. 5:13; Eph. 4:12.

foreign body in Pauline thought, any more than the idea of retribution was for Jesus himself (see above, section 16). But it plays a different rôle for Paul from what it did in Jewish theology. It is awaited but not feared;[22] it is a spur to moral endeavour, but not to self-righteousness and presumption. As with Jesus, it is a motive in moral exhortation, but not the principal motive.

Perhaps the best characterization of the position in which we Christians find ourselves with regard to salvation would be that of "hope", but our hope is not vague and empty; it is based on God's saving acts and the salvation already given us (cf. Rom. 5: 1–11). We are "saved by hope" (Rom. 8:24). Galatians 5:5 expresses it very compactly, "For we in the Spirit, wait for the hope of justice" (that is, the justice we hope for). Because we already possess the Spirit and with the Spirit the beginning of salvation, we can look forward "much more" surely (cf. Rom. 5:9f.; 2 Cor. 3:9f.) to the full inheritance and final justification. Like liberty, hope is both a blessing of salvation and a moral duty. It shows itself especially in readiness to suffer and in steadfastness (ὑπομονή: Rom. 5:3; 8:25; 12:12; 2 Cor. 1:6f.; 1 Thess. 1:3), in confidence (2 Cor. 3:12) and even in joy (Rom. 12:12), in the midst of all the tribulations of this world, of which the Christian may even "boast" (Rom. 5:3). The deeper reason why hope must be the specific Christian attitude and virtue "between the ages", is the fact that the Christian still lives in a body capable of death and suffering, and is still held fast in this world characterized by evil. We walk as yet in faith, not by sight (2 Cor. 5:7; cf. 1 Cor. 3:12) and so our faith is also a hope. "If we hope for that which we see not, we wait for it with patience" (Rom. 8:24). But our steadfastness must prove itself in the sufferings of this present world-epoch (Rom. 8:18).

---

[22] Paul speaks of the "frankness, confidence" (παρρησία) with which we approach God: 2 Cor. 3:12; Eph. 3:12; 1 Tim. 3:13; cf. H. Schlier in ThWB vol. V, pp. 881f.

This same thought lies behind many texts in which hope is not expressly mentioned but is presupposed, for example, 2 Corinthians 4:16–18, "For which cause we faint not; for though our outward man is corrupted, yet the inward man is renewed day by day. For that which is at present momentary and light of our tribulation worketh for us above measure exceedingly an eternal weight of glory; while we look not at the things which are seen, but at the things which are not seen. For the things which are seen are temporal; but the things which are not seen are eternal." In his exhausting activities, menaced every day by death, a "spectacle to the world, and to angels and to men" (1 Cor. 4:9), the apostle embodied in himself in the fullest possible way this power to suffer and this hope.

By his atoning death Jesus Christ has, indeed, saved us in principle from this "present evil world" (Gal. 1:4), so that we no longer need to walk according to the "course of this world" (Eph. 2:2), but "this world" (an equivalent expression) temporarily continues to exist, although its form is passing away (1 Cor. 7:31) and the end of the ages has come upon us (1 Cor. 10:11).[23] Hence, "this world" is still an evil place of temptation, all around us, and we need the admonition, "Be not conformed to this world, but be reformed in the newness of your mind" (Rom. 12:2). God has indeed "delivered us from the power of darkness and hath delivered into the kingdom of the Son of his love" (Col. 1:13); but Christ still rules hidden in heaven, and hence we are to seek the things that are above (Col. 3:1f.). We are, as it were, a colony of citizens of heaven, for "our conversation (that is, citizenship) is in heaven; from whence also we look for the Saviour, our Lord Jesus Christ, who will reform the body of our lowness, made like to the body of his

---

[23] These plurals should probably not be seen as intensifying the meaning. The thought here is not that the ends of the two ages touch (and intersect) — thus J. Héring and J. Weiss, *in loc.;* cf. G. Sasse in *ThWB* vol. I, pp. 203, 29ff. and n. 19; Bauer, *Wörterbuch,* p. 50.

glory" (Phil. 3:20f.).[24] "This age" or "this world" or "the world" is also used to designate men and things that have not been brought by Christ into the divine domain.[25] Hence St. Paul says that the world is crucified to him and he to the world (Gal. 6:14).

But above all there are still at work in this world super-human, spiritual powers, angelic-demonic forces, which in Paul's view opposed the dominion of God over the world openly and autocratically, and which were only subjugated by Christ, but again only in principle, as it were, so that they still have influence in this world. It is probably such "rulers of this world" that Paul describes as sharing in the crucifixion of Jesus (1 Cor. 2:6, 8). They, of course, failed to recognize the wisdom of God, who raised the crucified to be the "lord of glory". As Paul says in another metaphor, Jesus has despoiled these powers and forces of their weapons and has exposed them publicly, leading them in his triumph (Col. 2:15). At Ephesians 1:21 this triumph is described by saying that God has raised up Jesus to rule with him at his right hand, far above "all principality and power, virtue and dominion . . .". But the ruler "of this air" (under which image these powers are in part imagined) still works through the sons of disobedience (Eph. 2:2). The "god of this world" has blinded the minds of unbelievers (2 Cor. 4:4). Clearly this is Satan, against whom Paul warned those to whom he wrote because "we are not ignorant of his devices" (2 Cor. 2:11). Satan can clothe himself as an angel of light (2 Cor. 11:4), and has even worked outwardly against the apostle in his work (1 Thess. 2:18). Paul was afraid that this tempter had led the Thessalonians astray and his own work had been in vain (1 Thess. 3:5; cf. also 1 Cor. 7:5).

[24] Cf. M. Dibelius, *An die Thess. I–II, an die Phil.;* 3rd ed. *in loc.,* 1937; K. L. Schmidt, *Die Polis in Kirche und Welt,* 1939, pp. 21–24; E. Peterson, *Apostel und Zeuge Christi,* 1941, *in loc.* On the concept of strangers in Paul, cf. 2 Cor. 5:6 and 9.
[25] Cf. 1 Cor. 1:20; 2:6, 12; 3:18; 5:10; 1 Tim. 6:17; 2 Tim. 4:10.

Are these merely "mythological expressions"?[26] The language is often metaphorical and the ideas are in keeping with the old picture of the world ("the middle kingdom of the air"). But it cannot be denied that Paul saw spiritual realities behind these images. He shared this conviction about the kingdom of Satan with the whole of early Christianity and with Jesus himself.

The Christian must also fight these cosmic powers of evil afresh. This struggle is described most fully at Ephesians 6:10–17. In the strength of the Lord, with the armour of God, the Christian can withstand the onslaughts of the devil and all the "rulers of this world of darkness". The supernatural armament of the Christian is described in metaphors which are in the main taken from the language of the Old Testament: loins girt about with truth; clothed with the breastplate of justice; feet shod with the preparation of the gospel of peace. With the shield of faith, we are to extinguish all the fiery darts of the evil one. And in addition we wear the helmet of salvation and grip the sword of the Spirit, that is, the word of God.

One of the recently discovered Dead Sea manuscripts is a book of the "War of the Sons of Light against the Sons of Darkness" which in a similar strain describes by a warlike metaphor the eschatological struggle of the chosen ones of "God's Covenant" against the powers of darkness. God supports the sons of light. The superscriptions on the banners of the

---

[26] R. Bultmann, *Theology,* vol. I, p. 257. H. Schlier in *Der Brief an die Epheser, passim,* esp. pp. 112ff., is also convinced that as regards the letter to the Ephesians the teaching about the "ages" incorporates some ideas that are in appearance Gnostic (the "ages" seen as personal beings); but he interprets them in a theological way: "The 'ages' stand for the world as it rises from the hand of the Creator over the horizon of history, if it may be so expressed, but when it is not yet become the tool and expression of the principalities and powers", p. 113. The conception of ages as personal beings is difficult to justify in all cases (e.g. Eph. 2:7; 3:11). Where they appear personified (see Eph. 2:2) they tend more to the appearance of "principalities and powers". On these see the monograph by H. Schlier and the various literature in the bibliography.

army of God are characteristic. On the great banner carried into the battlefield there is written, "The army of God". On the banner of the Thousand, "The wrath of God is kindled against Belial (Satan) and all the men of his company without remnant". On the banner of the Hundred, "All the might of battle against all wicked flesh comes from God". Before the battle the High Priest encourages the troops: "Fear not, tremble not before them, do not give way", of the enemy he says, "They are a gathering of wickedness, they work in darkness, and their desire is for darkness". Finally he starts a warsong in which God himself is called on, as a valiant champion, to defeat the enemy.[27]

Was this only an eschatological picture, a collection of late Jewish eschatological ideas? Though the form of words may have been determined by the time in which they were written, the war of the divine forces against the forces hostile to God is a reality, and Christ is involved in it. But Paul was not merely filled with a conviction of victory like those Essene holy men who cut themselves off from the rest of human society. He also saw the outcome of the struggle as already decided by Christ and knew that in the midst of this world he was protected by the love of Christ and God and proof against all the powers of darkness. "But in all these things we overcome, because of him that hath loved us; for I am sure that neither death, nor life, nor angels, nor principalities nor powers, nor things present, nor things to come, nor might, nor height, nor depth, nor any other creature, shall be able to separate us from the love of God which is in Christ Jesus our Lord" (Rom. 8:37–39). The last enemy to be annihilated will be the power of death itself (1 Cor. 15:26) and then, at the general resurrection, the victory of the risen Lord will be complete (1 Cor. 15:54f.).

[27] The dating and meaning of the *War Rule* are still controverted; cf. L. Rost in *TLZ* 80 (1955), pp. 205–8; translation by G. Vermes, *The Dead Sea Scrolls in English*, 1962; see further esp. Y. Yadin, *The Scroll of the War*..., 1961; J. Carmignac, *La Règle de la Guerre*..., 1958; J. van der Ploeg, *Le Rouleau de la Guerre*, 1959.

§ 30. CONSCIENCE AND ITS FORMATION
AS A CONCERN OF ST. PAUL

H. Böhlig, "Das Gewissen bei Seneca und Paulus" in *TSK* 87 (1914) pp. 1–24; F. Tillmann, "Zur Geschichte des Begriffs 'Gewissen' bis zu den Paulinischen Briefen" in *Festschrift für S. Merkle,* 1922, pp. 336–47; T. Schneider, "Der paulinische Begriff des Gewissens (Syneidesis)" in *Bonner Zeitschrift für Theologie und Seelsorge* 6 (1929) pp. 153–211; *id.,* "Die Quellen des paulinischen Gewissensbegriffs", *ibid.* 7 (1930) pp. 97–112; M. Dibelius and H. Conzelmann, *Die Pastoralbriefe,* 3rd ed. 1955, Excursus pp. 16f.; J. Stelzenberger, *Die Beziehungen der frühchristlichen Sittenlehre zur Ethik der Stoa,* 1933, pp. 192–216; C. Spicq, "La conscience dans le Nouveau Testament" in *RB* 47 (1938) pp. 50–80; *id., Les épîtres Pastorales,* 1947, Excursus pp. 29–38 (with bibliog.); M. Pohlenz, "Paulus und die Stoa" *ZNW* 42 (1949) pp. 69–104, more especially pp. 77ff.; J. Dupont, "Syneidesis aux origines de la notion chrétienne de conscience morale" in *Studia Hellenistica* 5 (1948) pp. 119–53; C. A. Pierce, *Conscience in the New Testament,* 1955; O. Kuss, *Der Römerbrief,* 1st imp. 1957, pp. 76–82; J. Stelzenberger, *Syneidesis im Neuen Testament,* 1961.

PAUL was a Jew of the diaspora with a Jewish-Hellenistic upbringing, and in his writings we encounter an idea which was to be full of significance for Christian moral doctrine, the concept of conscience (συνείδησις). In speaking of it he was, of course, only giving us a definite name for something that had been known both to Old Testament Judaism and to Jesus.[28] But the great apostle of the gentiles had many things to say about conscience and the obligation it imposes that we do not yet hear in the gospels. The growing recognition that a clear concept of conscience and the cultivation and formation of this living witness, advocate and judge in our own heart is very im-

---

[28] Cf. P. Heinisch, *Theologie des Alten Testaments,* 1940, pp. 226f.; T. Schneider, art. in *Bonner Zeitschrift für Theologie und Seelsorge* 7 (1930) pp. 102–4. L. Köhler in his *Theologie des Alten Testaments,* 3rd. ed. 1953, p. 192, concludes that the concept of conscience was neither widespread nor significant in the Old Testament.

portant in moral education,[29] gives increased relevance today to Pauline doctrine. Yet we must be clear that the concept of συνείδησις in Paul is not yet or not yet entirely identical with what we call "conscience".

i. The Concept of συνείδησις in Paul

The word συνείδησις is to be found twenty times in St. Paul (five times in the pastoral epistles), as against only another ten times in the rest of the New Testament (in Acts twice, Hebrews five times and 1 Peter three times). In using it, Paul was taking up an idea which was frequently used from the first century before Christ onwards in the Greek vernacular (the koine) and in Latin popular philosophical writings (conscientia).[30] It was also familiar to Philo (τὸ συνειδός); but this Jew of Alexandria adapted it to suit his belief in revelation and his personal concept of God.[31] As it was used chiefly in popular ethics and not defined, we cannot expect absolute clarity in its use. Thus there is no differentiation between awareness of moral values and the actual function to which we might like to restrict the term "conscience" nowadays.[32] The characteristic mark of this spiritual function is, of course, the personal and spontaneous reaction before or after some moral decision; but awareness of moral values is, of course, necessarily presupposed as its foundation.

[29] Cf. T. Müncker, Die psychologischen Grundlagen der katholischen Sittenlehre in Tillmann's Handbuch (vol. II, 3rd ed. 1948): certainly the most thorough account of the whole complex of problems; J. Stelzenberger, Moraltheologie, 1953, pp. 89–99.

[30] After a thorough examination of the question, J. Dupont "Syneidesis", pp. 123–46, reaches the conclusion that the Pauline concept of conscience was rooted in popular philosophy, as may be demonstrated from the Latin writers of the first century B.C.

[31] Cf. E. Bréhier, Les idées philosophiques et religieuses de Philon d'Alexandrie, 3rd ed., 1950, pp. 295 ff.; W. Völker, Fortschritt und Vollendung bei Philo v. Alex., 1938, pp. 95 ff.

[32] Cf. Stelzenberger, Moraltheologie, pp. 94–99; id., Syneidesis im Neuen Testament, pp. 42–44.

But Paul seems to have been more concerned, in accordance with the original, etymological sense ("to be conscious of something" — cf. 1 Cor. 4:4) with this latter, although in fact at Romans 2:14f. he describes both the constitution and the functioning of conscience. Furthermore at 1 Corinthians 8:7ff. the apostle writes partly of moral judgement (we notice the reference to "knowledge"), and partly of the reaction to moral conduct, that is, subsequent conscience (the conscience of the weak is "defiled").

The fundamental meaning, awareness, is more closely adhered to than is usual with us, when St. Paul speaks of "commending ourselves to every man's conscience in the sight of God" (2 Cor. 4:2) or when he hopes he is "manifested" in the "consciences" of the Corinthians, that is, that his uprightness may be discernible to them (2 Cor. 5:11). The use of "for conscience's sake" as opposed to "for the sake of wrath" (cf. Rom. 13:5), is a reference to awareness of moral responsibility; and in 1 Corinthians 10:25, 27 and 28, Paul is thinking of moral scruples.

Most often conscience is characterized as a "witness" (Rom. 2:15; 9:1; 2 Cor. 1:12); it accompanies our actions as an incorruptible witness within us, and can also be called upon to attest the truth of our assertions. Subsequent conscience is probably what Paul is describing at Romans 2:15c under the image of mutually accusing and defending thoughts (see below).

It is noteworthy that such attributes as "a good conscience" (1 Tim. 1:5 and 19; cf. Acts 23:1; Heb. 13:18; 1 Pet. 3:16 and 21), or "a pure conscience" (1 Tim. 3:9; 2 Tim. 1:5; and the opposite at Tit. 1:15) are to be found only in the pastoral epistles, and they are more firmly established in later writings.[33] To say, as Dibelius did, that this marked the appearance of an ideal of "middle-class Christianity" is surely too harsh, yet it

[33] Cf. T. Schneider in "Begriff des Gewissens" pp. 193–211. M. Dibelius and H. Conzelmann, *Die Pastoralbriefe*, p. 17 would like to see this as a characteristic mark of a certain understanding of the faith; see also C. Spicq, *Épîtres Pastorales*, pp. 29–38.

cannot be denied that this mode of expression does not appear in the earlier Pauline epistles. Furthermore, there is also to be found in the pastoral epistles (which have the cause of sound teaching very much at heart) another noteworthy feature: conscience now stands generally like a watchful cherub before the portal of the faith, before the temple of religious doctrinal truth.[34]

ii. The Conscience as a Moral Endowment of all Men

In the well-known text Romans 2:14f., St. Paul shows he is convinced that "the Gentiles, who have not the law (of Moses), do by nature those things (the commandments) that are of the law" and hence "are a law to themselves". The next verse then seems to determine more precisely how far they can do acts fulfilling the moral law without knowledge of the written law: "They show the work of the law (that is, the acts demanded by the written law) written in their hearts, their conscience bearing witness to them, and their thoughts between themselves accusing, or also defending, one another." This text is usually quoted as the *locus classicus* for the existence of a natural moral law which even the natural man can observe. But this view must be qualified by certain exegetical reservations.

First it is clear from the context St. Paul certainly does not mean to say that such moral behaviour is normal among pagans. The whole passage Romans 1:18–3:20 serves rather to prove that "all have sinned and need the glory of God" (3:23). Only a few lines earlier Paul says, "Whosoever have sinned without the law, shall perish without the law; and whosoever have sinned in the law, shall be judged by the law" (2:12). And lastly v. 15c also shows that the apostle was thinking more of accusing than of defending voices. His reference to pagans who without knowing the revealed law fulfil the commandments of the law, serves only to show the emptiness of claims made by

[34] T. Schneider, *ibid.*, p. 201.

the Jews on the grounds of their possession and knowledge of the divine law "for not the hearers of the law are just before God; but (only) the doers of the law shall be justified" (2:13). Just as he did in connection with natural knowledge of God, (1:19f.), Paul admits the possibility here that even heathens might do good works on the basis of a natural knowledge of morality; but his purpose is not to use the noble pagan to shame sinful Jews, but only to destroy the Jew's pride in the law, his boasting about the revelation of the law without actual fulfilment of its commandments. Just as he adds to his acknowledgement of the fact of natural recognition of God the significant clause "so that they are inexcusable", so too when thinking of their moral judgement, he remained convinced that although they might do good moral actions, they would no more be able than the Jews to withstand the final judgement of God.[35]

Hence St. Paul's "by nature" cannot simply be equated with the moral *lex naturalis,* nor can this reference be seen as straightforward adoption of Stoic teaching. The Stoic was so certain that the *lex naturalis* was a part of human nature that he maintained that everyone who recognized it could also live by it.[36] That was definitely not St. Paul's opinion. He uses the expression φύσει in an unphilosophical, popular sense, as meaning perhaps "by what you are, of yourselves".[37] Thus the text does indeed

---

[35] In several essays G. Söhngen has displayed the religio-historical view taken in Rom. 1:20f. and 2:14ff. and clearly demonstrated its correspondence with the teaching of the Vatican. See *Die Einheit in der Theologie,* 1952, pp. 206ff.; 216ff.; 224f.; 252f. Cf. also G. Bornkamm, "Die Offenbarung des Zornes Gottes, Röm. 1–3", art. in *Das Ende des Gesetzes,* 1952, pp. 9–33.

[36] Cf. M. Pohlenz, "Paulus und die Stoa", pp. 75ff.; M. Lackmann, *Vom Geheimnis der Schöpfung,* 1952, pp. 217ff.

[37] Cf. Rom. 2:27 "that which by nature is uncircumcision"; Gal. 2:15 "We by nature are Jews"; Gal. 4:8 "them who, by nature, are not gods"; Eph. 2:3, "were by nature children of wrath"; also Rom. 1:26, "their women have changed the natural use (of the sexual instinct) into that use which is against nature".

say that pagans can do good acts (v. 14), that they possess within themselves the capacity to do them (v. 15a), but not that they are inclined to do them and are in fact people who, because of this, will be able to stand at God's judgement.

On the other hand we should reject various interpretations which give the text a completely different meaning, such as that suggested by Augustine, and recently again by W. Mundle, K. Barth, and F. Flückiger, interpreting ἔθνη as meaning gentile Christians.[38] In verses 15–16 many scholars find a single eschatological picture of the judgement.[39] According to M. Lackmann the ἔργον νόμου is a successful concern for the law, from the human viewpoint, which leaves its traces in the heart; but God will judge according to his own knowledge of the heart of man and will not account such justification by works as sufficient even from the heathen.[40] Even with these interpretations, however, the difficulties of the text do not entirely vanish.[41] Admittedly in the traditional exegesis of the passage the reference to the judgement at v. 16 gives an unexpected and disruptive effect; but perhaps Paul wanted to return to the

[38] St. Augustine, *De Spiritu et littera*, 26–28; *Contra Julian.*, IV, 23f. W. Mundle, "Zur Auslegung von Röm. 2:13ff.", art. in *TB* 13 (1934) 9; K. Barth, *Kirchl. Dogmatik*, vol. I, 2, 1939, p. 332; F. Flückiger, Die Werke des Gesetzes bei den Heiden (nach Rom. 2:14ff.)", art. in *TZ* 8 (1952) pp. 17–42. But Paul never said of gentile *Christians* that they did this φύσει, but rather that they did it πνεύματι. Besides his reference would lose all relation to the context. Cf. O. Kuss, *Der Römerbrief*, pp. 70f.

[39] H. Lietzmann and (differently) J. Sickenberger, *in loc.;* cf. also Lackmann (in text).

[40] *Op. cit.* pp. 221–35; similarly, A. Nygren, *Der Römerbrief,* 1951, *in loc.*

[41] Thus the subject of 15 c cannot be primarily "condemning (put first!) or defending thoughts". It cannot be concerned with morally weighing the facts before acting (Lackmann, p. 229), for condemning — and defending — depends on the act, presupposing it. But if it is a question of thoughts after the act, the condemnatory ones would deprive of all force the evidence brought forward that the law had been accomplished.

theme of vv. 6–10, or perhaps the verse should be thought of as a gloss.[42]

In any case this passage bears witness to St. Paul's view, a view perhaps not uninfluenced by Stoic thinking, but wholly translated into Christian terms, that everyone possesses a faculty of making moral judgements, and a conscience. If at the same time they are sinners who will not be able to stand at the judgement of God, this fact supports Paul's doctrine of justification: that there is only one way to salvation, redemption by the blood of Jesus. Recognition of the good and occasional fine actions are not enough to bring anyone to salvation. From this point of view man's natural ability is just as weak (Rom. 8:3), just as impotent to give life (Gal. 3:21) as the Mosaic law. Man's moral endowment assumes its true worth only when he becomes a Christian, when the Holy Spirit lays hold of his spirit and moves him to what is good.

iii. Conscience as the Ultimate Authority in Moral Judgement

That conscience is decisive for determining the moral quality of an act, was another clear insight of St. Paul. Being a human being capable of making mistakes, the Christian can find himself in inner conflicts. He may still not have enough "knowledge" *(gnosis)* and may think, for example, that the meat offered for sale in the public markets, meat from pagan sacrifices, is morally forbidden, although he should know that there are no "gods" and there is nothing against the meat from the sacrifices (cf. 1 Cor. 8:10). In Romans 14, Paul examines a similar problem. In the Roman community there were many Christians who believed that the use of meat and wine generally was forbidden (cf. vv. 2–21). Paul said that the others, the "strong", were

[42] Thus R. Bultmann in *TLZ* 72 (1947) pp. 200f.; H. Sahlin also advocates an emendation of the text in *TZ* 9 (1953) pp. 93–95, seeking to add ἡμέρᾳ in v. 16. Against this see Pohlenz, "Paulus und die Stoa", p 79.

right, that for Christians no food is "unclean". At Colossae he censured more severely similar opinions, because they were being spread by false teachers, and calls them the "precepts of men", and a fall back into slavery to the "elements of this world" (Col. 2:20ff.). Thus at Corinth and Rome the "weak" were really deficient in knowledge and Christian liberty. But if they had eaten things which, although mistakenly, they held to be forbidden, they had "defiled" their consciences (1 Cor. 8:7). The conclusion of these discussions in the Epistle to the Romans forms a statement which is also a precept: "All that is not of faith is sin" (14:23b). For moral theology this is a classical text demonstrating that the conscience, even if it judges wrongly, is the ultimate and decisive measure of morality. For biblical theology it is also noteworthy that St. Paul here uses the same word, πίστις, as he uses elsewhere for belief, faith. It is difficult to attribute a special sense to it here,[43] for to St. Paul, faith is the whole attitude of the Christian, assimilating his judgements of moral worth too. The Christian is not divided within himself, with a natural economy and a supernatural one; there is only one judgement of conscience, and it is determined by his belief.

iv. Formation and Training of the Conscience

In the discussion of the use of meat offered to idols St. Paul endeavours to teach those members of the community at Corinth who are asserting their liberty and boast of their knowledge, to be considerate towards the "weak",[44] not by external admonition but by giving them a motive that will

---

[43] Bultmann, *Theology*, vol. I, p. 220, rightly draws attention to the parallel forms used by Paul in 1 Cor. 8 and Rom. 14: what he says in 1 Cor. 8 about συνείδησις he repeats in similar words in Rom. 14 about πίστις. Cf. Bauer, *Wörterbuch*, 1317, "The freedom of faith; the powers of faith."

[44] On "the weak", see esp. J. Dupont, "Syneidesis", pp. 146ff.

touch their consciences. Such formation of conscience can only be interpreted as an attempt to refine and elevate their moral values (not the function of conscience as such), bringing them up to true Christian standards. Fraternal love stands at the top of the list (cf. section 23). If anyone who has full knowledge gives occasion, through his untroubled eating, to one of the weak brethren to eat like him the meat of sacrifices made to idols, and so defile his conscience, he should voluntarily renounce it. Christian liberty must not be a cause of stumbling to other brethren (1 Cor. 8:9). "Through thy knowledge *(gnosis)* shall the weak brother perish, for whom Christ hath died?" (1 Cor. 8:11). In the Epistle to the Romans, St. Paul calls that frankly an offence against charity (14:15). Under his frequently recurring image of the building he calls on all to put the community before their own wishes: "Therefore let us follow after the things that are of peace, and keep the things that are of edification, one towards another" (14:19). This is the only reason why Christian liberty is to be surrendered; the apostle expressly rejects the idea that those who eat the sacrificial meat without scruples should allow themselves to be changed by the condemnation of others (1 Cor. 10:29b–30).[45] Paul therefore, wants perfectly clear minds; but even more he wants loving hearts.[46]

In other ways, too, this man, who was sometimes so impulsive himself, tried to inculcate tact in the exercise of charity. With sensitive consideration, he told his Philippians that he prayed their charity might "more and more abound in knowledge and in all understanding" (Phil. 1:9). Probably he thought they still lacked proper harmony and selfless humility in their dealings with one another (cf. 2:3ff.; 4:2). This was, moreover, his constant concern, "Bearing with one another, and forgiving one another, if any have complaint against another" (Col. 3:13;

[45] On this point, cf. Bultmann, *Theology,* vol. I, pp. 219f.; Dupont, *op. cit.,* p. 151.

[46] Dupont, *op. cit.* p. 153 sees St. Paul's originality as consisting in the primacy of charity, not in the concept of conscience.

cf. Eph. 4:32). Sometimes he is even rather severe: "But if you bite and devour one another, take heed you be not consumed of one another" (Gal. 5:15).

With such admonitions Paul was training Christian consciences, that is, trying to make Christians clear-sighted and aware of true moral values. This is clearly shown by his continual demand that they examine themselves (1 Cor. 11:28; 2 Cor. 13:5; Gal. 6:4) or seek the will of God (Rom. 12:2; Eph. 5:10), or again, weigh carefully what is in question (Phil. 1:10).[47] He was not reintroducing the ideas of Jewish casuistry (cf. Rom. 2:18), but making Christian charity the key to knowledge, the sign pointing the way to morally good behaviour. From this point of view, Augustine with his advice, "Love and do what you will", follows and interprets Paul perfectly. Christian liberty springs from charity and at the same time bows under the light yoke of Christ.

§ 31. THE MORAL PREACHING
OF THE MISSIONARY TO THE GENTILES

See Stelzenberger's and Pohlenz's works in section 30. Also R. Bultmann, *Der Stil der paulinischen Predigt und die kynisch-stoische Diatribe*, 1910; A. Bonhöffer, *Epiktet und das Neue Testament*, 1911; H. Böhlig, *Die Geisteskultur von Tarsos*, 1913; M. S. Enslin, *The Ethics of Paul*, 1930, pp. 17–49; A. D. Nock, *Conversion*, 1933; C. H. Dodd, *The Bible and the Greeks*, 1935; W. L. Knox, *St. Paul and the Church of the Gentiles*, 1939 (on this see. R. Bultmann in *TLZ* 72, 1947, pp. 77–80); K. Prümm, *Der christliche Glaube und die altheidnische Welt*, 2 vols., 1935; A. Vögtle, *Die Tugend- und Lasterkataloge im Neuen Testament*, 1936; J. Dupont, *Gnosis, La connaissance religieuse dans les épîtres de saint Paul*, 1949; J. Munck, *Paulus und die Heilsgeschichte*, 1954; G. Schrenk, "Urchristliche Missionspredigt im 1. Jahrhundert" in *Studien zu Paulus*, 1954, pp. 131–48; P. Dalbert, *Die Theologie der hellenistisch-jüdischen Missionsliteratur unter Ausschluß*

---

[47] In all these texts Paul uses the word δοκιμάζειν. It is one of a group of words all concerned with the moral testing of Christians; cf. W. Grundmann in *ThWB* vol. II, pp. 260–4.

von Philo und Josephus, 1954; H. Thyen, *Der Stil der Jüdisch-Hellenistischen Homilie,* 1955.

PAUL was called to be the apostle of the gentiles (Acts 9:15; 22:11; 26:17f.) and looked upon himself as such (Gal. 1:15f.; Rom. 1:5; 15:16, 18). In discussions between him and the leaders of the Jerusalem community, it was decided that Peter should undertake the mission to the Jews and Paul the mission to the gentiles (Gal. 2:6-9). This man, on whom preaching lay like a compulsion (1 Cor. 9:16), this prototype of the labourer and soldier of Christ, knew only one method, that of being all things to all men, a Jew to the Jews, a gentile to the gentiles (1 Cor. 9:20ff.). We may, therefore, ask how he himself, with his origins in the Judaism of the diaspora, adapted his moral teaching to the requirements and understanding of his non-Jewish hearers. Did he change his emphasis for these heirs of a different spiritual outlook? Did he tone down many of the commandments for these children of an easy-going world? Did he adopt some of the popular material of the wandering pagan philosophers, or at least their way of talking to ordinary people? The fresh, unsophisticated language of his epistles, his lively interest in everything that concerned his young communities, the profound seriousness of this preaching and, in addition, his understanding of human weakness and vulnerability, give us insights it would be difficult to find in a theoretical treatment of ethics. We can examine only a few special questions here.

i. The Themes used in Exhortation of Gentile Christians and the Way these were handled

The first of Paul's epistles to the Churches which have come down to us, the two Epistles to the Thessalonians, at once give us some indication of the chief difficulties that the new Christians had to overcome in the moral sphere. Sexual purity and honesty in business life are the most urgent moral admonitions in these epistles. Paul puts both before the Thessalonians clearly as God's will (1 Thess. 4:3ff.). We have already noted the instruction in chastity (see above, section 26,2). It is important that the apostle requires something more from his hearers than pagan social or civic morality. "Every one of you should know how to possess his vessel in sanctification and honour, not in the passion of lust, like the Gentiles who know not God" (vv. 4–5). Whether "vessel" here refers to their own bodies or to their wives (cf. 1 Pet. 3:7) has been disputed since ancient times and can scarcely be determined with certainty. In the first case it would have to be understood as meaning, "learn to control your own body" and in the second, "possess your wife in sanctity and honour". It is unlikely that the passage refers to contracting marriage, for the apostle can hardly have been speaking to a limited circle of people. Although in Rabbinic Judaism the expression "vessel" can be shown to have been used for "wife", that was not the case in Hellenism. Yet, gentile Christians must have been able to understand the expression in this sense, as 1 Peter 3:7 shows. We must, therefore, leave the question open.[48]

Paul not only includes lasciviousness, "fornication", in the traditional lists of vices: he also attacks it on his own account with the strongest of Christian arguments (1 Cor. 6:12ff.; see above, section 28). It is noteworthy that he speaks much more often of unchastity or fornication (πορνεία) than of adultery (μοιχεία);[49] probably because Christian demands

---

[48] For Rabbinic usage see Billerbeck, vol. III, pp. 632f. and for the Greek, Liddell and Scott, *Lexicon*, vol. II, p. 1607; Bauer, *Wörterbuch*, pp. 1372f. (who leaves the question open). It is discussed by Dibelius, *Thess. Exk.* 21, who supports "flesh", as do Schlatter and Staab *in loc.*; a decisive view but with good evidence given by B. Rigaux, *S. Paul, Les Épîtres aux Thessaloniciens*, 1956, pp. 504ff. In contrast the meaning "wide" is supported by Juncker, *Ethik*, vol. II, pp. 200f.; Delling, *Paulus' Stellung zu Frau und Ehe*, p. 61, note 36; Meinertz, *Theologie*, vol. II, p. 202, note 1.
[49] Adulterer occurs in the Pauline lists of vices only at 1 Cor. 6:9.

went so much further than Stoic ethics. Frequenting of prostitutes and any kind of illegitimate satisfaction of desire is bound gravely to endanger the exclusive and close mystical relation of the Christian with the Lord (cf. 1 Cor. 6:17; 7:32ff.). Paul also urgently warns his readers against occasions of debauchery, for example, feasting and drunkenness (Rom. 13:13; 1 Cor. 5:11; Gal. 5:21), and pagan idolatry (1 Cor. 10:7, 14–22; see also the lists of vices at 1 Cor. 5:11; 6:9; Gal. 5:20).

Another important point in Pauline moral exhortation, was honesty in everyday life; he sees avarice as another vice typical of the pagans[50] and calls it "idolatry" (Col. 3:5; Eph. 5:5). Avarice can easily lead to falling away from the true God; that was the experience of Judaism too.[51] Paul brought esteem for poverty, moderation and liberality with him from Judaism, but he surely also knew Jesus' earnest words about the idol Mammon. And he based his precept to give freely and cheerfully (2 Cor. 9:5–7) on motives of his own, drawn from faith in Christ (2 Cor. 8:9; 9:8ff.).

Envy and strife, anger and discord belonged to the pattern of general Hellenistic moral teaching,[52] but Paul was not satisfied merely to enumerate them in the catalogue of vices. Because he had to fight hard against these evils in his communities, he had a great deal to say about concord and love in the

[50] Cf. Rom. 1:29; 1 Cor. 5:11; 6:10; Eph. 4:19; 5:3, 5; Kol. 3:5.
[51] Cf. the texts in E. Lohmeyer, *Die Briefe an die Phil., Kol., Phlm.,* 1930, on Col. 3:5. For a Christian judgement, cf. Polycarp, *ad Phil.* 11:2: "He who does not keep himself from avarice, will soil himself with the worship of idols and likewise will be numbered among the heathen."
[52] In the New Testament the same set phrases often occur in lists of vices and virtues; cf. Rom. 1:29; Gal. 5:20; Eph. 4:31; Col. 3:8; 1 Tim. 6:4; 2 Tim. 3:2f. For the pagan lists of vices see Vögtle, *Lasterkataloge,* pp. 78, 87 etc. (see index). For the Late Jewish catalogues of vices see S. Wibbing, *Die Tugend- und Lasterkataloge im NT,* 1959, pp. 91–99; but precisely the above-mentioned vices are here incapable of being substantiated (pp. 95ff.).

Lord, and adduces the highest motives (see sections 19 and 23 above).

Paul, then, accepted many things that were also taught by popular ethics; we might also notice obedience to authority, family duties and duties of state, the so-called household or domestic codes. But to what was often a coin worn smooth, the Christian missionary frequently, though not always, gave a new splendour. The method of presentation in popular instruction at that time was anything but faulty. It was a lively style delighting in argument and counter-argument, in replies to imaginary objections, exclamations, direct address to the audience, and in changing from "I" to "you" and from "we" to "you". St. Paul took over this art of the *diatribe* as it was cultivated in Cynic and Stoic popular philosophy, and it suited his scintillating mind, the compulsive plenitude of his thought, his ability to adapt himself to the readers, with whom he wanted to fall into "talk". In addition he used many metaphors, especially from the life of business and the law courts, sport and the army, but above all from everyday life. However, it cannot be denied that his application of them is not always felicitous.[53] At any rate Paul drew close to his hearers and readers, and his gift of sympathy, his delicacy and his ardent love for Christ and for them was more than enough to steady the waverers (the Galatians, for example) and give a firm footing to those who (like the Corinthians) were stumbling.

ii. The Motivation of his Demands

As the missionary to the gentiles, did Paul use, as well as the great motives of God's saving work, communion with Christ, possession of the Spirit and so on (see above, section 28), any special motives adapted to those who had once been pagans? Generally speaking, the answer is no. He did not employ two

[53] Cf. W. Straub, *Die Bildersprache des Apostels Paulus*, 1937.

levels of teaching, one for beginners, the other for advanced students; at most some adaptation to his hearers' capacity to grasp the truths of faith (cf. 1 Cor. 3:1 ff.). He drew everyone immediately into the soaring flight of his theology and sought to set them on fire with his own love for Christ. The old sinful man is laid aside (Rom. 6:6); those who belong to Christ have crucified their flesh, with its passions and lusts (Gal. 5:24); the Christian who lives "above" with Christ, has left his old vices on the earth, should mortify his sinful members (Col. 3:1-5); everyone must be guiltless when the Lord comes (1 Cor. 1:8; Phil. 1:10). These and other admonitions are addressed principally to gentile Christians.

It is, however, remarkable what a significant rôle the concept of judgement played in missionary preaching to the gentiles. According to 1 Thessalonians 1:10, one of the principal points in their initial instruction was "salvation from the wrath to come", and even in the actual epistle Paul reminds the Thessalonians of this (vv. 5-6). But no one can say that punishment by the gods in the world to come was a dominant concept in Hellenism; the Epicureans and Stoics were at one in rejecting the concept of the wrath of the gods.[54] The common people did, however, ascribe many chastisements in this world to angry gods, and ideas about the judgement of the dead in the next world had become deeply rooted through the Orphic religion and Platonic doctrines.[55] Paul was able to make contact with these rationally weak but emotionally strong convictions and announce the clear doctrine of Christian revelation. The pagan, too, could and must use his sense of justice to understand what to Jewish theology was axiomatic and what the early

---

[54] Cf. M. Pohlenz, *Vom Zorn Gottes,* 1909; E. Rohde, *Psyche,* 9th and 10th imp. 1925, vol. I, pp. 308 ff.; H. Braun, *Gerichtsgedanke,* pp. 2 ff.

[55] Cf. E. Rohde, *Psyche,* vol. II, pp. 127 ff.; 275 ff.; M. P. Nilsson, *Geschichte der griechischen Religion,* vol. I, 1941, pp. 651 ff., 772 ff.; vol. II, 1950, pp. 188 ff., 220 ff., 526, Eng. tr. *History of Greek Religion,* 1925; H. Kleinknecht, art. in *ThWB* vol. V, pp. 384-92.

Church firmly maintained: that at the end of time, God will hold a strict judgement of reward and punishment over the whole human race (cf. Acts 17:31).[56] This was also a topos in the Hellenistic-Jewish missionary preaching, although admittedly more in the sense of punishment for the sinful human race.[57] Such a powerful motive was certainly not unsuitable in the face of pagan immorality; but it is only the dark backcloth to the message of salvation, that the gentiles, too, had been "delivered from the power of darkness" (Col. 1:13) and become "the children of light" (Eph. 5:8). Now they should no longer share in the "unfruitful works of darkness", but should rather call shameful things by their right names, and lead their pagan fellow-citizens to the light of faith and salvation (cf. Eph. 5:3-17).[58]

Sometimes St. Paul did not despise certain "natural" motives. On occasion he turns to the unspoilt human being who felt the hatefulness of vice and the humiliating tyranny of the passions. The Stoic system of ethics, which praised virtue and moral freedom, duty fulfilled and service to the community as a great happiness, had prepared the ground for him in this. That age, not yet utterly depraved, found convincing an argument that Paul had no doubt borrowed from the Judaism of the diaspora: that unnatural vice was a degrading punishment from God on the heathen for their sacrilegious idolatry (Rom. 1:21-27), and the abundance of vices a folly and irrationality inflicted by God on these wicked people (1:28-31). This description does not,

---

[56] M. Dibelius too acknowledges the ending as a "uniquely Christian phrase" ("Paulus auf dem Areopag" in *Aufsätze zur Apostelgeschichte*, 1951, p. 53, Eng. tr. *Studies in the Acts of the Apostles*), although in other respects he attacks the genuineness of the narrative concerning the areopagus.

[57] This thought is stressed especially in the *Sibylline Oracles*, see III, 287, 686 ff.; IV, 40 ff., 183 ff.; V, 108 ff.; see also P. Dalbert, *Missionsliteratur*, pp. 119-23. Cf. also 2 Mach. 7:35; Wisdom 3:1-10; 4:20-5:14; 6:5 ff.

[58] The paraenesis of this section deals clearly with motifs which were alive in Qumran; cf. K. G. Kuhn, "Der Epheserbrief im Lichte der Qumrantexte" in *NTS* 7 (1960-61) pp. 334-46.

of course, come in the paraenetic section, but is intended to show the perdition of unredeemed mankind. In the paraenesis itself, "natural" motives occur only incidentally, as in the admonition against fornication (1 Cor. 6:18). Other fragmentary ideas of a similar kind are: drunkenness is debauchery and ruin (Eph. 5:18); anyone who will not work, shall not eat (2 Thess. 3:10). At Philippi, the Christian who has surrendered to sin, the enemy of God, is bluntly characterized by the apostle: "Whose God is their belly; and whose glory is in their shame" (Phil. 3:19). He had a good knowledge of men, as his use of the motive of propriety and good name reveals (cf. 1 Thess. 4:12; Rom. 14:18; Eph. 5:12); but it does him honour as a Christian teacher that he also called on his readers to discern what will please the Lord (Rom. 12:2; Eph. 5:10).

Those, however, are only secondary motives, incidental notes. Almost everywhere one can sense how the apostle strove to reach a deeper religious foundation. The household codes taken from popular ethics are instructive here (see above, section 26). That in Colossians 3:18 ff. has been only slightly christianized (e.g. "as it behoveth in the Lord", v. 18), whereas the exhortation to married people in Ephesians 5:22–23 is full of Christian matter.

iii. Concepts Borrowed from Popular Philosophy

A. Bonhöffer maintained that Paul received no essential influence from the Stoa and this conclusion has been confirmed by M. S. Enslin, M. Pohlenz and others. However, attention is often drawn to certain characteristic ideas already known from Stoic writings, which also occur in Paul.

For the concepts of conscience and nature see section 30 above. The careful investigations made of these expressions, seem to suggest that we should be very careful before we attribute to Paul a direct dependence on Stoic terminology. Furthermore, we should distinguish between philosophy as formulated in the schools and the popular form in which its ideas were disseminated. Much was a part of the common stock of ideas of the people living in Hellenistic cities, and it was this that St. Paul seems to have taken up, although he himself had clearly had an education above the average.

Attention has often been drawn to the concept of "what is fitting" (τὸ ἀνῆκον), used by St. Paul at Philemon 8; Colossians 3:18; and Ephesians 4:5. Closely related to this, is the concept of "what is seemly" (Eph. 5:3) and the negative "what is shameful" (Eph.5:12).[59] The Stoa spoke of what was "fitting" for human beings as the καθῆκον, that is, demands and actions arising for them from the claims of their environment, and which critical reason shows to correspond to their nature.[60] On the other hand with Paul, the objective and highest standard was not "what is in accordance with nature", but the will of God; consequently only genuine and moral values are appropriate and becoming to the Christian. Thus formal concepts, perhaps originally borrowed, receive new content.

Yet it remains doubtful whether Stoic ethics were the direct source even of such ethical ideas. The Stoa did not term conduct contrary to what was right τὰ μὴ καθήκοντα, as Paul does at Romans 1:28, but παρὰ τὸ καθῆκον.[61] The word for "virtue", which is found in only one Pauline text (Phil. 4:8), was in general use. It is significant that Paul did not make more use of it, but left it to Christian paraenesis after him. "The mark of Christian

[59] With this cf. *1 QS* X, 22f.: "And in my mouth shall be heard no folly or sinful deceit, no cunning or lies shall be found on my lips. The fruit of holiness be on my tongue and no abominations (schikkuzim) shall be found upon it." This expression must correspond to the αἰσχρότης of Eph. 5:4, as the warning against harmful thoughtless speaking (v. 3f.) corresponds in general very closely with the Qumran documents. See Kuhn, *loc. cit.,* p. 339.

[60] H. Schlier in *ThWB* vol. III, p. 441, 36ff.

[61] Cf. Schlier, *loc. cit.,* p. 443; Bonhöffer, *Epiktet,* p. 157; Pohlenz, *op. cit.,* p. 73. Paul was probably influenced more by the usage of the Septuagint; see this same use at 2 Mach. 6:4; 3 Mach. 4:16.

ethics is not the thought of the ideal (of virtue), but rather the thought that what is good, is God's demand."[62]

But in at least one text most scholars will acknowledge a concession on Paul's part to the ethics of Stoicism, namely in Philippians 4:8. The list here is terminologically colourful, containing some striking turns of phrase, some of them used by Paul nowhere else; but it is not a catalogue of virtues and does not lead the Christian to a civic ideal of virtue. Paul is rather calling, in an emphatic way, on his correspondents to think about what is good in itself and also enjoys a good name among men, and this for Christians is the will of God (cf. Rom. 12:2). That this was his meaning is shown by the following verse 9, where he recalls to the Philippians what they had learned and seen embodied in the apostle.[63] Elsewhere in this letter, of course, Paul shows his readers a quite different goal: the heavenly vocation (3:12–14), and a completely different picture of man: the man conformed to Christ (3:10), who is to be made like his glorified Lord even externally, by the power of God (3:21).

In that way a further important difference reveals itself. Paul is not concerned with an ideal of perfect humanity and not with any idealistic ethics at all. The Christian here on earth is to be bound to Christ and conformed to him, but precisely by suffering with him in order one day to be glorified with him. (Rom. 8:17); here we can still bear the image of the earthly man, the first Adam, in order one day also to obtain the image of the heavenly man, Christ, the second Adam (1 Cor. 15:49). It is true that even now through God's gracious deed and our own moral effort, we are to "put on the new man who is renewed unto (growing) knowledge according to the image of him that created him" (Col. 3:10; cf. Eph. 4:24). The process of moral development has a different ground and a different direction from any humanitarian ethics; the guiding principle

[62] Bultmann, *Theology,* vol. I, p. 119.
[63] On this whole text see Vögtle, *Lasterkataloge,* pp. 178–88.

is not the harmonious and perfect personality but the divinely-willed image of man renewed by Christ and brought to its eschatological accomplishment.

The terminology of the pastoral epistles, with its very great differences from that of the main epistles and those of the captivity, presents a special problem. It is characterized by specially selected, more rarely used words, and in the lists of qualifications for those seeking office in the Church (1 Tim. 3:2ff. and 8ff.; 5:9f.; Titus 1:7f.), and the admonitions for the various states of life (1 Tim. 2:8ff.; 5:3ff.; Titus 2:1ff.) comes much closer to the language of Hellenistic ethics.[64] As this problem, however, is very closely bound up with the question of authorship and the circumstances of its composition, we cannot discuss it here.

It is clear that on the whole the motives of popular ethics had "only a very limited significance" in Pauline moral exhortation and the concepts that sound similar were "mostly only formal borrowings from the formulae and vocabulary of rhetoric, almost always demonstrably filled with a new content and Christian ideas".[65] Hence it cannot be maintained that the missionary to the gentiles came down to the level of his hearers and curtailed the commandments; on the contrary, he wanted to bring them mature and irreproachable to meet the Lord.

[64] See Dibelius and Conzelmann, *Pastoralbriefe,* pp. 41ff.; Bultmann, *Theology,* vol. II, pp. 183ff.; and against these radical judgements, C. Spicq, *Épîtres Pastorales,* CVIIff.; CXLIff.; CXCIff.; pp. 234ff.; 257ff.
[65] L. Nieder, *Die Motive der religiös-sittlichen Paränese in den paulinischen Gemeindebriefen,* p. 135.

Chapter Two

JOHN

§ 32. THE SUMMONS TO MAN BY THE REVEALER AND SAVIOUR WHO HAS COME INTO THE WORLD

H. H. Huber, *Der Begriff der Offenbarung im Johannes-Evangelium*, 1934; W. von Loewenich, "Johanneisches Denken" in *TB* 15 (1936) pp. 260–75; E. Gaugler, "Das Christuszeugnis des Johannes-Evangeliums" in *Jesus Christus im Zeugnis der Heiligen Schrift und der Kirche*, 1936, pp. 34–67; E. Percy, *Untersuchungen über den Ursprung der joh. Theologie*, 1939; W. F. Howard, *Christianity according to St. John*, 1934; J. Huby, *Mystiques paulienne et johannique*, 1946; W. Groussouw, *Pour mieux comprendre saint Jean*, 1946; E. K. Lee, *The Religious Thought of St. John*, 1950; J. Dupont, *Essais sur la christologie de saint Jean*, 1951; R. Bultmann, *Theologie*, 4th ed., pp. 367–85, Eng. tr. *Theology*, vol. II, pp. 15–32; id., *Das Evangelium des Johannes*, 4th ed. 1953 (Suppl. vol. 1957) *passim;* F. Mussner, ΖΩΗ. *Die Anschauung vom "Leben" im 4. Evangelium*, 1952; C. H. Dodd, *The Interpretation of the Fourth Gospel*, 1953; F. M. Braun, "Morale et Mystique à l'école de saint Jean" in *Morale chrétienne et requêtes contemporaines*, pp. 71–84; O. Prunet, *La morale chrétienne d'après les écrits joh.*, 1957; W. Thüssing, *Die Erhöhung und Verherrlichung Jesu im Joh.-Evangelium*, 1960; S. Schulz, *Untersuchungen zur Menschensohn-Christologie im Joh.-Evangelium*, 1957; id., *Komposition und Herkunft der joh. Reden*, 1960; J. E. Davey, *The Jesus of St. John*, 1958; E. M. Sidebottom, *The Christ of the Fourth Gospel*, 1961; T. Müller, *Das Heilsgeschehen im Joh.-Evangelium*, 1961; J. Blank, *Krisis. Studien zur Christologie und Eschatologie des Joh.-Evangeliums* (unprinted dissertation, Würzburg, 1961).

JOHANNINE theology, which has left its mark on the gospel and three epistles of John, finds its focus in Christology. The main reason for the composition of the last canonical gospel may very well have been to give Johannine churches a picture of Christ which showed them in the earthly activity of Jesus the glory of their Christ already shining, that eschatological revealer and mediator of salvation through whom alone true information and knowledge of God and his world, genuine communion with God and share in the divine life, are to be obtained. This picture of Christ is outlined against a background of the intellectual trends at the turn of the first Christian century, and is addressed to a Christendom for which Christ's message had already become an interior and well-pondered possession, but which also had problems in its intellectual dealings with the world around it (Judaism, Hellenism, Gnosticism) and in defending itself against false teachers from its own ranks (1 John). The reflection on what is proper to, and characteristic of, Christian faith in an atmosphere that is intellectually alert and religiously full of life, involves as a consequence that the theological lines are more sharply drawn, the view is deeper, the thoughts simplified but directed to what is essential and permanent. As regards moral teaching that means that less prominence is given to more specialized questions such as we find in Paul's dealings with his churches, but there is a gain in comprehensive vision of principles and this is to the advantage of the picture of the world and of man, the understanding of reality and of salvation. In our age which has raised the question of the actual concrete human situation and directed attention more closely to man's historical lot, this Johannine message deserves increased reflection, all the more so as it has been given a special interpretation in terms of existential theology by R. Bultmann.[1]

[1] R. Bultmann, *Das Evangelium nach Johannes,* 4th ed. 1953, *passim;* compare his presentation in *Theology of the New Testament,* vol. II, pp.

In contrast to the synoptic gospels in which the message regarding the kingdom of God involves God's claim on man (cf. section 1), the emphasis in St. John's gospel becomes a Christological one. The summons to man follows from John's own claim as God's eschatological envoy. Because Jesus is the Messias in a sense that transcended all expectation, because he is the Son of God equal in nature to the Father (cf. 20:31), he in his person reveals the Father (14:8-11; 8:19; 12:45), and he designates himself as salvation (cf. 8:12), as the way (14:6), as life (11:25; cf. 6:35, 48, 51). As a consequence, however, he only makes the one demand, that men should believe in him (3:16, 18, 36; 5:24; 6:29), follow him (8:12; 12:26), keep and observe his word (8:51f.; 14:15, 21, 23; 15:10). The clear recognition that only one has "descended from heaven" and that only one "ascended" again in order to provide access for all to the heavenly world of light and life, namely the Son of man (cf. 3:13, 31; 6:33, 50f., 58, 62; 20:17), illumines at the same time the hopeless situation of the man in this world who trusts to himself (cf. 3:18, 36; 8:24; 12:35), and the only possibility of salvation, which is to pass from the domain of death to God's circle of light and life (5:24).

Thought of this kind presupposes God's infinite distance from all the transitoriness of creatures, the frailty of what is earthly (cf. the antitheses σάρξ — πνεῦμα 3:6f.; γῆ — οὐρανός 3:31; κάτω — ἄνω 8:23), and takes as an established fact that the "world"[2] has as a matter of history turned aside to evil. This thought, however, is only presented and sustained because God in the meantime has overcome the gulf and taken the initiative in deliverance by sending his Son into the world

1-92, especially pp. 75-92 "Faith as Eschatological Existence". For a critique (Protestant) see H. Ott, *Geschichte und Heilsgeschichte in der Theologie R. Bultmanns,* 1955; J. Körner, *Eschatologie und Geschichte,* 1957; T. Müller, *Heilsgeschehen;* J. Blank, *Krisis* (Catholic).

[2] Cf. Section 35 and its bibliography for the Johannine concept of "World".

(3:17; 12:47). The great eschatological event has taken place: the eternal Logos himself has become "flesh" (1:14), the heavenly witness and revealer has appeared on the earth (1:18; 3:32 ff.; 8:26), he who lives from a divine source has come in order to give life for ever to the world enslaved to death (4:14; 5:21, 25f.; 6:33, 51, 56; 7:38; 10:10; 11:25f.). Against the dark background of a "dualist" view of the world, the Christian message of salvation stands out all the more brightly. Besides, Johannine theology, despite dualistic modes of expression, is far removed from any extreme dualism. It is true that there is an opposition of contrasted concepts, life and death, light and darkness, truth and falsehood, freedom and slavery (only in John 8:31–6), being from above and being from below (8:23), children of God and children of the devil; but they are not traced back to two equally strong primordial powers, or understood metaphysically; it is not a cosmological dualism or one of principles. It is never forgotten that all that was made was created by God and by the Logos (1:3), that to God and the Son of God there belongs, even before "the foundation of the world" an inviolable glory (17:5) and that God is always stronger than his adversary "in the world" (1 John 4:4). The "world" is not, as in Gnosticism, the "plenitude of evil" (*Corpus Hermeticum* VI, 4), but is only full of evil tendencies such as the "concupiscence of the flesh, the concupiscence of the eyes and the pride of life" (1 John 2:15 ff.). What belongs to the body and to matter is not bad in itself or of less account in contrast to the soul and the spirit, but only weak and frail, so that even the Logos could become "flesh" (John 1:14) and "all flesh" (a Semitic expression for "all human beings") could be called to share in eternal life (cf. 17:2). The "dualistic" perspective borrowed by John derives from an historical conception of the "world" which has shut itself against God, developed away from him (cf. 1:5) and placed itself under the rule of the "evil one" (1 John 5:19), that is to say Satan, the "prince of this world" (John 12:31; 14:30; 16:11). There are no "children of the devil" by nature, but human beings who show themselves to be such by their desires and deeds (John 8:44). "He that committeth sin is of the devil, for the devil sinneth from the beginning" and through sin the "children of the devil" are manifest (1 John 3:8, 10).

This sharply contrasting opposition of two classes of men strongly recalls the Dead Sea manuscripts which speak of the "sons of light" in antithesis to the "sons of darkness". Those who joined the community of Qumran were obliged to "love all the sons of light each according to his lot (= place) in God's community and hate the sons of darkness, each according to his guilt in God's vengeance" (1 QS I, 9 ff.). The sons of light armed for the eschatological combat against the sons of darkness (1 QM passim). There is instruction about the two kinds of spirits according to which each class walks (the "spirits of truth and falsehood"), and in accordance with which men's deeds are determined. Each of these opposed classes of men is placed under a spiritual ruler ("an angel"): "In the hands of the prince of light lies rule over all the sons of truth, they walk in the ways of light; in the hands of the angel of darkness lies rule over the sons of falsehood and they walk in the ways of darkness" (3:20 f.). But even this dualism which itself extends into what is supra-human and cosmic, is subject to faith in the biblical God and creation. God "created the spirits of light and darkness" (3:25), and he retains dominion: "But God in the secrets of his understanding and in his glorious wisdom has set time (or, an end) to the continuance of falsehood; in the time of visitation he will destroy it for ever" (IV, 18 f.). The descriptions, though to a certain extent they sound deterministic, leave no doubt that it is a matter of the moral decision of men, in whose hearts "the spirits of truth and falsehood struggle" (IV, 23), and that they are not absolved of responsibility. This dualism of Qumran whose more specific nature and origin is, of course, still disputed,[3] is certainly close to Johannine thought, at least in its

[3] For the Old Testament and Late Judaism (apart from Qumran) see

formal structure and moral aspect. What is special and distinctive in Johannine theology derives from the sending of God's Son into the world. By his call, the sole intention of which is to serve the deliverance of all men, he summons men to a decision and this brings about a separation among them (cf. John 3:18–21; 8:47; 9:39; 12:44–50; 18:37).

This Johannine antithetical mode of thought not only places Jesus' mission in the clearest light from the point of view of the theology of redemption, by teaching that is to be understood as the outcome of God's love overcoming all distances (cf. John 3:16; 1 John 4:10), but also has important consequences for moral theology. Decision concerning faith in regard to the "Light" who has come into the world, calls for clear and resolute turning away from all works of darkness. "For every one that doth evil hateth the light and cometh not to the light, that his works may not be reproved. But he that doth truth cometh to the light, that his works may be made manifest; because they are done in God" (John 3:20f.). To this "Light" the whole man is transparent and he cannot conceal his moral attitude; belief and "doing the truth" are very closely linked. Just as believing acceptance of Jesus as the revealer who incorruptibly announces God's word and truth presupposes a pure disposition only concerned with God's honour (cf. 5:40–4; 8:43ff.; 12:43), so also "faith" signifies submission to all that Jesus teaches and prescribes as his commandments. "My doctrine is not mine, but his that sent me. If any man will do the will of him, he shall know of the doctrine, whether it be of God, or whether I speak of myself" (7:16f.). This saying refers in the first place to belief. God's will, the only "work" that he demands, is to

S. Aalen, *Die Begriffe "Licht" und "Finsternis" im AT, im Spätjudentum und im Rabbinismus,* 1951; for Qumran see especially F. Nötscher, *Zur theologischen Terminologie der Qumrantexte,* 1956, pp. 79–133; G. Baumbach, *Qumran und das Johannesevangelium,* 1958. H. W. Huppenbauer, *Der Mensch zwischen zwei Welten,* 1959 (Bibliog.); R. Mayer and J. Reuss, *Die Qumranfunde und die Bibel,* 1959, pp. 56–61, 114–19.

believe in him whom he has sent and to whom he has testified
(cf. 6:29); but belief in this unique plenipotentiary of God, in
whom God himself speaks, also involves faithfully holding to
his words and commandments, which are summed up in the
precept of mutual love (8:31, 51f.; 14:15, 21), and of abiding
in his love (15:7, 10). This very accomplishment of Christ's
commandments becomes a confirmation for the believer that
Jesus is the saviour who comes from God, a concrete proof by
experience of the truth of belief in Christ. From it there follows
the closest conceivable connection between religion and morality, between knowing God and keeping the commandments,
between communion with God and brotherly love, as the First
Epistle of St. John shows by its rejection of a pseudo-gnosis that
was morally a failure.[4] What Jesus aimed at establishing and
achieving by his double command of love of God and the
neighbour, the single structure of a moral religion and a religious morality, the obligation of all religious endeavour to
authenticate itself by pure moral action, and at the same time
the grounding of all moral activity on the nexus with God
(cf. section 11), was confirmed in a new way by John's Christological perspective. His Christ who lives in complete unity with
the Father, subject to him in love and obedience, seeking his
honour only and fulfilling his command (cf. 7:18; 8:29, 55;
10:17f.; 12:49; 14, 31), requires of his disciples the counterpart
of this, and is their direct example and guide: "If you keep my
commandments, you shall abide in my love; as I also have
kept my Father's commandments and do abide in his love"
(15:10). He draws his own into loving community with the
Father (17:26), but also expects that they will produce the
fruits of this communion with God bestowed by him (15:8f.,
16f.).

[4] Cf. Schnackenburg, *Die Johannesbriefe*, pp. 13–20 and *passim;* W.
Nauck, *Die Tradition und der Charakter des ersten Johannesbriefes,* 1957,
pp. 122–7; E. Haenchen in *Theologische Rundschau* 26 (1960) pp. 35–8.

Just as the Johannine presentation of Jesus' eschatological mission and message brings out with incomparable urgency the unity of the requirement of faith and love (cf. also section 33), it also emphasizes the negative judgement on unbelief and sin, and manifests the inner connection between them. Although the evangelist knows the old Jewish concept of sin (cf. 5:14; 9:2f., 34), sin only appears in its full horror when men refuse to believe and follow the Son of God who takes away sin (cf. 1:29). Anyone who in inexplicable blindness (9:39; 12:38 ff.), bars this, the sole way to deliverance, falls a victim totally and entirely to the dark domain of the "world". He remains in his sins and will die in his sins (8:21, 24). Only Jesus, the divine bringer of life, can lead him out of the lower world of death and ruin (cf. 3:16, 36; 5:24). Consequently, unbelief is sin absolutely as such. That is not only clearly stated in a saying regarding the Paraclete (16:9), but also forms the tacit presupposition of other passages in which instead of the many particular sins, only "sin" is mentioned (8:12; 9:41; 15:22, 24; 19:11).

John had reflected a great deal on the dark power of unbelief.[5] How was it that so many people, and precisely those who should most of all have recognized Jesus as the Messias, namely the leading circles among the Jews at that time (Pharisees, Scribes, high priests), shut their hearts to this messenger of God from the world of light and life? And although Jesus had done everything to bring them to belief? "If I had not come and spoken to them, they would not have sin; but now they have no excuse for their sin ... If I had not done among them the works that no other man hath done, they would not have sin; but now they have both seen and hated both me and my Father" (15:22, 24). It was a terrible, active and aggressive unbelief. From it developed blind hate against the man sent by

---

[5] Cf. A. Charue, *L'incrédulité des Juifs dans le NT*, 1929, pp. 225–63; A. Augustinovič, *Critica "determinismi" joannei*, 1947.

God, which did not rest until the latter was bleeding to death on the cross. How could men rage in such a way against God and their salvation? Precisely because they belong to that world hostile to God with which Jesus and his own have nothing to do (15:18f.); they come from "below" just as Jesus is from "above" (8:23). Because in this way it might sometimes seem as though this unbelief were due to lack of grace (6:44, 65) and to a hardening imposed by God (9:39; 12:39f.), it is stated in other passages that these obstinate enemies are themselves guilty of their own unbelief. They seek only their own honour, not the honour of God (5:44; cf. 12:43). They are already sunk in evil deeds and darkness (3:20f.), and share the desires of the liar and murderer from the beginning (8:44). To his unbelieving "brethren", too, Jesus declares that the world hates him because he has given testimony of it, that its works are evil (7:7).

John makes these judgements in view of the attitude of men to the historical Jesus in whom he confesses the Messias and the Son of God. But in addition his judgements gain additional weight for his readers also, the Church of his time (cf. section 35), and are important in general for the psychology and evaluation of unbelief. Unbelief in regard to Jesus Christ is and remains a dark, terrible enigma, a mystery of iniquity (cf. 1 John 3:4),[6] in which the essence of sin is manifest. Sin is not to be regarded superficially as an offence, an individual action or an omission of good; it springs from the whole attitude of a human being towards God, and only becomes visible in its true form to the eye of faith, as the great power hostile to God in the life of man and the course of history.

This narrower and yet profounder concept of sin which reveals the nature and historical range of evil, this antithesis between the world of evil and devil and God's world of light

[6] Cf. I. de la Potterie, "Le péché c'est l'iniquité" in *NRT* 78 (1956) pp. 785–97.

which is penetrated by his holiness (1 John 1:5; 2:10), gives to moral exhortation great seriousness and confronts those who hear it with a strict alternative. He who loves his brother dwells in light and there is no scandal from him (or in him?), but he who hates his brother is in darkness, not knowing where he is going because the darkness has blinded his eyes (1 John 2:10f.). There is no middle way between belief and unbelief, love and hate, any more than there is any other choice except that between salvation and perdition. He who has the Son possesses life; he who has not the Son does not possess life.

The clear, radiant motives, however, predominate: knowledge of God's will to save (John 3:17; 12:47), confidence in his saving power (1 John 4:4), faith in the victory already won by Christ which is asserting itself and ceaselessly prevailing (John 16:33; 1 John 5:4f.). "The darkness is past and the true light now shineth" (1 John 2:8). Yet the Church in the world is not spared conflict. Great tribulation is laid upon it and the individual Christian must also struggle with temptation, weakness and sin (cf. section 36).

§ 33. THE SYNTHESIS OF MORAL TEACHING
IN THE COMMANDMENT OF FAITH AND LOVE

See the bibliographies to section 32, for Faith to section 3, and for Love to section 9.

AFTER reading Paul, who in his letters decides moral problems of the most varied kinds, the Johannine message seems simple and uniform: faith and love, and that is all. But we have seen (section 32), that the reduction of all requirements to these two fundamental attitudes is deliberate and has its ground in the Christological focus. Belief in Jesus the Messias and Son of God is the only means and the only possible way to attain life; love, however, especially active, fraternal love, is the necessary consequence of adherence to Jesus in faith. St. John does once, in fact, summarize the "commandment of God" in the words, "that we should believe in the name of his Son Jesus Christ, and love one another" (1 John 3:23). Comparison of this with the synoptic gospels makes it appear even more impressive. Of Jesus' basic requirements for entry into the kingdom of God, only one has survived: faith. But this has acquired quite a different fullness and profundity from what it had in the synoptic gospels. "This is the (only) work of God: that you believe in him whom he hath sent" (John 6:29). In this reply to the Jews, Jesus was not meaning an achievement, a performance, like the Jewish works of the law, but rather was merely taking up the words of his interlocutors and explaining to them that instead of all the many human endeavours they had been prepared to undertake (v. 28), there is one fundamental decision to be made: to believe in him, whom God had sent. In the Johannine writings we frequently hear of the commandments of God;[7] but this does not indicate a rehabilitation of legalism. St. Paul himself could not have formulated the difference between the old and the new order of salvation more succinctly than it is expressed in the prologue to St. John's gospel: "For the law was given by Moses; grace and truth came by Jesus Christ" (1:17). When he speaks of the commandments of God or Christ it is with the sole intention of indicating the binding character of faith and love. Faith rightly understood also includes love for God, Christ, and the brethren, and the fulfilment of the moral duties springing from love.

More precisely, Johannine faith has assimilated two commandments of the Jesus of the synoptic gospels: repentance

---

[7] John 14:15 and 21; 1 John 2:3 and 4; 3:22 and 24; 5:2 and 3; 2 John 6. Cf. G. Schrenk in *ThWB* vol. II, pp. 550–2, who rightly says: "The ἐντολαί wholly summed up in the single commandment to love, do not mean the complete Jewish complex of prescribed definitions, but the influence flowing from the sole ἐντολή in the multiplicity of the life of obedience" (pp. 550, 36 ff.). See further O. Prunet, *Morale,* pp. 24–27.

and discipleship. It is noteworthy that the word "repent" does not occur in the Johannine writings (apart from the Apocalypse). But we must remember that in consequence of Johannine dualism, faith implies determined renunciation of the "world" hostile to God, rejection of all the works of darkness. The believer steps completely out of the dark realm of death into the bright expanse of the divine life (John 5:24). Anyone in this light, must also walk in light, that is, holy and without sin (cf. 1 John 1:6f.; 2:9–11). In the moral judgement of condemnation passed on the disbelief of the "Jews" (John 3:19–21; 5:44; 7:7; 12:43), there is contained the idea that they would have needed "repentance" in the sense of the first three evangelists, in order to begin to believe in Jesus. But these opponents, whose minds are closed to the word of God, are blind and obdurate. St. John's gospel nowhere describes or mentions an act of conversion (not even with the Samaritan woman in chapter four); but it does bring before us people who possess an outlook of a kind that disposes them to belief: Nathanael, who was at first sceptical, but whom Jesus called a "true Israelite . . . in whom there is no guile" (1:47); the Samaritan woman, who had fallen very deeply into sin, but who was a soul seeking God and thirsting for salvation (chapter 4); the man born blind, who would let neither remonstrance nor terrorization obscure his realization of Jesus' majesty and holiness (chapter 9); Martha, the sister of the dead Lazarus, who in spite of her severe shock on the human plane did not become confused about Jesus' person and mission (11:20–27); Jesus' close disciples themselves, who were so often puzzled and yet loyally continued in his company (cf. 6:66–69). They were all people whom Jesus did not have to accuse, as he accused his faithless enemies, of seeking their own glory, but not the glory of the one God (5:44; 12:43). Even the gloomy picture of the Jewish leading circles is somewhat relieved by the mention of the two councillors, Joseph of Arimathea and Nicodemus (19:38f.). If Jesus had believed that it was impossible for a man to turn to faith, he could not have cried to the multitude until the last moment, "Whilst you have the light, believe in the light, that you may be the children of light" (12:36).

Johannine faith binds the believer to adherence to Jesus, not always in that closest of bonds, that of the disciple, sharing in Jesus' wandering life and continuing his preaching, but, nevertheless, to a real "discipleship", as John himself could call it by using the word in a wider sense.[8] Jesus once cried out to a great multitude of people who were ready to believe, "If you continue in my word, you shall be my disciples indeed" (8:31). Expressions synonymous with "believing" in this gospel are, "keeping Jesus' words" (8:51), "hearing" and "keeping" them (12:47), and "following" Jesus (8:12; cf. 1:9ff.). Unbelief leads immediately to the end of one's "walking" with Jesus (6:67). The use of "keeping Jesus' words" (12:47) shows that adherence to him in faith also makes moral demands. Because faith is obedience (cf. 3:36b), perfect self-submission to the Son of God, it must lead to loving observance of all his instructions (cf. 14:15, 21, 23).

The believer must be resolved to accept even the ultimate consequence of following Jesus: he must be prepared for suffering and martyrdom. There is one text in the gospel of St. John which directly recalls the words of Jesus in the synoptic gospels on following the way of the cross (Mark 8:34f. par.; Matt. 10:38f. par.): "he that loveth his life (τὴν ψυχήν) shall lose it: and he that hateth his life in this world keepeth it unto life eternal (εἰς ζωὴν αἰώνιον). If any man minister to me, let him follow me. And where I am, there also shall my minister be" (12:25f.).

These words are not addressed directly to the Twelve, but are, it would seem, deliberately left undefined. Moreover, the saying has been recast by John.[9] The addition "in this world"

---

[8] The wider application of the word is evident in 4:1; 6:60, 61 and 66; 7:3; 8:31; 9:28; 18:19 (?); 19:38. Cf. Schnackenburg, *Der Glaube im vierten Evangelium,* pp. 32–4. K. H. Rengstorf, art. in *ThWB* vol. IV, p. 463.

[9] Cf. R. Bultmann, *Das Evangelium nach Johannes,* 1950, *in loc.*

is new, and correspondingly the promise "unto life eternal". The synoptic saying is more pithy, the Johannine clearer: compare the two different words for "life". John contrasts "this" cosmos of death with the true, divine realm of life. The second saying about "ministering" (with synoptic parallels at Mark 9:35 par.; 10:43 par.; Matt. 23:11) is already looking forward to Jesus' highest ministration of love in the washing of the disciples' feet and the sacrifice of the cross as it is interpreted in the gospel of St. John (cf. 13:1, 12–17). Another wholly Johannine idea here is that Jesus' servant will be where he himself is, that is, in the heavenly world of glory, into which Jesus leads the way for his followers (cf. 14:3; 17:24).

This text is all the more significant because just before it Jesus had applied to himself the image of the grain of wheat, which must fall into the soil and die, if it is to bring forth fruit. Here the Johannine Christ too is requiring of his disciples that, uniting themselves as intimately as possible with his own destiny, they should follow him even to death. What glory for the disciple whom the Lord deems worthy to follow him even to martyrdom (cf. John 21:18). In conjunction with the prophecies of sufferings for the disciples (15:18–20; 16:1–4), John 12:25f. is enough to show that John, too, was aware of the severity of serving Jesus, of the radical nature of his demands. He does not, however, offer the disciple a more fully elaborated moral doctrine. It seems to him enough to believe in a lively and unfading way in Jesus, and love him unto death (cf. 21:15–17). However, these words about love require special attention too.

It is only in the gospel of St. John that Jesus speaks of love for himself.[10] Faith and discipleship are perfected only in love, but this love of the disciple for his Master does not appear as a commandment, but as the consequence and fruit of true faith. The "first farewell discourse" (chapter 14) is especially informa-

---

[10] 8:42; 14:15, 21, 23, 24, 28; cf. 21:15f.

tive on this point. The whole of the first part of this (14:1–14) is concerned with the necessity and power of faith in Jesus, which makes the disciples proof against all the shocks of the coming hour of darkness (cf. 13:19; 14:29; 16:4). When such faith is fully mature, it leads to a loving community with Jesus. The second part of the discourse, treating of the mystical communion of the disciples with Jesus and the Father (esp. 14:18–24), replaces faith by love. The exhortation in these verses is that love for Jesus must be confirmed by keeping his commandments. So then effectual love grows out of the actual mystical union with him. This emerges even more clearly from the discourse in chapter fifteen, where John writes that the disciples should remain in Jesus (vv. 4ff.), especially in his love (v. 9f.), that is, they should do everything to preserve the love and community given them by Jesus.

Not even the first part of the great commandment, to love God with all one's heart and soul, is to be found in John's gospel in that form. Most of the texts which people used to like to interpret as referring to actual love for God are probably intended to refer to divine love, God's love, that is, to the love essentially characteristic of those who are God's and of which they have been made capable by the love they have received from God.[11] John is not merely thinking here of the willingness of human beings to love; he is convinced that the fire of love has to be enkindled by God himself. If God himself has begotten them "from above" and filled them with his holiness and love, they are, of course, to respond to him both in attitude of mind and in their actions. It is in this way, through the co-operation of God and man that God's love "is perfected" in the Christian (1 John 4:18), "his charity is perfected in us" (4:12) and we have "perfect charity" (4:18). Of those who are not God's it

---

[11] Such texts include John 5:42; 1 John 2:5; 3:17; 4:12; cf. John 15:9f. Cf. A. Wikenhauser, *Evangelium nach Johannes*, on John 5:42 and 15:9f.; Schnackenburg, *Johannesbriefe*, on the texts in 1 John. "Love for God" is clearly meant at 1 John 5:3 (cf. with 4:20f. and 5:1f.).

can be said that "you have not the love of God in you" (John 5:42). John is profoundly convinced that our love is a gift from God (cf. 1 John 3:1; 4:10). If we allow ourselves to be moved to a corresponding love and to obedience, the love of God will be bestowed on us even more fully (John 14:21, 23). At the moment of his departure, Christ prayed that the Father would draw us ever more deeply into communion with him (17:23, 26).

Strictly speaking, in St. John the plenitude of the moral commandments is summed up not in the double commandment to love God and one's neighbour, but in the "new" commandment to love the brethren alone. A single text in the first Epistle seems to contrast love for God with love for the "world": "Love not the world, nor the things which are in the world. If any man love the world, the charity of the Father is not in him. For all that is in the world is the concupiscence of the flesh and the concupiscence of the eyes and the pride of life, which is not of the. Father but is of the world" (1 John 2:15f.). In reality this text is meant neither to warn against certain vices nor to comprise all virtues in love for God. It is a dualistically coloured warning against toying with the world, that perilous temptress, and coming to terms with her, a warning in keeping with general early Christian paraenesis.[12] At every stage John remains faithful to his single-minded and urgent call to faith and love, a call that contains all that God requires of his children in this world.[13]

[12] Cf. Schnackenburg, *Johannesbriefe,* pp. 117–20.
[13] Cf. also W. F. Howard, *Christianity,* pp. 151–73; W. Grossouw, *Mieux comprendre,* pp. 111–17.

§ 34. ACTIVE LOVE FOR THE BRETHREN AS THE PROOF OF COMMUNION WITH CHRIST AND GOD

See the bibliography to section 23. Add H. v. Soden, art. "ἀδελφός" in *ThWB* vol. I, pp. 144–46; R. Schnackenburg, *Die Johannes-Briefe*, 1953, pp. 102–06; K. H. Schelkle, art. "Bruder" in *RAC* vol. II, pp. 631–40; O. Prunet, *La morale chrétienne d'après les écrits johanniques*, pp. 96–115.

THE EXHORTATION to love of the brethren is the characteristic feature of Johannine moral teaching. In the fourth gospel, even when Jesus is speaking of his commandments (14:15, 21), his primary aim is to urge on his disciples love for the brethren (13:34; 15:12, 17). "To keep Jesus' word" (14:23, or "words" v. 24) means the same thing, except when it refers to faith (8:51f.; 15:20). But in the last resort faith, keeping Jesus' word and loving the brethren are all different facets of obedience to the Son of God. In 1 John 2:3f., the commandments of God, or the word of God (2:5), are explicitly interpreted as relating to the old and yet new commandment of brotherly love (cf. 2:7–11). The (moral) message brought to Christians from the very beginning has been that they should love one another (3:11).

But why does Jesus call this crucial commandment a "new" commandment? Was not fraternal love already axiomatic in Judaism?[14] Was it not sincerely practised in many Jewish communities (the "fellowship" of the Pharisees, the monastic communities of the Essenes and Therapeutae, the Damascus sect and the closely-related brotherhood at Khirbet Qumran), and indeed in many pagan, Hellenistic religious societies?[15] Only the answer to this question, what the "new" element in Christian love of the brethren was, brings understanding of Johan-

---

[14] Cf. I. Abrahams, *Studies in Pharisaism and the Gospels,* vol. I, 1917, pp. 150–67; Billerbeck, vol. IV, pp. 536–58; 559–610; Moore, *Judaism,* vol. II, pp. 162–79.
[15] Cf. K. H. Schelkle, "Bruder".

nine thought. Jesus adds the words "as I have loved you" (13:34; 15:12)[16] and so provides the key to understanding: because he has loved his own in the world to the uttermost (13:1), so giving them an example (13:15), his disciples, acting explicitly as his disciples (13:35), should love one another in precisely the same way. Jesus is their precursor, their model, their master and their teacher. The act enshrining and revealing in an unparalleled way this loving attitude of Jesus, expressing his love and making it fruitful, was his voluntary loving sacrifice upon the cross (cf. 10:11, 15, 17f.; 15:13).

Probably, within the framework of the Johannine narrative, the washing of the feet is intended to be the pre-eminent "sign" of this and is to be seen (perhaps in addition to another interpretation cf. 13:10) as a model for love only in connection with Jesus' sacrificial death. The sacrificing of oneself for one's brethren, serving them selflessly in accordance with the great pattern of Jesus may be, in John's mind, the "new" element in the commandment to love.[17] Otherwise John could not have written, "Again a new commandment I write unto you; which thing is true both in him and in you, because the darkness is passed and the true light now shineth" (1 John 2:8).

It is also remarkable how strongly John emphasizes the example of Christ in his own moral exhortation (cf. 1 John 2:6; 3:3, 7; 4:17). And above all he draws from Jesus' highest proof of love the conclusion "We ought to lay down our lives

---

[16] The second clause, "that you also love one another" in 13:34 could be a repetition of Jesus' instruction under the idea "As I — so you too" (cf. the similar construction at 17:21); it can also be understood as the object of Jesus' love.

[17] On this frequently discussed pericope, cf. esp. H. Windisch, *Johannes und die Synoptiker,* 1926, pp. 72–78; P. H. Menoud, *L'Év. de Jean d'après les recherches récentes,* 2nd ed. 1947, pp. 54–56; R. Bultmann, *Johannes-Evangelium,* pp. 355–65; A. Wikenhauser, *Das Evangelium nach Johannes, in loc.;* F. Mussner, "Die Fußwaschung (Joh. 13:1–17)" in *Geist und Leben* 31 (1958) pp.25–30; (on 13:10) M. E. Boismard in *RB* 60 (1953), pp.353–6.

for the brethren" (1 John 3:16). In these words he bases the interpretation of the "new" commandment of love on faith, for only the believer realizes the uniqueness of the love of God expressed on the cross of Golgotha and the compelling force with which it binds us. There God revealed out of the primordial depths of his own nature, a love which the world did not know, and enkindled a movement of love that brought something new into the world (1 John 4:9f.). In obedience to his Father (John 10:18; 14:31), Jesus, the bearer and revealer of the divine nature, expressed this divine love in action. The result is that his commandment to love one another "according as I have loved you", cannot but seem to be something new.[18]

Consequently what is new in the Johannine commandment of love must consist in two things, the profoundly understood idea of discipleship, namely that of following Jesus' example and model to the utmost, in his loving disposition and activity, which is binding on the disciple and, closely connected with this, the eschatological novelty of such an attitude. For John such unselfish love which sacrifices itself to the utmost, has only been made possible and realized by God's initiative, by the eschatological mission and sacrifice of his Son, which is the consequence of his incomprehensible, paradoxical love for the sinful world. The "new" commandment has "become a reality in him (Christ) and in you, because the darkness is past and the new light is already shining" (1 John 2:8). In Jesus the love of God has become visibly perceptible and has entered this world as a divine power lightening the darkness and it is received, continued and put into practice by his disciples who are really worthy of the name. "We know that we have passed from death to life (that of God), because we love the brethren" (1 John 3:14). It is understandable how urgent the call for

[18] This is why parallels such as the death of Socrates are unconvincing. Socrates died loyal to the laws of his native city and gave an example of a lofty ethical attitude. The same is true of Mahatma Ghandi.

brotherly love is, since it is to manifest the new state of affairs that God has brought about.

In addition there were also historical grounds why St. John should esteem brotherly love so highly and make it the characteristic mark of those who are disciples of Christ and begotten of God. In his first and second Epistles at least he was warding off certain false teachers whose tendency was clearly towards gnosticism. They altogether despised the divine commandments (1 John 2:3ff.) and even claimed to be in communion with God without moral obligations of this kind (1:6ff.; 2:9ff.). They also seem to have maintained that they loved God, but St. John would have nothing to do with such bare assertions: "If any man say: I love God, and hateth his brother, he is a liar. For he that loveth not his brother whom he seeth, how can he love God whom he seeth not?" (4:20). Thus, outwardly perceptible love of the brethren becomes a proof of the interior love for God that cannot be directly tested. John deepens this thought (which can already be found in the writings of the noble Jew Philo)[19] still further, by his teaching about faith. Christians are the children of God in a very real sense (3:1), for, through baptism, they have been "begotten of God".[20] "Every one that loveth him who begot, loveth him also who is born of him" (5:1), that is, loves those who, like himself, are born of him, or in other words, his brothers: it is a fact and law of nature. But for the Christian it is also the express wish and will of his Father (4:21; cf. 3:23; 2 John 4). If in general it is true to say that the children of God must have love as a sign, as it were, of their relationship with God, "who is love" (1 John 4:7f., 16), so too this love must be made apparent in the concrete,

[19] *De Decal.* 120: "It is impossible for the invisible God to be honoured by those who dishonour the visible and near at hand." The saying relates to respect for parents.

[20] John 1:13; 1 John 2:29; 3:9; 4:7; 5:4, 18; cf. John 3:3ff.; and on this point, Schnackenburg, *Die Johannesbriefe,* pp. 155–62; K. H. Schelkle, *Die Petrusbriefe,* pp. 28–31.

in love for the brethren. In its nature their love is very similar to that revealed to us as proper to God's own essence by the mission and death of his Son (4:9–11), a completely unselfish, generous, merciful love, a love seeking the salvation of others, a love that for the most part does not correspond to the "natural" feelings of men, and surpasses all other human kinds of love.[21]

One often hears references to Johannine mysticism. It is indeed true that this great theologian did make our communion with Christ and God the central point in his thinking. But so that there should be no misunderstandings, no pantheistic, ecstatic, or magical mysticism, or any that fuses God and man, he demanded love of the brethren as the expression and realization of our exalted communion with God. "No man hath seen God at any time. If we love one another, God abideth in us; and his charity is perfected in us" (1 John 4:12).

But in spite of all his "mysticism", St. John also sees God as our Lord and judge. As a result of his sins, even the Christian's conscience may still prick and disturb him. Doubts can appear, if we belong wholly to God at all. It is then, however, that we recognize, through the operation of active, practical love, that we are "of the truth" (that is, participate in the divine nature) and calm our heart in the sight of God with regard to everything for which it condemns us, because God is greater than our hearts and knows everything (1 John 3:19f.). John is not saying here that loving good works on our part can outweigh previous guilt; his purpose is rather to give us a criterion for our participation in the life of God.

Fraternal love expressed in action is so great, so important, so indispensable; it is, as it were, the outer mark of our divine sonship, the unmistakable sign of our union with God. A simple act of true love is a rock on which the dreamer founders, but

[21] Cf. V. Warnach, *Agape. Die Liebe als Grundmotiv der neutestamentlichen Theologie*, 1951, esp. pp. 181 ff.; Schnackenburg, *Die Johannesbriefe*, pp. 260 ff.

those heavily burdened or in doubt find respite. Here St. John the "mystic" shows himself to be a very practical Christian realist.

The concrete demands of John's brotherly love were already appreciated within the framework of the charitable life of the early Church (see above, section 23.). But is it not true to say that in John the commandment to love one's neighbour is narrowed down into love of one's brethren? It has frequently been asserted that this is so, yet closer examination of the texts shows that it is not so. For John, love is the completely universal characteristic of the children of God, in contrast to hate, the token of the "world" (1 John 3:13f.). If he is reproaching the "world" for its hatred towards Christians, it would be unintelligible of him to limit the Christian's love to the circle of the community of the Church. He nowhere preaches hate or speaks of revenge. By comparing love for our human brethren whom we can see, with love for the invisible God (4:20), he is giving the title "brother" a comprehensive meaning; in the next verse he seems to be referring to Jesus' great commandment. Clearly, then, John has expressed the synoptics' "love of one's neighbour" as "love of the brethren", and hence he cannot be using this in any exclusive sense. All John does, is to point first to the community of his brethren in the faith, as a sphere in which the Christian may express his love. But in doing so, he does not mark any frontier. The fact that he orders that heretics be expelled and refused even a greeting (2 John 10f.) is due to his anxiety about the faith. It is self-evident, however, that he did not mean to forbid Christians to play the part of the Good Samaritan. We should not expect to find all Christ's teachings repeated in these occasional writings. But fresh prominence is given to one new duty, hospitality to brethren who are travelling and support for wandering missionaries (cf. 3 John 2–8). This passage reflects the changed, more complex situation of the Church at the end of the first century. A certain shift of emphasis is perceptible here, but no fundamental change in charitable attitude and practice. St. John is not only a loyal guardian of Christ's inheritance preserving his spirit but also a disciple of the Lord illumined by the Holy Spirit, giving added profundity to the commandment of love and raising it to be the ruling principle of Christian morality throughout all ages.

§ 35. CHRIST, CHURCH, AND WORLD

E. Gaugler, "Die Bedeutung der Kirche in den joh. Schriften" in *IKZ* 14 (1924) pp. 97–117, 181–219; 15 (1925) pp. 27–42; D. Faulhaber, *Das Joh.-Evangelium und die Kirche*, 1935; A. Correll, "*Consummatum est*". *Eschatology and Church in the Gospel of St. John*, 1958; E. Schweizer, "Der Kirchenbegriff im Evangelium und den Briefen des Johannes" in *Studia Evangelica* (*TU* 73), 1959, pp. 363–81; R. Schnackenburg, *Die Kirche im Neuen Testament*, 1961, pp. 93–102.—(On the concept "World") R. Loewe, *Kosmos und Aion*, 1935; H. Sasse in *ThWB* vol. III, pp. 894–6; R. Bultmann, *Theologie*, 4th ed., pp. 367–69, Eng. tr. *Theology*, vol. II pp. 15–17; R. Schnackenburg, *Die Johannesbriefe*, pp. 117–20; A. Wikenhauser, *Das Evangelium nach Johannes*, 2nd ed. 1957, pp. 174–6; R. Völkl, *Christ und Welt*, pp. 393–439.

BY THE message of the Johannine Christ, the individual human being is summoned to decide for salvation or to abide under the wrath of God (John 3:36). In accordance with thought of this eschatological stamp, it could not be otherwise. If Jesus is the definitive and complete revealer of salvation who has come down from heaven, and to believe in him is the only way to deliverance from the situation of perdition that hangs threateningly over man, the summons concerns each individual personally with inescapable rigour and urgency. Each faces an alternative and has to make up his mind. Hence the impression that in St. John's gospel more markedly than in the other New Testament writings, a turning to the individual has occurred, an individualism regarding salvation, which is not of course to be overlooked in the teaching of Jesus in the synoptics, but is noteworthy here by the very marked form it assumes, in view of the usual mode of thought in the New Testament which is linked with the redeemed community, the Church. This impression is strengthened by the stylistic form of "revelation discourse" which is found in St. John's gospel, together with majestic "I am" statements and apostrophes to the reader with pleas and also with warnings (cf. 6:35; 8:12, 24; 10:7–10; 11:25f.; 14:6; 15:5f.), or which makes the revealer in the third person but in a similar absolute manner (cf. 3:13–21, 31–6; 5:19–30; 12:44–50).[22] The same effect is produced by certain sharply antithetical sentences in the First Epistle of John which announce to the individual, communion with God and salvation or remoteness from God and perdition (cf. 1 John 2:4–6, 9–11; 2:22f.; 3:4–6; 4:2f.; 5:10–12). In form these may be analogous to "revelation discourse" or the formulas of baptismal vows, or the polemic against false teachers,[23] but at all events the individual is addressed in his personal responsibility, placed as it were directly before God and subjected to his judgement. It is not surprising that existential theology has taken John as a basis in order to work out the "situation of eschatological decision" of the individual under the summons of the Word of God. But if by that the revelation event is reduced

[22] Cf. E. Norden, *Agnostos Theos. Untersuchungen zur Formengeschichte religiöser Rede*, 1913; E. Schweizer, *Ego eimi . . .*, 1939; K. Kundziņš, *Charakter und Ursprünge der joh. Reden*, 1939; H. Becker, *Die Reden des Joh.-Evangeliums und der Stil der gnostischen Offenbarungsrede*, 1956; S. Schulz, *Komposition und Herkunft der joh. Reden*, 1960; H. Zimmermann, "Das absolute Ἐγώ εἰμι als die neutestamentliche Offenbarungsformel" in *BZ* 4 (1960) pp. 54–69, 266–76.

[23] R. Bultmann, "Analyse des 1. Johannesbriefes" in *Festschrift für A. Jülicher*, 1927, pp. 138–58, wanted to infer, just as he did for St. John's gospel, a source in Gnostic apocalyptic discourses; W. Nauck, *Die Tradition und der Character des 1. Johannesbriefes*, 1957, accounts for the stylistic forms from the tradition of another mode of literary composition (Jewish legal style; lists of antitheses in *1 QS*, cf. especially pp. 29–41), and considers their function and context in the life of the Church to have been baptismal paraenesis and refutation of false teachers.

to a meeting in personal relationship between the individual and God, and its binding character is made simply to mean the "radical obedience" of the individual in the particular situation that is his, essential aspects and interrelations of Johannine theology and ethics are lost from view. For all the claim he makes on the individual, John does not represent a moral individualism or an existential ethics. With all the early Church he always envisages the individual as a member of the Church which transmits to him Christ's instructions and calls for their realization within the Church. Reference to the community is not established only by the precept of brotherly love (which can also find place in an individualist existentialist ethics), but is much more deeply anchored in John's thought. The Church is constitutive and regulative of Johannine Christianity and permeates his theology more strongly than might at first sight appear.[24] Without the Church as believing and redeemed community, Christian life for John too is impossible of accomplishment. The Church, by its appearance and position in the midst of the "world", contributes most strongly to affect and determine the being and action of the individual. This must be made rather more plain, in view of some of the questions raised at the present time.

That the individual Christian necessarily belongs to and is bound to belong to the community of brethren in the faith (united in true confession of faith), is expressed as a clear conviction in the First Epistle of John, and is emphatically insisted upon. Community with God only receives its foundation through community with those who experienced a direct and believing encounter with the incarnate "Word of Life", that eternal life that was with the Father and appeared to men, and with those who bore witness to this and proclaimed it as the occurrence of salvation (1 John 1:4). From this follows the duty of all believers to accept the confession of Christ of

[24] Cf. the bibliography at the beginning of the chapter.

these legitimate and authoritative informants (2:22f.; 4:2f.; 5:1, 5f.); for only this Jesus Christ who has come in the flesh is "the true God and eternal life" (5:20), that is, to say, the revealer and saviour who bestows communion with God (1:3; 2:23; 4:15), and divine life (5:11f.). But in precisely the same way, however, they must take seriously and keep the commandments of God that he taught (2:3ff.), or with the eyes fixed on Jesus himself "also walk even as he walked" (2:6). That is ultimately only one commandment, that of brotherly love (2:7; 3:11), and only one example comprising everything else, namely "that he has laid down his life for us" (3:16). The spokesman and guarantor of this "old" yet "new" commandment, however, is the community of true believers, which was already looking back on a certain extent of time during which the gospel had been preached. "The old commandment is the word which you have heard" (2:7b). Precisely because those addressed possess this and nothing else "from the beginning" (2:7a), it must not be nullified. The same holds good of true belief in Christ. Just as they have heard it "from the beginning" they must abide in it in order to abide in the Son and in the Father. Confession of faith and conduct of life, an indissoluble unity, are therefore determined by what is proclaimed in the Church "from the beginning" as true and authoritative.

Incorporation of the individual in the Church and his living bond with it are viewed even more profoundly, in a supernatural way; membership of the redeemed community is ultimately a disposition of God's grace. This conviction emerges in reflection on the false teachers who left the Church. "They went out from us but they were not of us, for if they had been of us they would no doubt have remained with us; but that they may be manifest that they are not all of us", that is to say, by what they are, do not belong to us (2:19). Their departure, however, shows that despite their outward membership of the Church, they were not to be reckoned in the ranks of "the children of God" (cf. 3:10). The author, therefore, had a very clear and lofty conception of the nature of the Christian Church to which the individual Christian must belong externally and interiorily in order to make his way to salvation. Consequently it is not without reason that the society of the brethren is indicated to all as the most immediate field for the exercise of their love (4:21; cf. section 34).

This significance of the Church, which has also received the Spirit of God (3:24b; 4:13; cf. 2:20, 27), is of course particularly evident in the First Epistle of John, on account of the condemnation of false teachers and their moral indifferentism, but it can also be recognized in St. John's gospel. The farewell discourses in particular (John chapters 13–17), that is, in Jesus' instructions, admonitions and consolations addressed to the circle of close disciples which already prefigured the later Church, throw light on it. Jesus will reveal himself to the disciples, not to the "world" after the Resurrection (14:22). He will ask the Paraclete of the Father for them, "the Spirit of truth whom the world cannot receive" (14:16f.), and he himself in his living reality will be united with them (14:19). But associated with him they will also be able to bear fruit if they abide in him and his love and keep his commandments (15:1–10). At this moment of parting he gives them the "new commandment" (13:34f.; 15:12–17), which he intends to be understood very concretely, after his own example (13:1–17). That all these discourses to the community of disciples as such, are addressed to the later Church, can be recognized by the fact that even the operation of the Paraclete can only take place in the closest connection with the Church and through the Church. The Paraclete gives the Church that introduction into "all truth" (16:13; cf. 14:26), by which he will convince the world (16:8–11). So, too, the separation from Christ which leads to withering and ruin (15:6), must not only have meant abandonment of communion with Christ (by sin), but at the same time and perhaps chiefly, separation from the community linked with Christ. The metaphor of the vine and the branches certainly has ecclesiological significance. It is sufficient to recall the Old Testament background with Israel as God's vineyard (Isa. 5), or as his chosen vineyard (Jer. 2:21; Ps. 79, 9–16), and in the New Testament, the Pauline parallel of the "Body of Christ". The Church as the worshipping community of the New Covenant also finds a place in St. John's gospel. Jesus' glorified body after the Resurrection is the eschatological temple (2:21), and the worship introduced by him and made possible by him, the adoration "in spirit and truth" (4:23), is certainly accomplished in the community of those who are born "of God", "of water and the Spirit" (1:13; 3:5) and who are now also called to a priestly service of God in adoration and moral action.[25] Similarly the sacraments are to be kept in mind in more than one passage of St. John's gospel as the fundamental means of salvation which alone make possible a holy life free from sin (cf. section 36).[26]

Ultimately, therefore, the Johannine Christians do not take up their position in relation to the "world" on their own account, but within the Church to which they belong; and this is aware of itself as altogether separate from the unbelieving cosmos which denies Christ and is hostile to God. Once again the First Epistle of John is particularly clear. In face of the terrifying number of false prophets and their outwardly successful influence in the world (4:1–5), the author affirms: "You are of God, little children, and have overcome him, because greater is he that is in you than he that is in the world" (4:4). The Church in its

---

[25] Cf. Schnackenburg, "Die 'Anbetung in Geist und Wahrheit' (John 4:23) im Lichte von Qumrantexten" in *BZ* 3 (1959) pp. 88–94.
[26] Cf. O. Cullmann, *Urchristentum und Gottesdienst*, 2nd ed. 1950, Eng. tr. *Early Christian Worship* (who goes too far); P. Niewalda, *Sakramentssymbolik im Joh.-Evangelium?*, 1958; Schnackenburg, "Die Sakramente im Joh.-Evangelium" in *Sacra Pagina*, vol. II, 1959, pp. 235–54; H. Schürmann, "Die Eucharistie als Repräsentation und Applikation des Heilsgeschehens nach Johannes 6:53–58" in *TrTZ* 68 (1959) pp. 30–45, 108–18.

close unity and bond with God is the bastion which the "Antichrist" (cf. verse 5) cannot capture. Of course the "world" is also certainly envisaged in its seductive influence on the individual (2, 15ff.; cf. section 32), but the power to conquer "the wicked one" (2:13f.), springs not only from the individual's link with God, but also from the consciousness of standing in the society of those born of God. "We know that we are of God and the whole world is sealed in (the sphere of influence of) wickedness. We know that the Son of God is come; and he hath given us understanding that we may know 'him who is true' and we are in 'him who is true', in his Son, Jesus Christ" (5:19f.). The Johannine Church is engaged in a hard defensive struggle, but it also possesses an unconquerable sense of victory, as is shown by the repetition of "we know".

This knowledge of the situation of the Church in the world has already its foundation in the gospel. In the most pointed antithetical terms Jesus foretells to his disciples in the room of the Last Supper hatred and persecution by the "world". "If the world hate you, know ye that it hath hated me before you. If you had been of the world, the world would love its own; but because you are not of the world, but I have chosen you out of the world, therefore the world hateth you" (15:18f.). In what follows it is clear that what is meant is quite concretely the persecutions (on the part of the unbelieving Jews) in the time of the evangelist, or they are included (16:2-4). Christ's parting discourse to his disciples is also addressed to the later Church. "In the world you shall have distress. But have confidence. I have overcome the world" (16:33; cf. 1 John 5:4ff.).

For the position of the Church in the world the prayer of Christ before his departure (Jesus' sacerdotal prayer) in John 17 is also significant. As he himself is leaving the world and returning to the Father, he recommends his own to the immediate protection and care of the Father. "Thine they were and to me thou gavest them. And they have kept thy word" (verse 6). Here too, therefore, is the thought of the supernatural

335

call to the flock of Christ or God, which, of course, those who are called must themselves abide in (verse 12). In regard to God's "property", we even read words which it would be easy to misunderstand: "I pray not for the world, but for them whom thou hast given me, because they are thine" (verse 9). This band of Christ's disciples who belong to God stands in the midst of the world and is even sent into the world, but on that account needs God's special protection (verse 11), and the sanctification which is guaranteed by Christ's sacrificial consecration (verses 18f.). Christ says expressly, "I pray not that thou shouldst take them out of the world, but (only) that thou shouldst keep them from the evil one" (verse 15). For in fact the "world" hates them, the "evil one" lays snares for their purity and attachment to God, because they bear God's nature and are not of the nature of the "world", as was the case with Jesus before them (verses 14, 16). In this situation it is of particular importance that the community of Christ's disciples is united within itself, with that ultimate most profound unity which is an image and consequence of the unity that exists between the Father and the Son (verses 11, 21–23), and so becomes a proof of the divine origin of Christ's mission and work, in contrast to the destructive powers of the evil one disintegrating divine order in the "world". The missionary idea is also unmistakably present. Christ before his departure also prays for those "who through their word shall believe in me"; his mind is already directed to his future flock, to which other sheep as well as those of the house of Israel will belong (cf. 10:16). How the evangelist understood this, is shown by his interpretation of the unwitting prophecy of the high priest Caiaphas. By his death Jesus was to "gather together in one the children of God that were dispersed" (11:52). The "world" has "not known" God, but Christ possessed this "knowledge" of God and has bestowed it on those who have recognized and affirmed him to be God's envoy (17:25f.). Once again the conviction of the later Church is also expressed when Christ goes on to say

"And to them I will make your name more known, that the love wherewith thou hast loved me may be in them and I in them" (verse 26).

As well as showing Jesus' attitude, the words quoted are also clear evidence of how the Johannine Church saw itself and its position in regard to the "world". It does not exclude itself from the world but marks itself off from it.[27] If the question is once more raised, what kind of a concept of the "world" this presupposes, the answer must be that the "world" does not mean God's creation, nor the sum of existing things and conditions which man is called upon to care for, to administer in due order and to shape, but it means the "world" as an historical factor, existing in a particular historical condition, and precisely as the world of men in its relation to God and the moral order established and intended by him. Even more does it signify "this world" in its attitude to God's eschatological envoy Jesus Christ who was intended most profoundly to heal its shattered order, bring life and redemption to men, but against whom it shuts itself in unbelief and hatred. In face of it, the Johannine Church sees itself in the same strained and paradoxical situation as the fourth evangelist shows us in Jesus' encounter with his own nation, the Judaism of that time. Into this world in need of redemption, but encompassed with God's merciful love (cf. John 3:16; 1 John 4:9, 14), Jesus was sent and his Church is now sent. Yet like Jesus, the Church finds itself faced with incomprehensible rejection, blindness and enmity, which is only to be explained by the influence of God's adversary, the "evil one". This experience makes the judgement passed on "this world" a darker one, and also prompts scepticism regarding everything that is "in the world" (1 John 2:15 ff.). Yet at the same time it does not lead to any pessimism of principle; it is not forgotten that the "world" before all its history of perdition, was once God's creation, formed throughout by the

[27] See further R. Völkl, *Christ und Welt*, pp. 409–18; 430–9.

divine Logos (John 1:3), and that the latter came "into his own" (1:11), nor does the slightest doubt arise that Jesus Christ will bring to conclusion on the cosmic scale the victory won on the cross over the "prince of this world" (12:31; 16:33), and in fact will do so through his Church despite all resistance (1 John 4:4; 5:4f.). The struggle against the moral powers of perdition is waged simultaneously on two levels: in the life of the individual Christian (cf. section 36), and in the Church's encounter with the "world"; but once again those are not separate battlefields. The Church carries on its struggle in the world through its individual members, and in the same way the individual receives help and support in the community of brethren in the faith, the Church assisted and defended by the Paraclete.

§ 36. CHRIST AND SIN

A. Zahn, *De notione peccati, quam Johannes in prima epistola docet, commentatio* (dissertation), 1872; H. Windisch, *Taufe und Sünde in der ältesten Christenheit bis auf Origenes*, 1908; B. Poschmann, *Paenitentia secunda*, 1940; P. Galtier, "Le chrétien impeccable" in *MSR* 4 (1947) pp. 137–54; J. Herkenrath, "Sünde zum Tode (1 Joh. 5:16)" in *Aus Theologie und Philosophie* (Festschrift für F. Tillmann), 1950, pp. 119–38; A. Kirchgässner, *Erlösung und Sünde im Neuen Testament*, 1950, pp. 253–301; R. Schnackenburg, *Die Johannesbriefe*, 1953, pp. 253–8; I. de la Potterie, "Le péché, c'est l'iniquité (1 Joh. 3:4)" in *NRT* 78 (1956) pp. 785–97; S. Lyonnet, "De notione peccati . . . V" in *VD* 35 (1957) pp. 271–8; W. Nauck, *Die Tradition und der Charakter des 1. Johannesbriefes*, 1957, pp. 98–122.

THE CHRISTIAN in the world finds himself confronted with yet another serious and in fact harassing problem, that of overcoming sin. The more clearly God's nature as holiness without shadow (1 John 1:5) is recognized, the more deeply Christian union with God is understood as "being of God" (John 8:47; 1 John 3:10b; 4:2–6; 5:19), and as "being born of God" (John 1:13; 1 John 3:9; 4:7; 5:1, 4, 18), the more incomprehensible it becomes that the Christian himself has still to struggle with sin and is not infrequently overcome by it. In Johannine theology, sin is disclosed as of diabolical nature (1 John 3:8), and as eschatological power of "iniquity" (ἀνομία, 1 John 3:4), which is diametrically opposed to God and his radiant light. Christ, however, himself sinlessly holy, has brought that divine nature as a new power of life into the cosmos (cf. John 8:24, 34, 46; 1 John 3:5, 6, 8b, 9; 5:18). He is the "lamb of God who taketh away the sin of the world" (John 1:29), the "propitiation" for our sins and those of the whole world (1 John 2:2; 4:10). After the Resurrection he gave to his disciples the power of forgiving sins (John 20:23); the sins of Christians are forgiven for Jesus' name's sake (1 John 2:12). Jesus' intention of "destroying the works of the devil" is realized in those who are born of God (1 John 3:8f.). Nevertheless sin occurs even in the Christian life, and it would be self-deception and falsehood to say we are without sin (1 John 1:8, 10). Our heart can alarm us by reprehending us, that is to say, accusing us of sin and guilt (3:19f.). It also happens that the Christian sees his brother sin, whether it be "by sin not to death" or even "by sin unto death" (5:16). Sin is, therefore, a harsh and sinister fact in Christian life which it is impossible to ignore.

The depth of the problem is only fully realized when it is considered that God has imparted to the Christian powers which enable and bind him to lead a holy life without sin. "Whosoever is born of God committeth not sin, for his seed abideth in him. And he cannot sin, because he is born of God" (3:9). And the author of the First Epistle continues in logical accord with this, "In this the children of God are manifest, and the children of the devil. Whosoever is not just is not of God and (especially) not he that loveth not his brother" (verse 10). The author sees in the absence of sin, and positively in brotherly love, a criterion for distinguishing the children of God from the children of the devil; so convinced is he of the efficacy of the divine powers. At the end of the epistle this is again shown in the awareness of these Johannine Christians. "We know that whosoever is born of God sinneth not; but the man born of God preserveth him (or, 'the man born of God holds fast to him') [28] and the wicked one toucheth him not." It is, therefore, not only a question of the Christian's being still weak and sinful, and of his failing like a human being, but rather that what God has done in man ought really to prevent a new fall into sin, and yet, as experience teaches, often does not prevent it. How is this antinomy to be resolved?

It must first be inquired what was the context and function in the Church's life of the affirmations which seem so contradictory. They chiefly occur in the sections 1 John 1:6–2:2; 3:4–10; 5:16–18. In 1:6–2:2, the condemnation of the false Gnostic teachers who had fallen victims to moral indifferentism must have occasioned the sharp emphasis on the persistent sinfulness. In contrast to them the author had to stress that to genuine fellowship with God, there belongs "walking in the light" (cf. also 2:9-11); and "doing the truth". On the other hand, in view of their notion that they have "known God" (2:3f.), and are "in God" (2:5), he cannot admit that "We have no sin" (1:8), particularly as these Gnostics evidently thought little of brotherly love. No human being, not even the Christian, has completely overcome sin; he still needs to be cleansed by the Blood of Christ (cf. 1:7). But this explanation does not completely clear up the various statements; it only adds a difficulty; for in other passages, polemic against false teachers is quite absent. As the end of the epistle shows, the problem is also

---

[28] Not a few commentators take "engendered by God" (ὁ γεννηθεὶς ἐκ τοῦ θεοῦ) as referring to Christ, who is contrasted with the evil one, namely Satan, and preserves everyone who is born of God from sin (Cf. also John 17:12). Such a way of speaking of Christ would of course be rather strange. An acceptable meaning can be had if it is taken as referring to the Christian. "Anyone who has once been engendered by God (aorist tense!) holds fast to him (God)" (Bauer, *Wörterbuch*, p. 1513, under τηρεῖν 3); and cf. Schnackenburg, *Die Johannesbriefe*, on this text.

one within the Church. Unmastered sin is a burden on the Christian communities.

It has long been recognized that the question of sin in the Christian's life arises in view of baptism, the saving grace it bestows and the obligations it imposes. The "birth from God" occurs in the fundamental Christian sacrament which fills man in his weak frail "flesh" (σάρξ) as he is, with the divine Spirit (πνεῦμα) and "from above", from the heavenly, divine world, makes of him a new man (cf. John 1:13 with 3:3–8). God's "seed" is bestowed on him (cf. 1 John 3:9), and as an enduring vital power (ἐν αὐτῷ μένει), which makes him capable of life without sin.[29] Consequently it is now true to say that "Whoever abideth in him sinneth not" (3:6a). John is so thoroughly convinced of the reality and efficacy of the divine Spirit of life and holiness that he can write (3:6b), "Whosoever sinneth hath not seen him nor known him"; that is to say, with such a person there has not really been communion with Christ and God. If the "engendered of God" in 5:18b does mean Christ, the statement is made that Christ himself preserves the Christian from sin and defends him from the clutches of the evil one (Satan); if the expression refers to the baptized person, it testifies no less clearly that the latter holds fast to God by the power of God bestowed on him and that the evil one cannot touch him. Yet the need for human collaboration is never in doubt; the condition is always implied that the Christian "abides" in Christ and God. With insistence equal to that with which it is categorically stated that God's word "abides" in those addressed, and that they have "overcome" the wicked one (2:14), that God's "seed" abides in those born of God (3:9), that God himself abides in us, as can be recognized from the

---

[29] The σπέρμα αὐτοῦ can no doubt be taken as a metaphor signifying the Holy Spirit (like χρῖσμα in 2:20, 27), and suggested by the idea of being born of God. What is in fact in question is the permanence of the divine powers, the operation of the Holy Spirit in the baptized person.

341

fact that he has given us of his Spirit (5:13; cf. 3:24), the conditions for such continuance in fellowship with God are impressed on the recipients of the epistle. "(Only) he who keeps his commandments abides in him and he in him" (3:24); "If we love one another, God abides in us" (4:12); "he that abides in love abides in God and God in him" (4:16). From the point of view of right belief, which is also the work of the divine Spirit (the "unction"), and an obligation on man, indicative and imperative, statement and precept are even juxtaposed. "Let the unction which you have received from him abide in you . . . and as it has taught you, abide in him" (2:27). This Johannine "abiding" is like a bracket linking God's action and man's endeavour; the divine and the human side are each referred to equally definitely.

Consequently we are confronted with the same state of affairs as we have already observed in Pauline theology. The indicative sentences about redemption themselves involve the imperative moral precepts (cf. section 28), and we are obliged to give the same explanation as with Paul (cf. section 29). After the saving event has taken place by grace (in baptism), the Christian belongs as a child of God (cf. 1 John 3:1) to the holy world of God (cf. 3:3) — in Pauline terms he is a new creation in Christ —, and yet he is still in the "world" (cf. 1 John 2:15 ff.), — in Pauline terms in "this aeon" — and must now put to the proof and authenticate by his manner of life the divine life bestowed on him. In somewhat different categories from those of Paul, the fundamental experience of the Christian in the world is thus brought out. His existence is both earthly and heavenly, in history and yet eschatological. The tension manifest in the two sets of statements, one deriving from God and the other concerning man's situation in redemptive history, is not removed thereby, but to some degree rendered intelligible. Consequently all endeavours to weaken and harmonize hard sayings by drawing distinctions such as "impeccability in principle and human weakness", "incapable of mortal sin, impossibility of avoiding daily faults", "apostasy and moral lapse", are unsatisfactory and inadequate.[30] Clearly every baptized person is called to a perfectly sinless life (3:3, 9; 5:18), yet each is also threatened by sin, even by "sin unto death" (5:16) and total apostasy. Baptism as such does not guarantee final salvation, does not lead automatically to sinlessness, does not operate magically without moral effort on man's part. Only those who abide in what is given them, only those who give to others the love they have received (3:1, 11), only those who actively practise brotherly love have "eternal life abiding" in them (3:15). If the author of the First Epistle of John refuses to regard apostates and those who reject charity, as "born of God", and declares them to be "children of the devil" (cf. 3:8, 10; 4:3, 8), that says nothing against baptism but certainly concerns the abuse of baptism, disregard of the obligations imposed by baptism.

Only if this fundamental theological perspective is assured, is it permissible to note that "sin" and "sinning" are not used in the same sense in all passages in the First Epistle of John. There are texts which obviously refer to the "daily" sins that no Christian can avoid; these texts mirror no doubt the experience of Christians in the world. The passage 1:8–2:2 is one such text, and gives proof of sound Christian realism. Confession of "our" sins, that is, of those committed among Christians, is necessary, but takes place with trust in the faithful and merciful God who remits our sins and cleanses us from all iniquity (verse 9). In the paraenetic apostrophe to his readers (2:1), the author expresses the wish that they may not sin, yet "if any man sin, we have an advocate (Paraclete) with the Father, Jesus Christ the just" (2:1). The propitiation for the whole world (2:2), who now dwells at the right hand of the Father continues, therefore, to intervene on behalf of his weak sinful human brethren, a thought that is also found in Romans 8:34 and Hebrews 7:25. The trust expressed is directed to God

---

[30] On the various explanations, see the Commentaries and the bibliography to the present chapter.

himself who "is greater than our heart" (3:20), "if our heart reprehends us". The reason for the trouble of heart is not of course stated, but may most likely be considered to be sins that a Christian has committed out of weakness. We are to approach God at the judgement with "frankness" or confidence; yet we are not yet rid of fear of the divine judge, but we are to drive it out by perfect love (4:17f.). Here, too, it is not said what the cause of the fear is; but it is likely that sin and guilt are responsible. Finally, there is a passage in the last chapter which deals plainly enough with the failure of Christians: "He that knows his brother to sin a sin (which is) not to death, let him ask (for him) and (new) life shall be given to him (by God)" (5:16). The author only exhorts fraternal prayer of petition for such as do not "sin unto death". "All iniquity is sin. And (yet) there is a sin not (leading) unto death" (5:17).[31] Accordingly by that is meant an offence which does not remove the sinner entirely from the sphere of God's life, yet which weakens and endangers the divine life in him. For the intercession is to move God to "give life" (no article!), that is to say, to provide new strength which will unite him again more closely to God, and also permit him to overcome his condition of moral weakness. In contrast to this, there is also "sin unto death" and the author expressly excludes prayer of intercession for such sinners by their brethren (verse 16c).

There has been much discussion about how that is to be understood. Many commentators have suggested a hardening of the sinner in his attitude of hostility to God, which would make conversion impossible, a "sin against the Holy Spirit" (cf.

---

[31] The Vulgate here with many other authorities (33, 623, 1852, q, sy[h], sa, Tert.) omits the negative. That would intensify the statement: There is in fact (as was already said at the end of verse 16) a sin unto death. But the reading "sin not unto death" is critically better attested, and is also intelligible in the context. The thought returns here to the case under consideration where one of the brethren commits a sin "not to death" (verse 16a).

Mark 3:29 parallels), so-called unforgivable sins; but the text does not say that but simply excepts "sin unto death" from prayer of intercession. Not a few therefore would prefer to think it refers to apostasy, and especially to joining the false teachers with whom the author has already severed the bond of fellowship (cf. 2:19; 4:3, 6; also 2 John 10f.). But that is not certain either, for the author scarcely allows such apostates the name of brother any more. Consequently, other commentators suggest the offences later termed capital sins, apostasy, murder, graver kinds of unchastity, idolatry, or the sins of the "way of death" (*Didache* 1–5); but that is merely conjecture, which is excluded, for lack of more precise indications. The author takes for granted that those he is writing to will understand. So it is only possible to say that a way of acting is meant which "is the negation of full community of life with God, Christ and the brethren".[32]

Johannine thought regarding the antithetical spheres of life and death (cf. section 32) also influences the teaching about sin. Ultimately there is only the choice between walking in "light" or in "darkness"; but sober observation of Christian life as it is lived "in this world", though of course according to the way and pattern of Christ (cf. 1 John 2:6; 3:3; 4:17c), yet in human failure too, has led to realization that even the children of God still can and do fall into sins of both slight and serious kind. And it is to be hoped that it does not go as far as complete separation from God, the loss of divine life, "sin unto death"! Certainly later doctrine about sin is based on the fundamental distinction between mortal sin and venial sin; but it may be questioned whether the divisions, often too diagrammatically drawn, correspond to John the theologian's intention. Anyone who has any sense of the latter's horror of the domain of death far from God, will be cautious about rapid identification of "mortal sin" in the life of a seriously striving Christian. The author of the

[32] J. Herkenrath, "Sünde zum Tode", pp. 135f.

epistle who perhaps throws most light onto this set of problems, is convinced that God's "commandments are not heavy", for "whatsoever is born of God overcometh the world" (1 John 5:3f.). And this optimism based on the divine powers in the believing and loving Christian, should animate all who are painfully conscious of the "evil one". The same piece of writing which implacably reveals the seriousness of our situation in regard to salvation, is also full of hope and confidence and keeps pointing out to the struggling Christian the path of love. "But perfect love casts out fear" (4:18).

Chapter Three

JAMES

§ 37. THE "PERFECT LAW OF LIBERTY"

See the *Introductions* and *Commentaries;* see also A. Gaugusch, *Der Lehrgehalt der Jakobusepistel,* 1914; A. Meyer, *Das Rätsel der Jakobus-Briefe,* 1930; H. Schammberger, *Die Einheitlichkeit des Jakobus im anti-gnostischen Kampf,* 1936; G. Kittel, "Der Geschichtliche Ort des Jakobus" in *ZNW* 41 (1942) pp. 71–105; *id.,* "Der Jakobusbrief und die Apostolischen Väter" in *ZNW* 43 (1950–1951) pp. 54–112; A. T. Cadoux, *The Thought of St. James,* 1944; W. Bieder, "Christliche Existenz nach dem Zeugnis des Jakobus" in *TZ* 5 (1949) pp. 93–113; M. Lackmann, *Sola fide. Eine exegetische Studie über Jakobus 2,* 1949; J. Bonsirven, art. "Jacques" in *Dictionnaire de laBible,* Suppl. vol. IV, pp. 783–95; H. Rendtorff, *Hörer und Täter. Eine Einführung in Jakobus,* 1953; G. Eichholz, *Jakobus und Paulus,* 1953; J. Jeremias, "Paul and James" in *Expository Times* 66 (1954–1955) pp. 368–71; J. B. Souček, "Zu Problemen des Jakobusbriefes" in *EvTh* 18 (1958) pp. 460–68; J. Blinzler in *LThK* vol. V, 861–63.

THE AUTHOR of the Epistle of James has often been compared with Paul and said to have been overshadowed by him. His ideas have been variously criticized as a reversion to legalistic piety, as "moralism" devoid of theological profundity, as pedestrian preaching (Luther called this an "epistle of straw"). However, even among Protestants too there is now a growing realization that this man represents a Christianity which has a

347

right to existence as well as the "Pauline" kind, and has its salutary rôle to fulfil.[1]

As far as the almost wholly non-existent Christology of this epistle is concerned (one indication among others, according to some scholars, that we are here dealing with an originally Jewish writing, only lightly veneered with Christianity[2]) it must be remembered that in literary form the Epistle of James is a paraenetic work, consisting of a chain-like series of mutually dependent individual exhortations and makes no claim to lofty theological thoughts. This type of work had been very popular since the appearance of the proverb and wisdom literature of the Old Testament;[3] there was absolutely no reason why it should not have also been borrowed by a Christian writer. It has many similarities with other early Christian works, such as the *First Epistle of Clement,* the *Didache,* the *Epistle of Barnabas,* and the *Shepherd of Hermas.*

We should be able to say a great deal more about the significance of the Epistle of James if we knew more about the circumstances of its composition, and more precisely, where it appeared; who this James "the servant of God and of our Lord Jesus Christ" was, if we could explain "the twelve tribes which

[1] Cf. M. Dibelius, *Der Brief des Jakobus,* 1921, p. 168; W. Michaelis, *Einleitung in das NT,* 1946, p. 288 ("Luther's condemnation ... was occasioned by a comparison with the Epistles of Paul, and does not do the Epistle justice"); F. Hauck, *Die Briefe des Jakobus, Petrus, Judas und Joh.,* 4th ed. 1947, p. 5 ("a valuable supplement to Paul's thought on justification by faith"); H. Preisker in the appendix to Windisch, *Kommentar,* 3rd ed. 1951, pp. 149f.; H. Rendtorff, *Hörer und Täter,* pp. 46–50; J. Jeremias, "Paul and James".

[2] A. Meyer, *Das Rätsel,* following several predecessors, especially represents this viewpoint; cf. also Windisch in his *Kommentar;* the view is, however, generally rejected in more recent works.

[3] Cf. esp. the so-called "Testaments", particularly the *Testament of the Twelve Patriarchs.* A. Meyer tries to reconstruct a "Testament of the Patriarch Jacob" out of James, claiming it can still be recognized in outline.

JAMES

are scattered abroad" (1:1) and if we knew whether we should attribute its good Greek style to Hellenistic influences or must continue to see, under the garb of this language, a Jewish Christian mind of Semitic stamp. Its Christian origin and fundamentally Christian attitude are confirmed not only by its repeated allusion to the words of Jesus, by "the good Name (that is, Jesus Christ) that is invoked upon you (in baptism?)" (2:7), by its looking forward to the parousia (5:7), and by other individual characteristics, but also by its fundamental thought which, as we shall see below, is not purely Jewish.[4] For the rest, it is difficult to determine the precise Christian position of the epistle, for the preliminaries of history, literary questions, and those of religious history, and exegesis, mutually influence one another, and we have available only internal criteria which do not present an unambiguous picture. As it is impossible for us to investigate the whole complex of problems here,[5] we must limit ourselves to a cautious positive exposition.

One of the crucial questions is the attitude of James to the "law". The word "law" occurs ten times in the Epistle.[6] Especially noteworthy are the texts in which the author makes characteristic additions to the word: "the perfect law of liberty" (1:25), "the royal law" (2:8), "the law of liberty" (2:12). We may presume that under these texts at least there lies a unified view. Moreover, from the context of 1:25 it is clear that the "perfect law of liberty" is closely related to the "ingrafted word, which is able to save your souls" (1:21). But this is followed by the admonition to be, not merely hearers, but doers of the word

[4] Attention has been drawn to its similarity to the fundamental ethical attitude of Jesus. But Kittel's view (*ZNW* 1942), that in time and content James is not far removed from the collection of the Lord's utterances into the Sermon on the Mount, has frequently been disputed.
[5] Cf. F. W. Maier in *LThK* 1st ed. vol. V, 270f.; J. Bonsirven "Jacques"; M. Meinertz, *Einleitung in das NT*, 5th ed. 1950, pp. 247ff.; A. Wikenhauser, *New Testament Introduction*, pp. 472-87; J. Blinzler *LThK* vol. V, 861-3.   [6] 1:25, 2:8, 9, 10, 11, 12; 4:11 (four times).

(v. 23), and the demand that whoever looks into the "perfect law of liberty" should persevere in it, not becoming a "forgetful hearer" but a real "doer of the work" (v. 25). The "word of God ingrafted" in us can hardly be anything else but the Christian message of salvation (cf. also v. 18, "word of truth"), which thus becomes the law that binds us, the law called perfect and said either to bring liberty with it or to promise liberty. Similar ideas are to be found in both Hellenistic and Jewish-Hellenistic literature.[7] Recently it has been claimed that precisely the same expression can be recognized in the writings recently discovered near the Dead Sea, that is, in the writings of the Jewish "Community of God's Covenant", but this is probably a mistake due to incorrect punctuation.[8] However that may be, it can scarcely be doubted that our text is intended to refer to the gospel as such, and more precisely to the obligations it entails, as the perfect law of liberty.

There is no need to see even the "royal law" (2:8) as limited to the special commandment to love the brethren. It should rather be seen as the expression of the heart of the whole saving law of the New Testament. The author indicates this in the context, in which his purpose is to attack the neglect of the poor and false "respect of persons". Verses 10-11 seem to be wholly based on a Jewish point of view: anyone who fulfils the whole law, failing in only one (point), is guilty in all (points).[9] The argument is used here, however, only to prove

[7] See the texts in Dibelius, *Der Brief des Jakobus*, pp. 110–13; A. Meyer, *Rätsel*, pp. 153 ff.; Windisch, pp. 12 f. The frequently quoted text, *Aboth* VI, 2: "For there is no freedom for you, except when you occupy yourself in studying the law. Everyone who occupies himself with studying the Torah, rises ever higher" is part of the supplement to this tractate and is relatively late. Cf. Marti-Beer, *Aboth*, p. 165.

[8] E. Stauffer, "'Das Gesetz der Freiheit' in der Ordensregel von Jericho" in *TLZ* 77 (1952) pp. 327–32; an opposite view is given by F. Nötscher in *Biblica* 34 (1953) pp. 193 f. (that the controverted phrase does not mean "law of liberty" but "inherited law").

[9] Cf. the parallels in Billerbeck, vol. II, p. 755, *in loc.*

that there can be no exceptions to the "royal law" of love.[10] "So speak ye and so do, as being to be judged by the law of liberty" (2:12). Thus "the law of liberty" must be the same thing as the "royal law", an expression suggested perhaps by the kingly rule of God in v. 5, or recalling the royal lawgiver, but in any case (it may be a kind of formula), emphasizing the high dignity and significance of the law.

The chain of thought at 4:11f. is also based on old ideas about the law. The law is something holy; one may not think badly of it and condemn it. The author is actually concerned here with the thought that no one should calumniate or judge his brother or neighbour, for in doing so one is calumniating the law (which forbids such things). Such ideas could certainly have arisen in a Jewish milieu, but it seems more likely that the writer was thinking of Jesus' admonition at Matthew 7:1ff. (and par.), just as the previous sentence (v. 10), "Be humbled in the sight of the Lord, and he will exalt you" has a clear ring of Luke 14:11. If this is so, then he is using the old concept of the law (perhaps for the benefit of readers whose ideas are still rooted in Judaism) only as a vehicle; the true law that we must not calumniate is the words of Jesus.

From all this we may draw the following conclusion:

In so far as the message of salvation makes claims on men and imposes moral duties on them, James regards it as the new, and indeed the perfect, law. In fact, the expression "new" is not used, but it is unlikely that James was still referring to the old law of the Jews. That he was writing of some particular law is clear from the qualifications "perfect" and "of liberty". He seems to be contrasting it with the old, imperfect law,[11] although he in

---

[10] That the command to love at this point was only seen as one among many (Dibelius, Windisch, A. Meyer, *Rätsel,* p. 150) is not certain, since even "showing partiality" can be counted a breaking of the commandment to love alongside other transgressions of the same commandment; cf. W. Gutbrod in *ThWB* vol. IV, p. 1074.

[11] Cf. Gutbrod, *ibid.* pp. 1073, 29ff.; M. Goguel, *L'église primitive,* p. 525.

no way condemns or completely rejects the old law, but rather uses it in the course of several arguments and even quotes it (2:8, 11). But in using it he refers only to its moral commandments, nowhere mentioning its ritual precepts, which must, then, have lost all meaning for him.[12]

James nowhere gives his reasons for maintaining that this law is "perfect". But from his use of language elsewhere it would appear that by calling it perfect he means primarily that it has no shortcomings and that it is good from every point of view (cf. 1:4). Its excellence, its royal worth, lies, according to 2:8, in its contents, and according to verse 12, in its requiring us to love. Though he exhorts us on many separate points, it is clear that James, nevertheless, sees the law as culminating in love.[13]

For human beings who love God and are striving to attain everlasting life (cf. 1:12; 2:5), such a law is a "law of liberty". It is by nature a law of liberty and adapted to its task of guiding man to true freedom; but nevertheless, he will also be tried by the "law of liberty" (2:13). Not much separates this "law of liberty" from wisdom. For James, wisdom was a lofty ideal (cf. 1:5; 3:13, 15, 17), though, of course, he means here the real wisdom "coming from above", the kind he praises so eloquently (3:17), not earthly, sensual, diabolic "wisdom".[14] We may venture to conclude that what the author meant was

[12] Cf. in contrast 1:27! This is especially emphasized by Windisch, who sees this as a strong argument against the authorship of James, the brother of the Lord (*Kommentar* pp. 12f.); Kittel and Wikenhauser, *Introduction*, pp. 481 ff. try to show that it is invalid. Even if ritual precepts were not always mentioned in Judaism, the lack of such allusion in this epistle is striking.

[13] Controverted by A. Meyer, *Rätsel*, p. 150; for exegesis on James 2:8 ff. see note 10 above.

[14] This text is of great importance to those who try to identify anti-Gnostic tendencies in James (Schammberger, *Einheitlichkeit*, pp. 33 ff.; H. J. Schoeps, *Judenchristentum*, pp. 343 ff.). But the problem involved is a complex one.

that where the true wisdom, originating from God, holds sway, the law of liberty is accomplished, an idea that recalls Matthew 11: 28–30.

James' concept of the law approaches closely to the saying in the Sermon on the Mount, "Do not think that I am come to destroy the law or the prophets. I am come not to destroy, but to fulfil" (Matt. 5:17). James' view has the appearance of being an explanation of this saying: what Jesus has in fact given us is a new and perfect law, safeguarding and giving liberty, but we must fulfil it through our actions (cf. Matt. 5:19; Jas. 1:25; 2:14 ff.). Precepts concerning ritual, worship and purification are obviously passed over in silence. The *Epistle of Barnabas* probably gives the best definition: "the new law of our Lord Jesus Christ (a law) without the yoke of compulsion" (2:6). The *Shepherd of Hermas,* too, gives a similar account of it: "After he (the Son of God) had cleansed the people from sin, he showed them the path of life, by giving them the law he had received from his Father" (v. 6, 3). Irenaeus also speaks in this way of the *lex libertatis*.[15] The "new law of Christ" need not lead to ossification of the message of salvation and a new kind of justification by works, but, as long as it is accepted with the love and freedom proper to the children of God, it can impel us to an active and joyous Christianity. So at any rate James understood and taught.

§ 38. WORKS AS WELL AS FAITH

See the bibliography to section 37; add B. Bartmann, *St. Paulus und St. Jakobus über die Rechtfertigung,* 1897; M. Meinertz, *Jakobus,* 4th ed. 1932, pp. 35–37; *id., Theologie,* vol. I, pp. 240 ff.; T. ab Orbiso, "Fides sine

[15] *Adversus Haereses* IV, 56, 4 (Harvey, vol. II, p. 272); see further in Windisch on *Epistle of Barnabas* 2:6 (supplementary volume III to his *Handbuch zum NT,* 1920); V. Hasler, *Gesetz und Evangelium,* pp. 29 ff.; 52 f.

operibus mortua (Jac. 2:14–26)" in *VD* 20 (1940) pp. 265–77; J. Michl, *Die Katholischen Briefe,* 1953, pp. 156–9; E. Lohse, "Glaube und Werke. Zur Theologie des Jakobus" in *ZNW* 48 (1957) pp. 1–22; G. Eichholz, *Glaube und Werke bei Paulus und Jakobus,* 1961.

THE AUTHOR of the Epistle of James was as concerned about "works" as he was about the "law of freedom". Coming fresh from Paul, the reader is tempted to think that the author contradicts the latter apostle who inveighed passionately against the old Jewish system of justification by fulfilment of the works of the law. James 2:24, "Do you see that by works a man is justified, and not by faith only?" sounds like the very antithesis of the Pauline gospel, "We may be justified by the faith of Christ and not by works of the law" (Gal. 2:16; cf. Rom. 3:28). However, Paul and James do not contend for their place in the New Testament. We have already seen in the previous section that James did not even envisage the old Mosaic law as a guiding principle of action, and we may now observe that he did not want to return to the old way of salvation and the Jewish system of justification by works. The "works" that James requires are those the Christian should perform after receiving justification by the gracious mercy of God. "For of his own will hath he begotten us by the word of truth, that we might be some beginning of his creature" (1:18): for James, too, this is the beginning of the Christian way. It is striking, too, that James never speaks, as Paul does, of the "works of the law"; for him, "works" are not a substitute for faith, they are only the necessary completion of faith. His meaning becomes quite clear when he deduces from the example of Abraham, "Seest thou that faith did co-operate with his works, and by works faith was made perfect?" (2:22). He drives home to morally lax but believing Christians that they should not be forgetful hearers, but effectual doers (1:25). Anyone among them who wants to be understanding and wise should exhibit his works by his good manner of life (3:13); faith without works is dead (2:17, 26). What James is saying, then, is that a life in keeping with the faith is a part of living faith — but Paul said the same thing in his own way. The apostle of the gentiles wants a faith that becomes effective in love (Gal. 5:6); the Christian who is impelled by the Holy Spirit must "mortify the deeds of the flesh" in order to receive life (Rom. 8:13). St. James' thoughts were turned in a different theological direction; he does not oppose St. Paul.

How then, did he reach the sharply pointed expressions in 2:14–26? People have constantly tried to interpret this passage as meaning that he was opposing a false theological view that faith alone without subsequent works is enough to justify us (cf. vv. 14, 20, 24). This perverse idea, it is then said, was certainly not Paul's but was championed by people who appealed to Paul for support, understanding him wrongly and misapplying his words. What St. James was opposing, therefore, was a debased "Paulinism". Such exegesis would involve us in almost insoluble riddles. Was James in that case not indirectly attacking Paul himself, at least in his misunderstood forms of expression? Why did he not expound to these faulty followers of St. Paul the true doctrine of the apostle himself? Did he not know it or even not understand it? These questions have repercussion on the problems of the authorship and date of this work. On the grounds of its complete disregard of the Pauline ideas known to us from Galatians and Romans, G. Kittel, for example, suggests that the only choice open is between a very early date (even before the Apostolic Council), when Pauline doctrine was perhaps not yet fully familiar, and a very late date (perhaps in the middle of the second century), when the actual questions at issue for St. Paul were no longer understood and when no one was taking any pains to understand them properly either. Kittel argues energetically for the early date.[16]

[16] ZNW 41 (1942) pp. 96f.; see also his last treatment in ZNW 43 (1950–1). Among others who join them in the question of an early date are W. Michaelis, Einleitung in das NT, 2nd ed. 1954, pp. 279ff.; and M. Meinertz, Einleitung in das NT, 3rd ed. 1950, pp. 252ff.

But not a few scholars disagree with him; they would prefer, on account of the general picture presented, and several points of detail, to date the epistle in the second half of the first century.[17]

In fact, however, we cannot even say that the passage contains polemics against a Paulinism wrongly interpreted and misapplied. Its points are made not against any teaching, but against negligent Christian conduct.[18] If those attacked by James appealed to faith (vv. 14, 18) (most remarkably, their appeal was, it seems, to monotheistic faith in God, verse 19, and not to faith in Christ), they did so because, by his challenge to them to prove themselves in works, he forced them onto the defensive. It was James who unmasked their attitude as a dead faith, by demanding, for living faith, the addition of works. "James himself created the enemy, or at least, gave workless sloth a tongue and speech. This speaker is justly (2:20) called an empty, vain man, and not Paul or a follower of Paul. The texts in support which follow, also relate to him. He is not, of course, speaking merely for the sake of this imaginary opponent, or even for the indolent who are being blamed, but, of course, primarily for his readers."[19] St. James cites the example of Abraham in the traditional way; in Romans 4 and Galatians 3, St. Paul used these texts in a

---

[17] Cf. the criticisms by K. Aland in "Der Herrnbruder Jakobus und der Jakobusbrief" in *TLZ* 69 (1944) pp. 97ff.; Feine and Aland, *Theologie,* pp. 390–6; the commentaries by Dibelius, Hauck, Windisch, and others. A date between these extremes (*c.* 60, before the death of James, the brother of the Lord in 62) is supported among Catholics by J. Chaine, F. W. Maier, J. Bonsirven; and among Protestants by Feine and Behm, *Einleitung,* pp. 232ff.; cf. however J. Blinzler, *loc. cit.,* 862: "The strong emphasis of the work, however, which seems to presuppose signs of fatigue in the Christian conduct, agrees more with a date of composition in late apostolic times." But he thinks a date in the second century is impossible.
[18] Thus T. Zahn, but esp. A. Meyer, *Rätsel,* pp. 91ff.; cf. with what follows, his statements on pp. 86–108, 123–41.
[19] A. Meyer, *Rätsel,* p. 94.

consciously anti-Jewish way, which served his Christian exposition.

Another question that arises is, of course, how James and Paul could exist side by side. A. Meyer has accounted for their similarities (the same concepts and in part the same proof texts) and their differences (different conceptual content and different interpretations of Scripture) by suggesting they both belonged to the same Jewish school of thought.[20] The difficult riddle remains the date of the composition of this Epistle of James, a date when such different manners of presentation could co-exist in Christian circles, not mutually dependent, and noticeably at cross purposes with one another. In order to solve it, it would be necessary to examine the whole work, with all its problems, not merely our passage, 2:14–26. Its close relationship with writings such as *Didache,* 1 *Clem., Barnabas,* and *Hermas,* suggests rather the end of the first century. "The possibility that the Epistle of James comes from a Later Jewish Christian of the Hellenistic school who felt himself to be a spiritual relation of the great Brother of the Lord, does not allow of demonstration from the style."[21]

The formula "faith and works" forcefully represented by James, even though it does sound cold to many theologians, in comparison with Paul, must be assessed separately. We shall recognize its value if we realize that it was making its point against a form of Christianity in which charity was growing cold, excusing itself by pointing to its faith and piety (1:27). In James, we hear the voice of a Christian who had understood and kept his Lord's words, "Not every one that saith to me, Lord, Lord, shall enter into the kingdom of heaven; but he that doth the will of my Father who is in heaven" (Matt. 7:21). This

---

[20] *ibid.,* pp. 102, 107.

[21] J. Blinzler, *loc. cit.,* 862. Cf. also M. H. Shepherd Jr., "The Epistle of James and the Gospel of Matthew" in *JBL* 75 (1956) pp. 40–51 (James used Matthew as the only gospel; the epistle comes from Syria, close of the first century).

disciple of Christ had also realized that what mattered to Jesus were the "weightier things of the law" (Matt. 23:23), that is, love and mercy. Religion pure and undefiled before God the Father consists not of idle talk, but of effective care for orphans and widows (1:26f.); true charity consists not in giving cheap words to those in need of food and clothing but in offering them the necessities of life (2:15f.). "To him therefore, who knoweth to do good and doth it not, to him it is sin" (Jas. 4:17).

It is obvious that anyone so concerned with exhortation could not ignore the motive of judgement. "Judgement without mercy to him that hath not done mercy" (2:13). He asks for a simple, pure form of speech, without the protestation of oaths "that you fall not under judgement" (5:12). He cries out to the hard-hearted wealthy man with the shattering words, "You have stored up to yourselves wrath against the last days. Behold the reward of the labourers who have reaped down your fields, which by fraud has been kept back by you, crieth (to heaven); and the cry of them hath entered into the ears of the Lord of Sabbaoth. You have feasted upon earth; and in riotousness you have nourished your hearts, in the day of slaughter" (5:3–5). But he also reminds the brethren who murmur against one another, "Behold, the judge standeth before the door" (5:9). Thus his motive here is not the general Jewish motive of retribution, but the Christian thought of the Lord's second coming. Moreover, this last event should not instil fear, but should encourage Christians. St. James expects it to happen in the near future, but he does not fall victim to an apocalyptic fever. "Be you therefore also patient and strengthen your hearts; for the coming of the Lord is at hand" (5:8).

The Christianity that James preaches is not a comfortable religion. But his practical, virile teaching will remain salutary and necessary as long as Christians continue to miss the path from knowledge to action, from faith to charity, from piety to moral proof.

§ 39. Sober and Practical Admonitions

See the bibliographies to sections 37 and 38.

A GOOD place in which to study James' manner is in his admonition to his readers to govern their tongues (3:1–12). Ben Sirach had already used a forceful saying and revealing simile such as the people loved: "The stroke of a whip maketh a blue mark: but the stroke of the tongue will break the bones" (Ecclus. 28:21). James compares the tongue with the fire capable of burning down a great forest (3:5f.). Anyone who rules that little member, the tongue, has power over the whole body, just as we put the bit in the horse's mouth and guide its whole body, or steer a great ship by the rudder (v. 3f.). Practically and realistically, James realizes that the tongue generally serves evil. It defiles the whole body and sets the "wheel of our nativity"[22] on fire, with the fire of Gehenna itself (v. 6). We can tame wild beasts "but the tongue no man can tame, an unquiet evil, full of deadly poison" (v. 8). But the moral preacher must not paint too black a picture, for fear of crippling the will to improve. With the tongue we bless our Lord and Father, and curse men made in God's image. This should not be. More examples follow: that of the spring, which cannot emit both sweet and bitter water at one and the same time; that of the figtree, which cannot bear olives, and of the vine that cannot bear figs – this may be a reminiscence of the Lord's saying at Matthew 7:16 par.[23] – and that of the salt water,

[22] The phrase is used here as a technical expression (almost equivalent to "the course of our life"), and is significant from the point of view of religious history (it was Orphic in origin). G. Kittel has shown that it was also known in Rabbinic tradition; cf. *Probleme des Spätjudentums,* pp. 141–68. This much-discussed phrase does not, however, provide us with a starting-point for the study of the religious and temporal background of James. For bibliography, cf. Windisch and Preisker, *Kath. Briefe,* pp. 23, 147f.; Bauer, *Wörterbuch,* p. 1638.

[23] It is not a direct parallel, neither formally nor in content, for the

which no one can make sweet (vv. 9–12). Without going into the difficult question, where the nearest parallels to these sayings and expressions are to be found,[24] we can say that what we have here is a forceful and popular proverbial lore, looking life in the face and going about things in a lively way, making its points naturally and drastically, without deeper religious motives, concerned only with moral efficacy. Yet the real situation of the community is presupposed here, for at the beginning of the passage there stands the admonition, "Be ye not many masters, my brethren, knowing that you receive the greater judgement" (3:1).

"Moralizing" of precisely this kind was possible on the lips of a Jew or a gentile. Undoubtedly, then, the Christian writer has adopted the style of moral instruction customary in his own times and borrowed well-known images, without any visible effort to deepen the motives in a Christian way. Has such a method any real claim to a place in Christian instruction? Anyone who applies Pauline standards will deny it; but those who affirm "works" in the sense James speaks of them, will not find it inconsistent. Judged merely on these texts, the picture of the ideal that St. James sketches has no specifically Christian characteristics; he calls someone a "perfect man" for not falling into the general sins of speech (3:2). Paul demands more, and gives deeper motives: "In carefulness not slothful. In spirit fervent. Serving the Lord. Rejoicing in hope. Patient in tribulation. Instant in prayer . . ." (Rom. 12:11f.). But it should not be forgotten that James gives individual aphorisms and urges us to put them into effect.

meaning of James is that every tree can only bear one kind of fruit, its own kind, and not two different kinds.

[24] Windisch, *in loc.,* suggests this was a tradition of the Stoic schools; but such examples from nature were also used in Jewish tradition. A. Meyer, *Rätsel,* pp. 206f. suggests that this essay on the tongue is paraenesis based on Gen. 49:21: Naphthali, a hart let loose (but this is hardly likely).

The next two sections show that our author had deeper arguments in readiness, although even here he does not abandon his pithy and forcible language. In 3:13–18, where he contrasts the wisdom that is from above with the false wisdom of the world, he shows he is conscious that the roots of disorder and evil deeds lie in the mind, in the bitter jealousy and quarrelsomeness of the heart. In 4:1–12 he censures "wars and contentions" within the communities and identifies their source as the "concupiscences, which war in your members" (v. 1). Although these ideas might be a commonplace of the philosophy of the period,[25] the continuation of the passage reveals the religious point of view of its writer. Even prayer, he says, is ineffective if it is misused for our selfish desires (v. 3). Next he attacks some of his readers with the words, "Adulterers, know you not that the friendship of this world is the enemy of God?" (v. 4.) Unequivocally he uses the old image of Israel's prostitution (Osee 1–2; Ezech. 16:23 etc.), to reproach his communities with their disloyalty towards God. We have already several times indicated the low opinion of the "world" current in Judaism and early Christianity.[26] By portraying for his readers the danger and corruption of the world, the cunning attacks of Satan and the judgement of God, and admonishing them to cleanse their hands and sanctify their hearts, he was in his own way perpetuating the preaching of penance, on which Jesus himself was by no means silent in his preaching of salvation.

How far James was concerned with the actual state of affairs in the communities he was addressing, it is difficult to say.[27] One subject, however, was so close to his heart that we can come to

---

[25] Cf. the texts in Dibelius and Windisch, *in loc.,* A. Meyer (*op. cit.,* p. 106) assumes a "common Judaeo-Hellenistic school", where "Jewish and Greek ideas were woven together".

[26] See sections 22 (4), 27, 35.

[27] Cf. Dibelius, *op. cit.,* pp. 45f., whose judgement on this point is very reserved.

certain conclusions about it: the relation between rich and poor. The case he vividly describes, a rich man coming to church automatically given a good seat, while a poor man has to stay at the back or sit on the ground (2:2f.), may not have been a common practice, and may never have happened in exactly that way. But it does illustrate a danger St. James considered very serious, that the rich might become influential and corrupt the spirit of brotherhood. It seems clear that the majority of those James addressed must have been unimportant, simple, poor people, like those of the Corinthian community (1 Cor. 1:26ff.), except that James presupposes a rural and not an urban setting (cf. 5:4, 7). "Do not the rich oppress you by might? And do they not draw you before the judgement seats?" (2:6). How very true to life is the observation here, that such unimportant, oppressed people are at the same time compliant and servile, even thinking themselves honoured if their lordly exploiter visits them! St. James intervenes, not by whipping up class feeling, but by appealing to the Christian conscience for respect for the poor brother, who in fact, in God's sight, is worth just as much as a rich man or someone of high rank. More than one page of the Church's history illustrates how right he was to guard against the dominion of money and power even within the Church itself.

But in the question of poverty, James went still further. He extolled the dignity of those who are poor in the eyes of the world, but whom God has chosen to be "rich in faith and heirs of the kingdom which God hath promised to them that love him" (2:5). Poverty as such has a religious value, especially in view of the proximity of the judgement: "But let the brother of low condition glory in his exultation; and the rich in his being low, because as the flower of the grass he shall pass away" (1:9f.). Here we can catch the echo of a devotion to religious poverty which can be traced a long way back in Judaism: the poor are oppressed and in need, but they set all their hope on God. They are devout, the rich are the godless. Moreover, the poor are also the heirs to the kingdom of God, whilst God's judgement of condemnation will come upon the wicked rich.[28]

The composition of the class of the economically poor and socially weak changed from time to time. Thus the Pharisees, who had once belonged to it (cf. *Psalms of Solomon* 5:2, 13ff.; 10:7; 15:2; 16:13f.) had, according to the gospels, become in part more prosperous and influential. Jesus brought the gospel of salvation to the "poor" (Luke 4:18; Matt. 11:5 par.) and promised them his Messianic "salvation" (Matt. 5:3 par.). Although his chief concern was with religious and moral disposition the rich are, nevertheless, strongly criticized by him (see above, section 13). The ideal of poverty survived in the original Jerusalem community (see above, section 23), and St. Luke, who described the pious life of these "poor" Christians, was himself strongly imbued with it. With him, James was the most radical representative of this idea. All the indications point to Jewish Christianity as the guardian of this kind of religious poverty. Yet it is hardly possible to determine more accurately from this, which was the community to which the Epistle of St. James was first addressed, or when, for this conception of poverty continued to be influential for a long time, as Ebionitism shows.

The rich filled St. James with a fierce wrath: "Go now, ye rich men; weep and howl in your miseries, which shall come upon you. Your riches are corrupted, your garments are moth-eaten . . ." (5:1ff.); but it is a wrath against the unjust exploiter and conscienceless glutton (5:4f.), against men such as he and his readers knew. His words should no more be interpreted as a social manifesto and incitement to the disinherited to rebel than should the preaching of Jesus or the prophets. He depicts the

[28] Cf. Ps. 37:16ff.; 86:1ff.; 109:31; 113:6ff.; 132:15; Proverbs 15:16f.; 23:4f.; Sirach 11:14ff.; 20:21 etc. For woes on the godless rich see esp. 1 *Enoch* 94:6ff.; 95:4ff.; 96:4ff.; 97:7ff. etc. For bibliography, see section 13 above.

judgement of God on the whole human race. The only thing is that it will fall specially hard on those who have given themselves to mammon. Besides, he also warns another group as well as rich land-owners against vain striving for profit, namely, those in business (4:13-17). Materialism and the craving for pleasure are a threat in every class and any situation.

St. James' concern for religion is, therefore, perceptible behind all his moralizing. Christians should serve God in unpretentious, genuine piety and wait for the coming of their Lord. It is not by chance that religious instruction stands at both the beginning and the end of this book of proverbs. This too is practical, shaped to stand the test in the midst of a world inclined to evil and practising it. Besides, this "servant of God" sees temptations and trials as salutary if they are met with wisdom and endurance; at the end there shines the victor's crown of eternal life (1:2-12). He continually exhorts us to pray, which is to be done in faith, and with no hesitations or doubts whatsoever (1:5f.). The power of prayer will prove itself in times of tribulation; but in times of happiness we must praise God (5:13). The prayer of faith, if said by the elders of the community, will "save" the sick (probably the primary meaning here is, "will restore him to health");[29] the prayer of a just man can accomplish a great deal if it is assiduous (5:15f.). Piety of this kind, of course, knows nothing of Pauline ideas of being conformed to Christ, or of John's communion with Christ and God, but it can claim support from much of what Jesus said, such as his saying about faith free from doubt, faith that can move mountains (Mark 11:23 par.), childlike prayer (Matt. 7:7-12 par.) and persistent supplication (Luke 18:7). If, at the same time, the heart remains pure and humble, those who live like this may well be the "little ones", the "simple" people to whom Jesus has promised the kingdom of God (Matt. 11:25; 18:6, 10, 14 par.).

[29] Cf. F. Mussner, "Krankensalbung" in *LThK* vol. VI, 585f.

Chapter Four

OTHER EXAMPLES OF
EARLY CHRISTIAN EXHORTATION

§ 40. THE FIRST EPISTLE OF PETER

In addition to the *Commentaries* see R. Perdelwitz, *Die Mysterienreligion und das Problem des 1. Petrusbriefes,* 1911; T. Spörri, *Der Gemeindegedanke im 1. Petrusbrief,* 1925; J. Blinzler, " Ἱεράτευμα" in *Episcopus* (Festschrift für Kardinal Faulhaber), 1949, pp. 49–65; M. Meinertz, *Theologie,* vol. II, pp. 255 ff.; W. Brandt, "Wandel als Zeugnis nach dem 1. Petrusbrief" in *Verbum Dei manet in aeternum* (Festschrift für O. Schmitz) 1953, pp. 10–25; E. Lohse, "Paränese und Kerygma im 1. Petrusbrief" in *ZNW* 45 (1954) pp. 68–89; L. Cerfaux, "Regale Sacerdotium" in *Recueil L. Cerfaux,* vol. II, 1954, pp. 283–315; W. Nauck "Freude im Leiden" in *ZNW* 46 (1955) pp. 68–80; W. C. van Unnik, "The Teaching of Good Works in I Peter" in *NTS* 1 (1954–5) pp. 92–110; *id.,* "Christianity according to I Peter" in *Expository Times* 68 (1956–7) pp. 79–83; J. Ratzinger, *Die christliche Brüderlichkeit,* 1960; M.-E. Boismard, *Quatre hymnes baptismales dans la première épître de Pierre,* 1961; K. H. Schelkle, *Die Petrusbriefe. Der Judasbrief,* 1961 (Bibliog.).

READING the first Epistle of Peter immediately after the Epistle of James — and there are certain links between James and the pastoral letter from Rome (1 Pet. 5:13)[1] — one suddenly gains

[1] Cf. E. G. Selwyn, *The First Epistle of St. Peter,* 2nd ed. 1947 (repr. 1952), pp. 384 ff.; 462f. He refers these connections back to a common basic stock of early Christian tradition and instruction (cf. also 18–23); as against this, A. Meyer, *Rätsel,* pp. 72–82 and Meinertz (*op. cit.,* p. 255 and n. 5) see 1 Peter as directly dependent on James.

the impression of being enveloped in a much more ardent glow of faith. After the pithy, self-supporting admonitions of the Epistle of James, we find ourselves listening to an elevated, enthusiastic, sustained style of writing (1:3–12), which, nevertheless, soon (from v. 13 onwards) reveals that this writer's principal concern too is with religious moral exhortation. In comparison with James, 1 Peter is theologically much more profound and is steeped in Pauline theology, although it is also shot through with thoughts which gave life and movement to the early Church as a whole and, finally, it is enriched with original statements that we meet nowhere else. Once again, we should be able to say more about this work, composed under the auspices of the chief apostle, if we knew the details of the circumstances under which it appeared.[2] In fact, however, we are restricted to internal evidence. For our purposes, we need not accept any of the special theories, but we can learn a great deal from the fruitful discussion which has produced them.

Even if there is no justification for the supposition that the central passage 1:3–4, 11 records the address delivered at a baptism,[3] or even mirrors the celebration of a baptism,[4] it is quite conceivable that what is said here is an example of the exhortation given to neophytes in the early Church. Its readers are compared to new-born children (2:2). They have been "born again, not of corruptible seed, but of incorruptible,

[2] Cf. the introductory works by Feine and Behm, Michaelis, Meinertz, K. T. Schäfer, Wikenhauser — all of which demonstrate a remarkable unity of basic interpretation, seeing the epistle as of indirect Petrine origin (through Silvanus), being sent from Rome shortly before the outbreak of persecution under Nero.

[3] Since R. Perdelwitz the thesis that the epistle is a baptismal discourse has been constantly advocated. Against it see Feine and Behm, op. cit., p. 247; K. H. Schelkle, Petrusbrief, pp. 4f.

[4] Thus H. Preisker in the appendix to Windisch, Kath. Briefe, 3rd ed. 1951, pp. 156–61; similarly F. L. Cross, 1 Peter — A Paschal Liturgy, 1954; see also M. E. Boismard, Quatre hymnes.

by the word of God who liveth and remaineth for ever" (1:23), and they are "purifying" their "souls in the obedience of charity" (1:22). The titles of honour accorded to the old people of God have now been transferred to them: "You are a chosen generation, a kingly priesthood, a holy nation, a purchased people; that you may declare his virtues, who hath called you out of darkness into his marvellous light; who in time past were not a people; but are now the people of God . . ." (2:9f.). Before this there occurs the metaphor of the holy building (the temple), whose most precious stone is Jesus Christ himself, to whom, however, the faithful too are joined as living stones and in whom — with a change of metaphor — they function as a holy priesthood, offering up "spiritual sacrifices". But the joyful announcement of salvation always leads to moral exhortation. As obedient children, St. Peter's hearers should not be shaped by the desires that filled them while they were still ignorant, but having received God's call should be holy, as he is holy (1:14ff.). The first and most important goal of their sanctification, according to this epistle, is genuine love of the brethren; they should love one another constantly, from their hearts (1:22), avoiding all malice, guile, dissimulation, envy and slander (2:1). However great their dignity as God's people it also lays the obligation on them, as strangers and pilgrims, to refrain from "carnal desires which war against the soul" (2:11). Various individual exhortations follow, in the form of a "household code" (2:13–3:7), a shorter list of virtues with five characteristic "Christian" virtues, concord, compassion, love of the brethren, mercy and humility (3:8) and, as the climax, the precept to bless instead of repaying evil with evil and reviling the reviler (3:9). These admonitions are not new, and even the motives expressed are formulated in a way that is only partly unfamiliar. What is original, and proper to 1 Peter, is the effective linking of baptismal jubilation with serious exhortation, a further development and application of Pauline ideas.

1 Peter lives by hope. This epistle shows more compellingly than almost any other New Testament writing what strong moral stimulus hope gives. The great introductory eulogy (1:3–12) is one of the finest monuments to Christian hope. It praises God who, out of the riches of his mercy, has begotten us afresh to a living hope by the resurrection of Jesus Christ from the dead, so that we may receive an inheritance "incorruptible and undefiled and that fadeth not away", reserved for us in heaven. As with Paul, the perspective is that of the history of salvation; salvation is ready to be revealed in the last days (v. 5; cf. Col. 3:1–4; Eph. 2:7; Phil. 3:20). The present age is still full of tribulation and manifold trials for us, and is a trial of faith until the "appearing of Jesus Christ" (v. 7), that is, the parousia. The attractive thought, repeatedly expressed, that we are "strangers and sojourners" in the midst of this world (1:17; 2:11f.; cf. 1:1), a thought that recalls Philippians 3:20, seems also to be applicable to the lifespan of the individual (cf. 1:17 with 4:2), so that for Peter, as for Paul later, it seems unimportant whether the Christian attains salvation personally at death or with the Church at the end of this world. The moral inferences drawn, however, that we should keep ourselves from fleshly lusts (2:11), be sober (1:13; 4:7; 5:3) and watchful for the snares of the devil (5:8f.) illustrate the general reserve of the early Church towards the "world".

But in 1 Peter this view of the world is accompanied and intensified by the thought of the various sufferings to which Christians were exposed. What the epistle's first readers, the Christians of Asia Minor, had principally to endure from their pagan fellow-citizens seems to have been suspicion, slander and petty persecution (2:12; 3:13, 16). The pagans were disturbed because the converted would no longer lead the unprincipled and dissolute lives they did ("you run not with them into the same confusion of riotousness" as St. Peter puts it, 4:4), and "thinking it strange" of them, slandered them. The withdrawal of Christians from the world, their supposed hatred of the human race, was also one of the accusations brought against them in the persecution under Nero.[5] From the admonitions to show the authorities obedience and respect, however, we may obviously conclude that official persecution of Christians had not yet broken out (2:13–17). In a later passage (4:12–19) the writer does in fact discuss suffering "as a Christian", but this, as the context shows, means being brought before the courts for the sake of the Christian name.

This fact and the other, in 1:3–4, 11, where suffering is seen as a possibility because of the conditions existing in society, whilst on the other hand in 4:12–5:11 it seems already to have occurred, gave rise to the conjecture that the epistle is formed from two originally independent pieces.[6] However, on other grounds we are no longer so inclined today to try to interpret it in this way — the style is the same throughout and there are connections between the thought in both parts. Was the last section, in contrast to the main part, addressed to Christians of long standing? Yet it is sufficient to suppose that 4:12–5:11 was a later addition, perhaps on the receipt of disturbing news about law-suits brought against certain individual Christians. 4:12ff. does not, however, suggest that there was a general persecution. On the whole, the author is confident (5:6–10), consoling his readers by telling them that "the same affliction befalls your brethren who are in the (whole) world" (5:9). We still hear nothing about cruel martyrdoms. Social ostracism and the vexations of civil law-suits, the oppression of social

[5] According to M. Dibelius, *Rom und die Christen im 1. Jahrhundert*, 1942, p. 35, it may be taken as proof that in Tacitus' report on the Neronian Persecution (*Annals*, XV, 44), we read *odium humani generis* (hatred of the human race). Attacks of this kind had already been used in polemic against the Jews. Cf. H. Fuchs, "Tacitus über die Christen" in *Vigiliae christianae* 4 (1950) pp. 65–93; H. Hommel, "Tacitus und die Christen" in *Theol. viat.* III (1951) pp. 10–30.

[6] Thus, among others, Perdelwitz, Windisch, Hauck (*Kommentar*, p. 36), the writers in note 2 above take an opposite view.

dependents (slaves) and the economically weak were enough to be called the "burning heat" that was to fall on all Christians to tempt them (4:12).

The epistle puts forward an abundance of truly Christian motives for readiness to suffer and trial by suffering. Peter-Silvanus tells unprotected slaves that with God, suffering is a grace (2:20); and sets before them the example of Christ who "when he was reviled, did not revile: when he suffered, he threatened not" (2:23). Their Lord bears the features of the suffering Servant of God of Isaias 53, but is also their shepherd and protector, who found them when they were like lost sheep and took them under his protection (cf. v. 25). Later, they offer the same arguments to all Christians (3:17f.).

It is a complete misapprehension to regard the "passive virtues" so strongly emphasized and recommended in 1 Peter as weakness and a moral system for slaves. In fact, the imitation of Christ intensifies inner powers of self-control which even pagan Stoic ethics knew should be valued, though, of course, on different grounds. This power of suffering leads to the strength to withstand all kinds of evil, courage to swim against the stream, candour before the courts, and resistance to the unjust power of the state. Humbling oneself "under the mighty hand of God" is not an ethical admonition making a virtue of necessity, but springs from the religious insight, that God alone can change the ultimate darkness of this world era, that only he can "exalt you in the time of visitation" (5:6). And this fits very well with the demand that Christians, firm in the faith, should withstand the devil who "as a roaring lion, goeth about seeking whom he may devour" (5:8f.).

The strong emphasis on obedience is also in keeping with the manner of approach of this work, and maybe also with the character of its author. Slaves should be subject to their masters (2:18), women to their husbands (3:1ff.), the younger members of the community to their elders (5:5), and all Christians to public authority (2:13ff.). But on the other hand, husbands are exhorted to be full of understanding for their wives, the "weaker vessels", honouring them as co-heirs of the grace of life (3:7). And presbyters should not lord it over the "portions" (that is, the communities) entrusted to them, but give good example to their flocks (5:3). We can perceive here a feeling for genuine authority, intrinsically valued and hence able to claim proper respect. Once again, this ethical attitude is buttressed by the religious idea that God resists the proud but gives grace to the humble (5:5; cf. Prov. 3:34). In the last resort, the fear of Gòd (1:17; 2:17) is the foundation of respect for all kinds of authority.

Finally, prayer belongs to this kind of reverential attitude. Here too reason and calm good sense in view of the seriousness of the moment reached in the history of salvation, should be dominant. The end of all things has come (4:7). The author has not much opinion of excessive emotion; but that need not mean poverty in prayer. One is almost surprised to read in the admonition to husbands, "that your prayers be not hindered" (3:7). The fact that the style here is allusive makes it impossible to interpret this passage with certainty: is personal prayer meant, or prayer in common? Perhaps what the author really means is that "where the heart grows hard through lack of understanding in the highest and most sensitive of all human relationships, the relationship with God, as it finds expression in prayer, is also seriously disturbed."[7]

The tone of the whole work shows that the First Epistle of Peter does not lack religious warmth. Once, in a reference of a kind rare in the epistles of the New Testament, the author speaks of love for Christ: "Whom having not seen, you love" (1:8). His is a sound, virile and yet profound piety. We may well believe that it embodies the mind of Simon Peter himself.

[7] Selwyn, *in loc.* (p. 188); more prosaically, J. Michl, *in loc.*

§ 41. THE EPISTLE TO THE HEBREWS

See the *Introductions* and *Commentaries*. On the theology see E. Käsemann, *Das wandernde Gottesvolk*, 1939; M. Meinertz, *Theologie*, vol. II, pp. 253–4; A. Oepke, *Das neue Gottesvolk*, 1950, pp. 17–24; pp. 57–74; W. Manson, *The Epistle to the Hebrews*, 1951; C. Spicq, *L'Épître aux Hébreux*, vol. I, 1952, pp. 266–329; F. J. Schierse, *Verheißung und Heilsvollendung. Zur theologischen Grundfrage des Hebräerbriefes*, 1955; O. Kuss, "Der theologische Grundgedanke des Hebräerbriefes" in *MTZ* 7 (1956) pp. 233–71; *id.*, "Der Verfasser des Hebräerbriefes als Seelsorger" in *TrTZ* 67 (1958) pp. 1–12; pp. 65–80; C. E. Carlston, "Eschatology and Repentance in the Epistle to the Hebrews" in *JBL* 78 (1959) pp. 296–302; A. Wikgren, "Pattern of Perfection in the Epistle to the Hebrews" in *NTS* 6 (1959–60) pp. 159–67.

THE AUTHOR of the Epistle to the Hebrews, a man whose knowledge of Scripture was by no means limited and whose education had been Hellenistic (Alexandrian), takes us into the time of the second generation of Christians who received the gospel of salvation from witnesses who had actually heard the Lord (2:3). Nothing of his own personality is revealed to us, and we do not know to whom the work was originally addressed.[8] It was, however, a community that had accepted Christianity some time previously (5:12; 6:1). Its faith had already been tried (10:32ff.), but still more "discipline of the Lord" was to be expected (12:4ff.). The problem that led the author to make his long, theologically elaborate "word of consolation" (13:22) was the decay of the spirit of faith, piety and moral endurance. Those he was addressing seemed about to

---

[8] Cf. the *Introductions*. The old, traditional view, that the addressees must have been former Palestinian Jews (C. Spicq, *L'Épître aux Hébreux*, vol. I, 1952, pp. 220–52, suggests converted Jewish priests, perhaps in Caesarea, or perhaps, more likely, at Antioch in Syria), has to face considerable difficulties. Catholic scholars, too, are tending towards the recent widely advocated view that the recipients, who might even have been gentile Christians, should be looked for nearer Rome, and somewhere in Italy; cf. Wikenhauser, *Introduction*, pp. 53f., 57f.; O. Kuss, *Der Brief an die Hebräer*, 1953, pp. 19f.

faint; their souls were sleeping (12:3). He appealed to them in the words of the Prophet Isaias, "Lift up the hands which hang down, and the feeble knees" (12:12). What was important was to bring increasing religious indifference under control; many had already formed the habit of staying away from meetings of the community (10:25). In a period threatened by controversies and persecution it was also imperative to arouse new courage to confess the faith (10:32ff.; 11; 12:4ff.). Furthermore, some individuals were in danger of giving moral scandal (12:15f.). How did the author master this situation, which is just as topical today as then?

He was an early Christian theologian, at home in the Pauline school,[9] yet independent, and he chose a way which promised success with everyone who had not completely jettisoned his faith, working to enkindle in everyone new insight into faith and new ardour in it. His purposeful theological statements place Christ at the centre, in the form of the High Priest leading the people of God into the true celestial sanctuary (4:14–10:18). His typological method of exegesis and learned theology are not easily accessible to us, but we should not like to be without his voice in the choir of the New Testament as a whole. In the present study we can do no more than draw attention to the way in which, after profound theological exposition, he points out its relevance to the lives of his hearers.

In general, St. Paul constructed his paraenetic passages in such a way that each principal theological section was followed by a specific piece of exhortation. The author of Hebrews continually interrupts his theological treatise for the sake of exhortation (2:1–4; 5:11–6:3; 10:19–39) and interweaves into his admonitions theological considerations (cf. 12:18–24 within the context of chapter 12 as a whole), or even shows from his exegesis of Scripture that admonition is his principal concern (3:7–4:13). The whole epistle is a "reminder" based on the deepening of

---

[9] On this point, cf. particularly C. Spicq, *op. cit.*, pp. 144–68.

faith, rather as 1 Peter constructed his encouragement to be ready to suffer and to be tried by suffering, on the joyous thought of the Christian vocation, although the execution here is, of course, quite different.

As an example of the method of Hebrews we might take the exposition in 3:7–4:13 of the text of Psalm 94:7–11 (according to the Septuagint), "Today, if you shall hear his voice, harden not your hearts, as in the provocation, in the day of temptation in the desert". Out of the old people of God that wandered through the desert to reach the promised land of Canaan, there has emerged the new people of God, the multitude of Christ's faithful, to whom there has been promised, at the end of their journeyings, the "peace of God". In the psalm, however, it is said that in his wrath God swore with regard to the recalcitrant generation in the desert, "They shall not enter my rest", and this leads the writer to the earnest admonition, "Take heed, brethren, lest perhaps there be in any of you an evil heart of unbelief, to depart from the living God. But exhort one another every day, whilst it is called today" (3:12f.). But, and here the author reveals his theological profundity, this harmonizes with his Christological theme, for the people of God of the New Covenant is, in fact, led by Christ (whom, in the main section of his epistle, the author portrays as the High Priest going before us into the sanctuary). "For we are made partakers of Christ; yet so, if we hold the beginning of his substance firm unto the end" (3:14). The old people of Israel did not reach true "Sabbath rest"; we, being led by Christ, have every prospect of reaching it. "Let us hasten therefore to enter into that rest; lest any man fall into the same example of unbelief" (4:11).

Similarly, at the very beginning of his long discussion of Christ as our High Priest, this theologian and pastor writes, "Having therefore a great high priest that hath passed into the heavens, Jesus the Son of God; let us hold fast our confession" (4:14). And at the end of his exposition, which brings out for the people of God of the New Testament the glory of the way of salvation it follows with Christ, he immediately draws the conclusion, "Having therefore, brethren, a confidence in the entering into the Holies by the blood of Christ; a new and living way which he hath dedicated for us through the veil, that is, his flesh; and a high priest over the house of God; let us draw near with a true heart, in fulness of faith" (10:19ff.). Such salutary knowledge is bound to result in joyful zeal in the things of religion (v. 25, attendance at meetings for worship) and to renewed readiness for the battle of suffering as in earlier days (vv. 32ff.). In an imposing survey of the history of salvation under the Old Covenant which shows us something of the work of the early Church in biblical theology,[10] the author brings before his readers a long series of exemplary witnesses to living faith, which for him is essentially determined by hope (chapter 11).[11] The admonition that issues from this is, to defy the sufferings of this world and avoid sin. "And therefore we also, having so great a cloud of witnesses over our head, laying aside every weight and sin which surrounds us, let us run by patience to the fight proposed to us; looking on Jesus, the author and finisher of faith, who having joy set before him, endured the cross, despising the shame, and now sitteth on the right hand of the throne of God" (12:1f.). Just as it is said of Christ that "although Son he learned obedience by suffering" (5:8), the writer also warns those to whom he is writing, that on them as sons the "discipline" of the Lord is incumbent: "Persevere under discipline. God dealeth with you as with his sons . . . all chastisement for the present indeed seemeth not to bring with it joy but sorrow; but afterwards it will yield to them that are exercised by it the most peaceable fruit of justice" (12:5–11).[12]

---

[10] Cf. E. Stauffer, *Theology*, pp. 235 ff. (historico-theological summaries); F. Graber, *Der Glaubensweg des Volkes Gottes*, 1943.

[11] On the concept of faith in Hebrews, cf. O. Kuss, *op. cit.*, pp. 96–8; C. Spicq, *L'Épître aux Hébreux*, vol. II (Commentary), 1953, pp. 371–81 (with add. bibliography).

[12] On Hebr. 5:7–10 see J. Jeremias in *ZNW* 44 (1952–3) pp. 107–11;

But in addition to the attractive notes of Christian hope, the author also strikes the more serious notes of the threat of judgement, and from time to time these drown the more attractive melody. A fearful judgement awaits anyone who will not permit himself to be aroused by this admonition but sinks back into indifference and coldness, spurning the salvation offered him. The author warns against complete apostasy in words that are unmatched in severity: "For it is impossible for those who were once illuminated, have tasted also the heavenly gift and were made partakers of the Holy Ghost, have, moreover, tasted the good word of God and the powers of the world to come, and are fallen away; to be renewed again to penance, crucifying again to themselves the Son of God and making him a mockery" (6:4–6).

People have sometimes wanted to see in this text (together with 10:26–31; 12:16f.) a proof of a very strict early Christian penitential discipline. But it should be remembered, firstly that the author is not describing some enactment of ecclesiastical discipline but is setting forth his personal conviction; then that he is writing not from the point of view of the apostates, but from that of the pastor concerned with the religious and moral stimulation of those entrusted to him, with their "conversion"; and finally that he continues, "But my dearly beloved, we trust better things of you, and nearer to salvation; though we speak thus" (v. 9). So his concern here is rather with a pastoral and educational conviction than with dogmatic teaching.[13] An obstinate attitude of mind, firmly set against repentance ("sin against the Holy Spirit"), may also, perhaps, have been what is meant.

His warning to great sinners is equally severe and almost open to misunderstanding: "For if we sin wilfully after having the

on the idea of discipline see G. Bornkamm, "Sohnschaft und Leiden" in *Judentum, Urchristentum, Kirche* (Festschrift for J. Jeremias), 1960, pp. 188–98.

[13] Cf. B. Poschmann, *Paenitentia secunda*, 1940, pp. 40ff.; A. Kirchgässner, *Erlösung und Sünde im NT*, pp. 161–3; O. Kuss, *op. cit.*, pp. 114–16; C. Spicq, *op. cit.*, vol. II, pp. 167–78.

knowledge of the truth, there is now left no sacrifice for sins; but a certain dreadful expectation of judgement, and the rage of a fire which shall consume the adversaries" (10:26f.). Perhaps, with delicate pastoral tact, he himself felt that he had gone almost too far with this warning and should encourage his readers, for by way of conciliation he then adds a reference to their former testing in the battle of suffering (10:32ff.). Thus he warns and threatens his readers without depressing them, praises and encourages them without for a single moment allowing any lack of clarity about the present dangerous crisis. He is a profoundly solicitous and ardently loving teacher.

Another thing is noteworthy. The author is writing to the community as such. This is in accordance with his high conception of the "people of God" (2:17; 4:9; 5:3; 13:12). The recipients of the letter are themselves to watch diligently to see that none of them forfeit the grace of God "lest any root of bitterness springing up, do hinder and by it many be defiled" (12:15). The community as such is responsible for the sanctity of the people of God and each of its members. This awareness of the community, already noticed in St. Paul (cf. 1 Cor. 5:11, 30ff.) and in the early Church in general (see above, section 19), is perhaps intensified in Hebrews by the liturgical element, which here is to be understood as a purified, spiritual and moral ritual piety (cf. 13:9ff.), a "reasonable service" of God such as St. Paul too calls for (Rom. 12:1).[14] If we add the conviction that every Christian possesses the Spirit here and now (6:4; 10:29), as a blessing of salvation, not as a special charismatic endowment, and the unshaken expectation of the parousia in the near future (10:25, 37), and above all the strong hope, characteristic of the whole epistle (cf. 12:22f.; 13:14), of the eschatological consummation, we see in a living form in this paraenetic composition of the second generation, all the ideas and forces that filled the early Church as a whole.

[14] See P. Seidensticker, *Lebendiges Opfer (Röm. 12:1)*, 1954, pp. 280–320.

§ 42. The Seven Open Letters of the Apocalypse of John

See the *Commentaries;* also W. R. Ramsay, *Letters to the Seven Churches,* 1904; L. Poirier, *Les sept églises ou le premier septénaire prophétique de l'Apocalypse,* Montreal, 1943; I. Schuster, "La Chiesa e le sette chiese apocalittiche" in *Scuola Cattolica* 81 (1953) pp. 217–23; W. Barclay, *Letters to Seven Churches,* 1957; M. Hubert, "L'architecture des lettres aux Sept Églises (Apoc. II–III)" in *RB* 67 (1960) pp. 349–53.

The early Christian communities to which the Apocalypse is addressed were in a position similar to that of the recipients of 1 Peter and Hebrews, except that they were even more oppressed and threatened by the dark shadow of the cult of the emperor, which, out of loyalty to Christ, they had to reject. The blood of the martyrs had already flowed, and was to go on flowing. In heaven, those "that had been slain for the word of God and for the testimony which they held" were waiting for "their fellow servants and their brethren, who are to be slain even as they" (6:9, 11). But as in Hebrews, perceptible signs have appeared in some parts of the seven communities in Asia Minor to which these open letters in Apocalypse 2–3 are addressed, that strength of faith is withering and love diminishing. The whole of this New Testament Apocalypse, which, in spite of superficial appearances can hardly be a unity,[15] is intended to kindle a new ardour of faith, to awaken a readiness to suffer even violent death by martyrdom, to encourage a steadfast perseverance in the midst of all the terrors of the last evil time before the cosmic victory of Christ. Here, however, it will be enough to look at the open letters to the seven churches, intended probably for all the communities within the range of the seer's vision and over and beyond them for

[15] In addition to the introductions, see also on the Catholic side, M. E. Boismard, "'L'Apocalypse' ou 'les Apocalypses' de s. Jean", art. in *RB* 56 (1949) pp. 507–41 (arguing that two Apocalypses have been combined in chs. 4–22); Boismard, *Notes sur l'Apoc.* in *RB* 59 (1952) pp. 161–81; several essays by P. Gächter in *Theologische Studien* 1947–49 (assuming that a pupil of St. John put the book together from memory), and on this view, A. Wikenhauser, art. in *Theologische Revue* 48 (1952) pp. 57–60.

the whole Church of Christ in general of which the seven are representative.[16] These proclamations, which should not be thought of as real letters, but majestic utterances of the heavenly Lord to communities still involved in the terrestrial struggle, do form a unity. They throw light on "the things . . . which are" (1:19) and their sobriety excludes from the outset the erroneous interpretation that the later revelations couched in the apocalyptical language of symbolism and mystery (and in part at least in terrible and fantastic pictures), necessarily form part of the admonitions concerning the present.

In the past conclusions such as this were met with: "The fundamental mood of early Christianity was . . . apocalyptic. The more oppressive the position of the believers in the Messias appeared, the stronger grew their taste for this their inheritance from Judaism. On every side we meet with prophetic voices and spiritual proclamations, visions and revelations, borrowings from Jewish eschatology and the revival of apocalyptic traditions."[17] Today we are more inclined to differentiate between an "eschatological" attitude (orientated towards the end) and an "apocalyptic" one (concerned with visions, calculations, etc.). Although it can hardly be denied that apocalyptic tendencies of a kind totally unknown in the teaching of Jesus himself were manifested by isolated groups in early Christianity, the profound religious content of the "apocalyptic" element in the Apocalypse shows that it should be seen as the form adopted by the author for his book, partly under pressure from the political situation, and his visions on Patmos, and probably because the form was

[16] This emerges from the symbolic number seven and from the fact that there were other Christian communities in Asia — and also from 2:23, where all the "Churches of Christ" acknowledge his works, and lastly from the sayings beginning "He that hath an ear, let him hear", in which the Spirit speaks to all the Churches — cf. E. Lohmeyer, *Die Offenbarung des Johannes,* 2nd ed. 1953, pp. 42f.

[17] H. J. Holtzmann, *Lehrbuch der neutestamentlichen Theologie,* 2nd ed. 1911, vol. II, p. 539.

not out of keeping with his own gifts. But it did not represent for him anything essential in the message of Christ. He does not live by fantasies, but in the conviction that soon after "the great tribulation" (Mark 13:19ff. par.; cf. Apoc. 7:14), the Lord will appear, overwhelm his adversary and establish the kingdom of glory. Fundamentally he is only using different means to awaken to new life the Christian hope founded on Jesus' words and, like Jesus himself, deriving from it comfort and exhortation for the present.

What is immediately striking is the candour with which praise and blame are allotted to each community. The seer announces his judgement not as his own, but as that of the heavenly Lord of the communities, whom he had earlier described, in an impressive vision (1:12–16), as "the Son of man" (the reference here is principally to Daniel 10), and had characterized by traits significant to those addressed and criticized. The Son of man has a regal and sacerdotal dignity (in v. 13 he is described as wearing a long robe and with a golden girdle about his breast) and shines with the light of heaven (his head and hair are snow-white, his feet have a golden glitter, his face shines like the sun); his blazing glance pierces all things (v. 14b), and his words have power (his voice being like the rushing of many waters, v. 15b) and is like a sharp, two-edged sword (v. 16). In the sight of the heavenly Lord, who is enthroned in the midst of seven candle-sticks, that is, the seven communities, and holds in his right hand seven stars, the "angels" of the seven churches, the state of the seven communities lies like an open book. "I know thy works" are the first words the Lord says to the "angel" of each of the communities through the mouth of his prophet.

It is hardly possible to interpret the "angel" as the bishop, for the word is not found in this sense anywhere else in the Apocalypse. It means, rather, "guardian angel", just as the nations have angelic princes as their guardians according to Daniel 10:13, 20f.; 12:1; the message concerns the community on earth, which is addressed directly as well as through the "angel". Some understand the angel as the representative of the individual community, its personified spirit.[18] That is perhaps a modern way of thinking; probably real angels are meant through whom the Son of Man (who holds them in his right hand) guides his communities.[19] One thing is certain: every Christian community represents a living self-contained unity, and in spite of its various different individual members, and their personal responsibility, it can be the subject of a single criticism. For its own part it must care for the sanctity of all its elements. Hence praise and blame are not aimed here only at individual Christians within the separate communities, but also at them all as a body.

The state of the communities is judged by their "works", but these are not achievements like the Jewish works of the law. In the lines addressed to Thyatira they are mentioned together with "thy faith and thy charity and thy ministry and thy patience" (2:19). Clearly, "works" here must be interpreted in relation to these expressions that follow. So they refer to the total outcome of religious and moral action. This concept of "works" reminds us of St. James. In the promise to those who are victorious, contained in the same lines, we read, "And he that shall overcome, and keep my works unto the end, I will give him power over the nations" (2:26). The primary principles guiding action are no longer the commandments of God contained in the Old Testament or even the more fully developed law of Judaism, but the will of God proclaimed through Jesus. Hence we also find here the phrase "kept my (that is Jesus') word" — an unmistakable echo of the usage of the Gospel and Epistles of St. John.[20] But Jesus' sayings and instructions are no more felt

---

[18] Thus, among others, E. B. Allo, *S. Jean, L'Apocalypse,* 3rd ed. 1953; J. Behm, *Die Offenbarung des Johannes,* 5th ed. 1949; E. Lohmeyer, *Offenbarung,* on 1:20.

[19] Cf. A. Wikenhauser, *Die Offenbarung des Johannes,* 3rd ed. 1959, pp. 34ff.; J. Michl in *LThK* vol. III, 867.

[20] John 8:51f.; 14:15, 21, 23, 24; 15:10, 20; cf. 1 John 2:3–5; 3:22, 24; 5:3; cf. also Apoc. 12:17; 14:12.

to be an oppressive law than they are in St. James. Love is the driving force of all action and, at the same time, the one thing necessary. The community of Ephesus, which had given proof of its steadfastness in bearing trials for the sake of Jesus' name and had not weakened, was, nevertheless, not spared all reproach: "I have somewhat against thee, because thou hast left thy first charity" (2:4). Charity here can be restricted neither to "love for Jesus" (for they had shown this in their endurance) nor to "fraternal charity" (for this would certainly have been defined more explicitly), but certainly must be interpreted comprehensively, as an all-embracing attitude of charity, impelling to action (cf. 1 Cor. 13 and 1 John). And when, finally, the Lord's delegate exhorts the community to "do (again) the first works", "charity" and "works" appear to be almost identical, at least as far as external observation can detect. There are both good and evil works: Christ praises these same Ephesians because they hate the deeds of the Nicolaites "which I also hate" (2:6). Thus everyone will be requited according to his works (2:23; cf. 20:12f.; 22:12). In later visions, works even figure as independent companions of those dying in the Lord (14:13) and the "justifications of the saints" are the radiant white robe in which the Bride of the Lamb (that is the Church) clothes herself (19:8). It cannot be denied that in speaking of "works" without qualification in this way, the text is again coming close to Judaism;[21] but this last text itself shows clearly that there was no falling back into the kind of justification by works so sharply attacked by both Jesus and Paul. "It is granted" to the Bride of the Lamb to clothe herself in the linen of moral sanctity. Nowhere in the Apocalypse is it forgotten that Christ had first to release us from our sins by his blood (1:5) and redeem us for God (5:9); even those who have been tried by great tribulation are not extolled as heroes, but are characterized as those "who have washed their

[21] In Judaism, too, as in Apoc. 14:13, the dead were accompanied by their "works"; cf. Billerbeck, vol. III, p. 817, *in loc.*

robes and have made them white in the blood of the Lamb"
(7:14).

With unsparing candour the Lord reigning in heaven has his
churches told what displeases him in their works. Only two
communities are left entirely without reproach, the church of
Smyrna (2:8–11) and that of Philadelphia (3:7–13). It is no
accident that these were communities which had endured especially bitter tribulations, brought on them, in fact, by a group of
Jews who are here called a "synagogue of Satan" (2:9; 3:9).
With the Smyrniots their poverty is mentioned (2:9) and with
the Philadelphians, their limited power (3:8), that is, probably,
the weakness of their social influence. The Christians of these
prosperous cities were probably mostly members of the lower
classes. The evidence of these divinely attested documents confirms the ancient experience that poverty, want and tribulations
preserve a purer and more living charity and faith than peace
and prosperity (compare the reverse image presented by Laodicea at 3:17f.). The other communities receive serious warnings
because of the Lord's love for them: "Such as I live, I rebuke
and chastise. Be zealous, therefore, and do penance" (3:19).
It is also noteworthy that in all five letters the same warning to
repent is repeated (2:5, 16, 21f.; 3:3, 19). In this call to repentance (which recalls Jesus' fundamental demand, see above,
section 2) there is included everything that ought to be changed
in each individual case, for example in Pergamum toleration of
those Christians who eat flesh offered to idols in sacrifice and
commit fornication, and also, as in Thyatira (2:20ff.),[22] of the

[22] It is disputed whether these (clearly closely related) false teachers, the
Bileamites and Nicolaites, tended in an amoral, libertine direction
(when fornication would have to be interpreted literally) or towards an
unscrupulous approach to paganism (when fornication is a metaphor for
idolatry). "Knowing the depths of Satan" (2:24) might suggest a
movement towards Gnosticism, in which sin was perversely defended.
Cf. Lohmeyer, *op. cit.,* p. 31 (attacking this view); Wikenhauser, on
2:20ff. (defending it).

Nicolaites (2:14f.); in Sardis the interior deadness of many Christians in spite of the good repute of the community (3:1f.), and in Laodicea the tepidity and indifference that springs from prosperity and satiety (3:14ff.). Christ threatens that he will soon intervene, bringing punishment to the communities unwilling to repent: "Or else I come to thee and will move thy candlestick out of its place (among the circle of the other communities), except thou do penance" (2:5). "If not, I will come to thee quickly, and will fight against them (the members of the community favouring false doctrine) with the sword of my mouth" (2:16).

This "coming of Christ" is not the parousia, but an earlier, temporal chastisement (cf. 1 Cor. 11:29–32). Christ's "coming" is to the disadvantage of the communities affected, or those members who are failing. The same thought is to be found at 3:3. In the lines to Thyatira, there appears "Jezabel ... the prophetess" who was trying "to teach and seduce my servants, to commit fornication, and to eat of things sacrificed to idols" (the reference is probably to the same false teaching as at 2:6,14f.). Those who commit fornication with her are threatened with sickness and very great tribulation, including death for her children (2:22ff.). As the other churches are to recognize from this that Christ is "he that searcheth the reins and hearts", and so receive a terrible example, even "the death of her children" can scarcely be taken to mean eternal damnation.[23]

This preaching of penance and threats of this kind recall the old prophets, except that Christ now replaces God, watching over his churches in heaven. But the exhortation to penance here has a wholly new eschatological emphasis, for these are the last times before the parousia.

The fact that in the seven letters the expectation of the end provides very strong motives to action, is also evident from the promises to those who are victorious, which in every case close

---

[23] Many exegetes explain the expression "kill with death" as an allusion to Ezech. 33:27 and interpret "death" as plague or some other epidemic.

the letters. Like the writer of Hebrews, Christ's vigorous prophet John knows how to rekindle the hope of salvation. Under a variety of images and with the tersest of phrases, the victor who overcomes all tribulations, temptations and struggles, is promised a reward that can only be fulfilled in the coming kingdom of God. Over and above this, Christ appeals to the loyal members of the community of Thyatira: "Yet that which you have, hold fast till I come" (2:25). These promises to those who "overcome" are clear signals, perceptible to all Christians doing battle with the powers of darkness; they are promises from above, from Christ himself, who has already collected around him the triumphant confessors and martyrs, and they are also perhaps words used in the liturgy of the Church on earth to exhort the faithful to strive for their own future triumph and blessedness.[24] "To him that overcometh I will give to eat of the tree of life, which is in the paradise of my God" (2:7). "To him that overcometh I will give the hidden manna" (2:17). "He that overcometh shall thus be clothed in white garments" (3:5). "He that shall overcome, I will make him a pillar in the temple of my God" (3:12). "To him that shall overcome, I will give to sit with me in my throne" (3:21). All the faithful who hear these maxims are to pay constant heed to them and open their ears to the cry of the divine Spirit. The Apocalypse is not the esoteric book of a small, isolated group, but a book of faith for the whole Church. Its revelation, consolation and exhortation concern all believers, but at the same time, only believers will profit from the message of the seer of Patmos. For only the believers, to whom the celestial world where Christ is enthroned by his Father's side as the divine ruler of all, is the true and indestructible reality, and for whom the coming kingdom of God, the new Jerusalem, the new heaven

---

[24] The liturgical and ritual note in the Apocalypse is indisputable in the rhythmical hymns of the heavenly city and the triumphant Church. But it is also legitimate to see in them an echo of the earthly liturgy, in which the struggling and suffering Church on earth celebrates in prospect its own coming victory. Cf. the bibliography in section 24, note 15.

and the new earth are a certain expectation, can draw from the promise of them the strength to persevere in the darkness of this world's course and "follow the Lamb whithersoever he goeth" (14:4).

CONCLUSION

As the last section of our study has been intended to show, admonition in the early Church was by no means uniform, but bore the impress of the individual preacher. The men who speak to us in the epistles of the New Testament are strong, spiritually independent personalities, and yet they all bear the common mark of Jesus' spirit. They are conscious of being bound by what he said. Vigorously and unflinchingly, they proclaim Jesus' message to their own age, mitigating nothing of the Lord's commandments and demands. Never since that time has the voice of those who proclaim the Christian faith and preach Christian morals fallen silent; but their words were not always equally profound in faith or equally powerful. One reason for this was no doubt that many of them no longer understood Jesus' message in its eschatological urgency. But only when this is presupposed can we comprehend the radical demands made in the gospel, which have the holy will of God as their sole guiding principle and which could only be made in the light of the gospel of salvation, of the coming reign of God which, in Jesus, is already at hand. Our present generation of Christians seems once again more ready to accept the original words of the Bible, sensing in them the purity of a well-spring and the power of a root. But this means that they must be proclaimed without attenuation, and in the moral sphere this involves bringing the undiminished demands of Jesus into our own times and applying them to ourselves. That also means that we do not need to cling anxiously to the language of the New Testament authors. But the task which they performed then for their communities is still ours to fulfil in our own times: with equal ardour in the faith, equal moral earnestness and above all equal eschatological vigilance, to proclaim the gospel of Jesus.